Katherine,

Looking forward
to reading & engaging
with your work!

Alyandra

INFORMED POWER

INFORMED POWER

Communication in the Early
American South

Alejandra Dubcovsky

Harvard University Press

Cambridge, Massachusetts
London, England
2016

First printing

Published with the assistance of the Frederick W. Hilles Publication Fund of Yale University

Library of Congress Cataloging-in-Publication Data

Dubcovsky, Alejandra, 1983– author.
Informed power : communication in the early American South / Alejandra Dubcovsky.
pages cm
Includes bibliographical references and index.
ISBN 978-0-674-66018-2
1. Communication—Southern States—History.   2. Power (Social sciences)—Southern
States—History.   3. Southern States—History—Colonial period, ca. 1600–1775.   I. Title.
P92.U6D83 2016
302.20975—dc23
2015031060

For Ryan

CONTENTS

~

ILLUSTRATIONS

~

FIGURES

MAPS

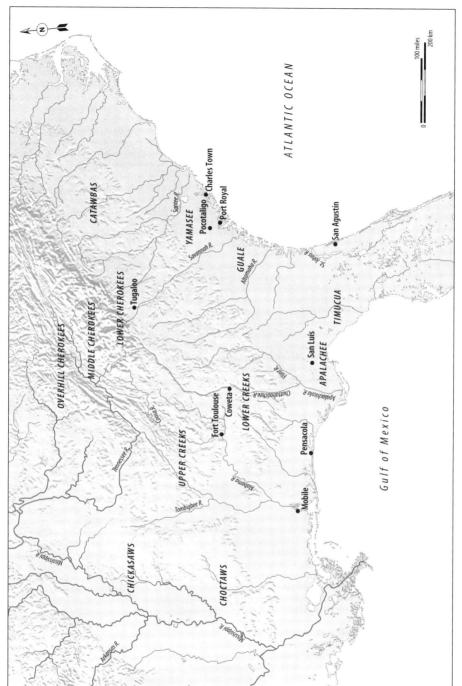

The early South

INTRODUCTION

~

THEY WENT SOUTH. In September 1739, a group of slaves near Charles Town, South Carolina, revolted against their masters, killing over twenty whites and destroying several plantations. William Bull, the Governor of South Carolina, reported with horror and dismay that "a great number of Negroes Arose in Rebellion." The slaves who led what became known as the Stono Rebellion hoped to reach Spanish Florida, a colony that promised freedom and protection to all runaway slaves.[1] The rebels did not make it very far before the South Carolina militia intercepted them. Some slaves were captured and others killed in the battle that followed, but a small group managed to escape and continue their flight south. The largest slave rebellion in colonial North America ended the following week, when the English and their Indian allies finally apprehended the remaining fugitives. But how did the slaves know to march south? How did they know that if they reached Spanish Florida, they would be freed?

The slaves' savvy or agency had nothing to do with it, or so Governor Bull insisted. He dismissed the rebels' ability to turn a Spanish "Proclamation . . . declaring Freedom to all Negroes who should desert" into armed rebellion as a lapse in South Carolina's regulation of information. But in the aftermath of the Stono Rebellion, the English proved more eager to punish and silence the slave perpetrators than curious about how news of a proclamation issued by a Spanish governor 300 miles away had made its way north. South Carolinians killed anyone who had participated in the rebellion or was assumed to be an accomplice. Without trials or proceedings and "for their own security, the said inhabitants . . . put such negroes to immediate death." The new slave code made "all and every act, matter and thing . . . committed and executed, in and about suppressing [the slave rebels] . . . lawful." Self-imposed

1

reticence became a common thread in contemporary English accounts of the rebellion.[2]

The English found an easy culprit in the Spanish. South Carolinians had long complained that the Spanish in Florida lured their slaves away. The Stono Rebellion confirmed that the threats to the English colony from their meddlesome Catholic neighbors were in fact real. When South Carolina officials blamed the slave rebellion on the Spanish, they spoke not in vague terms about Florida's fugitive slave policies or the long history of tensions and violence between the two colonies. Instead, the English pointed to a specific "bando" or edict. They linked the events of the Stono Rebellion to a bando passed by Florida's governor, Manuel de Montiano, seven months before the rebellion.

English officials in South Carolina accused Governor Montiano of issuing this bando with the clear goal of inspiring English slaves to flee for Spanish Florida. The bando, passed on February 16, 1739, did little more than reinforce two existing *cédulas* (laws) that had been adopted six years prior and had already guaranteed freedom to the fugitive slaves who reached San Agustín. For his part, Montiano insisted on the strategic value of this bando in broadcasting and reaffirming Spanish policies—particularly to enslaved Africans. Within a few months, Montiano had evidence that his plan was working. In May 1739, South Carolina suffered the "Desertion of 23 Negroes . . . to St. Augustine." Lewis Jones, an Anglican clergyman from St. Helen's Parish in South Carolina, explained how these twenty-three slaves had acted "on a Proclamation Publish'd there of freedom to all Slaves that Sh[all] Desert to them from Any of the English Plantations."[3] As Governor Montiano proudly reported, these slaves were "well informed" of Florida's policy to welcome and free runaways.[4]

No copies of Montiano's bando have been found, but it apparently made its way into the hands of several high-ranking English officials in the months leading up to the Stono Rebellion. The longest description historians have of the bando comes from a discussion of Florida's fugitive slave policies held in the South Carolina assembly.[5] Members of the South Carolina House of Commons considered the bando an attack against their property and livelihood not only because it encouraged slaves to flee but also because it required Spanish officials and their native allies, in particular Yamasees, to publicize it surreptitiously. Indian information networks connected the region, and the Spanish found relying on these native nodes and paths far easier than South Carolinians found regulating these multipolar connections. The growing number of fugitive slaves reaching San Agustín in 1739 suggested that the English were right to fret.

Information exchange in the colonial world was not easy. It was hard for the Spaniards to circulate Montiano's bando beyond the walls of San Agustín. It was difficult for South Carolinians to regulate how slaves (or anyone, for that matter) used information networks that operated and extended well beyond English control. It was trying for African slaves to acquire information on imperial and colonial policies that could transform their situation.[6] And it was complex for all parties involved to navigate these information exchanges that largely took place through Indian channels and were contingent on native geopolitics. The different and innovative ways that Indians, Africans, and Europeans stayed informed created lifelines of learning that transcended some of the cultural, political, and linguistic divides of the time. Recognizing these varied information strategies and approaches, which are quite often unobserved and unremarked upon, holds the potential to destabilize the image of the colonial world as an underinformed or uninformed place.[7]

These channels of communication and the relations they afforded were instrumental for disseminating news and ideas in the American South, a region that lacked a regular mail system and operated until the 1730s without a printing press.[8] Most of what historians know about the spread and acquisition of news in early America (for instance, the development of intellectual communities through the Republic of Letters or the reconstruction of networks bridging the Atlantic world) has relied primarily on research conducted in the mid-Atlantic or New England regions.[9] Based on these existing accounts, the focus here on Indian, European, and African networks might seem ancillary to a more formalized print or epistolary communication system. But these networks, neither centered on European towns nor dominated by European actors, uncover everyday articulations of power that gave shape to the early South.

Both *early* and *South* are terms that depend, of course, on perspective. This ambiguous temporal parameter—earlier than the founding of Jamestown in 1607; the establishment of San Agustín, Florida, in 1565; or even before Columbus sailed the ocean blue in 1492—requires some anchor. Cahokia, which is where this story begins, is perhaps the most readily discernible choice. Located on the confluences of the Mississippi, Illinois, and Missouri Rivers, this powerful and large chiefdom of approximately 40,000 people at the height of its population is considered the center of the early Mississippian world.[10] Although the rise of Cahokia in the eleventh century appears *early* only in comparison to later Mississippian societies like Etowah and Coosa, the point of starting here is to center the long and layered history of interactions among the composite societies who came to inhabit the colonies of South Carolina, Georgia, Florida, and parts of Louisiana.[11]

Bounding the region by the Mississippi River to the west and the Cumberland River to the north helps foreground different kinds of native experiences as well as different types of colonial spaces. The Indian nations in this region, unlike Indian groups in New England or even in the Chesapeake, had to reckon with far fewer numbers of colonists and, as a result, remained sizable, sovereign, and powerful for over three centuries after the first European incursions into their territories. The "early South" is thus not some projection backward in time of what would later become the Confederacy. It was a world shaped by African slavery but also populated by Spaniards, Timucuas, Apalachees, French, Creeks, and Cherokees. The early South functions as a social-cultural model that explicates the multivalent interactions that bound the region from the pre-Columbian era to the mid-eighteenth century and helps contextualize the latent historical complexities that arose from that multiethnic and increasingly multiracial world.

Communication networks were crucial to the creation, development, and growth of colonial spaces and the conflicts that emerged within them. As I employ the term, a *network* simply refers to the pattern of ties connecting discrete places or peoples. These patterns allow me to investigate the linkages between people and places and to look past the confines of contemporary geographic boundaries. Moreover, networks reveal as much about constraints as they do about opportunities. The networks that allowed the Stono slave rebels to acquire information about the prospects available in Spanish Florida, for example, show that slaves in South Carolina could learn and mobilize from faraway news. On the other hand, these same connections also emphasize slavery's role in shaping what information people cared about as well as who could spread it, and how. Networks are not separate or independent from the societies that sustain them; they are products and reflections of those worlds. Treating them as such, offers new ways to reconstruct the lived social relations of the early South.

Indian actors forged some of the main paths and connections that the Stono slave rebels used to learn of Montiano's bando. Uncovering how these enslaved men knew to march south requires looking beyond the rice plantations of South Carolina and toward the information networks that crisscrossed *la tierra adentro* (literally, "the land inside"). How were Creek Indians and South Carolina's fugitive slaves linked? Why were Yamasees at the center of Carolina–Florida debates about African slavery? Demography offers one answer. In 1739, as the Stono rebels readied to attack their masters and flee to Florida, the majority of the population within the English colony was both black and enslaved. But South Carolina's 20,000 African slaves and 10,000 whites were well outnumbered by the 11,000 Creeks, 10,000 Cherokees, 14,000 Choctaws and Chickasaws, and close to 5,000 other Indians living near Charles Town and San Agustín. In the 1730s, there were more Indians than Africans living in the early South—actually more Indians than black slaves *and* Europeans. Information networks reveal not just the large presence of Indian actors but also their importance.[12]

The English established Carolina in 1670 with hopes of replicating the slave plantation model for sugar production that had transformed the Caribbean islands into lucrative sites of empire. But sugar did not grow in Carolina (officially divided into North Carolina and South Carolina in 1712). Neither did tobacco or silk or any other profitable crop.[13] It took over forty years for rice plantations to develop and finally give South Carolina a staple commodity crop. During the first half-century of English presence in the region, trade with the neighboring and powerful Indian nations fueled the colony's economy. These commercial connections, first between the English and the Westos, then with the Savannahs, and eventually with the Yamasees and the Creeks, developed into an expansive, profitable, and violent trade for both deerskins and Indian slaves. Indians allied with the English raided rival and often neighbor Indian groups, exchanging captives for guns and other European commodities. By "[f]urnishing a bold and warlike people with arms and ammunition," explained the Lord Proprietors in 1681, the English were able to "tie them [neighboring Indians] to so strict a dependence upon us . . . that whenever that nation shall misbehave themselves towards us, we shall be able . . . by abstaining from supplying them with ammunition to ruin them."[14]

The Indian slave trade left no corner of the region untouched. Spanish mission Indians in Guale (present day Georgia), Timucua (north Florida), and Apalachee (northwest Florida) were especially vulnerable to these slaving raids. The Spanish had had refused to furnish their Indian allies with guns. Although the Spanish had a permanent colony in La Florida since 1565, their presence in *la tierra adentro* had remained limited to missionary activity. The Indian slave trade quickly destabilized Franciscan missions that, until 1655, had flourished and boasted over 20,000 neophytes.[15] By the 1710s, the crashing waves of violence, disease, and warfare brought on by Westo, Yamasee, Apalachicola, and Creek slaving raids had confined Spanish influence to San Agustín and its immediate surroundings. Florida officials could hardly make sense of the devastation of Indian slaving let alone mount an organized response to it. In a matter of decades, the Indian slave trade had led to the enslavement of over 50,000 Indians, removed most Spanish holdings from the area, and completely reshaped the region's geopolitics.[16]

The study of communication networks provides a new approach to early American history. It shows the links among peoples who shared no consensus of the physical or political boundaries of their worlds without losing sight of the differences and inequalities among them. Exploring these connections—and the entanglements that ensued within and between them—unpacks processes that resonate well beyond the early South: the perpetual tension between imperial ambitions and local arrangements, the uneven and unequal linkages that helped structure the social and political landscape, and the incongruent yet still coexisting articulations of power that permeated the region. Examined alongside each other, Indian, European, and African networks generate a story about communication in which the main takeaway is neither the lack of information that plagued the colonial world nor the technological advances that, as time went on, supposedly facilitated the circulation of news. These communication networks show the uneven, varied, and interconnected relations that not only bound the early South but also informed power.

∽

Communication itself is not a historical act because peoples in all times and places have communicated. Even so, peoples' relationship to information—to what mattered, to who spread and acquired news, and to how those exchanges unfolded and changed—has a history. Uncovering that history presents not only a more dynamic, fluid, and complex world but also one in which that dynamism, fluidity, and complexity matters.

Divided into three parts, *Informed Power: Communication in the Early American South* begins by first asking *what* information did people in the early South want? The first chapter offers a general overview of Indian networks before and after European colonization. Detailing the dynamic information networks that Indians had in place before 1492 helps recover some of the everyday practices of pre-Columbian peoples and, more important, shows how native paths and connections determined what information circulated, who could carry news, and the implications of both.

The next two chapters move forward in time, focusing on the period between the establishment of San Agustín and the founding of South Carolina, roughly from 1560 to 1670. Chronicling the efforts of European colonists to understand, record, and explain what and who La Florida was, these chapters argue that, when the Spanish looked outward, at the coming French threats or English pirate attacks, they understood La Florida to be at the center of a tug of war between imperial rivalries and colonial developments. When they looked in, at the state of the colony or at the success of the Franciscan missions, they found more divisions than connections. More than the objects or subjects of these information arrangements, Indians—in particular, Timucuas, Guales, and Apalachees—informed what the Spanish knew as well as how they knew it. By inquiring about *what* information people wanted, the story that unfolds—one that centers on the experiences of Indians—challenges historians' ideas of what as well as who mattered in the early South.

Part II focuses on *who* acquired and spread information. Resuming the story in the 1660s, this section describes some of the many and different peoples who carried news. The backdrop to a rather eclectic list of individuals, which included—but was not limited to—spies, diplomats, sentinels, messengers, scouts, traders, friars, and soldiers, was the Indian slave trade. The connections and asymmetrical relations fostered by the Indian slave trade illuminate the geographic reach and interdependence of the early South since Indians and Europeans raided peoples far beyond their lands or any political or economic arrangement that could mediate social and cultural differences. In answering *who* transmitted and moved information, this section not only describes the region as disordered and volatile but also examines *why* that entropy prevailed.

Part III examines *how* Indians, Europeans, and Africans used networks to move information. This section uses the Yamasee War of 1715–1717, which pitted Yamasees and Creeks against South Carolina, to study how communication networks functioned and faltered during wartime. In the wake of a conflict that destroyed or, at the very least, unsettled most of the existing connections that had linked the early South, older strategies and approaches for networking information no longer seemed sufficient. The conflict compelled Indians, Europeans, and Africans to reassess which connections to rely on and who to include in their networks. The Yamasee War offers a way to make sense of *how* different people understood, articulated, and defended their changing milieus. This final section argues that networking information was not simply about having the latest news or the quickest informer; it was a way of establishing parameters, articulating priorities, and enforcing both.

This book has no section labeled *why*. This absence is deliberate because the answer is clear: power, or "the ability of human groups to control space and resources, to create dependencies and neutralize rivals, to influence the behaviors and perceptions of others, and to initiate and resist change."[17] But saying that there was a relation, even a direct and intimate relation, between information and power is where this story begins, not ends. The book is intended to interrogate this relation by arguing that the simple and obvious correlation between information and power was anything but simple or obvious. The ebbs and flows of power can be both studied and historicized from how people, all sorts of different people, made sense of their worlds. Using both a chronological and thematic approach, *Informed Power* explores how different aspects of information were privileged at different times. In the process, it reveals the intricacies and contingencies that constituted the core of both personal experiences and historical processes in the early South.

PART I

WHAT

Making Sense of La Florida,
1560s–1670s

~

Who wants to go to Florida?
Let him go where I have been,
Returning gaunt and empty,
Collapsing from weakness,
The only benefit I have brought back,
Is one good white stick in my hand,
But I am safe and sound, not disheartened,
Let's eat: I'm starving.

Nicolas Le Challeux, carpenter of Fort Caroline (1565)

CHAPTER ONE

PATHS AND POWER

~

They will draw Maps, very exactly, of all the Rivers, Towns, Mountains, and Roads, or what you shall enquire of them.

John Lawson on Indian maps, 1709

INDIAN DELEGATES, TRADERS, and soldiers traveling to Cahokia would have immediately noticed the writing on the large, quartzite slab on the side of the Mississippi River. This rock in a narrow and rocky section of the river, about 150 miles south of present-day St. Louis, contained a map. The object historians now call the Commerce Map both welcomed and warned Indians heading toward Cahokia, one of the largest and most powerful chiefdoms in the Mississippian world. Carved sometime between 1200 and 1400 BCE, this rock map offered a visual representation of the vast yet asymmetrical connections that Indians in the early South needed to negotiate to exchange goods and information.

The Commerce Map, the oldest known cartographic representation in eastern North America, contains several engravings: a moccasin, an arrow, several dot clusters, and an ogee or eye, but the largest motif on the map is a bird—probably a falcon—which seems to represent Cahokia (Figure 1.1). All of the engravings in this rock map, from the small dots to the large glyphs, are placed in relation to the most pronounced feature of the map: a long, continuous, and deeply carved line, which probably refers to the Mississippi River.

The map argues for the interconnected nature of this world. But it also evinces that not all relationships were equal or of equal importance. From the size of the glyphs to their locations, the Commerce Map shows that some places were well connected and accessible, with others more remote. Many dots are carved beneath the falcon glyph, implying that some form of

FIGURE 1.1. Pre-Columbian rock map. Also referred to
as the "Commerce Map."
(Photo courtesy U.S. Army Corps of Engineers.)

tributary relation existed between the small towns these dots represented and the large chiefdom of Cahokia the falcon engraving depicted. The small towns, though located close together, were bound to the falcon, not to each other. These connections reflected and reinforced the centrality of Cahokia, but they also offered an explanation of how these imbalanced relations functioned in the Mississippian world.[1]

The Commerce Map opens up a larger story about the networks of information that linked and shaped the South before European colonization. Describing the different and varied ways Indian peoples chose to communicate (or not communicate) does more than create a long list of the trials and misadventures of intercultural exchange in the pre-Columbian world; it reveals how Indians understood their world and how that understanding changed over time. Change is crucial to this story. A focus on the modes and techniques that Indians developed to acquire and spread information reveals a world that was not only intricately connected but also incredibly dynamic.[2]

Indian information networks, much like the Indian societies that supported and constructed them, were undergoing massive transformations in the early sixteenth century, as the first Spanish conquistadores landed on the coast of La Florida.

As the hierarchical and relatively centralized connections that had once supported paramount chiefdoms like Cahokia, Moundville (1000–1400), and Etowah (1250–1500) gradually and unevenly gave way to more dispersed information arrangements, Indians, and the Europeans and Africans they encountered, faced an increasingly complex communication landscape. More people than ever before had access to timely information, but the depth and breadth of their information proved limited. Or, more simply put, in the sixteenth-century South, more people knew more about less.[3] Indian networks remained extensive and far-reaching, but they began operating in increasingly localized ways. Examining these fragmented networks and contending with these regional variations help paint a complex picture of native people on the eve of European exploration and colonization. It also, and perhaps more important, details how communication and miscommunication laid the foundations for early colonial relations.

Historians' emphasis on the written (and mostly printed) word has led to an incomplete understanding of information networks. Pulling evidence from a wide range of sources, including material culture, iconography, written accounts, oral traditions, and linguistics, offers a way into the many and varied strategies that Indians employed to stay connected and informed. Recent works on literacy and writing systems have shown that the juxtaposition between literate European societies and illiterate native societies is both too simplistic and wrong; the same can be said of the early South, where pre-Columbian native societies developed sophisticated ways to link information, communication, and power.[4] The story of information in the early modern world looks different when printed texts are decentralized and Indian networks are taken seriously.

"*Ish-la-cho?* (Are you come?)" the Chickasaw host asked the Indian entering the town. "*Alali-o* (I am come)," the traveler replied.[5] This brief exchange is how James Adair, an eighteenth-century trader and writer, described a "common Chickasaw greeting" he witnessed. In his effort to understand how the Chickasaw communicated, Adair recorded a set of practices that almost never receives attention from historians. Quietly folded into the routines of everyday life, the acquisition and spread of information, whether by Indians or Europeans, tends to occur without much fanfare. It is only when the networks that support communication fail to work properly that people usually take note of the modes and techniques necessary to communicate. When information can be sent and received without much struggle, few bother to ask how this challenging task was ever accomplished.

As Adair's brief example illustrates, a few Europeans did attempt to describe the many and varied strategies that Indians employed to stay connected and informed.[6] This is not to argue that only European sources can tell us about Indian communication or that they offer the best perspective on the topic; this is simply not the case. Europeans almost exclusively examined Indian communication vis-à-vis their own struggles to stay informed, which is to say that these sources reveal as much, if not more, of European perceptions of native practices than about the actual practices themselves. But by asking who, when, and how news moved, these European sources describe Indian information networks as they functioned, not simply when they failed.

Adair's translation captures the gist, but not the essence, of the Chickasaw greeting. In Chickasaw, the verb *ala* does mean "to come," but not in some general, unspecified way. A better translation might be: "have you arrived *here*?" That intended location, *here*, matters and mattered a great deal. In turn, *Alali*, the reply, did more than simply answer in the affirmative. Meaning, "I have arrived *here*," the response reiterated the host's original question by emphasizing the importance of place. The messenger had arrived *here*, at a Chickasaw town, the heart and center of the host's world, and to get *here*, the Indian messenger had not only departed an implied *there*, but, more important, had managed to find and travel through paths connecting there to here. This emphasis on place, which Adair missed, hinted at both the opened paths and the good communication between the traveler and the Chickasaw town he had just entered. This greeting acknowledged the physical as well as the social, political, and even emotional link between the host and the messenger without directly inquiring about who the messenger was, where he was coming from, or the nature of his news. If the paths had not been kept up, damaged by war or lack of kinship, the Indian traveler would never have "arrived here."[7]

Indians forged paths for communication. Although hardly recognizable as roads by today's standards, these narrow footpaths, often built on top of existing animal grazing paths, crisscrossed Indian country.[8] Topography played a paramount role in the course most paths could and did take, but it would be wrong to assume that Indians established trails simply where it was easiest to tread.[9] Overland trails tended to follow waterways, but in the South's long rainy season, creeks and rivers were (and are) prone to swell, flood, and render trails impassable. The most important aspect of a path was how it crossed the region's unpredictable waterways. One of the earliest Creek dictionaries includes both the words *nene,* meaning "a way or path" and, right below, the phrase *nene etohwvlvpke,* translated in the dictionary as "a crossed path" (Figure 1.2). A more literal translation, based on the root structure, might be "paths crossed on top of each other."[10] In a time before bridges were common, fords and natural crossings were of the utmost importance. If an Indian lost his way, he needed to search not for a path or a town but for a ford. A ford would almost always lead to a trail and that trail would eventually reach a town.[11] Indian trails thus required working with and through nature.

The major corridors of interregional trade and communication often splintered to meet local and political needs. Compiled from archeological as well as historical information, Map 1.1 shows the many paths that connected and demarcated the early South, circa 1720. The branches in the trails reveal several geographical focal points. The Great Indian Warpath, discussed in more detail below, allowed entrance to the Southeast through the Kanawha River in present-day West Virginia, then followed onto the New River, and finally headed west on the Holston River to present-day Tennessee, crossing Cherokee towns and present-day Chattanooga, a major trading hub. The eastern branch of the Great Indian Warpath led to the Shenandoah River, after crossing Catawba country. The southern branch reached Upper Creek towns. The Cumberland and Tennessee Rivers helped paths cross the Appalachian Range, offering unparalleled east–west movement across the region, with some sections connecting to both land trails and waterways that moved north to south. But the majority of east–west travel was done via overland paths.[12]

European sources are filled with descriptions of Indian pathways. When conquistadores imagined themselves exploring uncharted lands, they were actually traveling on Indian-made trails that conditioned where the Europeans could journey and who they met. Trails made by the Timucua and Apalachee, for example, determined where the Franciscans established

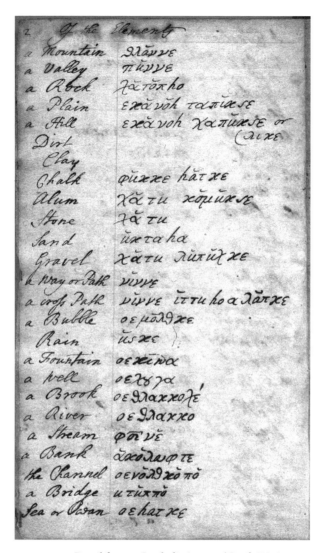

FIGURE 1.2. Detail from a Creek dictionary. (Creek Dictionary,
MS, "p. 2" [actually p. 7; incorrectly paginated by creator],
MissIND 3382.1, Moravian Archives, Bethlehem, Pa.)

their missions. Franciscan friars and other Spanish officials complained
about the roundabout nature of these trails and the difficulties they posed
for expanding mission activity, but it took close to one hundred years
(and a nasty rebellion) for the Spanish to realign these paths in a way that
privileged their, and not the Timucuas', interests. But even after Florida

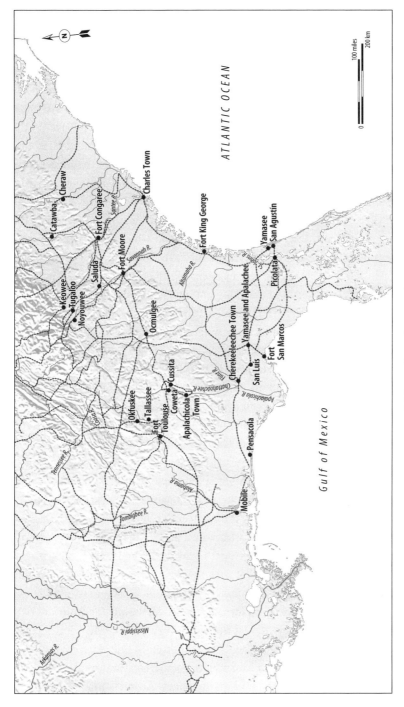

MAP 1.1. Major paths and towns, circa 1720

officials created a more streamlined Camino Real, which in theory connected San Agustín to northern México, Spanish ventures in *la tierra
adentro* remained dependent on Indian paths and guides.[13]

Both the French and the English, the other two major European players
in the colonial South, shared the Spaniards' reliance on Indian paths. The
French made extensive use of Chickasaw and Choctaw trails; these paths
allowed the French to go from the readily accessible Mississippi River to the
Tombigbee River, which in turn connected to the main overland trails that
led to the major Indian and European towns to the east of the Mississippi.
The English, for their part, primarily used Creek paths, many originating
from the Lower Creek town of Coweta, to venture westward.[14] Much like
the Franciscan friars who relied on Timucua-made paths to missionize the
region, French and English agents depended on Chickasaw, Choctaw, and
Creek trails to trade and travel around the early South.

For Indians, the trails served a variety of different purposes. They connected towns to other (and often larger) towns, they led to waterways and
hunting grounds, and they facilitated travel to both friendly and hostile
nations. There is, at first glance, nothing unusual about these descriptions.
After all, that is what trails do: They connect people of one place to people
of another. But these paths, leading to hunting grounds, enemy camps, and
major population centers, were the physical expressions of far deeper political, economic, cultural, and often spiritual linkages.[15]

The paths to and from Cahokia offer good examples. These paths reveal
first and foremost the centrality of Cahokia to the Mississippian world. With
its bustling market, extensive maize fields, and impressive earthwork mounds,
Cahokia was a sight to behold. Rather, it was *the* sight to behold. Cahokia was
unparalleled in size, religious activity, economic productivity, and even political influence.[16] From the tenth to the fourteenth century, tens of thousands of
Indians came to this imposing city from near and far, carrying salt, pinewood,
flintclay, and chert from the Missouri Ozarks; marine shells from the Gulf
of México; copper from Lake Superior; and mica from the Appalachian
Mountains. As raw materials moved into Cahokia, manufactured goods
made their way out. Traders, diplomats, and leaders returning from Cahokia
carried with them Ramey-incised pots, Chunkey stones, and copper plates
showcasing birdman iconography. They also brought Cahokian mythologies
(such as Long-Nose God and Morning Star), architectural models, govern-
mental structures, and social-ranking practices. Artifacts made in Cahokia

began appearing all over the Southeast in the twelve and thirteenth centuries. Cahokian networks had created "a Mississippian horizon," stretching from what is now eastern Oklahoma to western Tennessee, and from southern Minnesota down to Georgia. Cahokia was the sun, the most prominent and defining feature of this "horizon."[17]

But the rays of this Cahokia sun did not shine evenly. Both in their external relations and internal structures, Cahokia networks emphasized exclusivity and exclusion. Tributary towns, for example, could communicate with each other and, at times, could seek access to chiefdoms other than Cahokia, but these intracommunity and even interchiefdom connections were not encouraged. All the main trails led to Cahokia.

Networks were even further limited once inside the city. Cahokia's society was highly stratified, and its networks reflected these internal hierarchies. Goods, information, and power concentrated in the hands of a few; in a self-reinforcing way, the select people who had access to these far-reaching networks legitimized and promoted their power by displaying their exclusive connections.[18] By importing and then flaunting items like gorgets, effigy pipes, feathers, shells, and beads, Cahokia elites demonstrated their access to and influence over distant and sometimes even otherworldly places, peoples, and beliefs. These exotic goods—and more important, the esoteric knowledge these goods helped to mobilize— buttressed elite power. Cahokia chiefs depended on these items and information to fulfill their most important obligation, which was to establish harmony between the social and the natural (and often the supernatural) worlds.[19] Cahokia leaders were in constant dialogue with the larger Mississippian world, renewing, maintaining, and expanding the range of their connections—connections that placed disproportionate amounts of resources and information back in their hands. Following Cahokia's paths thus reveals extensive networks with rather exclusive access points.[20]

The same paths that provided a snapshot of Cahokia's power in the tenth to the thirteenth centuries also help tell the story of its decline. Etowah, a chiefdom located in present-day northern Georgia, had once actively traded with Cahokia. Cahokia-made items have been found in the mounds of Etowah and in the graves of its elites and chiefs, evincing a common belief system and a shared history of trade and diplomatic relations. When Cahokia's power waned after 1250 through a combination of war, drought, and probably a spiritual crisis (as Cahokian chiefs failed to appease these

violent forces), the paths between Etowah and Cahokia became less traveled. During this moment of transition, Etowah was even abandoned for
fifty years. The Etowah elite who returned and ruled from 1250 to 1375
worked to rebuild a far-reaching exchange networks. Excavations of Mound
C in Etowah have uncovered over 350 burials that contain objects from distant places decorated in nonlocal styles.[21] But in the late fourteenth century,
this network collapsed once again when Etowah was abruptly abandoned,
possibly due to a violent military attack.

The people who reoccupied Etowah in 1450 resumed their connections
to the larger Mississippian world along more regional paths, very few of
which extended as far as Cahokia. The practices and artifacts from Etowah's
third occupation reflect this reorganization. Mortuary traditions, for example,
placed less emphasis on the power of key individuals and the value of their
distant connections—gone were the ornate burials with headdresses, copper
tools, and fancy regalia found in Mound C. Items from southeastern chiefdoms, though never stylistically uniform, had once more closely resembled
each other. But as chiefdoms like Etowah started prioritizing more local
networks, their material culture became increasingly regionalized and distinct. Instead of a common iconographic tradition, materials were now
decorated with almost exclusively local symbols. Diversification trumped
centralization. These artifacts pointed to the growing autonomy of each
town and displayed the shrinking influence of individual chiefdoms.[22]

This localism only intensified with time. The chiefdoms that arose in
Etowah's wake, like Coosa and Ocute, were plagued by violence and frag-
mentation. These were the polities Hernando de Soto encountered in 1539.
The contested multipolarity of the early South is visible in the prestige
goods Coosa and Ocute elites valued. On the one hand, these items—shells,
feathers, and copper ornaments—echo the goods and distant connections
Etowah and even Cahokia elites had employed to display their authority.
On the other hand, the prestige goods in Coosa and Ocute were less widely
but more evenly spread than they had been in the past. In other words,
prestige goods and the knowledge, relations, and influence these goods
implied had both a shorter geographical reach and a broader distribution in
sixteenth-century chiefdoms than they had even two centuries earlier. The
paths and connections that bound Coosa and Ocute allowed more people
to access these goods and information, but the range and influence of both
were circumscribed. The polities that coalesced in the late fifteenth and

early sixteenth centuries, though far from autarkic, were built through regionalized and fractal paths.[23]

Indians in the early South used communication networks to demarcate both the scope and limits of their worlds. By creating trails that led to particular and often exclusive hunting grounds, for example, Indians transformed what was already an important subsistence activity into a way of articulating and delineating their territorial claims.[24] Consider, for instance, a series of conflicts that ensued in 1695 after Ivitachuco Indians marched through trails that led into the hunting grounds of San Pedro Indians. The two neighboring towns in the border between Timucua and Apalachee (Indian provinces to the north and west of San Agustín) regarded Ivitachuco's actions as a declaration of war. Though the conflict ended in stalemate, the value both Timucuas and Apalachees placed on defending their exclusive rights to these paths was clear. It was worth fighting over *who* could traverse these routes and *where* rival Indian groups could venture.[25]

Paths also played a vital role in allowing those fights to take place.[26] Warpaths, for instance, existed for the sole purpose of making war. In James Oglethorpe's first and somewhat rudimentary map of Georgia, he included a mention of "the Road of the Ochese going to War with the Floridians."[27] Though Oglethorpe was only beginning to explore this region, he made special note of the importance of these paths. The Great Indian Warpath, a major corridor between the southern and northern Indian groups, would make repeated appearances in European- and then American-made maps through the late nineteenth century. Though its name (given not by Indian contemporaries but rather by nineteenth-century anthropologists) suggests a single trail, the Great Indian Warpath was a composite of several roads that cut across the current states of Alabama, Georgia, Tennessee, Pennsylvania, and Ohio. Some of the main branches included the Warrior Path in the Chesapeake, the Kanawha Trail that linked to the Ohio River and continued to Lake Erie, and the Seneca Trail. These paths bound distant Indian nations together, even as they pitted them against each other.[28]

Because open paths and good communication went together, the role of these Indian-made trails could and did change. The Chickasaws had long traveled the Great Indian Warpath to make war on the Iroquois. In the late 1730s, when the Chickasaws decided they wanted trade rather than conflict with this powerful northern nation, they signaled their change of intentions by transforming the well-tread warpath into a path for peace. The

Chickasaws placed corn and other welcoming items along the trail as a way to convey that friendship, not violence, awaited the Iroquois who reached Chickasaw towns.[29] But if warpaths could be made white or peaceful, peaceful paths could also be turned into red warpaths. During Hernando de Soto's 1539 *entrada,* the chief of Ocale closed the paths leading to his town to prevent the Spanish conquistador from gaining access to his people. Instead of decorating the trail with corn, he dug up recently buried Spanish bodies and hung them along the trail. The chief of Ocale had dealt with "Castilians" in the past and, having received a "large noticia" (long communication) of de Soto's character and cruelty, this Indian leader wanted nothing to do with a man who harmed "people who have given [them] no offense." With mutilated corpses serving as grim trail markers, the Spaniards had no difficulty understanding that the paths to Ocale were closed.[30]

For Spanish conquistadores, the trouble then was not only in finding paths but in finding open and good paths. After all, de Soto had located the trails that led to Ocale, but a violent death awaited him and his men if he chose to follow them. To travel safely, Europeans and Indians needed access to paths undamaged by war and preserved by kinship, alliance, and trade. De Soto was forced to learn this lesson time and time again. Early in his expedition, he tried journeying from Ocute to Cofitachequi, two chiefdoms embroiled in war. At first, the conquistador was not too concerned with this interpolity conflict. Cofitachequi and Ocute were fighting each other, not the Spanish. De Soto had assumed he could readily make his way between the chiefdoms, which were only about 100 miles apart. But de Soto found no open paths between them. Without Indian aid or consent, the Spaniards could not travel or send word from Ocute to Cofitachequi, explain their peaceful intentions and neutrality in the ongoing struggle, or open a closed path.[31]

Beyond the binary of open or closed, paths could also convey the wide spectrum of relations that bound the Indian world. Paths contoured with the sinews of power. During Tristán de Luna's 1559 *entrada* into the Southeast, the Coosa Indians approached the Spanish leader and asked for help to "preserve . . . use of the[ir] roads and passes." The Coosas had been having problems with the Napochies. Once a tributary to Coosa, the Napochies were now in open rebellion and obstructing the paths of "communication, trade, and intercourse."[32] Instead of weapons or men, the Coosas wanted Spanish aid in "preserving" Coosas' ability to move freely through these "roads and passes." The Napochies had pushed too far in blocking the roads, limiting the reach of the Coosas' influence. Sensing that the balance of power was shifting, the Coosas sought to regain control over the region's main paths. They focused on reopening these routes not merely because they prized their ability to trade and travel throughout the region but also because maintaining these networks was a key source of power for the Coosas.

Traveling through the Carolinas in 1700, John Lawson quickly learned the value of Indian paths. Lawson, who was born in London, had a long apprenticeship with an apothecary that granted him some basic scientific training. He had lived in Carolina for only six months when he decided to venture on an overland expedition to Virginia, a feat few Europeans had attempted. Lawson remarked on the precision and accuracy with which Indians represented their lands: "they will draw Maps, very exactly, of all the Rivers, Towns, Mountains, and Roads, or what you shall enquire of them." In the same breath, however, he bemoaned Indian reluctance to share their knowledge: "you must be very much in their Favour, otherwise they will never make these Discoveries to you; especially, if it be in their own Quarters." Lawson understood the importance of Indian "draw[n] Maps," for "these Discoveries" exposed much more than the location of "rivers, towns . . . [and] Mountains." They revealed which paths were open, which towns were friendly, and the alliances of the Indians conveying the information. Knowing which paths to take, Lawson realized, was not only convenient; it was a matter of life and death. He and his companions avoided capture and possibly even death at the hands of an Iroquois raiding party when they learned that the paths they were using were stained red. Finding an open and friendly trail to the east, Lawson abandoned his goal of reaching Virginia and marched safely to an English plantation on the Pamlico River.[33]

As representations of geopolitical as well as geographical space, Indian maps offer a great deal of insight into how Indians understood and balanced their worlds. The Catawba Deerskin Map, made around 1721, over two decades after Lawson's journey, describes the relation between the English and Siouan-speaking groups, which South Carolinians collectively referred to as Catawbas (Figure 1.3).[34] Presented to South Carolina's governor in the wake of the devastating Yamasee War (1715–1717), the Catawba Deerskin Map was intended to serve as a didactic tool. It instructed the English on which paths were open, who was included in this network, and how the towns were connected.[35]

The Catawba Deerskin Map used circles to represent distinct towns or

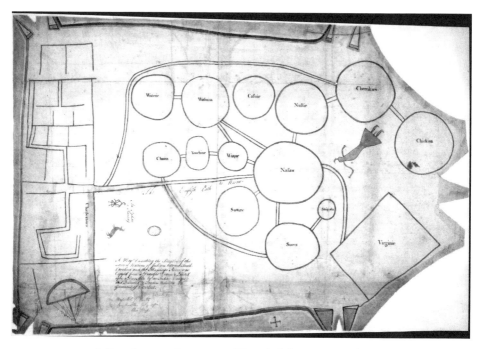

FIGURE 1.3. A Catawba map. Anonymous [Catawba], "A Map Describing the Situation of the several Nations of Indians between South Carolina and the Massisipi River." (Photo courtesy National Archives, Kew.)

nations and lines to illustrate the connections among them. This map further differentiated between Europeans and Indians by using a square rather than a circular motif to describe English holdings. The circles, much like the groups and places they represented, were of different sizes and displayed different levels of connectivity. Take the town of Nasaw. Its importance was emphasized not only by its placement at the center and its noticeably bigger size but also through its links to all places on the map.[36] The Catawba Deerskin Map included trails from Catawba towns to the English in Charles Town, to the Cherokees, and, through them, to the Chickasaws. Connections to the Creeks, the enemies of the Cherokees and the Catawbas, were not drawn. The Catawbas were neither oblivious to nor in denial of the existence of relations between the Creeks and the English; the ethnocentric approach of the mapmakers, however, centered Catawba towns and experiences, privileging only the communication networks Catawbas considered open. The Catawba Deerskin Map reflected that understanding and worldview.

Paths mattered. They mattered for trade, kinship, diplomacy, hunting, the transmittal of esoteric knowledge, warfare, and so much more.[37] Balance—balanced relationships to both earthly and spiritual worlds—was the organizing force of these Indian paths and communication. Balance was a highly practical goal based on the need to bring together, not equalize, parties with incredibly uneven levels of power. Mobilizing and organizing (and sometimes reorganizing) how goods, knowledge, and power operated in native societies, Indian paths reveal working, and often competing, indigenous epistemologies.

～

Indian communication took many forms other than paths. Maps, knotted strings, hieroglyphs, tree carvings, wampum, ritualized greetings and gestures, the capture and interrogation of prisoners, secret and public oaths, ceremonies, town councils, and even "news whoops" helped share and spread information.[38] The sheer number and diversity of these examples demonstrates, first, the emphasis that Indians placed on being informed and on having information, and second, the social specificity and cultural sensibility with which that exchange unfolded.

In his journey through the interior of Carolina, Lawson made careful notes of the Indians he encountered. Lawson recorded their traditions, clothing, dwellings, and political structure. Though he did not include a separate discussion on how Indians communicated, his journal is filled with references to the ways Indians acquired and shared information. In his section on "the Burial of their Dead," Lawson's descriptions move away from the elaborate ceremony itself and toward how the Indians talked once they gathered. Lawson was particularly impressed by the Indians' ability to recall their history.

> To prove the times more exactly, he produces the Records of the Country, which are a Parcel of Reeds, of different Lengths, with several distinct Marks, known to none but themselves; by which they seem to guess, very exactly, at Accidents that happen'd many Years ago; nay two or three Ages or more . . . I have been at the Meetings of several *Indian* Nations; and they agreed, in relating the same Circumstances, as to Time, very exactly; as, for Example, they say, there was so hard a Winter in *Carolina*, 105 years ago, that the great Sound was frozen over, and the Wild Geese

came into the Woods to eat Acorns, and that they were so tame, (I suppose, through Want) that they kill'd abundance in the Woods, by
knocking them on the Head with Sticks.[39]

Lawson remarked that the meaning of the reeds' lengths and markings
was only discernible to these Indians, "known to none but themselves."
With reeds of different lengths, the Indians spoke about the past both with
precision and with some level of secrecy.

Accurate and relevant, this means of communication seemed to Lawson
both important and perplexing. Lawson's mention of these Indian reeds
appears as a passing aside within a long description of burial practices.
He does not bother to explain why he included the information. Instead,
Lawson bluntly concludes his description of Indian communication by
stating: "*But,* to return to the dead Man."[40] That "but" was important. The
sole connecting link between funeral rites and communication, "but"
referred not to a contrast or an exception; it served as a segue between two
practices unfolding in plain sight, both of recognizable importance and
both deeply influenced by local variations. *But,* and here let's employ
Lawson's own conjunction against him, he could not properly account for
both. For Lawson, the dead man made more sense.

Lawson also found the speed of Indian communication confusing. He
was taken aback when news of his arrival reached Indian towns well before
he did. He commented on how the Indians had "heard that we were coming,
above twenty days before [we arrived]. It is very odd, that News should fly
so swiftly among these People."[41] It was baffling to Lawson how a group of
people who "never value Time" and could talk "as long as you please," and
be thus detained from "going out to hunt, fish, or any other indifferent
Business," could move faster than English traders. Lawson concluded that,
for Indians, the "value [of] time" and swiftness of communication did not
go together, and nothing made that disjuncture more evident than the
length and ritual of Indian councils.

If time seemed to collapse for Indian messengers, who traveled at speeds
seemingly impossible to the English, time slowed almost to a halt during
the elaborate, confusing, and long rituals of council meetings. Captain Jean
Bernard Bossu, a French explorer and prolific letter writer who spent many
years among the Mississippian Indians, explained, "[I]t is in such assem-
blies . . . that they [the Indian chiefs] relate all of their news and deliberate

over their political business, concerning war or peace."[42] In these exclusive
gatherings "into which they (the women) are never admitted," Indian chiefs
performed a variety of rituals that allowed them to "relat[e] all their news"
and learn the latest political and military developments. Though large,
intertown councils convened at moments of need, smaller councils met
more regularly and, more often than not, attended to basic and everyday
demands of the communities they served. Benjamin Hawkins, a longtime
Indian agent, described how "the Micco [chief], counselors . . . and warriors meet every day, in the public square; sit and drink . . . [the] black
drink; talk of news, the public and domestic concerns."[43] In this open space
at the center of town, a small group of easily recognizable men gathered and
addressed a wide range of issues, from personal quarrels to larger "domestic
concerns." These interpersonal exchanges were intended to assuage any tensions, strengthen local alliances, and foster a shared set of priorities.

Delving into how Europeans construed these exchanges requires pausing
at the mention, or rather the exclusion, of women, who "are never admitted."
Women are absent from most European sources detailing information
exchange. There are a few instances, however, when women are included, as
in the paintings of Timucuas made in the 1560s by Jacques Le Moyne and
later engraved by Theodor de Bry. De Bry's Plate XXIX, titled "Proceedings
of the Floridians in Deliberating on Important Affairs," depicts a council
meeting (Figure 1.4). Timucua women appear at the bottom corner of the
image and are briefly mentioned in the text accompanying the engraving:
"the king orders the women to prepare some casina which is a beverage
made from the leaves of a certain plant passed through a strainer." "The
women" are not even the subjects of the only sentence that mentions their
presence. Their role in the council was to make the black drink, not to share
their expertise or "deliberat[e] on important affairs." De Bry later under-
scores the importance of casina both during the council meeting and in
choosing native leadership, but never again mentions those responsible for
making the sacred drink.[44] In matrilineal societies, as in the one depicted in
the engraving, women played integral roles in economic, cultural, and even
political realms. But in most historical sources, women appear only in the
background and often in an implicit background at that.

Material sources, like ceramic pots, provide some access into the active
community of practice in which native women found themselves. In some
instances, these women-made material artifacts echo the existing political

FIGURE 1.4. Timucua council meeting. Theodor de Bry engraving. Plate XXIX,
"Proceedings of the Floridians in Deliberating on Important Affairs."
(Michael W. and Dr. Linda Fisher Collection, courtesy State Archives of Florida.)

realities, supporting the predominance of specific groups and artistic traditions. But in other cases, these ceramics suggest rather different concerns.
The ceramics made by Yamasee women from 1660 until the 1680s, when the
Yamasees lived in former Guale and Mocama mission towns along the
Georgia coast, offer a different way to view the struggles of a community
fleeing Westo slaving raids. Unlike testimonies from Yamasee men that
fiercely defend their threatened autonomy, the pots made by Yamasee
women reflect a quick ability to adapt to the current circumstances in
Mocama and Guale worlds.[45] The absence of women in most historical
accounts does not mean that women were uninvolved in the spread and
transmission of information. It simply reminds us that the story of communication was recoded through an opaquely gendered lens. For every
male runner, chief, spy, trader, and diplomat that the archive has rendered
visible, it has obscured many more female agents and approaches to information exchange.

The town council described by de Bry and those depicted by Lawson over a century later shared many commonalities. Ritualized gatherings that followed a "strict order of protocol," council meetings were about sharing information as well as reaffirming social hierarchies. De Bry described an information exchange in which "the Indians . . . never make any decisions without first having listened to all the various opinions and discussed them." Lawson hinted at the difficulties of this endeavor.

> Whensoever an Aged Man is speaking, none ever interrupts him, (the contrary Practice the English, and other Europeans, too much use) the Company yielding a great deal of Attention to his Tale, with a continued Silence, and an exact Demeanour, during the Oration. Indeed, the Indians are a People that never interrupt one another in their Discourse; no Man so much as offering to open his Mouth, till the Speaker has utter'd his Intent: When an English-Man comes amongst them, perhaps every one is acquainted with him, yet, first, the King bids him Welcome, after him the War-Captain, so on gradually from High to Low; not one of all these speaking to the White Guest, till his Supexcriour has ended his Salutation.[46]

Council communications depended on proper protocol. Though not as involved as the Iroquois Greeting Ceremony, the interactions Lawson described reveal clear procedure and organization.[47] Lawson observed how the older men spoke first. Others needed to be silent and patient; the order of speech, from "High to Low," indicated rank within Indian society. Lawson learned never to interrupt and acquired a comfort with not understanding the particulars of what was being conveyed.

Lawson quickly realized that he was not the only one confused. He explained that Tuscarora Indians "have such a Way of abbreviating their Speech, when in their great Councils and Debates, that the young Men do not understand what they treat about, when they hear them argue."[48] The "young Men" knew the language and were invited to the council, but they lacked the proper training and knowledge, and thus often failed to grasp all the intricacies of the speaker's message. Lawson might have found these different levels of speech frustrating, but he probably did not find them surprising. The idea that religious or elite members of society spoke in ways that were not widely accessible probably resonated with Lawson.[49] Lawson, like the Indians gathered at the council, understood that there was power in the chief's ability to know and use this complex language. In a world where most information moved orally, chiefs not only had to develop creative ways of transmitting information but also had to find ways to make information both controllable and reliable. This "abbreviating," as Lawson called it, displayed and validated the chief's authority.[50]

Other Indian groups used similarly complex communication structures in their internal affairs. Who the speaker was and how he performed his speech mattered as much as the information he presented. Historian James Merrell has shown that, while the English did not trust or particularly value the go-betweens who served as their intermediaries to the Indians, the opposite was true for the Indians, who often sent high-ranking and well-respected members of their society to speechify and otherwise communicate with the English. In a circular logic, the high rank and respectability of native agents hinged on their ability to communicate and speak in these public settings.[51]

The close connection between the ability to speak and the authority to share news made communication all the more difficult in the multilingual South. The region was a patchwork of mutually unintelligible languages. Home to at least five major language groups (Iroquoian, Muskogean, Siouan, Caddoan, and Timucua), the Southeast also boasted many more dialects, with a lot of regional diversity.[52] Lawson complained how "it often appears, that every dozen Miles, you meet with an Indian Town, that is quite different from the others you last parted withal."[53]

This was a common predicament in the South. In his 1605 reconnaissance of the Florida coast, Captain Francisco Fernández de Ecija found himself constantly having to employ new interpreters. In St. Catherine's Island he hired Felipe Christian, but when the Spaniards reached Santa Elena, only forty miles away, Ecija was forced to find a new interpreter to communicate with Orista and Cayagua Indians. The language Indians chose to speak (or not speak) conveyed a great deal about both the identity of any particular group and its relationship to its neighbors.[54] In this divided landscape, finding a common language had more to do with power than with community. In Timucua, place names like Ceibamocha ("speaking Place by the Ceiba Tree" or "mo-cha Speaking place") as well as Utinamocha ("speaking place of the lord of the land") reveal the role of language (and of changes in the language) in articulating the limits of specific territory.[55]

Language did more than demarcate space; it also revealed who was in control. "The most powerful Nation of these Savages," explained John Lawson, "scorns to treat or trade with any others (of fewer Numbers and less Power) in any other Tongue but their own which serves for the Lingua of the Country, with which we travel and deal . . . the Tuskeruro's [Tuscaroras] are most numerous in North-Carolina, therefore their Tongue is understood by some in every Town of all the Indians near us." Trade was conducted in the Tuscaroras' tongue because "they are the most numerous" and "the most powerful." The Tuscaroras' refusal "to treat or trade" in any tongue but their own was a sign of their strength and influence.[56]

Lawson may have understood the deep implications of Tuscarora serving as the "Lingua of the Country," but most European conquistadores and traders simply heard what they wanted. In the 1680s, Henry Woodward, one of the earliest Indian agents and traders based in South Carolina, recorded some of the different methods Westos used to communicate. From the Westos' "long speeches" and drawings "uppon trees (the barke being hewed away) the effigies of a beaver, a man, on horseback and guns," Woodward concluded that these Indians were keen on South Carolina and wanted to open trade: "[i]ntimating thereby as I suppose, their desire for freinship [sic.], and comerse wth us."[57] Though Woodward's interpretation may have been right, his reading of the Westos' messages had more to do with English interests in "commerce" than with the "desires" of the Westos.

Listening for what they wanted, Europeans often failed to hear correctly. Most of the early conquistadores heeded only the language of gold. Juan de Añasco, a scout for Hernando de Soto, proved no different in this sense. As de Añasco searched for a good landing site for de Soto's sizable party, an Indian he captured told him about Juan Ortiz, a survivor of an earlier Spanish *entrada* living in a coastal Indian town since the late 1520s. When de Añasco "heard him [the Indian captive] say Orotiz," he stopped listening and began celebrating certain that he had found *oro* (gold). Brushing aside any "further interpretation," the Spaniards completely missed the "meaning and sense" of the Indians' message. de Añasco's "principal aim was to go in search for gold," and he looked for it everywhere, even in reports of Spanish captives. The Spaniards only later realized their mistake when Ortiz, but no *oro,* appeared.[58]

De Soto proved an even slower learner than de Añasco. The conquistador had a long career in the Americas before he arrived in La Florida. At the age of fourteen, de Soto had left Spain and served in expeditions in Panamá, Nicaragua, and Ecuador. His exploits, especially under Francisco Pizarro, had made him wealthy. De Soto had used his fortune to win favor in the Spanish court and secure a contract to lead his own expedition. Late in the spring of 1539, at the age of forty-three, he sailed from Cuba to Florida with about 600 men and 240 horses. For all his experience and preparation, or maybe because he had so much experience in other parts of America, de Soto found even the least reliable reports of gold convincing. Perico, a young Indian boy captured by de Soto in Napituca, had promised to take the Spanish to Cofitachequi, where riches awaited. De Soto's other Indian guides questioned Perico's claims, but de Soto dismissed their concerns, favoring the alluring reports of this young boy. After a long and strenuous march through desolate lands, the dreams de Soto had built on Perico's promises began to disappear. Perico had misled the Spanish, probably in the hopes of reaching a land and people he was familiar with. De Soto was forced to contend not only with the consequences of a disingenuous informer but also with finding reliable information to regroup his increasingly discouraged party. The Spanish did not suffer from a dearth of information. On the contrary, the Spanish had to make sense of many and different reports. As with the multiple paths that lay before de Soto, the trick was not simply finding a route or news but securing an open path and "*buenas nuevas.*"[59]

The disorientation the Spanish felt as they traversed the early South was rivaled only by the intense violence with which they responded to it. The bloody chronicles of de Soto's 1540 march draw an implicit link between the Spaniards' lack of information (or their imagined and feared lack of information) and the violence with which they retaliated against false or misleading reports. De Soto killed, burned, tortured, and even fed Indian guides and interpreters to the dogs if he suspected them of lying or even of withholding key information.[60] The Spanish were unable to make much headway without Indian aid, but even after they secured what seemed like relevant information, they did not know how to evaluate it properly. Unsurprisingly, de Soto marched his men toward more mirages than oases. From 1539 to 1542, de Soto led his men north to Apalachee (Tampa Bay), then east, through modern-day Georgia, South Carolina, and North Carolina. Next they turned south and west, where they trekked through present-day Alabama, Mississippi, and eventually Arkansas. Their long, winding journey, violent confrontations (most famously at Mabila), and rapidly diminishing supplies heightened Spanish dependence on Indian information.[61]

Not all Indians betrayed the Spaniards. De Soto owed his handful of victories in great part to the Indian guides who decided to share valuable and timely information. In Napituca, de Soto avoided certain death when four Indian interpreters disclosed the Indians' plan to attack the Spanish. Vitachuco, the cacique of Napituca, had welcomed de Soto and his men but quietly revealed to the Indian interpreters that his intentions were far from amicable. The four interpreters at first agreed to go along with Vitachuco's attack, but after some debate they reconsidered the feasibility of the plan for "the undertaking now appeared difficult and a victory in it impossible." Instead of joining Vitachuco, the four interpreters decided to disclose the plan to de Soto.[62] The Spaniards wasted no time mounting a preemptive strike, foiling the Napitucas' attack and capturing many Indians as slaves. This experience—having reliable information and, more important, being able to act on it—proved to be an exception rather than the norm for most Spanish conquistadores.

Indians made it their business to learn about the foreigners marching through the South. Indians wanted to know about the intentions, the strengths and weaknesses, and the sources of power, both natural and supernatural, of the Europeans. Disease, in particular, proved an important subject. In his *Briefe and True Report of the New Found Land of Virginia*, John White, who had first traveled to North America in 1585 to establish a colony on Roanoke Island, noted that Indians quickly learned about European diseases and that this knowledge complicated early Indian–English relations. "The disease also so strange, that they neither knew what it was, nor how to cure it . . . all the countrie wrought so strange opinions of us."[63] The movement of information about illnesses "so strange" overlays the devastating story of population decline in the sixteenth- and seventeenth-century South with native efforts to understand what those illnesses were and, more important, how they could be cured.[64] Álvar Nuñez Cabeza de Vaca, one of the four survivors of the disastrous Pánfilo de Narváez's *entrada* in 1528, remarked on Indians' keen interest on this topic. In his eight-year overland journey from Florida to northern México, Cabeza de Vaca repeatedly met Indians who knew a great deal about him and his supposed power to cure illness, even though neither he nor any of the surviving members of his expedition had visited those towns.[65]

The ability of Indians to acquire and transmit information about the Spanish, even without having direct contact with the conquistadores, made quite an impression on explorers and chroniclers alike. Garcilaso de la Vega, also known as El Inca, was the son of a Spanish conquistador and an Inca noblewoman. In 1605, he published *La Florida del Inca*, a rich and complex account of Hernando de Soto's *entrada* based on firsthand accounts.[66]

Garcilaso's narrative depicts the Spanish conquistadores in a favorable light but also treats native people as fully fleshed actors, deserving of consideration and respect. He reported that news of Spanish practices and beliefs traveled quickly among Indian towns. Garcilaso made special note of the power of information in his description of de Soto's travels through Guancane.[67] Garcilaso describes how, as de Soto marched,

> from land to land, [he] reached the province of Guancane. And since the Indians here had learned . . . and had heard it said that the Christians had brought the cross in their hands as a device, and that all benefits performed by them in curing the sick were accomplished by making above them the sign of the cross, there arose the pious practice of putting this symbol over their houses, for they believed that just as it had cured those sick, so it would also deliver everyone from all evil and danger.[68]

In Guancane the Spaniards encountered Indian houses decorated with crosses and Indians doing "the sign of the cross." De Soto and his men did not know what to make of Indians practicing Christianity without instruction from priests or guidance from other Spaniards. Guancane is not mentioned in any other historical or linguistic sources from the time, however, which perhaps suggests that Garcilaso invented this province as a literary device (probably by combining oral testimonies of de Soto's expedition with Cabeza de Vaca's earlier account).[69] Creating Guancane enabled Garcilaso to show his readers several things: first the power of Christianity or at least of the power of the symbol of the cross; second, the willingness of Indians to embrace Christianity; and third, how quickly and far Indians moved information, even information the Spanish thought they controlled—a fact that unsettled more than delighted European travelers.[70]

The Spanish struggled to decipher Indian communication correctly. "They [the Cayagua Indians] never left off making the smoke signals to us," recalled Captain Ecija as he reconnoitered the coastline north of San Agustín, Florida.[71] The unmistakable pillar of smoke scorching in the distance both reassured and disturbed Ecija in 1605. The smoke revealed that there were Indians present, but what those Indians wanted to convey was not always clear. Ecija wondered whether these were "smoke signals *to us* [the Spaniards]" or whether they were admonitions to stay away. Sometimes trade, and other times arrows, greeted the Spanish captain as he sailed toward the smoke signals. The only certain meaning Ecija surmised from the smoke signals was that his expedition had not gone unnoticed. The Cayagua Indians seemed to know more about the Spaniards than Ecija would ever learn about them.[72]

Unlike the Spanish conquistadores, who tended to repeat the mistakes of their predecessors, Indians paid attention. Cabeza de Vaca recalled that in one of the first Indian towns the Spaniards had visited, they had "found samples of gold. Through signs we asked the Indians where they had gotten those things. They indicated to us that very far from there was a province called Apalachee, in which there was much gold, and they gestured that it had a great quantity of everything we valued."[73] Although Cabeza de Vaca would go on to have many more and far more complex interactions with southeastern Indians, this early conversation struck him as significant. The Indians not only displayed their geographical knowledge of and connections to "a very far . . . province called Apalachee" but also revealed their awareness of who the Spanish were and "of everything we valued."

Vitachuco, the chief of Napituca who planned the failed attack on de Soto, explained to an approaching Spanish delegation that his dislike of the Europeans was well informed. Vitachuco remembered the "many cruelties" carried out by the Spanish during their previous incursions into the region. The chief of Napituca also knew "very well what [Spanish] customs and behavior are like"; he would not be fooled by promises of friendship from these "sons of the devil."[74] Sixty years later Gaspar de Salas attempted to journey to Napituca. The cacique of Ocute warned Salas not to continue because, "if they went forth they would be killed by the Indians, for long time ago . . . Soto had gone by . . . [and the Indians] had killed them, and it was likely that they would kill" any Spanish party that entered their land.[75] Salas probably did not know the details of de Sotos' *entrada*, but the Ocute and Napituca had not forgotten. Salas wisely heeded the Indians' threat and turned back.

The Spanish had to go to great lengths to communicate in ways that would prove indecipherable to the Indians. In 1559, for example, Tristán de Luna had to find a way to leave a message for a small group of men he had sent to reconnoiter the land. He needed to inform them that the Spanish colony had moved from Nanipacana back to the coast. Because Luna did not know or particularly trust the local Indian population, he did not wish to share his plans with them. Instead, Luna placed a placard on a tree that read: "dig below." Buried beneath the sign was an urn with a letter and instructions inside.[76] Hernando de Soto had tried a similar approach twenty years earlier near the town of Aymay, in present-day South Carolina. He "left a letter buried at the foot of a pine tree and on the pine some words cut on the bark . . . [which read] 'Dig at the foot of this pine tree and you will find a letter.'" De Soto hoped his men, and only his men, "might learn what the governor had done and where he had gone." In the letter, de Soto provided further instructions, describing the particular "marks left cut on the trees by Juan de Añasco" that would guide the small group of men who had ventured inland in search of supplies back to the main group.[77] The Spanish strategically employed letters to exchange information in a way that restricted native involvement, even as they traveled on Indian-made paths.

But Indians were not disarmed by the written word. They quickly understood its value. Carved on trees, buried in an urn, or printed in a letter, European written texts were only as incomprehensible to the Indians as the drawings on tree bark was to Woodward or the mention of *oro* was to Juan de Añasco. The capture of that same Juan Ortiz, a member of the hapless Pánfilo de Narváez's 1528 expedition, showed how quickly Indians learned to manipulate European communication techniques. By the time Narváez embarked for Florida, he was in his fifties and had already served in the conquests of Jamaica and Cuba. He was deeply embittered when Hernán Cortés took his place as commander of the lucrative expedition to México. Narváez spent the followings years petitioning for a new commission that would grant him the right to conquer a part of North America (and would afford him the same gold and glory that had welcomed Cortés). But Narváez, who proved a brash and inept leader, did not have Cortés's fortune. Narváez made one mistake after another, at one point fatefully dividing his already weakened crew into two groups. The two Spanish parties spent more time searching for news of one another than exploring the land and its resources. This vulnerability afforded the chief of Ucita an opportunity. Preying on the Spanish want for news, Ucita attached something that resembled a letter to a stick near the shore, where the Spaniards were sure to see it. To further convince the Spaniards of the letter's legitimacy, Ucita arranged the sticks holding the letter in the shape of a cross. When the Spaniards spotted the piece of paper hanging from a cross, they assumed it contained news of Narváez's whereabouts. Ortiz went to retrieve the letter; as soon as he reached the shore, Ucita's men apprehended him. For the next eleven years, Ortiz remained captive, until the announcement of his presence inspired false hope of gold among de Soto's men.[78]

Chief Ucita had exploited the inherent risk of gathering information. His trap revealed the Indians' keen ability to understand Spanish desires, in this case information about the rest of the Narváez party. Perhaps more interesting, his cunning ploy reveals a deep familiarity with the Spanish means of conveying information. Chief Ucita had acquired paper, created something that resembled a letter, and placed it on the most easily identifiable Catholic symbol: the cross.[79] Clearly, Ucita knew how the Spaniards exchanged *nuevas*.

This is not to say that Indians always understood perfectly either who the Spaniards were or what they wanted. Their frustrations in communicating with Spaniards become palpable in the testimony of Hernando de Escalante Fontaneda. Shipwrecked around 1549 at the age of thirteen, Fontaneda lived primarily with Calusa Indians for over seventeen years. In 1566, Pedro Menéndez de Avilés, the first governor of Florida, negotiated for his return, though it is possible that French Huguenots had rescued him a year earlier and Fontaneda rejoined the Spanish when Menéndez destroyed the French fort. For three years, Fontaneda served as an interpreter for Menéndez de Avilés, after which he returned to Spain and penned his memoir. He recalled how the cacique of Calusa became irritated when his "newly captured" Spanish prisoners failed to understand him and disobeyed his requests. "When we tell these, your companions, to dance and sing, and do other things, why are they so mean and rebellious that they will not?" the cacique of Calusa asked Fontaneda. "Is it that they do not fear death, or will not yield to a people unlike them in their religion?"[80] Fontaneda attempted to explain that the "rebellious" Spaniards were nothing of the sort. The prisoners did not comply simply because they did not understand. The cacique of Calusa remained unconvinced. He did not believe that linguistic limitations bore all the blame. After all, "he would command them to do things, and sometimes they would obey him, and at others they would not." The unpredictable responses of the Spanish prisoners led the cacique of Calusa to distrust his captives' intentions.

In their inability to make sense of what the other was saying, the Spanish and the Calusas had something in common. The Spaniards, like the Calusa, proved incapable of processing the conflicting responses of their Indian captives, allies, and guides. Labeling Indians as *gente sin razón* ("people without reason"), the Spanish understood that whatever information arrangement they established between themselves and the Indians would be imperfect. Apparently, as Fontaneda's testimony showed, Indians thought so too. In the end, it took another interpreter, who confirmed Fontaneda's

response, to convince the cacique of Calusa that confusion, not insubordi-
nation, had driven the Spanish captives.[81]

Both Europeans and Indians struggled to remain informed and attuned to
a world in flux. Navigating this world required Europeans to reconcile new
and sometimes inexplicable developments with not knowing how to gather or
process reliable information. Making sense of these new forces required
Indians to work through increasingly localized and fragmented channels of
communication, an unstable and often violent political climate, and a reduc-
tion in the size and influence of most existing polities. Though communication and the need to communicate predated any European incursion, the
Spanish *entradas* put Indian approaches to information networking to the test.
That de Soto's massive, hundred-strong army managed to surprise a small
number of Indian towns hinted at the limits of Indian information networks.
As the Spanish soldiers traveled past Toalli, in central Georgia, they reached "a
little stream where a small footbridge was made . . . As soon as the Governor
had crossed the stream, he found a village called Achese [Ichisi] a short distance on . . . [where] the Indians had never heard of Christians." The testimony
of Ichisi's leader echoed this confusion, admitting that the Spanish had gained
"entrance into my land . . . without me [the cacique] having known of [their]
coming." De Soto was taken aback, dumbfounded by the idea that the Spaniards
had managed to surprise the town. These Indians were lying, the conquistador
concluded, because his arrival could not possibly have been missed.[82]

The surprise of the Ichisi attests to the increasingly localized nature of
Indian information networks in the mid-sixteenth century.[83] It is easy to
blame the conquistadores for their failure to find information. Their brazen,
violent, and culturally insensitive recourses make their struggles to communicate perfectly explicable. But this is only part of the story—a part that
is perhaps more readily recognizable because the conquistadores authored
the bulk of the sources. The Spanish were not alone in their struggles. The
communication shortcomings of the Spaniards and later the French and
the English also reflected the limitations and problems that constrained the
particular Indian networks that these Europeans managed to access. Ichisi
was on the outer rim of Ocute's sphere of influence, and Ocute itself was a
smaller polity than the mightier and more expansive Cofitachequi or Coosa.
Neither its location nor its language made Ichisi a particularly accessible
site; it is entirely possible that de Soto's men could have marched near Ichisi
without the Indians having received a detailed warning.

Tristán de Luna, the last Spanish conquistador to arrive before the founding of the first permanent European colony in the region, left detailed accounts of the changing native networks in the mid-sixteenth century. Luna was a seasoned Spanish explorer who had accompanied Coronado on his ill-fated search for *Cíbola* in 1542 and had quickly learned the value of preparedness and administrative savvy. In 1558, having been chosen to command a new expedition to Florida, Luna was determined to avoid the failures of previous expeditions. He landed in Ochuse Bay with an exceedingly well-supplied fleet and over 1,500 colonists under his command.[84] Unlike Juan Ponce de León's 1513 expedition, which had barely been able to reach land before it was attacked by Calusa Indians, or Lucas Vázquez de Ayllón's short-lived 1526 colony, which had suffered constant harassment from Guale Indians, Luna managed to avoid hostile encounters with local populations. "Until now," Luna wrote in his report to the king, "there have appeared in this bay a few Indian fishermen only."[85] No Indian encounters implied that no violence had befallen the young colony, but also that the Spanish had gathered very little information about their surroundings. "Concerning the country," Luna confessed, "I have up to now learned no secret."[86]

The emptiness Luna sensed was real. The Indians in Ochuse Bay were leaving their towns in large numbers in an attempt to limit Luna's access to food and supplies as well as to any information the Spanish could gather about the resources and people beyond the coast. It wasn't that Luna was avoiding Indian entanglements; it was that the Indians were avoiding him. On September 19, 1559, the lack of Indian presence suddenly became a major problem. "A fierce tempest" decimated the month-old Spanish settlement and "did irreparable damage to the ships of the fleet."[87] As the wind blew with unimaginable force, the heavy rain drowned Luna's high hopes. The supplies, ammunitions, and population intended to support the Spanish endeavor were gone.

Luna needed to find Indian allies, and he needed to find them quickly. The *adelantado* sent parties inland to locate "information of the character of the country and the towns they may find."[88] Luna had searched in vain for food and he misguidedly relocated the colony twice: once to Nanipacana and then again back to Pensacola.[89] Luna could no longer wait in the dark. He needed to learn "the secrets" of the country, and he believed that the Coosa were the answer to his prayers. Twenty years earlier, the Coosas had welcomed de Soto and had helped the Spanish party travel through the region. Some of Luna's men had even participated in de Soto's 1539-1542 expedition and probably remembered the kindness of the Coosas. The Gentleman of Elvas, one of the chroniclers of de Soto's march, reported that Coosa was "very populous and had many large towns and planted fields which reached from one town to the other. It was a charming and fertile land." Coosa, according to de Soto, was a large chiefdom, with clear boundaries and a powerful ruler.[90]

But Luna never found this Coosa. The supposedly "well-populated land with abundant food" actually had few towns and even fewer supplies. Though there was still a cacique of Coosa who commanded significant authority—which he displayed before the terrified Spaniards in an oath-swearing ceremony—the chiefdom was far less centralized than it had been two decades earlier, plagued by internal conflicts and rife with division.[91] Luna's pleas to the Coosas for aid were neither fulfilled nor denied, but countered with requests for Spanish help. Luna needed food and supplies, but the Coosas needed Luna's men to fight or at least intimidate the Napochies. This request reflected a significant shift from what de Soto had seen during his *entrada*. In 1540, the Coosas were keen to display the reach and influence of their paths; in 1559, the Coosas approached Luna for help in keeping those very connections open.[92]

The Coosas remembered their prior dealings with the Spaniards well. Though the Tascaluzas, a neighboring paramount chiefdom on the upper Alabama River, and not the Coosas had decided to attack de Soto and his men at Mabila, some Coosa soldiers had participated in the battle and many more had suffered from the food shortages, the ravaging diseases, and the violence that followed de Soto's *entrada*. When Luna sent Mateo del Sauz into Coosa to find supplies and Indian allies, the Coosas had to decide whether the benefits of welcoming the Spanish outweighed the costs. They had a difficult, but informed, choice to make. The starving Spanish soldiers, on the other hand, were far more desperate.

Sauz first entered the chiefdom of Coosa through the town of Onachiqui, heading then to Apica and finally to the big city of Ulibahali, which de Soto had visited two decades prior.[93] The Ulibahali at first offered to help Luna's men. But when Sauz and his party overextended their welcome and ate most of the town's corn supply, the Ulibahali wanted the Spanish gone. They deviced a plan to remove the Spaniards from their town in a peaceful and expedient manner: They staged a seemingly important but ultimately fake delegation to usher Sauz and his men away from Ulibahali. The delegation was comprised of a principal man carrying a cane adorned with a white feather and four well-dressed attendants. The pretend delegates came with a message from the "lord of Coza," which invited the Spaniards to his town.

The Spaniards were at first delighted by this invitation. As Fray Agustín Dávila Padilla, one of the main chroniclers of the Luna expedition recorded, "the captains and priests were quite innocent of cunning[;] they were overjoyed by this embassy." But after the initial joy came doubt. According to Padilla, Sauz and his men hesitated. The promises made by this Indian ambassador—promises of food, friendship, and welcome—were almost too good to be true. Having had endured one misfortune after another, the Spaniards did well to question their sudden change of fate. But questioning is all they could really do. Sauz had little choice but to follow the Indian ambassador because he could not risk offending the "lord of Coza" who was asking them "to hurry." To Sauz's dismay, his misgivings were quickly proven right. The Indian delegates promptly abandoned the Spanish party once they reached the outer limits of Ulibahali. The trick had worked. The Indians at Ulibahali had managed to remain friendly with the Spanish, all the while forcing Sauz and his men to continue onward to the town of Coosa.[94]

Nothing about the Spanish–Ulibahali exchange had been as it seemed. The welcoming Ulibahali actually wanted the Spaniards gone, the Indian ambassador was a fake, the promises of Coosa's friendship and support were a ruse, and the duped Spaniards were not as naive as they appeared. Looking closely at how Indians and Spaniards sought to understand one another on their own terms helps uncover the dynamics of cross-cultural contact. On the one hand, these exchanges emphasize the different expectations, approaches, and understandings arising from a singular moment. On the other, they show the conceptual mechanisms working at the point of exchange, with neither the Spaniards nor the Indians impervious to the difficulties of communication.

Sauz's delegation failed to gather the needed supplies, and soon thereafter Luna found himself governor of a mutinous colony. By July 1561, the Spanish had departed from Pensacola and would not return to the region for another four years. In 1565, when the Spaniards established a permanent town in La Florida, they entered a world where the struggle to communicate was exactly that: a struggle.[95]

CHAPTER TWO

INFORMATION CONTESTS

~

And although it is true that all this time I have spent seeking for
people knowledgeable of those provinces, I have not found one . . .
capable of informing me of those territories with any detail.

Captian Antonio Argüelles to Governor Manuel de Cendoya, 1671

THE FIRST PERMANENT Spanish colony in La Florida began with the
French. If the expeditions of Pánfilo de Narváéz (1528), Hernando de Soto
(1539), and Tristán de Luna y Arrellano (1559) had taught the Spanish anything, it was that Florida was a magnet for destruction, failure, and death—a
magnet that, for about fifty years, had only attracted Spaniards. In the summer
of 1564, all that changed. As the latest Spanish expedition to Florida struggled
to depart, plagued by problems of supplies, desertion, and licensing, word
reached Spain that the French had founded an outpost in La Florida. Under
the leadership of Jean Ribault, the French had established Charlesfort, a
Huguenot colony on the coast of present-day South Carolina, only to abandon
it shortly thereafter. Before the implications of these failed French efforts
could be assessed, a flurry of conflicting reports reached Spanish officials
about additional expeditions—English, possibly Portuguese, or perhaps even
more French ventures—sailing for Florida. These foreign threats gave the
Spanish colonial project in this region a certain level of immediacy that had
been absent from the earlier *entradas*.

Pedro Menéndez de Avilés had a keen and personal interest in Florida.
Appointed as Captain General of the Fleet of the Indies by King Philip II,
Menéndez had escorted treasure fleets from the Americas back to Spain for
several years. Loaded with precious cargo, these vessels followed the gulf
current back to Europe, which meant that they passed along the coast of
Florida. Menéndez understood and wrote forcibly about the strategic

importance of La Florida. In a 1564 *Memorial* to the King, Menéndez explained that "if the . . . French or the English or any other nation should want to make a settlement in Florida, it would be a great harm to these kingdoms, because [that could] . . . enable them to establish a site and fortifications that would enable them . . . to take the flotas and other ships which should come from the Indies."[1] But Menéndez had another reason for wanting to return to Florida: his son, Juan. On Menéndez's last voyage as captain general, a ship carrying Juan had wrecked near the coast of Florida. Menéndez had long hoped to return and search for both his son and the missing cargo, but all his earlier petitions to return to the area had been denied.

By the time Menéndez received permission to sail to Florida in 1565, his cargo and son were lost forever. To make matters worse, René de Goulaine de Laudonnière had already departed from the French port of Havre-de-Grâce to establish Fort Caroline, a new French colony. Though the instructions Menéndez received from King Phillip II made no explicit mention of the French, Laudonnière's activities informed practically every aspect of Menéndez's plan.[2] Menéndez was still preparing for his journey when the testimony of Roberto Meleneche, a seaman and soldier who sailed with and then mutinied against Laudonnière, reached Spain. Meleneche confirmed what had previously been only speculation: There was a French garrison in Florida and the French had every intention of making Fort Caroline a permanent colony. Meleneche described how the French had "built a fort of timber . . . [and] Into the fort they put eight artillery pieces, the two medium-sized cannon[s] . . . and great quantities of all kinds of ammunition."[3] The establishment of a French fort in La Florida added another layer of uncertainty and strife to a region already riddled with contests for authority.[4] That contestation shaped *what* the Spanish wanted to know about La Florida, its lands, and its peoples.

To compare and differentiate the information practices of European rivals in La Florida—first the Spanish, then the French, followed eventually by the English—requires employing a long yet punctuated chronology that covers a little over a century, from the 1560s to the 1670s. Examining these three colonial powers alongside each other reveals a shared understanding of *nuevas* as concerned with foreign and, more often than not, bellicose matters. Moreover, this approach emphasizes the many, different and local strategies of information exchange that coexisted in La Florida. And finally, it shows how most European efforts to acquire news in the early South demanded interaction with yet another *other:* Indians.[5] In seeking news, Spanish, French, and English colonists all depended on native informers and information.

And what of the Indians? Did they also associate news with what was foreign? Unlike languages such as English, Spanish, or French, in which "news" often refers to an account of a recent or noteworthy event, Indian words for *news* were more closely associated with notions of language and speaking. The Creek language had no particular word for *news;* the word *opunvkv,* which refers to a lecture or speech, probably is the closest in meaning and use. Creeks, Chickasaws, and Choctaws used verbs for *news* that could be modified with affixes and suffixes; these morphemes added to the beginning or the end of a word helped indicate, with remarkable precision, whether any particular item of news had been completed or was ongoing, whether it was deliberate or accidental, and even if the speaker had seen it firsthand or had acquired the report through hearsay.[6] Timucua, a non-Muskogean language spoken in the region, similarly linked *news* with the ability to speak and with the person speaking (the speaker). The Timucua word for *news* was probably *heba,* meaning "language," "word," or "a speech." While hardly conclusive given the diversity of Indian languages, these definitions suggest that some Indians at least partially connected news to discourse rather than to novelty.

We can make some assumptions about *what* Indians thought qualified as news before European colonization based on events that required action-able information. Burial sites from the twelfth to fifteenth centuries, for example, document the rise of armed conflict, the valorization of military might, and the consequences of that mounting violence—elites were increasingly laid to rest alongside their weapons, and the number of corpses displaying signs of traumatic death grew as well.[7] Palisades, which serve no other purpose than protection, also became a fixture of large Indian towns by the fourteenth century.[8] Issues of food and substance posed another set of information problems for large chiefdoms. Information about a harvest surplus or shortage was necessary to employ workers, distribute or store maize, and appease the powerful spiritual forces that balanced the uni-verse.[9] But beyond some general glean about the state of the harvest or the destabilizing force of war, we are left mostly to speculate about what Indians in the early South regarded as news before the Spanish *entradas* of the sixteenth century.

Indian place names offer perhaps the most enduring clue to how Indians conceived their world.[10] Although most native place names tend to be ethnocentric and specific, placing the concerns and understandings of the group in question ahead of a greater social, historical, or even geographic context, the Indian place names of La Florida show an ethnocentrism that was supported not by isolation but rather was fostered by a deep awareness of others.[11] Even the name Timucua, which means "enemy," functioned not as self-designation but as a way of underscoring the rivalries characteristic of Timucua-speaking polities. These Indian names and demarcations make it very clear that, while Indians cared deeply about external threats, the *other* they worried about most often was not Spanish, English, or French. It was Indian.[12] Florida Indians in the late sixteenth and seventeenth century expressed more concern about intra- and inter-Indian violence than about European attacks.

Indian approaches to information had a long history that influenced *what* news native people prioritized as well as what they communicated when they encountered Europeans. Most *nuevas* in the early South moved through Indian hands and voices. It was Indian networks that connected (and sometimes divided) the competing European players in the region. The question of *what* information mattered in the early South thus reveals a tension between imperial ambitions and on-the-ground power dynamics that underlay practically all colonial endeavors. The case of La Florida shows the interconnections among Spanish, French, and English colonial projects and, more important, the centrality of Indian networks in forging those connections.

La Florida held "the key to the Spanish empire," or so *adelantado* Pedro Menéndez de Avilés declared.[13] Though not many sixteenth-century Spanish officials agreed with Menéndez's rather hyperbolic assessment, all concurred that the French could not be allowed to stay in Florida. Menéndez was born to a well-respected family that had participated in the Catholic reconquest of Granada. As the youngest of twenty children, he had little chance of receiving a large inheritance and had turned to the sea to make his living. He worked as a corsair, sailor, and eventually as an officer in the Spanish armada—occupations that had taken him across the Atlantic many times. But in his 1565 voyage to Florida, Menéndez's vast experience proved no match for the tempestuous ocean. He endured a disastrous journey only to arrive after the French supply vessels he had been sent to intercept. Unsure of where the French had established the fort, Menéndez sailed too close to the coast. Instead of gaining important information about Fort Caroline, he was spotted by French soldiers and lost his tactical advantage. As French and Spanish ships exchanged fire, Menéndez climbed on deck and boldly declared that he was "Pedro Menéndez, Sent by order of Your Majesty to this coast and land to burn and hang the French Lutherans who were found here."[14] Menéndez's spirit was high, but the skirmish ended in neither burning nor hanging. Uncertainty and retreat were all that the Spanish could muster.

Fort Caroline stood. Laudonnière and the other French officers rejoiced. Laudonnière had participated in both of France's colonization efforts in Florida. He had served as second in command to Jean Ribault in 1562, and in 1564 he spearheaded the building of Fort Caroline, a Huguenot colony of about 200 people. Like Menéndez, Laudonnière was an experienced sailor with a deep commitment to his faith, though in his case it was Calvinism rather than Catholicism. But Laudonnière, who had fled to England during the outbreak of the French War of Religion in 1562, lacked both military expertise and political charisma. By September 1564, when Ribault returned to Florida with reinforcements and orders to replace Laudonnière as the colony's commander, the outpost was in a state of disarray.

The Spanish had gathered as much intelligence about the French as possible before reaching La Florida in 1565. From a deposition taken from captured Frenchmen, the Spanish had learned about the accomplishments as well as the problems at Fort Caroline. Stefano de Rojomonte, who had sailed with Laudonnière in 1564, provided information about the size of the fort, with its "300 men—soldiers and sailors," and on its armament, with its "10 pieces of heavy guns and many other medium-sized ones, and miscellaneous artillery, and many arquebuses, powder, and ammunition." The Spanish cared about more than weapons and fortifications, however. Three-quarters of the interrogation focused on French-Indian interactions. De Rojomonte commented on how "for the first two months after they had arrived in the country they had great friendship with them [the Indians] . . . [and that] the Indians had always brought them [the French] fish and many fruits of the soil and they had safely entered and left their villages and homes."[15] But then French–Indians relations began to deteriorate. Though de Rojomonte blamed Laudonnière's inept leadership skills for this situation, his testimony alluded to Indian politics operating beyond French control.

Menéndez's access to this information determined his next moves. Discouraged but not defeated by the initial skirmish with the French at sea, he landed his fleet thirty-five miles south at what would become San Agustín. For almost two weeks the two commanders cohabitated on the Florida coast, estranged but aware of each other's existence. Ribault's safe arrival prior to Menéndez's meant that Fort Caroline had been resupplied. The French officers decided that their best bet against the Spanish was to launch an immediate attack. Though some French colonists feared that this attack would leave Fort Caroline too exposed, Ribault's forces departed quickly, hoping to catch the Spaniards off guard. Meanwhile, Menéndez's crew had started digging trenches and creating some line of defense. Had it not been for the foul weather and the shallow waters of the harbor that sheltered Menéndez and his recently arrived crew, Ribault's attack might have succeeded. But it did not. The crushing French defeat gave the Spanish time to regroup and, more important, left Fort Caroline utterly unprotected, as some French soldiers had feared. The Spaniards saw divine providence in Ribault's defeat. Menéndez, like Ribault before him, wanted to retaliate quickly and transform the recent French loss into an even larger Spanish advantage.[16]

But not all members of Menéndez's crew were so confident. Gonzalo Solís de Merás, Menéndez's brother-in-law, thought the plan poorly conceived. Anticipating Menéndez's failure, he started preparing to withdraw from the barely established Spanish foothold, writing, "I swear to God that I am expecting the news that all our soldiers have been killed, so that we who remain here may embark on these three ships and go to the Indies."[17] Solís de Merás was right to worry. Even with Ribault's defeat, the Spanish had to overcome many other challenges, not least of which was finding and reaching Fort Caroline without significant loss to the already weakened Spanish forces.

The hurricane rains that had thwarted Ribault's attack also impeded Menéndez's journey. The Spaniards marched slowly; they would never have located the fort without the guidance of François Jean, a captured French mutineer. Laudonnière's own accounts were conspicuously silent on this topic, but the importance of these French informers was readily apparent to the French, the Spanish, and even the English. In his 1587 English reprint of Laudonnière's *Voyages,* Richard Hakluyt included a notation in the margins that drew particular attention to the French mutineers: "One of these mariners, named Francis Jean," explained Hakluyt, "betrayed his own countrymen to the Spaniard and brought them into Florida."[18] Once they reached Fort Caroline, the Spanish forces quickly overwhelmed it. "His Divine Majesty had mercy upon us and guided us in such a way that without losing one man and with only one injured (who is now well), we took the Fort with all it contained," proudly recalled Menéndez.[19] God had once again intervened on Spanish behalf, Menéndez concluded, allowing them to capture several French prisoners and ample bounty. Laudonnière, who was in Fort Caroline at the time of the attack, managed to elude Menéndez's forces, secure a small vessel, and sail across the Atlantic with a group of survivors. Ribault was less fortunate. Spanish forces apprehended and killed him, along with a large group other French refugees, near Matanzas Bay.

Laudonnière and his soldiers had done their best to prepare for an attack they knew was coming. They had repaired their meager fortifications, distributed the newly arrived supplies, and ordered sentinels to keep watch. But the French struggled to stay informed of when or how this foreseeable Spanish attack would materialize. Although Spanish weapons, not French lack of information, delivered the final blow against Laudonnière and his colony, Spanish and French efforts to learn about each other offers a new way to look at this bloody encounter. Unlike Menéndez, Laudonnière did not have any Spanish prisoners who could reveal specific information about the number and type of forces in San Agustín. Instead of *nuevas,* Laudonnière spoke of "*rapports.*"[20] In the English editions of Laudonnière's works, *rapport* is usually translated as "report," but the word has all sorts of other connotations. *Rapport* usually implies a type of favorable connection or relations. Laudonnière's reports, relations, and connections came not via Spanish captives but via Indians.[21]

The French had taken as many steps forward as they had backward in their dealings with Florida Indians, in particular with the Timucuas. On the eve of Spanish exploration in the region, Timucua, in what is now northeast and central Florida, boasted a population of about 200,000.[22] Timucua Indians were divided into thirty-five separate chiefdoms that spoke nine to ten different dialects. Expert hunters and fishermen, Timucuas also planted a variety of crops, including maize and beans. Timucuas lived in villages that housed 200 to 300 people, with clear and hierarchical political organizations. As Theodor de Bry's engravings reveal, Timucuas, much like their European counterparts, used dress and adornments to communicate their social rank and standing. Timucuas' early interactions with Spanish conquistadores and French colonists had profound consequences for all three groups. The drastic population decline was probably the most notable: By the late sixteenth century only about 27,000 Timucuas remained, a population loss of close to 90 percent. At the time that the French established Fort Caroline, however, the Timucuas were a formidable force in La Florida.[23]

Laudonnière and his predecessors understood the importance of establishing and maintaining Indian relations, but these interactions proved easier to envision than to establish. In 1562, Ribault had erected a column to demonstrate the French claim to the region, but when Laudonnière revisited the site two years later, he found Timucuas worshipping the column itself, unaware or unmoved by its symbolic representation of French power. Communicating with the Indians was easy; communicating *what* the French wanted to communicate was a different matter altogether.

This ambivalence characterized the *rapport* the French had with the Timucuas. In their brief time in Florida, the French dealt with several distinct and competing Timucua polities. The French had first established relations with *paracoussi* Saturiwa, chief of the Eastern Timucua, whose land was located between the French and Spanish garrisons.[24] The food and favor Laudonnière had secured from Saturiwa, however, came at a price. In return for Saturiwa's friendship, the French had agreed to supply both men and ammunition in an attack against Saturiwa's main rival: the *olata* Outina.[25] Saturiwa's descriptions of Outina presented Laudonnière with a dilemma. He needed Saturiwa's food, but the chief's depiction of Outina as a menacing threat suggested that he might prove a more powerful ally than Saturiwa. Laudonnière's limited supplies and crew forced him to choose between backing Saturiwa, as he had promised, and trying to court the perhaps more powerful Outina. In the end, Laudonnière decided to switch alliances, abandoning Saturiwa and agreeing to help the *olata* Outina. In Outina, Laudonnière gained a powerful ally, but he also inherited several of his enemies, including Saturiwa and Potano Timucuas, who lived away from the coast.

For a very brief while, the French seemed capable of maintaining peaceful relations with the different Timucua groups. Laudonnière pledged military support to his allies, but by not actually providing any aid, he managed to keep the other Timucua factions from attacking the French colony. All that changed when Outina demanded that the French participate in an attack against Potano. Laudonnière agreed, but he hoped that the French involvement would remain minimal and, with any luck, unnoticed by Saturiwa. Outina, however, had other plans (Figure 2.1). After a series of victories against Potano, Outina sent messengers throughout the region publicizing both his military success and his ability to mobilize French forces on his behalf. An appalled Laudonnière suddenly found himself with no room to maneuver, bound to Outina and no longer able to convince Saturiwa of French friendliness or even neutrality. Outina's success was both military and political. Laudonnière conceded that he was no longer in charge because Outina "had begun to treat us like other Indians."[26]

FIGURE 2.1. Outina attacks Potano. Theodor de Bry engraving. Plate XIII, "Outina, with the Help of the French, Gains a Victory over His Enemy Potanou." (Michael W. and Dr. Linda Fisher Collection, courtesy State Archives of Florida.)

The French did not control this information or the connections it revealed; Laudonnière and his men were simply one more node in the networks sustained by Outina and Saturiwa. Stefano de Rojomonte, one of the French deserters captured by the Spanish, commented on the ever-changing intra-Timucua political jockeying that thrust the French into a "very cruel warfare."[27] A Spanish epic poem written in 1571 to commemorate the Spanish victory in Florida also referenced the political conflicts within Timucua. While praising Pedro Menéndez, the poem suddenly pauses and mentions the tense relations between two Indian kings: "Satriba [Saturiwa] and Autina [Outina]." These verses appear disconnected from the rest of the poem—as if the author understood that internal Timucua dynamics were important but could not explicate their connection to Menéndez's victory over the French. This gap is understandable because, after all, it was not immediately apparent to either Menéndez or Laudonnière how these inter-Indian struggles affected their ability to colonize La Florida. But Saturiwa's fights with Outina, Outina's struggles with Potano and Saturiwa, and the tensions between coastal and inland Timucua groups shaped the Indian alliances (and enmities) the Spanish and French made.[28]

Timucua rivalries were central to the competing imperial projects in La Florida. Saturiwa appears in brief mentions in both the Spanish and the French colonial archives, first as an informer for Laudonnière and then for Menéndez, only to return once more to French favor in the late 1560s. The French decision to fight for Outina, or rather, Outina's ability to compel the French to fight for him, left Saturiwa feeling betrayed. With the arrival of the Spanish, Saturiwa saw an opportunity to undermine the French. Laudonnière had betrayed Saturiwa, and now Saturiwa would betray Laudonnière. The *paracoussi* welcomed the Spanish, supplying Menéndez not just with men and food but also with *nuevas* about the location, size, and number of men residing in Fort Caroline. The Timucuas under his command guided the Spanish to the ruins of the first and quickly abandoned French fort.[29] Saturiwa's Timucuas also helped the Spanish find and retrieve the French soldiers and colonists who had escaped before Menéndez destroyed Fort Caroline.[30]

But not all Timucuas agreed to help San Agustín officials. Emoloa, a leader who was supposedly a subject of Saturiwa (now loyal to the Spanish), kept Laudonnière informed about Spanish plans.[31] Even Saturiwa himself proved a fickle ally. After the Spanish defeated the French at Fort Caroline,

Menéndez began building San Agustín and interacting more regularly with local Indian groups, including Timucuas and Guales. Within a matter of months, the Spanish, like the French before them, had become entangled in inter-Indian struggles. Violence between the Timucuas under Saturiwa and Menéndez's precarious presidio erupted with months of the destruction of Fort Caroline.

In the fall of 1566, a party of Spanish soldiers met an unarmed group of Indians who displayed their friendly intentions through signs and appeared eager to communicate news. But these Indians had been merely "feigning friendship," and as they bowed before the Spanish, instead of "kissing their hands," the Indians disarmed the soldiers and killed the Spaniards with their own swords. The "betrayal of these Indians," which had happened in the middle of the day and within walking distance of the San Agustín presidio, spoke of the dangers the Spaniards faced in Florida.[32] Not only had the Indians tricked the Spanish with promises of *nuevas,* but the Spanish had been unable to distinguish Indian friend from foe, *buenas nuevas* ("good news") from *malas nuevas* ("bad or deceiving news").

In a surprising turn, Governor Menéndez chose not to punish the Indian attackers, despite Spanish protests and the violent nature of the crime. In justifying his decision, the governor cited two related issues. First, there were the delicate relations between San Agustín and its Indian neighbors; launching a punitive raid would not improve the already tense situation. Then there was the issue of news. If the Spanish attacked the local Indians, San Agustín would be left disconnected from the rest of La Florida, uninformed of imminent dangers and threats. Instead of seeking revenge, Menéndez blamed the Spanish soldiers for misreading the Indians' message. Had these soldiers followed the governor's orders and stayed within the presidio walls or traveled with an interpreter, this deadly encounter would have not taken place.

Many Spanish officials criticized Menéndez's leniency. Pedro Valdés, the interim governor, did not think that the Spaniards had "misread" the situation. On the contrary, the soldiers had been purposely misled. Valdés insisted that Indians were not to be trusted; Florida officials needed to find other ways to stay informed. While Menéndez argued that the Spanish could not afford to lose Indian allies, Valdés believed that Indian informers compromised the very safety of the new colony. Both sides used Spanish dealings with Saturiwa to support their position. From Menéndez's vantage point, interactions with this *paracoussi* emphasized the value of Indian *nuevas*. In Valdés's opinion, San Agustín's dealing with Saturiwa had shown only Spanish inability to control Indian informers and information. But both sides drew a similar conclusion from the 1566 murder of Spanish soldiers and subsequent exchanges with Timucuas: Indians had their own ambitions and goals. Native intentions could be difficult to read, hidden, or even deceptive, but they were always present.

In 1568, Saturiwa made his priorities perfectly clear when he decided to aid Dominique de Gourgues, a French pirate who wanted to destroy the Spanish presidio in retaliation for Menéndez's brutal attack against Fort Caroline in 1565.[33] Saturiwa gave Gourgues a detailed report about the state and military capacity of San Agustín. Gourgues thanked the Timucua chief and praised the Indians' ongoing commitment to France. But the paracoussi's actions were not, as Gourgues declared, a sign of devotion to the French. Saturiwa's *nuevas* were an expression of his continued influence over the region. By sharing information about the Spanish with the French, Saturiwa demonstrated that he could communicate with both groups, that he understood the type of information both sides wanted and valued, and that he alone could determine how to mobilize this information. Gourgues interpreted Saturiwa's offer of information as a sign of friendship; Saturiwa probably saw it as a display of power.[34]

The Spanish often had a limited selection in choosing with whom to communicate. To get a basic handle on the world that surrounded them, they had to rely on people who seemed less than trustworthy. In 1572, the *adelantado* Menéndez sent Don Diego Velsaco, his son-in-law, to uncover the fate of a distant Jesuit mission in Ajacán (the Chesapeake Bay).[35] Against the advice of Florida's government, Father Juan Baptista de Segura and his assistant Luís de Quirós had erected a mission far from San Agustín and Santa Elena, the two fortified Spanish outposts in La Florida. Frustrated by their failed missionizing efforts near the Spanish presidio, the Jesuits believed they would have greater success converting Indians away from the meddlesome interference of San Agustín officials. The Jesuits had traveled to Ajacán without the customary military entourage, placing their lives in the hands of Don Luís, an Algonquian-speaking Indian who years earlier had been taken, either by force or by trade, from the Chesapeake Bay and was now a supposedly devout Catholic.[36] Don Luís had awed the Jesuits with descriptions of the bountiful Ajacán and persuaded them to establish missions in his homeland. Once they arrived at the intended site, however, this native guide promptly abandoned the Jesuits.[37] Left without an envoy or an interpreter, the Jesuits saw their relations with local Indians, which had been tense from the onset, quickly fall apart. Before long, the Ajacán Indians, much like Don Luís himself, turned on the Jesuits.[38]

It took almost a year for Florida officials to send an expedition to investigate the fate of the Jesuits. Velsaco and his men found only hints of what undoubtedly was a violent massacre.[39] But aside from rescuing Alonso de Olmos, a young Spanish boy who had been spared from the Jesuits' fate, Velasco could not learn much about what had happened.[40] The Indians who had murdered the Jesuits showed no interest in helping another group of Spaniards interpret the situation. Sent to both reconnoiter "the condition of the land" and learn the fate of the Jesuit mission, Velasco found the latter of the two tasks harder to accomplish. The rescue party came back to San Agustín with information about the rich territory, but "with little or no news considering the things they desired to know for the frightened Indians had fled." Though not necessarily dependable or controllable, Indians were the best and sometimes only sources of *nuevas*.[41]

A particularly telling incident occurred in the summer of 1580, when the San Agustín officials welcomed the *nuevas* of an unnamed Indian. He "told the general that he brought a *Nueva:* he had seen a French vessel." The Spanish, eager to learn more about these intruding forces, asked about the weaponry, number of troops, and location of the French ship. Through these queries, the Spanish attempted to squeeze as many details as possible from the Indian. It was not atypical for a short, out-of-breath comment from an Indian about having spotted a foreign sail to transform into a long interview.[42] For all their questions, however, the Spanish tended to interrogate the news itself, not the informer. During this 1580 exchange, San Agustín officials recorded many specific details about the French vessel, but there is no mention of the informer's name or tribal affiliation—I know that the Indian messenger was male only because Spanish is a gendered language.

But the informer mattered. In this particular case, the unnamed Indian messenger carried his own secrets along with the *nuevas* of an enemy ship lurking in the area. As this Indian recounted with surprising precision details about the invading French forces, the Spanish interviewers became curious as to how he had come by such specific information. To the dismay of the Spanish governor, the Indian calmly declared that he had been on board the French vessel and had even conversed with the enemy forces.

At this point in the "very faithful Relation," the tone of the interrogation suddenly changes. Though the Spanish had been grateful to this man for gathering *nuevas,* they were less receptive to the notion that he might have also exchanged news. The Spanish left behind their worries about the size and firepower of the French forces and pressed the man on what he had told the French about San Agustín. "The Indian said that he told them [the French] that in the fort there were no vessels . . . and that in the port there were not many people and those [who were there were] sick."[43] This reply shocked the Spanish. What the Indian had communicated to the French was neither true nor false; it was a strange mixture of both. The Spanish had indeed endured a difficult summer, but there were several vessels docked in the San Agustín harbor. Furthermore, the Spanish population, though small, was more sizable than in the past. The Spanish "asked the Indian why he said there were few people [and that they were] sick since he knew there were many [people] and he knew that there were two large ships in the port." The Indian replied that he had misinformed the French on purpose. He had lied about the poor state of the Spanish presidio to encourage a French attack against San Agustín. The Indian had wagered that, with a decent population and "two ships in the port," the Spanish could defeat the French, who would thus lose their vessel or at least many of the armaments and supplies it carried. This bounty would then become readily available to the Spanish and to their Indian allies—Indians like himself.[44]

In the process of obtaining the latest and newest reports about the French, the Spanish had become entangled in this Indian's own ambitions. After revealing "his *Nuevas*" and his plot to capture French bounty, the unnamed Indian awaited the response of Governor Pedro Menéndez Marqués, nephew of the *adelantado* Pedro Menéndez de Avilés. The Spanish carefully debated the best course of action. They had two options: wait for the invasion to materialize, which was what the Indian had suggested, or chase out the French ships before they could attack. The governor opted for the latter. Governor Menéndez Marqués refused to become a pawn in this informant's plan. An Indian could provide Florida officials with news about the French, but an Indian could not dictate Spanish policy. Menéndez Marqués decided to expel the French before they could cause any major damage to the Spanish presidio, making a point that he was not following the plan devised by the Indian messenger.

This unidentified Indian was not the only Indian informer in play. The invading French forces, who attempted to attack at least three times during the summer of 1580, had their own Indian intelligence. A deposition of a French prisoner, Francisco Manuel, taken in San Agustín on July 24, 1580, mentions "friendly" French–Indian relations. "The Frenchmen asked the Indians what sort of people were in this fort [San Agustín] and if they [the French] could capture it, and the Indians answered they could take it easily and that it contained few men, and they themselves would come to help." Testimony from Master Julio Jilberto confirmed these claims; "when he was asked what the Indians said about the Spaniards he [Jilberto] said that they [the Indians] told many evil things about us and that we were few." Another French captive argued that the Indians had encouraged the attack against the Spanish; the Indians had talked repeatedly of Spanish weaknesses and promised "that they [the Indians] would help them [the French] because they [the Spanish] were evil men who made much war on them." These Indian informers not only shaped *what* the French knew about the Spanish but had also used this information to convince the French to launch a raid against San Agustín.[45]

The French attacks failed. San Agustín was not a formidable garrison, but it was far stronger then these French-informing Indians had insinuated. Or maybe that had been their plan all along. Perhaps, like the Indian who had informed the Spanish about the nearby French vessel, they wanted to plunder the defeated French ships. Or maybe they had told the truth. These Indians could have wanted to rid themselves of their "evil" Spanish neighbors "who made much war on them;" after observing the Spanish colonists struggle to even feed themselves, these Indians had concluded that the San Agustín presidio would fall easily. In either case, the Indians had mobilized the information that had facilitated these attacks. These informers, whose names no one bothered to record, had not only provided tactical and geographic reports to both French and Spanish officials but had also played a leading role in orchestrating violent clashes between rival imperial powers.

No sooner had the Spanish rid themselves of the French than the sails of Sir Francis Drake flew near the coast of Florida.[46] Drake had made a career as a privateer, raiding Spanish colonies and vessels. He had circumnavigated the globe from 1577 to 1580. In the fall of 1585, after a brief return to England, he organized a fleet of seven large ships and over twenty smaller vessels against Spanish holdings in the Caribbean, including Santo Domingo and

Cartagena. Before returning to England, Drake followed the Caribbean currents northwest to one final stop in San Agustín in the summer of 1586.

To prepare for this English attack, the Spanish sent Captain Vicente González to gather information about the dreaded English pirate and his forces. González traveled to "the coast to talk with the Indians to inform [him]self from them if any vessel or vessels had traveled there." But the captain could not locate any coastal Indians, so he continued his "search for other . . . Indians and for news." Indians and news went together.[47] If González wanted to uncover Drake's latest position, the Spanish captain needed to find Indians who had seen (or interacted with) this pirate and, more important, were willing to communicate with the Spanish. Drake, for his part, was doing the same.[48]

Drake's 1586 attack on San Agustín proved devastating. He burned not only the Spanish presidio but also the nearby fields and trees. Although the English forces destroyed San Agustín, they failed to find the Santa Elena outpost in Port Royal, leaving the strategic fort unharmed.[49] Drake's unintentional sparing of Santa Elena offered little comfort to the residents of San Agustín. As their town burned, the nearby Indians quickly plundered what little had survived the flames. Were these Indians working with the English pirate? Had they shown Drake where to attack? Would they do so again? The Spanish were not sure. San Agustín officials realized that their uncertainty had its roots in Indian silence. During the earlier French attacks, Indians had parlayed information to both sides, and though the Spanish had disliked and reprimanded this duplicity, they very much preferred it to the eerie quiet that they realized—in retrospect—had preceded Drake's attack. The Spanish learned a simple lesson from the 1586 attack: San Agustín officials needed to find Indians who would not stay quiet.

But as the Spanish already knew from their prior encounters with Indian informants, Indians who knew or shared too much also posed a threat. It was one thing for local *nuevas* to have imperial overtones. It was quite another for Indian informers to try to mold inter-European rivalries. In 1605, Florida officials had to contend with both when a delegation of Ais Indians arrived with news of war. Little is known about the Ais (also spelled Ays), who inhabited the southern tip of Florida from present-day Cape Canaveral to the Saint Lucie Inlet. During the first two centuries of European colonization, the Ais seem to enter and exit the Spanish, French, and English archives at their own will, leaving only scattered details about who they were and how they lived. The brief descriptions of thatched palmetto leaf dwellings, fishing practices, and military conflicts with the Calusa Indians offer only glimpses into what was a far more complex world.[50] Though Ais elites adorned themselves in silver and gold, French and Spanish colonists discovered—much to their disappointment—that these metals came not from inland mines but from shipwrecked vessels that sailed to and from the Caribbean.[51]

The location of the Ais granted them access to a great deal of goods and news. Governor Pedro Ibarra explained that every formality and sign of friendship had to be extended to the Ais because they live "in a port where all vessels, friend and enemy, disembark and tend to come to shore."[52] Ibarra believed that an alliance with the Ais, who could easily spot, identify, and report on vessels sailing from the Caribbean, would provide the Spanish with a regular supply of news. In 1605, then, the governor was understandably pleased when Capitan Chico, a leader of the Ais, arrived with words of friendship from the elusive Capitan Grande, their main leader.

In their dealings with the Spanish, the Ais purposefully emphasized their access to valuable and strategic information. Capitan Chico therefore began his meeting with the Spanish governor by sharing the latest *nuevas*. Capitan Chico's information concerned neither French vessels nor English pirates. Instead, he brought news of Spain. To Governor Ibarra's surprise, the Capitan Grande had received news of war between Spain and England and, fearing for the safety of San Agustín, had sent a delegation to defend the Spanish garrison. Sending these *nuevas* along with thirty soldiers, the Ais cacique was not only showing his ability to obtain news but also his power to respond as he saw fit.[53] The Spanish governor, who otherwise needed and wanted "relations and communications with the caciques of Ais, Horruque, Oruba, and the others," was taken aback by both the cacique's interpretation and initiative.[54] Though *nuevas* went from Indians to the Spanish, decisions and policy were supposed to travel in the other direction—at least in the governor's estimation. The complete reversal in the dynamics surprised the Spanish governor and hinted at the Ais's own understanding of their role as gatekeepers of information.

The Ais worked hard to maintain these far-reaching connections. Almost a century after they surprised the governor of San Agustín with *nuevas* from Spain, Ais from Saint Lucie Inlet used their access to European news and trade goods to capture a group of shipwrecked Englishmen. Jonathan Dickinson, a Quaker merchant who was sailing from Jamaica to Philadelphia, left an account of this failed voyage, his captivity by Ais Indians, and his difficult journey through Florida. Dickinson noted the many European goods held by the Ais and their keen ability to differentiate among European groups. The English crew had at first tried to convince the Ais that they were Spaniards and thus friendly, or at least friendlier than the English, who were leading devastating slave raids into the region. Dickinson explained how "we hailed them [the Ais] in Spanish" and made signs of the cross as a testament of their Catholic devotion. The Ais immediately saw through the charades and identified Dickinson and his party by shouting, "Nicklaeer! Nicklaeer!," meaning English.[55]

The Ais were not the only Florida Indians paying attention to the English. In early 1608, word of an English colony in Virginia reached San Agustín. Governor Ibarra, eager to gather information about the English, began by asking Guale Indians, whose homelands were along the Georgia coast north of the Altamaha River, if they had heard about or seen this new colony.[56] After organizing several small and unofficial reconnoitering missions, Ibarra sent Captain Francisco Fernández de Ecija to learn what he could about these new "settlements."[57] Ecija was familiar with the area, having led an earlier expedition to Virginia in 1605. Instead of sailing directly to Jamestown, the Spanish captain stopped along the Georgia coast and offered to reward Indians for any news they could bring regarding the English. He would pay them for "observing everything." Although at one point in his voyage Ecija placed an Indian "in irons," convinced that he was withholding vital information about the English colony, the Spanish captain quickly found that the carrot worked better than the stick when requesting news.[58]

Ecija's promise of a reward at first solicited little information about Jamestown. He received only fragmented reports that confirmed English presence but not much more. Determined to gather better *nuevas,* Ecija instructed some Cayagua Indians to spy on the English, complementing Spanish reconnaissance with a parallel native effort. The Cayagua Indians were to travel to English towns "without letting them know that they were sent by the Spaniards, or even that they had seen them or were acquainted with them, and that they should conduct themselves as simple Indians."[59] Ecija quickly realized, however, that he did not need to provide an incentive for Indians to spy on the English.

Most of the Guale groups Ecija encountered had been trying to figure out who these strangers in Virginia were before the Spanish showed any interest in them. Cayagua Indians were already spying on "the fortress that they have as well as the people and the ships and artillery," and although Ecija instructed them that reconnaissance should be done "without letting them [Virginians] know that they were sent by the Spaniards," the Cayaguas needed no such reminders. These "simple Indians" had no intention of disclosing any of their alliances to the English or, as Ecija unpleasantly discovered, to the Spanish.

After much pressing, a Cayagua cacique finally admitted that he had traveled to the English town. "It was true," the cacique explained, "that he had gone to a village that was named (Daxe), and that there he had heard from the natives of that village that near there, there was a settlement of Englishmen." Ecija then inquired "why he [the cacique] had not admitted [this] at the start and told what he knew, he replied that [it was] out of fear." What exactly did the cacique fear? The Spanish discovering that he dealt with the English? Or the Virginians learning of his connections to San Agustín? Both, Ecija came to realize. The Cayagua cacique wanted access to "the one and the other" without choosing sides. Ecija was frustrated, but the few details he could gather about Virginia did much to calm Spanish fears. The situation in the English colony was bleak, and the Spanish were certain that Jamestown would suffer the same fate as Roanoke. After Ecija's journey, San Agustín officials only sparingly mentioned the English.[60]

Until the mid-seventeenth century, that is. In the 1660s, the English began aggressively reconnoitering the region to the south of Virginia. San Agustín officials quickly tried to gather *nuevas* about this new English threat. In 1657, Governor Diego de Rebolledo sent "some Indians with their weapons until there was news [of the English]" to confirm rumors of their activities in the area. This was standard procedure, de Rebolledo explained in a dispatch to the Spanish king, adding that "the same would have been done in other situations of less risk and suspicion since this [using Indians to gather news] was the quickest and the most immediate relief that can be found to resist the enemy that was so close."[61] More than a century after the *adelantado* Menéndez and French leaders Ribault and Laudonnière had learned about each other's intentions through Timucua informers, the Spanish and the English found themselves in a similar situation. Now, however, it was Guale, Orista, Escamaçu, Sewee, Edisto, and Yspo Indians, among others, who kept the Spaniards informed of the early English expeditions into Carolina and kept the English aware of San Agustín's plans and alliances.

~

The English sent several expeditions to the region before establishing Charles Town in 1670. In their promotional tracts about Carolina, the English describe the area as lush, abundant, and full of potential.[62] But for all their promises of wealth and fortune, the English actually knew very little about the land and the native groups who lived in the area. William Edmundson, a Quaker preacher, simply described his 1676 journey through the region as "perillous travelling, for the Indians were not yet subdued."[63] But the English faced another problem beyond unfriendly Indians and dangerous lands: the Spanish. One of the earliest English letters from South Carolina described the precarious state of the new colony, "here settled in the very chaps of the Spaniard whose clandestine actions both domesticke and forraigne are not unknown."[64] Historians have often cited this quote to emphasize the proximity between the Spanish and English colonies— Charles Town was less than 300 miles from San Agustín but more than 500 miles from Jamestown, the nearest English town. The remark by Joseph Dalton, one of the first colonists to arrive in the new English colony, however, commented on more than geography. Dalton's observation made clear that Charles Town was "Settled in the very chaps" of a known enemy. Uncertain about the fate of the new English colony, Dalton had no doubts about the threat posed by the Spaniards and their "clandestine actions."

To begin to make sense of a world they knew little about, the early English explorers and colonists in Carolina turned their gaze to their Spanish neighbors. San Agustín became a point of reference through which the English evaluated both their surroundings and their native neighbors. While physical closeness did little to foster amity between Spanish and English colonists, the "not unknown" Spanish threat afforded English a tangible way to render a vast and unfamiliar world legible. In an early letter to Lord Ashley, one of the Lord Proprietors of Carolina, William Owen, explained how the English used mentions of Spanish Florida to distinguish friendly Indians from hostile ones. Indians who associated with the Spanish and in particular mission Indians were deemed unsuitable allies and untrustworthy:

> The great point in this design is security for they [the Spanish] are near
> a zealous and potent neighbour. The Spanish friars will never cease to

promote their tragic ends by the Indians whom they instruct only to admire the Spanish nation and pay them adoration equal to a deity. These have the advantage of the Indian tongue and incline the Indians to do anything and make war by these Indians upon those who disoblige them.[65]

Indians allied with the Spanish, or rather (from the English perspective) deceived by Spanish "instruction," meant only trouble for the recently arrived English colonists. Even if the Spanish were not physically present, their influence and ability to "incline the Indians to doe anything" could transform the most cordial of encounters into a dangerous exchange. Maurice Mathews, a well-respected Englishman who launched a successful political career in South Carolina, recalled how the sudden appearance of Spanish Indians could turn what had been peaceful trading relations into "a cloud of arrows."[66] Matthews, like most South Carolinians, was quick to blame the Spanish as the true culprits in these violent Indian–English confrontations, and just as quick to dismiss the possibility that English abuse, a misreading of the Indians' intentions, or even the Indians' own belligerence could be at fault.

The concept of Spanish Florida offered the English a simple way to process complicated information and relations.[67] But this simplicity biased *what* information the English sought and welcomed. As they searched for news of hostile Spanish Indians and calculating Spanish officials, the English were more inclined to believe reports that confirmed their assumptions than those that challenged them. William Hilton experienced firsthand the limitations of this information bias during his 1663 exploration of Carolina. Born in England, Hilton had moved with his family to the Massachusetts Bay colony and had spent a good deal of his young life working at sea. He had already reconnoitered the area near Cape Fear for an expedition sponsored by the "Committee for Cape Faire at Boston" when the Lord Proprietors, who had just secured Charles II's new charter for the region, asked him to command a subsequent exploratory voyage farther south.[68]

Sailing along the Combahee River (near St. Helena Sound), Hilton encountered a party of Edisto Indians. The Edisto Indians were a smaller group that had ties to larger Indian polities, possibly to the Cusabo Indians. The Edistos that Hilton encountered most likely spoke a Muskogean dialect, but little is known about their cultural and social organization. In 1562, a group of Edistos had aided the French; a few years later, the Edistos had first helped construct and then quickly attacked a fort erected by the Spanish in Edisto lands.[69] In stark contrast with Hilton and his men, the Edistos were not new to the area; they had a little over a century of practice with Euro–Indian relations.

The Edistos approached the English party with confidence, requesting goods for the safe return of some English castaways they had taken prisoner. Hilton quickly dismissed the Edistos' requests, convinced that there were no English hostages and that the Edistos were part of a devious Spanish ploy to undermine English exploration. He confidently declared that if there had been other English vessels in the area, he would have known about them. Hilton was certain he had made the right decision until the next day, when the Edistos produced an English captive. This unnamed prisoner readily confirmed the Indians' assertions. The Edistos held several other English captive and, to make matters more complicated, the Spanish had nothing to do with either the prisoners' capture or their promised release.[70]

Hilton had been wrong in his assessment of the Edistos. San Agustín officials had not instructed the Edistos to intimidate the English. The Indians had approached Hilton on their own initiative. Although Spanish metals adorned almost every Indian delegate who came aboard the English vessel, Spanish presents did not translate into Spanish ability to influence or control this Indian group. The Edistos interacted with, but were not close allies of, the Spanish. After several failed attempts to use Edisto Indians to open communications with San Agustín officials, Hilton began to understand that the simple dichotomy he had assumed to govern the region— that Indians with ties to the Spanish would be hostile to the English and that Indians with no connections to San Agustín would prove loyal friends—did not have traction. The European items worn by the Edistos were not a sign that these Indians had collaborated with the Spanish but that the Spanish had collaborated with the Edistos.

Not long after his clumsy exchange with the Edistos, Hilton received a letter from San Agustín officials advising him on how to deal with Florida Indians and recover any English prisoners from the Edistos or neighboring Indians. "Wherefore I advise you," wrote Captain Antonio Argüelles to Hilton, "that if these Indians (although Infidels and Barbarians) have not killed any of the Christians, and do require as a gift or courtesie for those four men, four Spades, and four Axes, some Knives, and some Beads," the English should oblige.[71] Not only were San Agustín officials complying with Edisto terms of exchange, but the Spanish were also urging the English to do the same. Argüelles explained that he had been ransoming captives held by the Edistos for quite some time. The Indians were not (simply) asking for payment "but only . . . an acknowledgement of kindness for having saved their [the captive's] lives." Although he was surprised by this information, Hilton felt that he had no choice but to follow Argüelles's advice and furnish the Indians with the artifacts they desired. Rather than foiling some evil Catholic ploy or defeating Indians corrupted by Spanish ambitions, Hilton had discovered the power of Edisto Indians to dictate the terms of exchange.

Hilton's understanding of Spanish Florida was neither wrong nor accurate; it was simply myopic. While the Spanish did "instruct" a large number of Indians in Catholic teachings, Florida officials could not make these roots take hold everywhere or necessarily grow in the direction they wanted. The Spanish recognized their limitations and even acquiesced to Edisto demands, but they had no intention of facilitating English–Indian relations. Captain Argüelles's correspondence with Hilton showcased Spanish authority over the area. Argüelles argued that the Spanish, unlike the English, had if not command, knowledge of the people, the relationships, and the practices that governed the region. Florida officials would continue to mention the miscommunication between the English and the Edistos in their subsequent correspondence with Hilton. Without their support, the Spanish taunted, Hilton and his men would still be at a loss, incapable of distinguishing Indian *nuevas* from Indian lies.

In one of his final letters Argüelles repeated an earlier request that Hilton write in Spanish but sneeringly added, "if you have none that can interpret the Spanish Tongue, you may write in your own, for here are your Countrey-men that can understand it." Argüelles's comment was intended to deride the linguistic limitations of the English party and to remind Hilton that the Spanish held several English "Countrey-men" captive. The exchange with the Edistos and subsequently with the Spanish had done much to expose Hilton's restrictive information lens and his limited ability to gather news.

The English had much to learn; but then, so did the Edistos. The Edistos' early attempts to communicate with the English as they had with the Spanish failed to achieve the results they desired. Indians living in what the English began calling Carolina needed to find ways of exchanging information with the English without the intervention of San Agustín officials. This was not a simple endeavor, especially because English distrust of the Spanish colored not only what the South Carolina colonists saw and heard but also how they interpreted what they saw and heard.

While the Edistos struggled to reckon with this English bias, other Indians managed to insert their needs and concerns into this framework. Some of the first native groups that the English encountered, like the Sewee, managed to transform English fear of Spanish Florida into an advantage. The Sewees were a coastal group that was perhaps Siouan speaking, as evidenced by their eventual decision to join the Siouan-speaking Catawba nation. Though repeatedly mentioned in English sources, almost no ethnographical details about the Sewee survive.[72] As was the case for so many other coastal Indian groups, the Sewees' population declined precipitously in the late 1600s as a result of European diseases, most notably from smallpox. But before smallpox, alcohol, and the loss of their lands, the Sewees were "a large Nation" that had wanted to ally with the English newcomers.[73]

Stephen Bull, deputy to Lord Ashley and one of the first English colonists to South Carolina, recounted an early instance in Albemarle Point in which presumably Sewee Indians saved the English from danger. In the summer of 1670, Henry Brayne, captain of the English frigate *Carolina,* had encountered a group of Indians and, assuming that they were friendly, began to approach them.[74] Brayne was quickly stopped by "one of our owne Indians" who cried out "those are enemy Indians!" Brayne had almost fallen victim to a simple ambuscade. Brayne does not properly identify either Indian but, based on the location of this exchange as well as later descriptions of this event, it seems likely that this loyal Indian informer was Sewee. The English captain remained unaware of the peril at hand until "one of our Indians" had warned the trusting captain.[75] To convince the English that they were walking into a trap, the Sewee simply explained that the approaching Indians were "Spanishe Indians."[76]

Stephen Bull would later use this very encounter as an example of English strength, explaining how the "Spanishe Indians" had fled in haste after "seeing the scalinge of our great gunns." These were hardly the only lessons to be drawn from this encounter. Brayne's ill-advised welcome of "Spanishe Indians" exposed a lapse in English understanding. The Sewee both saw and filled that information gap. They helped the English make an elemental distinction between Indian friend and Indian threat. Bull praised the Sewees' efforts and "relation [which] wee doe much credditt."[77] Unlike the Edistos, who had multiple alliances and no clear European loyalties, the

Sewees kept their news simple. They had identified hostile Indians not by name or language, but by their affiliations to the Spanish—that is, in a way that made sense to the new English colonists.[78]

Spanish actions and influences, both real and perceived, appear everywhere in English sources from this period. Though South Carolina would eventually become a powerhouse in the region and the Spanish would ultimately relinquish their claim to Florida (first temporarily in 1763 and then permanently in 1821), in the late seventeenth century, the English looked to the Spanish to make sense of the early South—to determine good landing site from bad, Indian friend from dangerous threat, and news from lie. The impact of the Spanish on English colonization comes not simply from the earlier establishment of La Florida but from the foundational connections between the networks of the two colonial projects.[79]

The relation between Indians and news was neither obvious nor permanent, as a group of Guale Indians unhappily discovered in their dealings with the English in South Carolina. In the winter of 1678, a Guale spying party had a chance encounter with Joseph West, governor of South Carolina. West stopped the Spanish Indians and proceeded to "ask them of the said Florida and of the disposition of San Augustine and its presidio." Governor West wanted the latest information about the size, military capacity, and threat posed by the Spanish. The Guales were probably not surprised by this line of questioning because Florida officials also used Guale spies to learn about the English colony. But they did not anticipate what happened next. Before the Indians could respond, Henry Woodward, an English trader who had been developing an extensive trade network with Westo and Savannah Indians, responded that "it was not necessary, that he would relate [the news] and that he would do it quite well," as he knew the area well and had been at San Agustín.[80]

The Guales found this exchange most troubling. Upon their return to Florida, they recounted the events to Captain Antonio Argüelles. The Spanish captain was more concerned with what the spies had learned about Charles Town than about West's attitude toward Indian *nuevas*. But the Guales insisted that West's dismissal of their reports was of consequence to the Spanish. The English had managed to establish information arrangements that circumvented Spanish Indians, ending or, at the very least, destabilizing an important

however, were more than objects or subjects in these missionary endeavors. They were actors in their own right. Indian chiefs saw missions as a way to become better attuned to and integrated with San Agustín's political, economic, and spiritual networks. In most instances, Indian chiefs, not Franciscan friars or Spanish officials, decided when and where missions could be erected. Indian leaders risked much by welcoming Franciscans into their towns, but they also stood to benefit from these arrangements. Having more direct access to San Agustín implied a better and often more regular supply of European goods—goods the chiefs could both display and distribute to promote their spiritual as well as physical authority.

Franciscan missions were the nodes in an emerging Spanish network built through Indian paths and relations. As concrete symbols of Franciscan presence and influence, missions also underscored the finite range of Spanish power. Franciscans and other officials who ventured to *la tierra adentro* were confined to clearly designated sites bound by Indian trails and authority. These missions, networked through Indian paths, did not always work to Spanish advantage. In the summer of 1656, the clashing interests of Timucuas, Franciscans, and San Agustín officials all came to a head. This was not the first time an Indian rebellion had swept through La Florida, but it was the first time a conflict transformed these networks of Spanish nodes and Indian ties.

What caused the 1656 Timucua Rebellion? Everyone in La Florida had a different answer. To make matters more complicated, each party mobilized different information to assert and justify its specific explanation. The Spanish governor, Diego de Rebolledo, accused the Franciscans of causing the unrest. In his detailed *visita* (investigation) of Timucua, de Rebolledo divorced himself and his administration from the uprising and placed most (and possibly all) of the blame on the Franciscans. The Franciscans pointed to the governor and attributed the rebellion to de Rebolledo's abusive policies toward mission Indians. Timucuas offered their own explanations, sometimes in less than open and free conditions, for the decisions and actions they took during the rebellion. Some Timucuas spoke of their dislike of government policies, in particular of having to serve as *cargadores*—workers carrying food and supply across La Florida for Spanish officials.[4] Other Timucuas expressed frustration with the Franciscans, who interfered with their everyday practices and forbade important ceremonies and rituals. But many Timucuas paid little heed to San Agustín officials or the Franciscans, focusing instead on their deteriorating relations with their Apalachee neighbors.

Incorporating these Indian testimonies into our understanding of the events of the summer of 1656 reveals a different geopolitical sensibility, one that involves peoples and places not accessible from San Agustín. Calling the incident a "rebellion" makes sense only if the Timucuas' relation to Spanish authority is considered vis-à-vis Spanish recognition of the Timucuas' own sovereignty and power. The Timucua Rebellion was as much resistance to an established colonial authority as a struggle over what any of those forces—established, colonial, and authority—implied.

The rebellion in Timucua was a multilayered event. As the governor, the Franciscans, and the Timucuas tried to explain what caused the uprising, they all strove to legitimate their version of the truth. Information about the rebellion proved exceedingly malleable; it was both product and reflection of the different power structures that coexisted in La Florida. As a single case study, the Timucua Rebellion offers unprecedented access into the competing struggles to find, gather, and present information inside colonial Florida. It also shows how an information network built through Spanish missions and Indian paths functioned and ultimately faltered. The debate about *what* information was needed exposed a bitter struggle among the governor, the missionaries, and the Indians over who should control La Florida (and in what terms). The Indian rebellion in Timucua offers a story about the power of information to define and challenge colonial authority.

⌇

As far as Indian rebellions are concerned, the Timucua Rebellion was not particularly bloody. By the end of the summer of 1656, three Spanish soldiers, one Spanish servant, two African slaves, and one Indian from México had been killed—seven deaths in total. In retribution, the Spanish executed eleven Timucua chiefs. But there are other numbers to take into account beyond the eighteen men who died directly in the rebellion. By the 1680s, the 13,500 to 27,000 Timucuas who had lived in or near Spanish missions at the beginning of the seventeenth century had been reduced to around 2,000. Waves of epidemics and slaving raids had left the Timucuas' population in serious decline.[5] During the mid-seventeenth century, the number of Franciscan missionaries in Florida had nearly doubled, from forty-three to seventy. Of these, probably thirty lived in Timucua on the eve of the rebellion.[6] Beyond missionaries however, there were hardly any Spanish in the Timucua province. When Captain Agustín Pérez de Villa Real and his interpreter Esteban Solana marched into the region in 1656, they basically doubled the Spanish military presence in western Timucua, where Captain Antonio de Sartucha and two soldiers, both named Bartolomé, were stationed. In other words, there were thousands of Timucuas, tens of Franciscans, and practically no Spanish soldiers in Timucua in the mid-seventeenth century.

The situation in Timucua reproduced La Florida in miniature (see Map 3.1). The San Agustín presidio, the main Spanish stronghold in Florida, could sustain only 300 to 500 *plazas* (positions), with very limited resources and men at its disposal.[7] The *peninsulares* (Spanish-born, comprising roughly one-third of the population) and the *criollos* (born both in Florida and other Spanish colonies, mostly from México) who made up the Spanish population worked generally as soldiers, officers, or government officials, not as planters or farmers.[8] Having never succeeded in establishing any sort of profitable economic venture, San Agustín depended on the *situado,* a subsidy from the crown that was often delayed in coming.[9] Unable to support itself, La Florida quickly became a burden to the Spanish Crown. Suárez Toledo, a well-connected resident of Havana who had sailed with *adelantado* Menéndez de Avilés, explained to the king that "to maintain Florida is merely to incur expense because it is and has been entirely unprofitable nor can it sustain its own population."[10] The strategically located colony was often on the brink of starvation and destitution.[11]

The Franciscans established their missions in Timucua just as an uprising threatened their gains and livelihood in Guale, to the north of San Agustín along the present-day Georgia coast. Guale was home to the earliest Franciscan missions in Florida. The Franciscans had moved into the area after the Jesuits departed in 1572. Most descriptions of mission life in seventeenth-century Timucua and Guale come from the visitation and writings of Fray Luís Gerónimo de Oré, who detailed Franciscan activities in the colony, from celebrating mass, preaching the Gospel, and administering the Sacraments to eradicating native cultural and religious practices and using corporal punishment to maintain order. Devoted to "holy poverty," the Franciscans, clothed in robes, cowls, and sandals, were to live on the alms they begged even as they furnished their smallest churches with silver chalices, gold altar pieces, and decorated crosses.[12] Given the precarious living conditions in Florida, the Spanish crown assumed responsibility for supplying the missions and

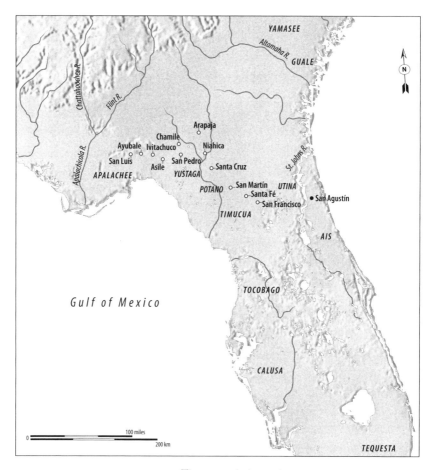

MAP 3.1. Timucua missions, 1650s

required the San Agustín government to pay the friars a regular wage, establishing a codependent relation that was tense from the start.[13]

By 1595, thirty years after the founding of San Agustín, six Franciscan
friars had managed to establish five missions.[14] Gonzalo Méndez de Canzo
had barely assumed the governorship of Florida when reports reached him
about a possible uprising in Guale. Tensions between a Tolomato cacique
named Juanillo and the friars escalated in the fall of 1597, culminating in a
revolt that specifically targeted the Franciscans. Fray Pedro Fernández de
Chozas, who served as a missionary in San Pedro Island, wrote an alarming
letter describing how "the Indians from Guale province, located 40 leagues

from this garrison, had murdered six Franciscan friars who served in their missions."[15] As the newly arrived governor tried to grapple with the rapidly deteriorating conditions of a people and a region utterly unfamiliar to him, a group of Timucuas marched into San Agustín. The cacique leading the Timucuas pledged loyalty to the Spanish and asked for a friar as well as supplies to build a mission in his town of San Martín. The Timucuas' timing might have been coincidental, but it is just as likely that the cacique of San Martín was using the unrest in Guale to promote the stability and promise of Timucua.[16]

Even in this context of uncertainty and anxiety, or perhaps because of it, Governor Canzo and the resident Franciscans eagerly welcomed the opportunity to forge an alliance with the Timucua. As the Spanish struggled to subdue the unrest in Guale, Fray Baltasár López traveled to Timucua. Fray Martín Prieto, who established the province's first *doctrina* and secured for the Spanish a continuous and growing presence in Timucua, quickly followed. San Agustín officials soon came to consider Timucua under their control. But it was not. While Timucua caciques proved receptive to Spanish initiatives, there were real differences between Spanish claims to Timucua and the Timucuas' understanding of Spanish activities in lands that they continued to regard as sovereign and bounded.

From the Spanish perspective, the success of the missions hinged on the *reducción* of Timucua. *Reducción,* required the Timucuas to live like Christians. Meaning, they had to convert to Catholicism and adopt economic and cultural Spanish practices. Merely introducing Catholic rituals, such as baptism and confession, would not be enough; the Franciscans had to dismantle Timucua traditions, healing ceremonies, dances, and ballgames.[17] But as anthropologist John Worth has shown, Franciscans needed to work within existing native power hierarchies if they were to gain converts; run successful missions; and, more important, live long enough to achieve any of their goals.[18] To reach Timucua souls, the Franciscans needed to respect the chief's power. Timucua chiefs determined where Franciscans could establish their churches, how the *gasto de Indios* ("Indian expenses" and gifts) were distributed, and who would be required to journey to San Agustín to comply with the Spanish *repartimiento* (labor draft).

On the eve of the rebellion, Timucua missions were scattered throughout the province and away from the Camino Real, the main road that led directly to San Agustín. Connected only by Indian trails and networks, the missions' locations testified to the control Timucua caciques exerted over missionary activity in their lands.[19] Timucua encompassed close to 20,000 square miles and included three different environmental zones as diverse as the people who inhabited them.[20] There were coastal groups, like the ones led by Saturiwa in the late-sixteenth century, which settled the areas north of San Agustín to the Altamaha River. There were inland Timucuas, whom the Spanish would come to identify as the Potano, Timucua, and Yustaga. These inland groups, who relied on freshwater resources, forest products, farming, and hunting, were by far the most numerous of the various Timucuas. A third group of river-dwelling Timucuas lived around the drainage of the St. John's River basin. These Timucua groups all spoke different dialects, and Timucua's connection to other languages remains unclear.[21] For all their differences, Timucuan peoples shared many cultural traits, central ideologies, and political practices. They were a matrilineal society. Rank and clan were inherited through the mother's brother and only certain clans performed leadership roles. The divisions and bitter rivalries within Timucua groups about the successions within leading clans reveal the contours of a highly ranked society, in which *paracausi, olata, inihama,* and other official roles were fiercely contested and retained only by the politically savvy.[22] The Franciscan missionaries both used and reinforced the Timucuas' clearly demarcated and hierarchical social structure.

In their attempts to replace, or *reducir* as the friars would say, Timucua beliefs and lifestyles with Christian mores, the Franciscans managed to introduce a far more destabilizing force into the region: pathogens.[23] The destructive effects and demographic loss caused by epidemic disease in La Florida cannot be overstated, but specific references about the consequences for the Timucuas are hard to come by. A vague report made by a Franciscan council in 1617 briefly mentioned a great *peste* (plague) that had struck a newly converted Indian population. From the timing of the report, the locations it referenced, and the high mortality rates in certain missions at this precise moment, it seems reasonable to deduce that whatever this *peste* was, it was devastating Potano and Timucua. It would be close to forty years before the Spanish made note of another epidemic in Timucua. "There are very few Indians," lamented Governor de Rebolledo of the demographic decline in Timucua, "because they have been wiped out with the sickness of the plague and smallpox which have overtaken them in the past years."[24]

This later wave of smallpox came in 1655, only several months before the Timucua Rebellion.

The two events were connected. The drastic population decline brought on by the *peste* contributed to the brewing unrest in Timucua. With a shrinking number of people under their command, Timucua caciques struggled to retain their sources of power, relevancy, and livelihood as they reckoned with the distress and disorientation of losing their families and friends. San Agustín officials offered little help; in fact, they made matters worse. Instead of providing aid to the Timucuas, Governor de Rebolledo used the *gasto de Indios* to win favors from the Ais and the Apalachee Indians, both of whom resided in strategically important locations. The Ais lived on the southern tip of Florida with access to the Caribbean, and the Apalachees were to the west of Timucua and were a grain producing province with connections both to the overland deerskin trade and to the maritime trade with México and Cuba. Despite the fact that neither group was missionized, de Rebolledo had favored these potentially more lucrative alliances over San Agustín's supposed commitment to Christianized Indians. Timucua leaders took notice. Lucas Menéndez, chief of the town of San Martín in Timucua, complained that while he had no Spanish goods "if he were cacique of Ays, or another pagan, that the Governor would give it to him."[25]

A shortsighted governor, an increasingly discontented Indian leadership, and a devastating epidemic would have been a bad combination under any circumstances. But an event happening hundreds of miles from Florida further damaged Spanish relations with the Timucuas. In May 1655, the English invaded and eventually took control of Jamaica.[26] By November of that year, word reached San Agustín that the English were planning subsequent invasions of vulnerable Spanish colonies. de Rebolledo sprang into action, repairing the decrepit garrison, recruiting and arming soldiers, and gathering enough food to endure a siege. The governor now demanded the Timucuas help defend San Agustín. That de Rebolledo would turn to Timucua for men and supplies was not surprising, but the manner in which he proceeded exposed both his inexperience and the changing conditions in Spanish missions.

De Rebolledo issued an order for 500 Timucua and Apalachee soldiers to march to San Agustín. Twenty years earlier, Governor Luís Rojas y Borjas had also used the language of *repartimiento* to draft Indian soldiers to defend the Spanish garrison. But de Rebolledo's order went further: He also demanded that each warrior carry his own food. This request also had a clear precedent. Ten years earlier, Governor Damián de Vega Castro y Pardo had ordered Indian *cargadores* to carry corn into the city. But by combining a call for soldiers with one involving food, de Rebolledo was requiring Timucua and Apalachee soldiers, essentially Indian elites, to perform tasks associated with the lowest echelons of Timucua and Apalachee society.[27] De Rebolledo, focused on preparing for an imminent English attack, did not understand or particularly care that he had affronted Timucuan chiefly authority.

Lucas Menéndez, a principal of Timucua, refused to obey either order. He had sent men and supplies to San Agustín only a couple of months before to comply with an earlier *repartimiento*. Given the smallpox epidemic, Lucas had struggled to meet the *repartimiento*'s demands, which called for the same number of laborers as before the *peste* struck. Now a new order had arrived demanding more men and food, even as de Rebolledo had ceased supplying Lucas and other Timucua caciques with gifts and goods. The Spanish provided their native allies with less but required more from them. Lucas was furious. His anger resonated with the caciques of Chuaquin, Santa Fé, Tarihica, San Francisco de Potano, San Pedro, and Santa Helena de Machava, who all began openly opposing de Rebolledo's order. With momentum quickly building, Lucas left his mission town of San Martín and convened a council meeting with other Timucuas and Apalachees in San Pedro, a town further to the west. While there are no records of this meeting, later testimony provides fragmentary insights into how Lucas rallied other Timucuas against Spanish authority—a matter to which I will return at the end of the chapter.[28]

After the meeting in San Pedro, the Timucua Rebellion unfolded in three distinct fronts: the establishment of alliances among rebelling towns across Timucua, the appeals to Apalachee leaders to join the fight, and finally an ongoing negotiation with de Rebolledo. The Timucuas began by asking the governor to modify his latest order. They wanted de Rebolledo to either decrease the number of men required to serve in the presidio or remove the requirement that Indian soldiers carry their own corn. But when it became clear that de Rebolledo had no plans of acquiescing, the rebellion began. The first attacks took place in Yustaga, the western part of Timucua, but the violence soon spread east to Potano. The subsequent killings took place closer to San Agustín, when Lucas led an attack on the hacienda at La Chua.[29]

It is not clear exactly when de Rebolledo received word of the unrest in Timucua. Rumblings of growing frustration and even threats of a coming rebellion had probably reached the governor before Bartolomé Francisco, a soldier who had been stationed in Ivitachuco, the western edge of Timucua and the border with Apalachee, arrived in San Agustín early in the summer of 1656. Bartolomé had witnessed the start of the rebellion with his own eyes, forcing the governor to contend with the reality of what had previously been only unfounded rumor. De Rebolledo faced a difficult choice. Sending men west, away from San Agustín and the coast, would leave the presidio far too exposed in the event of an English attack, but an unchecked Indian rebellion posed an equally alarming threat.

De Rebolledo waited. He was certain the enemy fleet from Jamaica was just beyond the horizon. But as days turned to weeks and then to months, the governor's demands for more men and food, which most in San Agustín believed had triggered the rebellion, now seemed completely unnecessary and even hurtful. After three months of wavering, de Rebolledo finally agreed to send Sergeant Major Adrián Cañizares y Osorio with a force of 60 Spanish and 200 Apalachee soldiers to suppress the Timucua rebels. Cañizares followed the Camino Real to Ivitachuco, at the western edge of Timucua, where he met Captain Antonio de Sartucha and Captain Agustín Pérez. Both men— the messengers de Rebolledo had sent to make his demands—had been stranded there since the start of the rebellion.

Cañizares had come prepared to fight, but by the time he arrived in Timucua towns, most of the initial fervor had died down. The Timucuas who had built and were manning a makeshift palisade outside the mission town of Santa Elena de Machava were weak and isolated from their former Indian allies. The increasingly unpopular rebellion affected the entire political structure of Timucua. By failing to foster support for their struggle, the principal caciques undermined their authority, and some secondary Timucua leaders began taking advantage of the power vacuum to secure better positions for themselves and their communities. Diego Heva was one such cacique. He had been the cacique of Ayepacano, a tributary of San Pedro, when the rebellion had started. Heva had dissociated himself from the rebellious San Pedro leadership, and had helped the Spanish find and pacify the rebels in Machava. By early 1657, Diego Heva was no longer in charge of Ayepacano; he was now the cacique principal of San Pedro.[30] Some Timucuas, especially those who were chiefs of smaller and tributary towns, stood to benefit by turning their backs on the rebellion.

The biggest threats to the Timucua rebels, however, did not come from within Timucua itself. The Apalachees, the Timucuas' western neighbors and sometime allies, had refused to join the uprising. The Apalachees, apprehensive from the start about the rebellion, were ultimately not persuaded to join the Timucuas. Spanish relations with the Apalachees, unlike with the Timucuas, were in good shape. The Apalachees were not eager to relinquish their relatively new and privileged position with San Agustín. When the Timucuas decided to rebel, the Apalachees sided with the Spanish, helping attack and apprehend Timucuas. With Spanish forces marching from the east and hostile Apalachee towns to the west, the Timucua rebels felt surrounded.

By the time Governor de Rebolledo joined Cañizares in Ivitachuco in early December, the sergeant major had successfully negotiated the surrender of the rebel stronghold on the outskirts of Machava, imprisoned most leaders (except Lucas, who remained at large), and killed one Timucua who openly confessed to murdering a Spaniard and refused to repent for his actions. Cañizares then took the remaining rebel leaders to Ivitachuco, away from the center of Timucua and the heart of the rebellion, and closer to Apalachee, which had remained loyal to the Spanish.[31]

At Ivitachuco, de Rebolledo put the leaders on trial. Though the transcripts of this interrogation have not been found, certain bits of information about these proceedings can be discerned from de Rebolledo's *residencia* (an official inquiry into the conduct of the governor while in office).[32] Roughly twenty Indians were tried; more than half of those who faced de Rebolledo were caciques. From these interrogations, two points become clear. First, and most obviously, the Timucuas had become increasingly discontented with the way the Spanish treated them. Second, Lucas was the mastermind behind the rebellion; he had channeled Timucua dissatisfaction into a violent course of action. The governor sentenced to death at least six caciques and four other Indians—bringing the Indian death toll to eleven (including the Timucua Indian Cañizares had garroted after his unapologetic confession). The bodies of the executed caciques were put on display as a warning. But this attempt to intimidate the Timucuas also served as a reminder to San Agustín officials that their control over Indian peoples, even those long regarded as close allies, was incomplete.

After the Timucua Rebellion, the Spanish took a more proactive role in regulating the province. de Rebolledo worked on establishing a new Timucua leadership. In collaboration with key Timucua elites, like Diego Heva, the governor promoted many of the Timucua leaders who had helped the Spaniards during the rebellion and demoted caciques involved, even tangentially, in the uprising. de Rebolledo also ordered the destruction of any town that had been a major hub during the rebellion and, more important, relocated all remaining Timucua missions and placed them along the Camino Real. Timucua missions would no longer be "far apart from one another" or connected "along crosswise paths (caminos trasbexsales)." The Camino Real would closely and more clearly tie Timucua missions to San Agustín. This geographic and political reorganization had a deep effect on Timucua, which would never operate or look the same as it did before the uprising.[33]

It was far more difficult at the time to explain what had happened in Timucua than this tidy account suggests. As the governor, the Franciscans, and the Timucuas struggled to report on and authenticate their own versions of events, they created conflicting and at times competing narratives of the Timucua Rebellion.

~

After the trials of the Timucua rebels, Governor de Rebolledo commenced a detailed investigation of the causes of the uprising. The rebellion proved to be a mere pretext, however, for de Rebolledo to collect information about how the Franciscans, and not his own, poorly timed policies, had led to the uprising. The governor conducted a two-month *visita* "in the Provinces of Apalachee and Timucua," or so the document proclaims in its title page.[34] In practice, de Rebolledo spent most of his time in Apalachee—visiting about ten towns and taking the testimonies of over forty Apalachee caciques and principales. The governor did not travel through Timucua, ordering instead that Timucua Indians gather for a general assembly in San Pedro de Potohiriba. By the time this meeting convened, the Spanish governor had significantly transformed the Timucua province and leadership; the list of Indian caciques, cacicas, and principales in attendance included many newly appointed Timucua leaders.[35] Once gathered, the Timucuas were not asked about the rebellion. Instead the governor inquired about the *repartimiento* and the Timucuas' relations with the friars.[36] De Rebolledo showed little interest in what the Timucuas had to say, grouping all the caciques together and giving them no opportunity to discuss their individual grievances. He probably felt compelled to include this section in his report, for he could not justify an investigation into the Timucua Rebellion without at least acknowledging Timucua. Nevertheless, the bulk of the governor's 130-page *visita* was devoted to the Apalachees.

The Muskogean-speaking Indians who lived mostly between the Aucilla and Ochlockonee Rivers had interacted with the Spaniards since Hernando de Soto's 1539–1540 *entrada*. But at the time of the Timucua Rebellion, the Spanish presence in Apalachee was minimal as well as liminal. De Rebolledo provided no explanation for why he devoted so much of his investigation to a region and a people who had not played a significant role in this violent resistance; however, the Apalachees' testimonies offer reason enough. In Apalachee, Indian cacique after Indian cacique willingly came before the governor with reproaches against the Franciscan missionaries. This information allowed de Rebolledo to craft a particular narrative about the Timucua uprising that praised his administration only slightly more than it lambasted the Franciscans. This narrative mattered to de Rebolledo not merely because he wanted to exonerate himself or because it gave him ammunition to attack a powerful group of people he greatly disliked. This information allowed him to articulate new government policies that increased the military presence in *la tierra adentro,* regulated Franciscan missionary activity, and streamlined the roads connecting the San Agustín presidio to the Indian missions. In other words, policies that gave de Rebolledo more access and power.[37]

The testimonies in the *visita* followed a predictable pattern. De Rebolledo began by introducing the Indian caciques and principales of each town he visited before inquiring about the state of affairs in Apalachee. The replies were as formulaic as the questions. In the testimonies from Bacucua, Patali, Aspagala, Xinayca, San Luís, Tholome, Ocuya, Ocone, Ivitachuco, and Asile, the Apalachee first thanked the governor for taking an interest in their plight, then commented on the value of having Spanish soldiers stationed in or nearby their towns. They concluded by detailing some horrible maltreatment suffered at the hands of the Franciscans. Depicted as meddlesome and ignorant, if not blatantly disrespectful, the Franciscans in Apalachee appear as nothing more than a roadblock on the path to good Indian–Spanish relations. The main inconsistency within these testimonies comes in the form of the Apalachees' praise of de Rebolledo, which varied from a great deal to a great deal more. The following testimony is typical.

> In the place of San Luís de Nixaxipa on the twenty-second day of the
> month of January of the year one thousand six hundred and fifty-
> seven . . . assembled Alonso, principal cacique of the place of San Juan
> de Aspalaga; Manuel, cacique of Pensacola; Xpobal, cacique of Sabe;
> and Santiago, heir of the chieftainship of Jipe, and other Indian leaders
> of the jurisdiction of this place . . . To this [the *auto* issued by de Rebolledo],
> and to other questions put to them in connection with this visitation
> they responded, that the lieutenant [Sartucha] who had been in this
> provinces and soldiers who have arrived at this place have respected
> them; and, that neither they nor the other Indians have received any
> injuries or vexations . . . And that the complaints that all of them have to
> offer are . . . [with] the priest that they have presently [who] took them
> [Indian dances] away with incivility, treating them [the Indians] insult-
> ingly, entering into the principal council house, and because they were
> dancing, grabbed a fat stick and thrashed a leading man named Feliciano,
> who is present, brother-in-law of the principal cacique, until he broke it
> on his ribs.[38]

This testimony, like others recorded by de Rebolledo, describes helpful
Spanish soldiers and evil Franciscans. Its form and content, though seemingly prescribed, is not necessarily false. Just because the Apalachee caciques told the governor exactly *what* he wanted to hear does not mean that
they were lying.

De Rebolledo interpreted these testimonies of Franciscan abuse as a call for
government regulation, but the Apalachees did not ask for Spanish supervi-
sion. The Apalachees complained that the Franciscans eroded *their*, not de
Rebolledo's, credibility and power. In his testimony, Alonso, the principal of
Bacucua, recalled an incident similar to one described above by the cacique
of San Luís. Alonso explained that the friar "broke them all with a stick, an
event that set everyone running, because of the disrespect that they had
been subjected to, inasmuch as it was public." The Franciscans were not just
forbidding native rituals and dances; they were publicly disrespecting
Indian authority. Both the governor and the Apalachees rallied against the
missionaries, but they did so for their own, distinct purposes.[39]

The Apalachee testimonies became a dual performance. The Apalachees
spoke first. In emotional speeches, they described the vicious and erratic

behavior of the Franciscans. Then it was the governor's turn. As he listened to the Apalachees' complaints, de Rebolledo became mortified by the behavior of the friars and promised to come to the Apalachees' defense. Consider, for example, Apalachee testimony on the subject of carrying supplies. The Apalachees protested that "the religious obliged and forced them to carry trade goods to pagan villages in order to bring back deerskins and other things." The work as *cargadores* was not only time consuming but also uncompensated. Refusing or failing to perform these tasks had serious repercussions, as Alonso the cacique of Aspalaga explained through a case involving a sick Indian who had been whipped until "bathed in blood" after not carrying a load. The governor, conveniently forgetting that he had also issued an order requiring Indians to carry food to San Agustín at the eve of the rebellion, argued that the Franciscans' actions were reprehensible. "The Indians are not slaves," de Rebolledo stated plainly. The bottom line was that the governor could not afford to lose Apalachee friendship or grain. If the Apalachees were to choose sides, de Rebolledo wanted to make sure that they chose the Spanish.[40]

De Rebolledo's *visita* barely mentions the Timucua Rebellion. He only inquired, in the broadest possible way, about "murders, disputes, and tumults among them in their place." Clearly, the purpose of the *visita* was not to understand the causes of the Timucua uprising but rather to create de Rebolledo's *own* vision of La Florida. This Florida was more centralized, as seen in the reorganization of Timucua missions, and also boasted more soldiers and forts in *la tierra adentro* for protecting the governor's interests and limiting the influence of the Franciscans. De Rebolledo used his *visita* to construct a web of loyal Timucua and Apalachee caciques all bound directly to him (Figure 3.1).[41]

De Rebolledo was not the first Spanish official to produce an investigative report designed to keep the Franciscans in their place. In 1602, Don Fernando Valdés, son of the governor of Cuba, arrived in San Agustín with orders to evaluate the state of the colony and determine Florida's investment potential. With a royal *cédula* in hand, Valdés summoned military personnel, prominent citizens, government officials, and members of the clergy. The eighteen testimonies he collected stressed similar themes: the difficulty of making ends meet; the harsh conditions of the land; and the tense relations with neighboring Indians, in particular with the Guale. But for all their shared experiences, these witnesses disagreed about who bore the blame for Florida's difficulties. While the friars reproached the

FIGURE 3.1. Spanish information networks, 1656. I used the list of Timucua caciques
who attended the general assembly in San Pedro on February 13, 1657, to visualize
how Governor Rebolledo wanted to network Florida. Rebolledo's envisioned
communication network places the governor as the central and most important node.
("Visitation to San Pedro," February 13, 1657, in *Visita*. Worth, *The Timucuan
Chiefdoms of Spanish Florida, Volume 2: Resistance and Destruction*, 91.)

gubernatorial body for failing to colonize and supply the lands beyond the
coast, most of the interviewed San Agustín officials accused the Franciscans
of instigating unrest.[42] In particular, San Agustín officials worried about the
Franciscans "unsettling" and misguiding the Indian populations. Governor
Pedro Ibarra bluntly reminded the friars that he "and not another [could]
order" the Indians, for he was the governor and thus the person in charge.[43]
This was a sentiment de Rebolledo wholeheartedly embraced.

Other San Agustín officials had a rather different outlook. Some of the most
revealing yet understudied sources for colonial Florida are the *residencias*.[44]
These royally sanctioned audits were intended to give the incoming governor
an overview of the colony as well as insight into the officers under his service.
Don Diego Ranjel, a royal inquisitor, interviewed over seventy-five individuals for the *residencia* into de Rebolledo's government, conducted in 1660
after the governor's sudden death. Colonial officials testified against the
governor and then against each other. Everyone had different ideas about
governing San Agustín; distributing the *gasto de Indios*; managing the

Franciscan expansion into Apalachee; and, of course, explaining the Timucua Rebellion. The *residencia* exposed the internal quarrels, some political and more personal, that divided Spanish officials.[45] This lengthy document, which took months to complete, described de Rebolledo as greedy, inexperienced, self-serving, and opportunistic. Despite de Rebolledo's detailed *visita,* almost no Spanish official blamed the Franciscans for the Timucua Rebellion.

In San Agustín, the government and the Catholic Church saw each other more as competitors than allies. They each fought over who was best suited to interpret unfolding events. Secular and religious leaders vied for this privileged position, arguing that their particular vantage point afforded them the best information about the land, the people, and the struggles of colonial Florida.

~

If government officials in colonial Florida had a long history of blaming their misfortunes on missionaries, missionaries had an equally long history of trying to work away from government oversight. One of the most famous examples of this phenomenon is also one of the earliest. In 1570, a small group of Jesuits, weary of their limited success converting native peoples in La Florida, became convinced that they would fare better if they established a mission away from San Agustín's watch. But Father Juan Baptista de Segura's mission to Ajacán (in present-day Virginia) proved a complete failure that ended in the violent murder of the Jesuits.[46] San Agustín officials interpreted the fiasco as proof that mission projects must not be located too far from San Agustín or operated without military protection. But the Jesuits, and later the Franciscans, saw it differently. The friars of Ajacán had been brave, resolute, and, above all else, willing. Francisco Alonso de Jesús's 1630 *Memorial,* a publication intended to recruit more missionaries to La Florida, extolled the Franciscans and credited them with rescuing La Florida from certain failure. Fray Alonso portrayed the Franciscans as Florida's best and, in most instances, only line of defense; they alone had transformed the provinces of Guale, Timucua, and Apalachee into places of "unbelievable devotion and notable spiritual benefit."[47]

Unbelievable was perhaps the optimal word. Mission activity did grow in the 1630s and 1640s, but the impressive numbers projected more the desires of the missionaries than the number of converts in La Florida. Bishop Gabriel Díaz Vara Calderón, who in 1675 produced the most comprehensive report of missionary activity in Florida, tallied 13,152 converted Indians in the region. Calderón's estimate, though far more conservative than earlier claims, reveals the significant impact of the Franciscan initiatives in *la tierra adentro*. Even by the lowest approximation, the Franciscans were managing a population more than ten times the size of the population of Spaniards living in San Agustín.[48] In his eight-month journey, Calderón traveled along the Camino Real to many missions in Timucua, Apalachee, and Apalachicola, praising the commitment of the Franciscans and their converts. Though the government had failed to adequately support or supply them, the Franciscans had established functioning and well-connected missions.[49]

In the middle of this generally positive and favorable report, Calderón made a passing complaint about the limits of the Camino Real. The bishop had wanted to reach and converse with Chacato and Chisca Indians, hoping to placate their recent and violent rejection of missionization. But these Indians, who did not live physically far from the Timucua missions, were beyond Franciscan reach. "[I]n spite of having made different inquiries," the bishop lamented, "I have been unable to find anyone who could give me information concerning the[se] territories."[50] Calderón offered no suggestions for how to improve the Franciscans' communication network, short of having more friars and building more missions, but his brief remark was a keen one. The Franciscan network was built through Spanish missions yet dependent on Indian paths and ties.

The 1656 Timucua Rebellion assured the Franciscans that their mission network, for all its problems and inefficiencies, had fostered better relations in Timucua than had the activities of the officials from San Agustín. After all, the Timucua rebels did not target or kill any Franciscans. The Indians went directly after government officials and soldiers—proof enough, according to the friars, that the San Agustín government and Governor de Rebolledo in particular had overstepped their authority. For the Franciscans, answering the question of *what* caused the rebellion required looking no further than the government's abusive native labor policies or its blatant disregard for indigenous leadership structures. If these grievances sound familiar, it is because they were the same ones that Governor de Rebolledo levied against the Franciscans.[51]

"It is widely known," the Franciscans argued in their own report on the 1656 rebellion, "that in this province a governor can make the information he wants."[52] De Rebolledo wanted information to implicate the Franciscans in the uprising; he wanted information that cleared him from any wrong-doing; and, above all else, he wanted information that validated his vision for a more centralized and militarized Florida. De Rebolledo had simply made-up his findings on the Timucua Rebellion, the Franciscans alleged. De Rebolledo's so-called *visita* was not a legitimate evaluation of the situation, but an attack that merely "described his [governor's] ill will and opposition he harvested against the ministers of god for instead of trying to find the guilty among the living, he conducted a residencia against the dead."[53] The missionaries accused de Rebolledo of using the guise of an investigation to manipulate the truth and fabricate lies.

Unlike de Rebolledo's *visita,* which had focused on Apalachee, the Franciscans' report spent the majority of its text on Timucua. In the Franciscans' account of the rebellion, the governor's ill-advised policies and interference had pushed the good Christian Timucuas to the breaking point. The Timucua testimonies collected by the Franciscans recite long lists of complaints against de Rebolledo. If none of the Apalachee reports that de Rebolledo had compiled criticized his administration, all of the Timucuas interviewed by the Franciscans rallied against the governor. To account for the difference between their reports and de Rebolledo's findings, the friars simply stated that the Indians *they* had interviewed told the truth while those interrogated by de Rebolledo either were Apalachee, and thus not involved in the rebellion, or had testified under duress and had therefore lied. Through these Timucua testimonies, the Franciscans created an alternate narrative of the Timucua uprising. In their version, the Franciscans were innocent and, more important, the *repartimiento* and the oppressive government policies had caused the rebellion.[54]

The Franciscans' accusations did not stop there. They turned Timucua testimonies into a platform from which to question de Rebolledo's ability to govern and promote their own, more competent administration of Indian affairs. The Franciscans criticized the government's regulation of Indian labor and advocated for Franciscan control of the *repartimiento.* The friars protested against the governor's final judicial authority over Indian crimes and transgressions, calling for the transfer of that regulatory power to Franciscan hands. They particularly condemned de Rebolledo's interference in religious matters, for instance, his acquiescing to Indian dances and the ballgame, and argued that only Franciscans could supervise Timucua lives and practices.[55]

Even in Apalachee, a supposedly staunch pro-de Rebolledo province, the Franciscans managed to gather information that contradicted the governor's *visita*. The friars never organized an official investigation into Apalachee, but after reading de Rebolledo's scathing report of the Apalachee missions, Father Provincial San Antonio became determined to disprove these accusations. Unsurprisingly, he only recorded the interviews with Indians who saved their ill words for Spanish soldiers and officials, not Franciscans.[56]

The Franciscan compilation of Timucua and Apalachee testimonies, much like the one recorded by de Rebolledo, echoed the interviewers' wants and arguments. The Apalachees' call to remove Spanish soldiers from their lands reiterated, almost verbatim, the demands made by Fray Alonso del Moral, the *definitor* of Apalachee, earlier that month. Moral had argued that the soldiers that de Rebolledo had sent into Apalachee after the Timucua Rebellion not only interfered with mission activity but also antagonized the local populations. It is unclear if the Apalachees, who according to de Rebolledo had welcomed the soldiers, actually believed the Spanish militia a nuisance, as the friars' accounts insisted. But the amount of ink the Franciscans spilled about the twelve soldiers de Rebolledo had ordered to Apalachee reveals that, whatever the Apalachees thought, the Franciscans despised them. The soldiers were an unwanted reminder that the Franciscans were not the only, nor the final, authority in the region.[57]

If the Franciscans felt monitored and even intimidated by the soldiers, that was de Rebolledo's intent. In the wake of the Timucua Rebellion, missionaries had pressured their Indian allies to mobilize against the governor. Moral and Fray Garçon de los Cobos went as far as to encourage Apalachees to refuse participation in Spanish military efforts to suppress the rebellion.[58] Sergeant Major Cañizares, who de Rebolledo had sent to *la tierra adentro* to put an end to the rebellion, angrily reported how "the damned priest" interfered with his plans. Cañizares found that the friars had been "pressing these chiefs so that they may speak and complain about their not consenting that this place not be settled by Spaniards."[59] Instead of trying to help San Agustín end the uprising, the friars fomented unrest. Instead of securing Indian allies, the friars encouraged the Apalachees to bar Spanish soldiers from entering their towns. And instead of trying to uncover *what* had caused the Timucua Rebellion, the Franciscans spread lies. These missionaries, Cañizares found, were more concerned with proving de Rebolledo wrong than with producing a truthful or accurate account.

Testimony against testimony, and report against report, the governor and the Franciscans battled over the cause, the meaning, and the aftermath of the Timucua Rebellion until de Rebolledo's death in 1660.[60] There were no winners in these debates, only inimical competitors. But beyond the all-too-familiar distrust between the church and the state, the competing reports show the ties between European information-gathering practices and the local Indian populations.[61] While the struggle between de Rebolledo and the Franciscans can be viewed as an internal colonial debate that happened to manipulate Indian voices, Indian testimonies can also be seen as the framework that enabled the arguments between these competing powers to take place.

In this intense, well-documented struggle between Governor de Rebolledo and the Franciscans, the Timucuas are but shadows cast. Though the nominal focal point of both sets of reports, the perspective of the Timucuas proves the most difficult to uncover. The main but least surprising problem comes from the evidentiary base. Compared to the plethora of documents generated by de Rebolledo's investigation and the Franciscans' complaints, Timucuas produced only a handful of sources. But that very verb, *produced*, is reason enough to pause. Timucuas who both supported and opposed the uprising did more than leave records of their experience. They created them. However small and fragmentary these sources are compared to the narratives that have traditionally helped explain this rebellion, Timucua letters and testimony offer a deep and nuanced understanding of their violent resistance to Spanish power.

The complexity of Timucua sources presents a problem far deeper than their dearth. Unlike the governor's reports or the Franciscans' accounts, the Timucuas' reports had to be careful in the way that they distributed blame and how they framed their arguments. Speaking and writing before an attentive, armed, and unforgiving Spanish audience, Timucuas could point their fingers neither at the crown nor at the church. Blaming one, then the other, and sometimes both, the Timucuas situated their resistance in a context of fear and enslavement that underscored the power of Spanish colonialism even as it emphasized its limits.

But before exploring Timucua explanations for the rebellion, it is important to consider what Timucuas said and did as their violent resistance took shape. Lucas, one of the earliest proponents of an organized attack against the Spanish, kept himself informed of San Agustín's plans and policies. Lucas corresponded regularly with both Governor de Rebolledo and Don Juan Menéndez Márquez, owner of La Chua hacienda, located to the west of San Agustín. Just as de Rebolledo employed Captain Agustín Pérez de Villa Real and Esteban Solana as regular couriers to Timucua, Lucas relied on his own messengers, Juan Alejo, an Acuera Timucua from Santa Lucía, and Alonso, the son of the cacique Lázaro from Chamile, to carry information to and from San Agustín. These messengers, as well as the *nuevas* they carried, helped start the Timucua Rebellion.

The Timucuas did not immediately resort to violence, however. After refusing to comply with de Rebolledo's call for more men and supplies, Lucas convened an Indian council in San Pedro. Lucas quickly learned that he was not the only cacique who opposed the governor's order. Though the Timucua leaders gathered at San Pedro were all furious with de Rebolledo, their first order of business was to write a letter to the governor requesting modifications to his edict. These Indian leaders were at first more interested in repairing relations with the Spanish than in ending them. As the caciques crafted this letter, Lucas and Diego, the cacique of San Pedro, consulted with the resident friar, Fray Escudero. Escudero attempted to calm the mounting anger, but he proved sympathetic to the Timucuas' plight. He feared that, unless de Rebolledo lessened his demands, Timucua would erupt in violence. Fray Escudero penned a letter to the governor describing both the dire situation in Timucua and the infeasibility of de Rebolledo's order—a letter that accompanied the Timucuas' own pleas. Juan Alejo and Alonso, Lucas's appointed messengers, carried these letters back to San Agustín, with instructions to wait for de Rebolledo's response.

The governor answered quickly with two letters. One was a reply to Lucas and the caciques gathered in San Pedro. It promised to consider the Timucuas' requests with care. The other was a letter for Captain Pérez, de Rebolledo's messenger. This second letter instructed Pérez to continue his journey through Timucua towns demanding men and supplies. Though it is not clear if Juan Alejo and Alonso knew the content of either of the letters de Rebolledo gave them, it is clear that Captain Pérez never received the governor's letter.[62] Lucas intercepted it and, upon reading the instructions, realized that the governor had no intention of heeding the Timucuas' pleas. At that moment, the Timucuas stopped talking about maintaining relations with San Agustín officials and issued a new rally cry: rebellion.

Lucas's action set in motion an information frenzy, and both Spanish officials and Franciscans realized that they did not fully understand the situation in Timucua. Solana, de Rebolledo's second regular messenger to Timucua, tried to warn the governor that a rebellion had begun, but he never made it back to San Agustín. Instead, he became the earliest casualty of the Timucua Rebellion. Juan Gómez Pérez de Engraba, a friar who had been in Santa Cruz when Solana read de Rebolledo's orders, had also heard the quiet mumblings of rebellion grow louder and louder. Engraba began preparing for the worst. Fray Joseph Bamba went a step further and tried to caution the few Spanish soldiers garrisoned in Asile that a rebellion was starting. But Bamba was too late. By the time Bamba arrived, the Timucua rebels had already attacked the Spanish and killed Bartolomé Pérez, a soldier in Asile.[63]

The Timucua rebels were a step ahead of the Spanish. Captain Alonso de Argüelles recalled that "when they [the Timucuas] found out about news that the enemy was coming by sea, [they] wished to take advantage of the occasion and rise up." The same English threat that had compelled de Rebolledo to demand more Timucua soldiers and supplies enabled Timucuas to imagine that they were part of a two-front assault against San Agustín. The English would attack "by sea," and the Timucuas would "rise up" by land.[64] Though Captain Argüelles did not stipulate how the Timucuas acquired this "news," caciques like Lucas were well-attuned to the developments, changes, and threats affecting the region. Lucas operated a communications network linked to Spanish friars and officials as well as other Indians. We know he corresponded regularly with Diego, the cacique of San Pedro, and the meeting he organized in San Pedro certainly suggests an ability to communicate with other Timucua and perhaps even Apalachee principals via messengers and letters.[65] As a third-generation mission Indian, Lucas's ability to read and write in at least two languages would not have surprised many officials in colonial Florida, but his use of literacy to organize and coordinate an Indian rebellion certainty did.[66]

Lucas may not have had anything to do with the rebellion's first murders— the record on that is unclear—but he did organize the subsequent attack in La Chua, Don Juan Menéndez's hacienda. Don Juan left no personal account of this attack and departed for New Spain soon after the rebellion broke out. But the testimonies of several Spanish soldiers who knew Don Juan revealed how at first the La Chua owner was pleased to see his correspondent Lucas near his home, if somewhat surprised that the cacique was complying with de Rebolledo's new orders so expediently. Don Juan greeted Lucas by inquiring: "So quickly have you departed and gone toward the presidio?" But Don Juan had not finished asking this question when Lucas dragged him outside the hacienda and said, *"desta te quedo que a ti no te hemos de matar"* ("From this I spare you; we will not kill you").[67] Lucas destroyed La Chua and killed the soldier Juan de Osuna and two black slaves who worked at the hacienda, but true to his word, he did not kill Don Juan. The attack on La Chua proved one of the last before Lucas and his men retreated back to Indian country. By early September, Sergeant Major Cañizares had pacified and imprisoned most of the rebel caciques, except Lucas and the cacique of San Francisco. Lucas eluded Spanish capture and execution for another two months.[68]

Afterward, the Timucua, just like de Rebolledo and the Franciscans, attempted to reconstruct *what* had caused the Timucua Rebellion. At their initial meeting in San Pedro, the Timucua caciques had blamed Governor de Rebolledo, who demanded too much and provided too little. But Lucas had also pointed to other inciting causes. Clemente Bernal, the cacique of San Juan del Puerto, recalled how

> Lucas Menéndez, had made a meeting of *caciques* in the said village of San Pedro de Potohiriba, the cause which moved him, according to what he said, was a letter that he said he had intercepted from the said Governor [. . . .] he said he wrote it, and that in it, the sending to call upon the principals and the rest of the people of the said provinces of Apalachee and Timucua for the aid of this city was in order to make them slaves, and not because there was news of enemies, and that an Indian who knew Spanish had read the said letter.[69]

Touting the intercepted letter from Governor de Rebolledo, Lucas declared that the Spanish did not need Timucua soldiers for protection; the governor had ordered Indians to march into San Agustín "to make them slaves." When talking to other Timucuas and Apalachees, it was not the government's abusive policies, the *repartimiento,* or the Franciscans' meddling that Lucas credited with sparking the uprising. The "cause which moved him" to rebel was fear that he and his men would be enslaved.

The extent to which Lucas truly believed this threat is unclear. Lucas, just like de Rebolledo and the Franciscans, manipulated the facts to make his contentions more relevant.[70] But in the wake of de Rebolledo's excessive and now seemingly inflexible order for more men and supplies, the claim that the Spanish planned to enslave Timucua and Apalachee Indians—to remove them from their homes and kin and force them to work in degrading tasks—had traction.

Unlike de Rebolledo's policies, which did not affect Indian country evenly, slavery was a great equalizer. It had the potential to devastate Timucuas as well as Apalachees—an important point in Lucas's bid for Apalachee cooperation. Timucua and Apalachee relations had been unbalanced for close to a century. Mission activity had pushed Timucua toward the Spanish and away from the Apalachees. In 1647, when Apalachee Indians killed three Franciscans and destroyed seven of the eight mission sites in their lands, Spanish and Timucua soldiers joined forces to suppress the violence. But the tide had now changed. Governor de Rebolledo, in need of grain, trade, and men, had started favoring Apalachees over Timucuas. Timucua elites, who had rallied against their neighbors less than a decade ago, now needed their support.[71] These shifting alliances perhaps hint at why Lucas focused on slavery.

Lucas's definition of enslavement was a native one. He described slavery as the absence of kin and clan support, as the forced removal from a native space to a European one, and as a new labor exigency that upset the structural pillars of the Timucuas' sociocultural hierarchies. Timucuas had their own history of slavery and captivity. Before Spanish colonization, Timucuas had seized enemies during wartime as a way to both display strength and intimidate their rivals. They also had dealt firsthand with Spanish slaving raids during the sixteenth-century *entradas*.[72] Native slaving practices and the memory and lived experience of Spanish enslavement converged when de Rebolledo issued his new order for men and supplies. In less than three generations, Timucua had undergone an almost incomprehensive population decline, with death and disease as twin forces of colonialism. But as the testimonies of Lucas and the other caciques at San Pedro made clear, the hierarchical rankings of Timucuas' social structure had endured and helped maintain native autonomy. Now the Spanish threatened to take that away as well, compromising Indian leadership and one of the Timucuas' remaining sources of sovereign power.

Lucas declared that Governor de Rebolledo's plan was already underway. He claimed that the governor had already enslaved one of the Apalachees' principal caciques, Don Luís of Ivitachuco. At the time of the council in San Pedro, Don Luís was not in Ivitachuco but in San Agustín receiving gifts and supplies from de Rebolledo. Lúcas knew of Don Luís's journey to the Spanish presidio and probably also knew the reason behind the cacique's travel, but he nevertheless made Don Luís's absence appear as something far more nefarious. The Apalachee leaders gathered at San Pedro listened with care. They knew that Timucuas were wary of the improving Apalachee–Spanish relations, but they also knew that Lucas's connections were extensive and that Timucua networks had linked Timucua to San Agustín for over half a century. The Apalachees in San Pedro feared that Lucas was privy to *nuevas* they did not yet possess.[73] In the end, Lucas did not convince the Apalachees to join his cause, but he did manage to persuade them that Don Luís was in danger. Lucas's claims about Spanish slavery were not so inconceivable after all.

After hearing Lucas's report, the Apalachees sent a messenger directly to San Agustín. The Apalachees confronted the governor and wanted proof that neither their cacique nor the men he had sent to fulfill the *repartimiento* had been enslaved.[74] With the Timucua Rebellion gaining momentum, de Rebolledo took the time to refute these accusations personally and thoroughly. The governor recognized the persuasive power of this rumor. This time, fear of Spanish enslavement had sent a delegation of Apalachees rushing to San Agustín to verify the information; who knew what might happen the next time?

The particular *nuevas* that San Agustín officials intended to enslave the Indians moved through both Timucua and Spanish nodes. The Timucuas first discussed this news in San Pedro, but Franciscans helped perpetuate and validate the report. At least one friar faced charges for telling Indians that the San Agustín governor intended to enslave all Indians.[75] There were lots of different people with competing agendas moving through the same roads, making news easier to spread than to regulate (see Figure 3.2). This was a tense time in *la tierra adentro.*[76]

Rumors of enslavement as a trigger for rebellion are particular noteworthy for two reasons. First, they remain an exclusively Indian explanation used by both Timucuas and Apalachees, but one that is never mentioned by

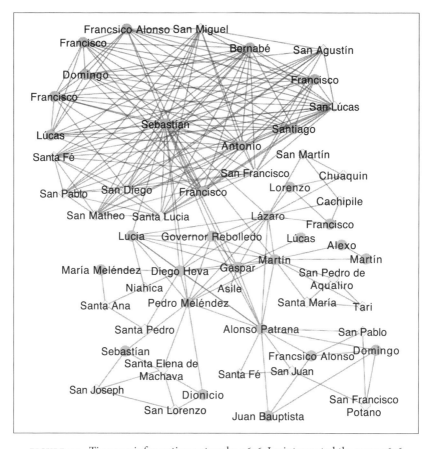

FIGURE 3.2. Timucua information networks, 1656. I reinterpreted the same 1656
San Pedro list used to recreate Governor Rebolledo's network by privileging
inter-Timucua relations. The Timucua information network has several
important nodes, far more connections, and no clear center.

Franciscans or government officials. And second, the claim evolved over
time. In 1656, Lucas called for a rebellion against a Spanish enslaver—against
a Spanish governor who had not only challenged Timucua leadership by
demanding more men and food than it could supply but had also insulted
soldiers and elites by requiring them to perform degrading tasks.[77] Three
years later, when San Agustín officials recorded Timucua and Apalachee testimonies of the rebellion, the talk of slavery remained but had taken on a
radically new shape. Slavery was no longer a potential threat by a Spanish
oppressor but an actual one being carried out by English and English Indians.

These testimonies about the Timucua Rebellion contain some of the earliest accounts of slaving raids carried out by Indians allied with Virginia colonists. de Rebolledo, it so happened, was not the only one afraid of an English attack. As the Florida governor searched the Atlantic horizon for the hostile fleet from Jamaica that never came, the Timucua and Apalachee Indians clamored for aid against a more local and imminent English threat.

The sense of fear and uncertainty over English slaving raids can be seen in the testimonies taken during de Rebolledo's *visita* and *residencia*. In San Luís de Xinaycal, the Indians welcomed de Rebolledo's initiative to build a new garrison precisely because they feared English raids. "A blockhouse (*fuerte*) to shelter them, for the defense of these provinces . . . all those of this place requested it and desire it even more as being in their interest, so that they may defend them from the English enemy, who has come to these provinces."[78] Martín, a principal of Ayubale, and his brother, Alonso, also spoke in favor of a new Spanish garrison in the context of English raids. "And they desire it [the fort] strongly, so that they may defend them[selves] from their enemies . . . as happened two years ago, when the Englishmen arrived in these parts . . . and, likewise, so that they may defend them from pagan Indians."[79] The comments by the cacique of Ayubale reveal that the English and English-sponsored raids were not some phantasmagorical threat but rather a growing problem in Timucua and Apalachee.

Neither Spanish officials nor Franciscans blamed Indian slavery for inciting the Timucua Rebellion. Nor, for that matter, would Timucuas or Apalachees point to it exclusively as their reason for joining or resisting the uprising. But slavery was nevertheless a key part of what Timucuas used in 1656 to convince other Timucuas and Apalachees that something needed to be done. Later Timucua and Apalachee testimonies taken in 1659 and 1660 repeatedly mention slavery when describing native life after the rebellion. The threat of enslavement not only shifts the discussion about the implications of the Timucua Rebellion back to *la tierra adentro* but also situates it in a different context. Indian answers to *what* caused the Timucua Rebellion revealed that, even though Indian relations and Indian rebellions were locally conditioned, they unfolded in increasingly transimperial landscapes. And, in the case of this 1656 Indian rebellion, those landscapes become most visible from Timucua, not from San Agustín.

~

Contemporary interpretations of the Timucua Rebellion of 1656 were varied. The government's abusive labor demands, the Franciscans' disruption of native society, the fear of English raids, slavery, disease, population loss, and the reorganization of local alliances: all received part of the blame. A simple question—*what* caused the Timucua Rebellion?—produced myriad responses, revealing first and foremost the competing and at times clashing preoccupations of those living in La Florida.

These alternative explanations depended as much on the sources and paths used to gather information as on individual perspective. For de Rebolledo, the rebellion offered an opportunity to travel beyond Timucua to collect testimonies of loyal Indian caciques and Spanish soldiers. This information allowed the governor to craft a narrative about the uprising that both blamed the missionaries and sanctioned his initiatives to centralize *la tierra adentro*. For the Franciscans, the rebellion offered a way to challenge de Rebolledo's policies. By gathering news that disputed the official *visita*'s rendition of the uprising, the friars displayed their ability to bypass the governor's network and influence. For the Timucuas, the 1656 rebellion tested the reach and the power of their connections. The Timucuas had relied on extensive networks that reached further and included more nodes than those originating from San Agustín to organize the uprising. These alliances proved more elastic than cohesive, affording individual Timucua towns and leaders significant leeway in how they understood and reacted to the rebellion. The different versions of the uprising reflect more than contrasting perspectives or sensibilities among the governor, the Franciscans, and the Timucuas. They expose the multiple ways that information was gathered, interpreted, and networked in the early South.

PART II

WHO

The Many Faces of Information,
1660s–1710s

⁓

Then he inquired of them as to what provinces they came from, and in order that they might realize that he too had been in Florida, asked if they were from Vitachuco, Apalache, Mauvila, Chicaza or other places where the Spaniards had fought great battles. The Indians thereupon recognized that he was one of those who had accompanied Governor Hernando de Soto, and regarding him with evil eyes, replied: "Having left those provinces as desolate as you did, do you want us to give you news of them?" And they would not answer him another word, but in speaking among themselves they did say . . . "We would more willingly give him arrow blows than the information he requests of us."

Florida Indians to Gonzalo Vicente, as recounted in
***La Florida del Inca* (1605)**

CHAPTER FOUR

INFORMERS AND SLAVES

 ~

No matter how much he cultivated the Indians, they did not respond,
but rather drew apart totally from communication with the Spaniards
and protected the English.

Alonso de Leturiondo, Memorial to the King, circa 1700

IN MAY 1675, an Indian woman raced through the gates of San Agustín,
Florida.[1] She looked exhausted and was out of breath; it was clear she had
seen better days. She revealed that her town had been destroyed.[2] The attack
came by night, and the woman was not sure what remained of her town or
how many people had escaped. The fact that she had arrived in San Agustín
alone, unaccompanied by family members or other refugees, hinted at the
brutality of the attack. Florida's governor Pablo de Hita Salazar listened to
her report in silence. He was furious. In his few months in office he
had received similar reports from Timucua, Mocama, Guale, and Yamasee
Indians. Making matters worse, when the governor asked "*¿quién hizo
esto?*" (Who did this?), the Indians answered, "*No sé*" (I do not know).[3] It
was the same with this woman. She had been there, seen the attackers, and
witnessed the destruction; yet she did not know who was responsible.[4] No
one in San Agustín seemed to know for certain.

The English knew. The attackers were Westos, or Chichimecos, as the
Spanish called them, a relatively new force in the region. Having fled from
Iroquois raids, the Westos migrated south to find more stable living conditions.[5] The Westos hoped a partnership with the English would grant them
better access to trade, goods, and, of course, guns. They had firsthand experience with the destabilizing power of Indian slaving, and now they wanted
to reap its profits. In the 1660s and 1670s, the Westos repeatedly raided
Spanish missions, capturing Spanish Indians and selling them into slavery.

99

Slavery had long been a feature of southeastern native societies, but the cycle of violence and devastation created by the selling of people for guns to the English radically altered the region's geopolitics. New groups like the Westos, then the Savannahs, followed by the Yamasees and finally the Creeks, rose quickly to power, only to experience an equally precipitous usurpation of their newfound privilege. These raiding parties systematically attacked and destroyed Spanish missions in Guale, Timucua, and Apalachee. Within fifty years of the first Westo raids, more than 50,000 Indians had been sold into slavery.[6]

But in the early 1670s, all Governor Hita Salazar could gather was that this force destroyed Spanish towns, killed Spanish friars, and kidnapped Spanish Indians. Who these Indian attackers were, where they were going to strike next, and how they might be negotiated with (if that was even possible) proved most uncertain. Indian groups on both ends of slaving raids also struggled to stay informed in their rapidly transforming world. Even English traders who had helped precipitate these changes were unsure who their native allies were or how long those alliances would last. More than a story of violence and displacement, the Indian slave trade exposes both the diversity of actors in the early South and the dynamic nature of their interactions.

Posing the question of *who* spread news during this critical fifty-year period allows us to reexamine some of the most familiar narratives about the early South. To be sure, centering informers and the spread of news does not change the fact that the English established South Carolina in 1670, that the Indian slave trade grew and engulfed the region in the late seventeenth century, or even that the contests over the lands and peoples in *la tierra adentro* reshaped imperial rivalries. Nevertheless, chronicling the struggles of those who were themselves trying to make sense of this complicated milieu allows me to describe the early South without homogenizing or flattening the experiences of Indians, Africans, and Europeans.

Examining *who* carried information thus serves two goals. First, it shows how communication structured the different relations among the region's many and often competing actors. And second, it helps reconstruct how these different peoples and groups exercised agency, what they worked toward, and why they acted the way they did. In other words, the focus on *who* transmitted news combines both narrative and analysis, forging cohesion from a time and a place that was anything but coherent.

～

The first indications that something had changed were subtle and disjointed. The fleeting references to the abrupt relocation of an Indian town, the murmurs about bands of roaming Indians wielding guns, and even the earliest mentions of violence offered little hint of the monumental destruction to come. In the late 1650s, Timucuas and Apalachees noted a growing threat posed by native groups trading with Virginia.[7] But San Agustín officials did not mention slaving raids for another two years, recording this destabilizing force only when the Westos started targeting Spanish holdings directly. The Westos, originally a group of Eries who had come south via the Ohio River, had formed a partnership first with the Susqueannock Indians and then with Jamestown traders and slavers. Within a decade, the Westos had moved near the Savannah River (in present-day Georgia) and began raiding Spanish missions. Spanish nodes in *la tierra adentro,* primarily in the provinces of Guale and Timucua but also in Apalachee and Apalachicola, began disappearing. To escape Westo raids, these mission towns and native communities were forced to relocate. Some chose to come closer to San Agustín, while many others moved away from Spanish influence.[8]

San Agustín officials had a hard time making sense of it all. In 1662, Governor Alonso de Aranguiz y Cortés wrote a letter to the king reporting how "in the province of Guale adjacent to this presidio some Indians said to be the Chichimecos have made inroads." The governor devoted less time to explaining the "inroads" made by the Westos than he did to describing *who* had given him this information. "This news," Aranguiz y Cortés explained, "had been acquired from other, non-Christian Indians who had been fleeing them [the Westos]." Piecing together this information was difficult, for "there was no one in these provinces who could understand" these fugitives.[9] As the Spaniards struggled to communicate with people identified only by what they were not (Christians), the extent of the Westos' disruption became clearer. The problem for the governor was not merely that a gun-toting Indian group from Virginia was launching slaving raids into Spanish Florida; it was that the Spanish had to learn about the Westos from Indians who had only minor or no direct contact with the Spanish. For San Agustín officials, *who* carried news of these slaving raids proved as foreign and unpredictable as the attackers themselves.

The only certain reports about these early English endeavors and slaving raids seemed to come too late for the Spanish to intervene. San Agustín felt as if they were standing on the edge of a sinkhole. Alliances they had made, missions they had established, and friendships they had secured began disappearing, as if swallowed up by the earth. "They seek to destroy the provinces and terrorize the Indians, pagan as well as Christian," decried Spanish officials.[10] That unspecified "they" referred to both the English and their Indian allies—Westos, Savannahs, or Apalachicola.[11] Though not untrue, these descriptions of incomprehensibly violent foes and unraveling alliances reveal the devastation of the Indian slave trade as experienced from the perspective of San Agustín. The Spanish were losing land, allies, and influence; their *nuevas* seemed to come from people who were themselves at a loss.[12]

The Spanish tried to stay informed. Since the founding of San Agustín in the mid-sixteenth century, Spanish officials had relied on sentinels stationed throughout La Florida to warn of coming or potential threats.[13] The sentinels' responsibilities as well as their livelihoods depended on their ability to read the rhythms of the early South, noting fluctuations in the expected patterns of trade, migration, and movement. By the late seventeenth century, however, the most common pattern observed by the sentinels was one of change. Surrounded by constantly mobile if not threatened or threatening populations, sentinels did not know where to look. Quite often, they looked in the wrong direction. Spanish sentinels not only proved incapable of warning of coming English raids but also fell victim to them.[14]

One of the earliest reports of English activity in Guale came via a sentinel who was captured and then released. During his short time as both a lookout and a captive, this unidentified sentinel uncovered a great deal of information about the English. Among other things, he learned that the English had established a town near Santa Elena and that "they have [allied with] Indians who had previously sworn their devotion to his [Spanish] Majesty."[15] The English were using these former Spanish allies to launch raids into Timucua. Though South Carolinians had denied involvement in these early slaving raids, this sentinel had found tangible proof. He had seen church bells in the English town, almost certainly looted from a Spanish mission. But far more worrisome was the presence of Timucua Indians, in particular women and children, in chains, clearly intended to be sold as slaves.

In 1683, a series of English attacks exposed the ineffectiveness of Spanish sentinels. First, a group of five sentinels simply abandoned their post in the face of invading forces. Captain Andrés Pérez, Manuel Risso, Juan Ruíz de Canizares, Joseph de Cardenas, and Pedro de Tejeda subsequently spent two years avoiding both the enemy and their obligations to the Spanish crown.[16]

When they finally returned to San Agustín in 1685, Captain Pérez and his men offered no excuse for fleeing and even demanded back pay for the service they had supposedly performed while wandering around the province.[17] Though not amused by the sentinels' request, Governor Juan Márquez Cabrera was relieved that, at the very least, these men had eluded capture.

The same could not be said of another group of five soldiers who left the mission of Santa Catalina that same year. These five soldiers left "without thinking of the risks that were to come" and marched directly into English hands. After getting caught, the Spaniards realized that the only weapon at their disposal was the very ineptitude that had led to their capture in the first place. The sentinels "pretended having known of" the English presence, and claimed to have "already sent warning about the enemy's whereabouts." The sentinels declared that the English would "be captured with ease and in no time" because Spanish reinforcements were on their way and would arrive before "the enemy had a chance to secure his piraguas."[18] The English believed the five soldiers' story, even though—or maybe because—they had overpowered the Spanish forces without any difficulty. The English quickly released their Spanish prisoners and sailed away, fearing the reinforcements who were supposedly on the way. The Spanish had been lucky—this time.

Florida officials were playing a constant game of catch-up in terms of the *nuevas*. But while the view from San Agustín appeared bleak, from Charles Town it seemed quite promising. In a letter to the Lord Proprietors, William Owen, a leading figure in the new English colony, reported in 1670 that San Agustín was "but an Impotent Garrison having not about 200 soldiers." Since the Spanish only "have 3 files of men whom they place there [as sentinels] for Intelligence of what shall happen of Importance on the coast, the Spaniard cannot affect our settling here [and] neither can he tell which way to Impede it."[19] The only thing the Spanish could do was watch, Owen argued, and with only three sentinels in place, they could not even do that well.

The English had established Charles Town in 1670. Eager to find a staple crop to cultivate and export, the Carolina colonists endured much trial and even more error. The colony's first engine of growth came from the deerskin and slave trade with nearby native groups. South Carolinians worked quickly to disentangle Spanish–Indian alliances, reorient the Indian trade away from their English neighbors in Virginia, and develop their own extensive and profitable commercial connections.[20] The South Carolina

English found willing partners first in the Westos (1670s) and soon thereafter in the Savannahs (1680s), Yamasees (1690s), and Ocheses (1700s).
Trading guns, alcohol, and other European goods for deerskins and increasingly for slaves, South Carolinians used the Indian trade as a way to network the region. Unlike the Spanish, who received their *nuevas* from hapless sentinels and Indians fleeing enslavement, the English were dealing
almost exclusively with those doing the slaving.[21]

South Carolina's information networks differed from those of San
Agustín. Trade, not missions, diplomacy, or gifts, became proxy for communication. This commercial exchange was "the Original great tye between
the Indians and Europeans."[22] This "great tye" offered three core advantages.
First, it created far-reaching networks. By the mid-1680s, Henry Woodward,
as well as other traders like John Stewart, had developed relations with
Indians all around Charles Town; by the mid-1700s, agents like Thomas
Nairne and John Wright had made connections with distant groups such
as the Choctaws, Chickasaws, and eventually the Cherokees.[23] Important
Indian paths and key nodes began supporting South Carolina's trade.
Within three decades, English traders and their native allies accomplished
what the Spanish had failed to do in over a century. South Carolinians
were participating in networks extending from the Atlantic coast to the
Mississippi and from native towns once trading with Virginia agents to the
missions in La Florida.

Second, these trade connections were lucrative.[24] South Carolina officials
and traders, who were often one and the same, considered this Indian trade
network "of the greatest Importance to the Wellfare of this Province."[25] "It
is the Means by which we keep and maintain the several Nations of the
Indians surrounding this Province in Amity and Friendship with us,"
explained a *South Carolina Gazette* article, "and thereby prevent their falling
into the Interest of France and Spain."[26] The Indian slave trade protected
and expanded English connections, even as it limited Spanish and French
influence.

Third, these commercial connections made South Carolina powerful. In
1704, when Apalachee Indians entered South Carolina's trading network,
the English used trade to negotiate the terms of this new friendship. "[A]
free trade for guns and ammunition shall not be granted them," the South
Carolina government explained, "till we are better assured of their sincerity
to us."[27] Guns and ammunition would come only after loyalty. The Indian

slave trade, the English quickly realized, could be used not only to create networks but also to control how these connections worked.

The first efforts to monitor this trade network came from above. Carolina was a proprietary colony, chartered by Charles II to a group of aristocrats in 1663—the most involved of whom was Lord Anthony Ashley Cooper, who later became the first Earl of Shaftesbury. The Lord Proprietors first tried establishing a monopoly over the Indian slave trade. They wanted to regulate the profitable enterprise as well as the myriad interactions this trade produced. Their attempts encountered immediate opposition from the Goose Creek Men. Members of this faction, like James Moore, Maurice Matthews, and Arthur Middleton, not only held positions of power within the colony but were also preeminent traders and slavers.[28] These individuals accused the Lord Proprietors of interfering with colonial matters and merely wanting to reap the profits from the Indian slave trade. The Lord Proprietors argued that their efforts to regulate the trade concerned the colony's greater safety. Conflicts during the colony's first two years had shown South Carolinians to be more eager than capable of directing the Indian slave trade. In the Kussoe War (1671) and then in the Westo War (1680–1682), South Carolinians had first "furnish[ed] a bold and warlike nation with arms and ammunition," and then found themselves fighting the very Indians they had just armed. The Lord Proprietors did not doubt the value and connections brought by the Indian slave trade, but they feared that this network placed the needs of "Particular persons" ahead of "the preservation of the Colony."[29]

They were not wrong. But despite the challenges of the Kussoe and Westoe wars, the English colonists, unlike the Spanish officials, saw their alliances and networks continue to grow. South Carolinians recognized the potential and power in their expanding commercial connections.[30] In 1700, a planter overheard two unnamed Indians trying to recruit "a small nation of Indians living" near Charles Town to join the "Great many Nations of Indians [that] had already agreed and confederated to make war & cut off all ye white men . . . [and] Came to Charles Town and there reported it in such a frightful manner as his fear had suggested it to him, not leaving room for any doubt ye Truth thereof." The members of the House of Commons listened to this man's frantic rendition of coming events, but they responded with calm. They explained that this "small nation of Indians" traded actively with South Carolina and instead of joining "the great many

Nations," these Indians had not only kept the English appraised of the developing plot but had also vowed to remain loyal. As frightening as the prospect of a "confederated" Indian force bent on "mak[ing] war & cut[ing] off all the white men" was, the English had confidence in their networks and believed that their trade alliances would protect them.[31]

Spanish and French officials viewed English advances with dread. Sieur de Bienville, governor of the new French colony in Louisiana, described South Carolina's commercial connections as "enterprising." The French governor understood how the English used trade to forge friendships and exert control over the whole region. South Carolina traders, he observed, "embark upon very difficult wars and voyages in order to corrupt our allies and give aid to our enemies, and they derive from this conduct all the advantages that they could derive from the most favorable war without having to fear reprisals from us."[32] Trade had enabled the English to "corrupt" French–Indian relations, cause "difficult wars," and profit from French loss.

The Spanish had a similar experience with English "enterprise." In 1707, a large force of over 100 Indians armed by the English easily overwhelmed the meager Spanish garrison in Pensacola. Juan Gabriel de Vangar and Joseph de Roxas were among the soldiers who managed to escape, but their journey back to San Agustín proved more terrifying than the original attack. They saw English soldiers and weapons in every town. The Spanish found that "all Indians had fire arms." Though the sheer numbers alone were alarming—the Tallapoosas had over 600 shotguns, the Apicas boasted 300 firearms, and the Ayabamos had more than 500—the Spanish soldiers were horrified by the betrayal of mission Indians. In the "four Christian Apalachee pueblos, Thomole, Escambe, Patale and Baququa," the Spanish found English goods, and "in all these places . . . there was [also] an English lieutenant."[33] South Carolinians were not merely destabilizing the region; they were infiltrating every node.

Charles Town officials understood the power of the Indian slave trade. In 1708, the Lord Proprietors sent an inquiry about the state of the colony, asking about its demography, geography, and commerce. "[H]aving answered the several queries stated to us by Your Lords in the best manner we are at present capable of," explained members of the House of Commons, "[we] humbly crave leave to superadd an account of the Indians or allies our Trade and Commerce with one another and their Consumption of our Goods." This unsolicited response was the longest and most detailed of the whole questionnaire. It described both the Indian populations that surrounded Charles Town and the intricate "Trade and Commerce" these groups had with each other and with the English.[34] A large part of the colony's growth and wealth, the South Carolina officials explained, was intricately linked to the Indian slave trade.

Traders and enslavers proved, as the Lord Proprietors had long feared, rather myopic network makers. Worrying more about profits and sales than about the long-term security of the colony, traders saw little merit in sharing information with one another. They stood to gain by competing rather than collaborating. In November 1700, months after South Carolinians had supposedly prevented a coordinated Indian attack through the power of their trade networks, the House of Commons had to issue an order compelling both Indian and European traders to communicate any pertinent information with the South Carolina government.[35] Robert Stevens, who represented the Goose Creek community, detailed the many crimes committed by traders. According to Stevens, withholding timely news was the least of the traders' growing list of offenses.[36] Gideon Johnston, a missionary of the Society for the Propagation of the Gospel (SPG), concurred. Johnson described South Carolina traders as "the Vilest race of Men upon Earth," who managed their business as if they had complete impunity from the law.[37] Francis Le Jau, a prominent SPG missionary, offered a slightly less critical view. He acknowledged that traders were a necessary and an important part of South Carolina's economy, but he called on the colonial government to regulate the Indian slave trade more vigorously. Le Jau saw only danger in the traders' far-reaching connections—connections that Charles Town officials could not control or even properly discern.[38]

Traders fueled South Carolina's expansion. They were also the ones *who* informed English officials about what this growth implied, who it included, and how it progressed. As Florida officials struggled to maintain their shrinking alliances, South Carolinians experienced a proliferation of allies and connections. These were not unconnected developments. The shifting topologies of the Spanish and English networks were muddled echoes of each other. But these seemingly bifurcated reactions, loss for Florida and gain for South Carolina, account only for European experiences. Native responses to the situation proved far more complex.

~

The cacica Pamini came to power during the early years of the Indian slave trade.[39] About fifty years old, the cacica commanded the Yspo and exerted significant influence over the Escamcu, the Cambe, and other native peoples who resided near Santa Catalina. Almost no ethnographic information about the Yspo has survived. There are hints that the people under Pamini's command were mostly Muskogean-speaking refugees who had come together as a way to cope with the devastation caused by Westo slaving raids. Pamini's experiences shed light on native efforts to understand and manipulate the changing geopolitics that had redrawn major alliances, pushed allies into war with each other, and depopulated vast parts of the early South in the late seventeenth century.

In 1670, Pamini met Captain Antonio Argüelles. The Spanish captain was in Port Royal investigating, or at least trying to investigate, English activities in the region. Argüelles was having a hard time distinguishing truth from rumor. Port Royal Indians offered little help. Eager to trade with the new English colonists, they were not too keen on Spanish interference. Even before South Carolinians made inroads into Port Royal, Spanish relations with Cusabo, Cayagua, and other nearby Indians had been lukewarm at best. These native groups had long refused Spanish missionization and colonization.[40] Then Pamini appeared. She immediately impressed Argüelles. The cacica had no affinities for the Port Royal Indians and, though not Christian, she also seemed unimpressed by English advances.

Pamini had put care and thought into how she introduced herself to Argüelles. The cacica's image as distinct from yet somehow intricately connected to the complex Port Royal politics came not from the Spanish, the English, or even the Port Royal Indians but rather from herself. In her first meeting with Captain Argüelles, Pamini preempted her *nuevas* on the English by stating that "she had not come to help." Insisting that she was not doing the Spanish any favors, the cacica proceeded to inform Argüelles that the Port Royal "Indians were deceiving him." These Indians had tried to intimidate the Spanish by overstating the military capacity of the English. Pamini had visited their town several times and could report, from firsthand experience, that it was far less equipped than the Port Royal Indians had insinuated.[41] Her testimony both pleased and angered Argüelles. The English were weaker than he had anticipated, which was good news for Florida, but the Port Royal Indians had no intentions of joining or even helping the Spanish.[42] Pamini, Argüelles concluded, was the most reliable informer he was going to find. He decided to entrust the cacica to *"hacer ynformazion,"* literally to "make information."[43]

Pamini became a news broker. From late 1670 to 1672, she furnished the Spanish with information about the English and, as later testimony would reveal, she also supplied the English with news about the Spanish. Her news centered on Port Royal; she reported on the weaponry, vessels, and soldiers stationed at the town. Given her role as dual informant, Pamini had to be careful. During her first meeting with the Spanish, the cacica urged Captain Argüelles to "keep secret" her role. She did not want the English to consider her a "friend of the Spanish" because that association would limit her access to Port Royal, which was both her source of news and leverage.[44] Through the information she supplied, Pamini secured trade and promises of relative nonaggression from both the Spanish and the English. At a time when slaving raids decimated most of Guale, Pamini's ability to protect the autonomy of her people was remarkable. News was a powerful weapon—it was both the sword Pamini used to defend her authority and the shield she wielded to protect her town.

It is not clear exactly when or why the English turned on Pamini. Their distrust of Indians they considered friendly with the Spanish offers the only hint at their actions.[45] In the early months of 1672, the English threatened the cacica's life; to show their resolve, they captured several members of her family.[46] The cacica had to regroup. In December 1672, she marched directly to San Agustín, circumventing the much closer fort in Santa Catalina. She justified her unannounced appearance in San Agustín and her breach of standard protocol by communicating supposedly pressing news: The English were planning an attack on San Agustín.[47] But Governor Manuel de Cendoya was not convinced. Reports of a coming English attack had circulated in San Agustín since the founding of Charles Town and, despite Pamini's insistence, her *nuevas* seemed more desperate than real.

Pamini had hoped to strengthen her position as an informant, and therefore reassert her importance, by heightening the sense of tension between the Spanish and the English.[48] Instead, her plan backfired. Within months of her testimony, a couple of Chiluque Indians arraigned Pamini for lying to Governor de Cendoya. The Chiluques accused Pamini not only of purposefully misrepresenting English intentions but also of trying to incite unrest.[49] The longer the Spanish waited for the English attack Pamini swore was coming, the more it seemed that the cacica had deceived them. By the time of her final testimony before the San Agustín governor, Pamini lacked much of her former strength. Westos had attacked her town and, unable to rally a military response, she eventually abandoned her settlement, her people, and thus her stance as ruler. The cacica's *nuevas*, more woeful than notable, no longer afforded her protection or influence.

Pamini was not, of course, the only native leader trying to mold the confusion and violence engulfing the region into a source of power. The Yamasees, much like the Yspo, had come together in response to the early slaving raids. Though more ethnographical information is known about the Yamasee than about some of the other native groups previously mentioned, there are still many critical details lacking. The language the Yamasees spoke (possibly Muskogean, but there is also evidence of Timucua and Guale influences), the boundaries of their territory (Ichisi, Alatamaha, and Ocute were all important early towns, but mobility rather than stability proved a defining Yamasee characteristic), and the sociopolitical organizations of their towns remains unclear.[50]

In the early 1660s, Yamasee refugees no longer capable of hunting or farming in their lands fled into La Florida. By the 1670s, there were at least twelve Yamasee towns within Spanish jurisdiction. Many Yamasees moved into abandoned or previously raided Guale and Mocama missions. But relations between the Spanish and the Yamasees remained tepid. The Yamasees rejected missionization and guarded their autonomy from San Agustín. For their part, the Spanish refused to arm Indians; for all their welcome of native refugees escaping English slaving raids, Florida officials offered very little physical protection. The Yamasees quickly understood that Spanish kindness would not ensure their safety.

The Yamasees sought a more permanent, and more autonomous, footing. When the South Carolina government allowed a group of Scottish colonists to establish Stuart's Town in the Port Royal area, the Yamasees saw their chance to redefine their relations with both the English and the Spanish.[51] Led by the cacique Altamaha, a group of Yamasees moved closer to Stuart's Town and expressed interest in trading with the new town as well as with Charles Town. The Scottish colonists had wanted autonomy from Charles Town and its politics, but South Carolina traders and officials had other plans; they sought to capitalize on Stuart's Town's strategic location and promising native alliances, especially with the Yamasees. The Yamasees, for their part, welcomed both Scottish and English traders, creating a network that accommodated Carolina's diverse European and indigenous populations and linked together some the region's most important nodes.[52]

In March 1685, within a couple months of this new Yamasee–English alliance, the cacique Altamaha led a deadly attack against the Mission of Santa Catalina de Ahoica. John Chaplin, an English trader from Port Royal, reported that after receiving "arms and other things," the Yamasee cacique had "gone against the Timechoes [Timucuas]."[53] Caleb Westbrooke, another of the traders who worked with the Yamasees, confirmed that the enslaved Timucuas "are Christians" and that attacks had targeted "the Chapell and the Fryers' house and killed fifty of the Timechoes."[54] Supported and supplied by the English, Altamaha and his men killed over fifty people, including a Spanish friar, and captured twenty-two Spanish Indians as slaves.

The attack shocked the Spanish. Until then, San Agustín officials had regarded the Yamasees as allies—distant, autonomous, and nonmissionized allies but allies nonetheless. Violence and unrest had long surrounded discussions of the Yamasees, but the Spanish considered these Indians victims, not instigators. Only a few years before the 1685 attack on Santa Catalina, Yamasees had poured into other Spanish missions and towns seeking asylum. San Agustín officials were bewildered by how Indians they had not long ago sheltered had transferred their loyalty to the English.

The Yamasees' political as well as geographical relocation had unfolded along their own indigenous networks. Their decisions were not merely about embracing English trade or rejecting Spanish missions. The Yamasees were comprised of Upper and Lower Towns. The connections between Upper Towns, the most important of which was Pocotaligo but also included the towns of Pocosabo, Huspah, Sadketche, and Tulafina, and the Lower Towns, the largest one led by cacique Altamaha, allowed the Yamasees to open several different paths. Some Yamasee roads extended along the coast, and some towns even kept their trails to San Agustín open for several years after 1685. Other Yamasee paths led to Muskogean-speaking groups farther inland. The Yamasee developed a network that was not only expansive but also flexible and adaptive.[55]

As Florida and South Carolina officials attempted to determine the strengths, intentions, and allegiances of the Yamasees, the Yamasees were doing the same for the Spanish and English. The Yamasees were also redefining and expanding *who* could be included in their networks. The links the Yamasees established with Scottish and English traders were as new as their connections with Muskogean-speaking towns. These towns, in what the Spanish considered the northern part of the "province of Apalachicole" and the English simply considered the "interior," were at the heart of coalescing Muskogean growth and power.[56] It is interesting, but not surprising, that the Yamasees, whose language resembled the Hitchi language spoken in the southern part of the "province of Apalachicole," searched for allies not in Sabacola, Ocuti, Talupasli, or Apalachicole but in the Muskogean-speaking towns of the north. The Yamasees forged alliances with Coweta and Cussita, which were, if not the largest, certainly the most influential towns in the region.[57] The Yamasees wanted powerful friends—friends who would provide aid in times of need and help them better connect to the rapidly changing region.

Proto-Creek towns were also active in negotiating the Yamasees' new arrangements. The Yamasees' connections to Coweta offered the Creeks a strategic vantage from which to engage in the growing deerskin and slave trade.[58] Though there are no records of Yamasee delegates struggling to learn Muskogean languages and only glimpses of them going to the Hitchi-speaking southern Apalachicola towns to seek allies, their willingness to cross linguistic and geographic divides shows that the Yamasees not only understood the importance of the new English and Scottish trading towns but also that the Yamasees were working hard to connect with the emerging Indian polities.[59]

Violence made these connections harder to sustain. In the 1670 Treaty of Madrid, the Spanish vowed to recognize English claims to Carolina. In return, the English promised not to attack the Spanish. But Florida–Carolina relations continued to be marked by conflict. By 1686, San Agustín officials had grown weary of English aggression and launched a series of attacks against South Carolina. Governor Juan Márquez Cabrera organized a small fleet and 150 men to march against the English colony. The Yamasees, though not the intended target, were a motivating factor in Cabrera's decision. James Colleton, the recently arrived English governor, believed that the Spanish had acted "in revenge of those Indians falling upon, and plundering some Spanish Settlements."[60] Colleton was partly right: Governor Cabrera did want "revenge" for the Yamasees' "plundering" of Spanish missions. But the Spanish governor also had longer-term ambitions. He hoped that crippling Port Royal and then Charles Town would convince South Carolina's Indian allies, especially the Yamasees, to shift their alliances back to Florida.[61] The first part of Governor Cabrera's plan succeeded: The Spanish destroyed Port Royal and burned English plantations along the coast. But a storm stopped the advancing forces before they could reach Charles Town.[62] The Spanish encountered similarly mixed success in manipulating Indian loyalties.

For the Yamasees, the destruction of Port Royal revealed the vulnerability of their new connections with Scottish and English traders and the danger still posed by their former allies. The Yamasee cacique Altamaha personifies this ambivalence.[63] He had led some of the earliest raids against Spanish missions and Indians, but he declined to assist Captain William Dunlop in reclaiming some of the African slaves who had fled to San Agustín during the 1686 attack. At first, Altamaha told Dunlop that he was "not willing to proceed" because "his people were not willing." An unconvinced Dunlop "soon found it was only himself [Altamaha] who was the cause of all" this delay; his men were "very willing" to march to San Agustín. When confronted, Altamaha "told plainly he wold not goe kill Spaniards for they had never killed any of his people." In the process, the cacique incurred the ire of both Dunlop and the soldiers under his command, who "chid[ed] him for his unfaithfulness" to the English. Only a year earlier, Altamaha had burned Spanish missions, captured and sold Timucuas as slaves, and sanctioned the death of a Franciscan friar, but the 1686 attack on Port Royal forced him to reevaluate the strength of his English allies.[64]

Altamaha did not want to bind his people permanently to a weakening node or put the Yamasees in open opposition to a Florida administration on a warpath. Altamaha was a cacique and had to think as one. Altamaha decided neither to rally behind the English, as Dunlop thought their friendship demanded, nor to abandon his English allies, as the Spanish had hoped. Balancing Spanish and English threats, Altamaha maintained open paths to both Lower and Upper Yamasee towns; these intra-Yamasee and inter-Indian connections were the ones that best served his peoples' interests.

The Spanish, meanwhile, realized that the destruction of Stuart's Town proved insufficient. Governor Diego de Quiroga Losada, who inherited the problems caused by the 1686 attack ordered by his predecessor, concluded that protecting San Agustín required more than destroying English holdings. The Spanish needed to foster their own connections, expand their networks and, at the very least, maintain their existing allies. Though sound, this logic proved futile. The attack of 1686 failed to recruit key Indian groups, such as the Yamasees, or curtail subsequent slaving raids on Spanish missions. On the contrary, the destruction of Port Royal had given an increased urgency to South Carolina's desire to eliminate its Spanish neighbor. As Governor Quiroga Losada struggled to prepare San Agustín for South Carolina's retaliation, the Spanish received a boost from an unexpected source: fugitive slaves.

The African presence in the colonial South can be traced back to the earliest Spanish *entradas* of the sixteenth century. Both in Florida and in South Carolina, African slaves performed a wide variety of tasks and were a visible presence in practically every facet of Spanish and English societies. But the ever-growing size of the enslaved population in Charles Town marked a noticeable difference between South Carolina and Florida. In one of Pamini's earliest communications with the Spanish, the cacica of Yspo made special note of the "many negroes who work and who were there" in Charles Town. The "many negroes" did more than labor in English fields and town. As Pamini succinctly explained, African slaves "were there." They were an integral part of the town, of *who* the English included in their colonial project. In the 1670s, there were less than 500 black slaves in Carolina, but those numbers multiplied fivefold within the decade. Pamini had immediately discerned the importance of African slaves for the English colony as did other Indians who moved in and out of these European spaces. Her descriptions of Charles Town offer a glimpse into the inchoate beginnings of English networks—networks connected through trade and Indian slavery but intended also to support or, at the very least to protect, another emerging system of slavery.[65]

The 1686 attack on Port Royal thrust runaway slaves into the heart of Spanish–English conflicts. Eleven slaves were taken from Port Royal (or willingly left). Within a couple of months, nine others followed, seeking both asylum and conversion to Catholicism in San Agustín.[66] Governor Quiroga Losada had not yet decided if he should employ, sell, or return these runaways when Captain Dunlop arrived in the Spanish presidio demanding the immediate return of English property.[67] A tense negotiation ensued. Though the fate of these runaways in San Agustín remained uncertain, Quiroga Losada refused to return them to the English.

South Carolina officials were furious. Their efforts to reacquire their human property proved unrelenting. Their persistence, however, did not lead to the return of these men and women; instead, it encouraged Spanish officials to protect and eventually to free these slaves. On November 7, 1693, five years after the arrival of the first fugitives, the Spanish issued a *cédula* (edict) freeing runaway slaves who reached San Agustín and vowed to convert to Catholicism.[68] As a result, African slaves became defining players in these imperial and colonial struggles. They were one the most sought-after and simultaneously heavily regulated group of informers in the early South.[69]

African slaves, like Indian leaders, used their role as informers to advance their own interests. Thomás de la Torre, a slave in Spanish Florida who had participated in the 1686 attack against Port Royal, left a brief testimony of his experiences as news broker. His colorful account is filled with adventure and chance encounters, but it was his ability to know and communicate timely information that pushed Torre along his journey—enabling him to join the Spanish expedition against the English, escape the Charles Town gallows, join a Dutch pirate ship, trick a French trader, and forge an alliance with Apalachee Indians. But for all his travels and cunning, Torre returned to San Agustín exactly as he had left: as a slave. Slavery shaped and circumscribed the experience of all African informers in the early South, whether they were enslaved; free; or, in Torre's case, somewhere along that spectrum.[70]

Officials in South Carolina also struggled with how to treat information provided by slaves. The House of Commons issued a law promising to reward anyone who reported on criminal activity, but when a group of slaves came forth bearing this type of information, English officials were caught in a bind. Should slaves be treated and compensated as any other informant? After debate, they finally ruled to accept "the Intelligence to be given by a Negro." But members of the House went on to reiterate the slave code. They issued reminders that "no Slave [was] permitted to go out of his Master's House or Plantation without a Ticket," and that any unsanctioned mobility would be punished.[71] The destruction of Port Royal and the prospect of runaway slaves allying themselves with the Spanish forced South Carolinians to reckon with the limited control they wielded over information networks built through and by the Indian slave trade. The English began to view the Indian slave trade and African slavery as linked, not because one gave way to the other but because the connections and contestations fostered by the former conditioned the feasibility of the latter.

For the English, the 1686 attack on Port Royal had come as a surprise. They recalled how "the few Inhabitants of that Towne having scarcely given the Alurm to their Neighbors by fyring great guns, when the Spanish came running tho' the woods."[72] The Spanish had easily destroyed the southernmost English holding in North America. Joseph Morton, the governor of South

Carolina, lost his brother-in-law, his Edisto plantation, and thirteen slaves. The English attempted to rally a military response, but the Spanish were nowhere to be found. Captain Robert Daniell, who led the counterattack, first received "information that the Enemie was at" Captain Benjamin Blake's plantation on Stono River, but when Daniell arrived, the Spaniards "were not there."[73] Daniell's intelligence had either been tardy or wrong. The situation then repeated itself, with multiple informants providing inaccurate information. Every time South Carolina soldiers got word of the whereabouts of the invading forces, the Spanish had either departed from that location days prior—"gone a day or two before in great hast[e]" because they had received "intelligence hearing of his [English governor's] persueing"—or had never actually been there. Chasing "false intelligences" through an uncooperative landscape, the English failed to capture their elusive attackers.[74]

After the 1686 attack, fear ran rampant in South Carolina. The investors of the devastated Stuart's Town worried about the unprofitability of their venture; the inhabitants of Charles Town feared a subsequent Spanish invasion; and English traders dreaded that powerful Indian groups, like the Yamasees, would treat the destruction of Port Royal as a sign of English weakness and choose to take their business elsewhere.[75] The English needed to be better prepared. Though talk of vigilance mostly centered on better armaments and military structures, it also generated a discussion about the role and value of information. The 1686 attack became a rare moment in which the English thought out loud about how to improve their communication networks:

> Whereas, our enemy the Spaniard hath, in a hostile manner several tymes made incursion into this his Majestie's Colony, robbing and burning several of the inhabitant's Houses, pillaging their stores, murthering and carrying away divers of his Majestie's subjects, all which, or the great part thereof, hath happened *for want of a speedy communication* of the allarum to the northern inhabitants of this Collony.[76]

In an act passed by the South Carolina government, "all . . . or the great part" of the blame for this attack rested on English, not Spanish, shoulders. The English lack "of speedy communication" had enabled or, at the very least, facilitated the Spanish destruction of Port Royal.[77] The Carolina assembly then pondered what would happen if "French and Spaniards may have notice of the war between the Crown of France and Spaine five or six months before we may." Without "speedy communication," South Carolina could fall. It would "be too late to raise money to finish places of Defence, and to provide other necessaries when the enemy is in sight."[78] The attack of 1686 pushed questions of information into the limelight.

The lessons learned from the destruction of Port Royal were as varied as those it involved. Florida officials realized that the violence they could muster was not enough to intimidate the English and their Indian allies. The Spanish needed to establish new connections and new network nodes. Their lack of success in recruiting and maintaining Indian ties was partially offset when fugitive slaves entered Spanish networks.[79] South Carolinians did not take that inclusion lightly. Even more than the attack on Port Royal, the presence of fugitive slaves in San Agustín exposed a critical vulnerability in English networks. South Carolinians responded quickly. The same year the Spanish issued an edict promising freedom to any fugitives who reached San Agustín, South Carolinians decided to employ Indians to apprehend and return runaway saves.[80] "Wee doe Conceive that the Indians will be of great Use to ye Inhabitants of our province," argued South Carolina officials, "for the fetching in againe of such Negroe Slaves as shall Runn away from their masters."[81] The English understood the need to protect and expand *who* comprised their networks, strengthening their connections to the Yamasees and, increasingly, to the Apalachicola and Creek Indians. For their part, Yamasees and Apalachicolas did much to foster the value of their own alliances and connections. But not every native group was successful in adapting their networks after the 1686 attack, and subsequent tests would prove even less forgiving.[82]

Rumors of war had circulated for years, but the death of Charles II in 1700 without an heir helped to catalyze the already escalating conflict among England, France, and Spain that soon engulfed large parts of Europe. One consequence of the War of Spanish Succession, known as Queen Anne's War in the English colonies, was a marked improvement of English transatlantic communication networks. The English had entertained the notion of using packet boats to speed the exchange of news between England and its colonies for at least a decade. The need to spread news quickly during wartime pushed this plan into place. Barbados received official news of war on June 23, 1702, a little over a month after the declaration in Europe. On June 29, the HMS *Swift* arrived in Boston from London with news of war, and from there word spread quickly among the other English colonies in North America. According to historian Ian Steele, the most notable change in English communications practices was not so much the increase in speed as the diligence with which the government in London approached the problem of information exchange with its colonies. The contrast with what was happening on the ground in the early South could not be greater.[83]

Colonists in South Carolina welcomed news of war. The conflict between England and Spain finally allowed South Carolinians to exact revenge for the 1686 attack on Port Royal. In August 1702, roughly four months after war had been declared in Europe, Governor James Moore came before the South Carolina assembly asking for men and supplies to invade San Agustín. In November, Moore led 500 English and 300 Yamasee Indians against the Spanish presidio. The plan of attack was simple. The English would lead two units, one by land, led by Colonel Robert Daniell, and the other by sea, under the leadership of Moore himself. With its main fort surrounded and its access to the ocean blocked, Florida would quickly capitulate. Or so Moore believed.

Thanks to an Apalachee informant, Florida's governor had word of Moore's forces. A Chacato Indian woman had heard the plan discussed at a town council in Achito, a town in Apalachicola. She had witnessed Apalachicola and Apalachee Indians, both supposedly Spanish allies, weighing the costs and benefits of attacking San Agustín. Under cover of night, the Chacato woman raced to San Luís, the main mission in Apalachee. She reported her news to Captain Francisco Romo de Uriza, who quickly sent word to Governor José de Zúñiga y Cerda. The governor ordered all Floridians to come inside the Spanish presidio and started gathering food and supplies to withstand a siege. The Spanish had less than a week to prepare. English victory would hinge on isolating San Agustín; Spanish survival would depend on receiving additional aid before their supplies ran out. Almost two months after the siege began, reinforcements arrived from Havana. The English forces, tired and no closer to breaching the San Agustín defenses, had to retreat.[84]

Moore returned to Charles Town in shame. The siege lasted longer than anticipated and failed to capture San Agustín; it had cost almost four times more than expected; and instead of showcasing English strength, it had unintentionally improved Florida's reputation. The Spanish now appeared strong and capable of withstanding the powerful English. Already dubbed an inept leader, Moore faced further disgrace when rumors surfaced that he had kept plunder from the expedition for his personal enrichment.[85]

Back in San Agustín, Governor Zúñiga y Cerda did not celebrate. Florida's governor did not know when, or how soon, but he was certain that the English would return. With war raging between England and Spain, Florida could not be safe. With very limited resources and men at his disposal, Zúñiga y Cerda needed to be strategic. The governor decided to reinforce the main Spanish stronghold, centralize scattered mission towns, and ask allied Indians to relocate closer to San Agustín. These networks had proven instrumental to withstanding the 1702 attack; if the Spanish wanted to survive any other invasion, their nodes and alliances needed to hold.

In the first weeks of 1703, Florida's governor sent Diego de Florencia to French Mobile to ask for aid. Florencia at first struggled to find sufficient men to accompany him to Mobile. Once his journey was underway, he had difficulty traveling on paths that had not been kept up as a result of the ongoing slaving raids. After a hard journey, Florencia was pleased by the warm French reception. Florencia reported, "from the French governor of Mobile I secure one hundred new and good guns, one thousand pounds of powder . . . and one thousand flints for guns . . . [but] the Frenchman did not have men to spare." Some men were ill, and the others were busy strengthening the French fort in anticipation of the Indian–English raids that were sure to come.[86]

The Spanish agent then suggested a different course of action. If the French were not willing to go on the offense to attack the English, then perhaps they might join with "Chickasas, Aibamos, and other neighboring tribes" to "make war on the Apalachicolos, which would be very advantageous." Florencia's plan was to attack the Apalachicolas (Creeks), a key ally in South Carolina's slave trading network. Even if the Spanish and the French could not invade South Carolina directly, "mak[ing] war on the Apalachicolos" could drastically curtail the advances made by the English. The French agreed. The Apalachicolas were strong, and both Spanish and French forces would benefit if the Apalachicolas could be intimidated or turned away from an English alliance.[87]

The Apalachicolas were already involved in a multi-front conflict. In the fall of 1702, as Moore's forces attacked San Agustín, 800 Apalachees marched against Apalachicola Indians. The Apalachee had decided to attack their neighbors because they were "now fearful of the hostilities and injuries which their villages ... suffer from the raids [by Apalachicolas]." The Apalachicolas needed to be "curbed and punished until they ceased their invasions." Weary and weak from Apalachicola slaving raids, the Apalachee now wanted to retaliate. The casualties, however, fell on the large Apalachee army instead. Near the Flint River, about 400 Apalachicolas ambushed the 800 Apalachees, who were accompanied by 20 Spanish soldiers under the command of Captain Francisco Romo de Uriza.[88] Though most of the Spanish officers managed to escape, at least 500 Apalachees were killed or captured. The joint Apalachee–Spanish offensive had failed miserably, and the Apalachicolas seemed stronger than ever.

With Apalachee towns in turmoil and Apalachee-Apalachicola relations at a breaking point, James Moore decided that the time was ripe to attack Florida once again. Moore, eager to clear his tarnished reputation, inserted himself into an ongoing inter-Indian conflict. In the process, he rallied Apalachicola support to attack the weakened Spanish holdings in Apalachee.[89] At first, most South Carolina officials were unenthusiastic about Moore's proposal given the failed and costly siege of 1702. But Moore proved insistent. He argued that unfortified Apalachee was a much easier target than San Agustín. More important, there was plenty of Indian support for the attack, especially because Yamasees and Apalachicolas were already raiding the Apalachees. Moore promised these Indian allies bounty from the Spanish missions, Indian slaves, and control over the paths across Florida. Successfully executed, Moore's proposal would all but ensure the collapse of Spanish Florida. The House of Commons eventually conceded but refused to organize or supply the expedition—which is perhaps why the only English accounts about the devastating set of raids against Apalachee come from Moore himself.[90]

Moore's first target was Nuestra Señora de la Concepción de Ayubale. In the early morning of January 24, 1704, the former governor of South Carolina marched on Ayubale "with a force of 1,500 Indians and 50 English, desolating the country, and assaulting the place." The attack proved quick: Ayubale fell as soon as the South Carolinians and the Ocheses breached the mission walls.[91] In response, the Spanish quickly mobilized. They had to stop Moore's army before the English–Creek forces struck again. From San Luís, the main Spanish mission in Apalachee, Captain Juan Ruíz Mexía led 23 Spaniards and 400 Apalachee soldiers.[92] But Mexía marched his men to their deaths. Of the 400 Apalachee who came to Ayubale's rescue, half were killed in battle, and the other half were enslaved.[93] After the fighting ended,

Captain Roque, who had been stationed in San Luís, sent a small party to assess the damage. "They found many burned bodies and [those] of some women pierced by sticks and half roasted, many children impaled in poles, and other killed with arrows, their arms and legs cut off."[94] Father Parga, who had accompanied the troops and performed last rites as the battle waged on, had been decapitated. The Battle of Ayubale had been horrific.

After their loss at Ayubale, the Spaniards struggled to form a coherent response to what felt like incomprehensible violence and destruction.[95] Terror of Moore's forces spread like wildfire through Apalachee. Panicked, many mission Indians fled their towns, trying to find safety. Some Indians went as far as Mobile or Pensacola; others "have fled into the woods, as well as many of those who willingly went over to the enemy."[96] The reports of Moore's raids were shocking: towns scorched, women and children beaten and enslaved, bodies so burned and mutilated that "they could not be identified."[97] When Spanish soldier Manuel Solana encountered a group of Indians fleeing from Apalachee, he could not convince them to wait for an official envoy from San Agustín to escort them to safety. They "were weary of waiting for aid from the Spaniards" and had taken matters into their own hands because "they did not wish to merely die" hoping for salvation that would never come.[98]

Though slaving raids had threatened Apalachee since the 1670s, the scale and violence of the attacks on Apalachee was new. From 1704 to 1706, over 1,300 Apalachee Indians were enslaved and taken to Charles Town—an amount rivaled only by the number of casualties, which came close to 1,500. Taken together, the total makes English raids into Apalachee one of the most devastating assaults in all of early America.[99] "Wholly laid waste being destroyed by the Carolinians," is how one of the few contemporary English maps of the region described northern Florida. This 1721 map, a detail of which is shown in Figure 4.1, memorialized South Carolina's forays into Apalachee and contains a long description of the Battle of Ayubale.

> Ayavally, on the 15th Jan. 1703 was a battle fought between the Carolinians commanded by Col. Moore and Indians commanded by Don Juan Mexia Gov. of Apalatchee, wherein 800 Spanyards were killed and taken with the said Mexia when upon the whole country submitted & being destroyed 1400 Apalatches Indians were removed to the Savana region under the English Government.[100]

Though this description greatly exaggerates the number of Spanish casualties, it provides a good estimate for the number of Apalachee Indians enslaved and a succinct description of the harrowing attacks that "submitted" and "destroyed" the "whole country."[101]

Perhaps the most interesting raid is one that did not take place. Ivitachuco was the only town in Apalachee not attacked during this paroxysm of violence. The chief of this Indian town on the border of Apalachee and Timucua, Don Patricio de Hinachuba, worked tirelessly to ensure the town's survival. Born in a mission town, Don Patricio was a devout Catholic and a member of a leading Indian family. He spoke several Indian languages and was literate. The historical record contains only scattered mentions of Don Patricio before the attack on Ayubale. From the council meetings and his letters to both the Florida governor and the Spanish crown, a complex figure emerges. Loyal to the Spanish, Don Patricio complied with the *repartimiento,* complained when there were not enough friars in Apalachee, and fought to protect Spanish interest in Apalachee. But his roots were not in San Agustín or even in the much closer mission of San Luís. His true interest and focus was on his hometown: Ivitachuco.

FIGURE 4.1. Indian slave raids. Section from William Hammerton (d. 1732) after John Barnwell (ca. 1671–1724), *Map of the Southeastern Part of North America,* 1721. (Pen and black and brown ink, with red, yellow, and blue-gray wash, Yale Center for British Art, Gift of the Acorn Foundation, Inc., Alexander O. Vietor ('36), President, in honor of Paul Mellon.)

When disaster struck Ayubale, Don Patricio called all his people back into the mission at Ivitachuco. Anticipating the worst, Don Patricio then rode out to meet Moore. Don Patricio, unarmed and alone on a horse, must have seemed a curious sight to Moore and his forces. After a short introduction, Don Patricio calmly explained to the former governor that Ivitachuco was a "strong and well-made" town. Attacking Ivitachuco, Don Patricio insisted, would prove a long and costly affair. This report troubled Moore, who had no intention of repeating the mistakes of his first expedition. After some thought, Moore agreed to a compromise. He would not attack Ivitachuco in exchange for the "church plate and . . . horses leaden with provisions."[102] Don Patricio readily agreed. He rode back to town, stripped the mission of all its silver and valuable artifacts, and gave them all to the English.[103] Ivitachuco was unharmed.

After ensuring the safety of his town, Don Patricio joined a Spanish military expedition against Moore's forces. But he never wandered far from Ivitachuco and, "observing that the enemy had retired to Patale, and not knowing his intentions, [but] fearful that he might hone to Ivitachuco and would capture the women and children who had been left with only a few men to protect them, he decided to return with his force."[104] For the next year, Don Patricio kept his town secure from subsequent raids. When he finally conceded to relocate closer to a Spanish stronghold, Don Patricio chose not to move inside San Agustín but instead settled the people of Ivitachuco near La Chua Ranchería. It took another year of fighting and a devastating attack on the refugee town he had established to convince Don Patricio to move the people of Ivitachuco inside a Spanish fort. His relentless determination to preserve the well-being and autonomy of his people reveals, at an individual level, the incredible story of dedication, struggle, and eventual loss that consumed Apalachee.

By January 1706, Ivitachuco was no longer an independent town; Don Patricio no longer a chief; and Apalachee, for all intents and purposes, no longer under Spanish control. An investigation of Spanish activity in Apalachee bluntly concluded, "in the said province of Apalachee there are no people remaining . . . there were fourteen villages, in which were a total of eight thousand persons, of whom not two hundred remain; and these are prone to leave, some to the woods and other to the enemy." The western province was a decimated land, with no more fortifications standing, missions working, or "people remaining."[105]

Already weakened, Spanish networks were falling to pieces. Amid the disarray, Moore's forces "destroyed the provinces and terrorized the Indians." Moore would later dismiss such reports, insisting that "I did not make slave, or put to death one man, woman or child but what were taken in the fight, or in the Fort I took by storm."[106] As one Apalachee town after another fell, Moore began promising leniency if the Apalachees transferred their alliances to the English and relocated closer to South Carolina. Many Apalachee towns apparently agreed to this offer and relocated to the Savannah and Ocmulgee Rivers, near the homes of the very Indians who had devastated their lands.[107] These slaving raids allowed English networks to grow exponentially, first by empowering and emboldening their existing Indian allies and then by incorporating new nodes and connections into the network. Thomas Nairne, one of the leading English traders, viewed the attacks on Apalachee as a great source of strength for Carolina:

> These Expeditions have added very much to our Strength and Safety; First by reducing the *Spanish* Power in *Florida* so low, that they are altogether uncapable of ever hurting us . . . [and then] by drawing over to our Side, or destroying, all the Indians within 700 miles of Charleston. This makes it impracticable for any *European* Nation to settle on that Coast.[108]

Moore's expedition had "reduc[ed] the Spanish Power" and, more important, it had created an impenetrable English network that stretched for over 700 miles. The English controlled *who* moved and traded in the region, thus eliminating any potential threat.

But this "added . . . Strength" came at a price. South Carolinian officials had to balance the demands of new "Indian Subjects" with the requests and needs of their already established Indian allies—some of whom, like the Yamasees and Apalachicolas (in particular the Alabama and Tallapoosa Creeks), had very troubled relations with these distant groups. English networks were becoming more diverse and also more unruly. To regulate this diversity, the House of Commons passed "An Act for Regulating the Indian Trade and Making Safe to the Public."[109] This act sought to manage the growing number of Indian nations trading with South Carolina by establishing tighter limits of where English traders could venture, what they could sell, and how much they could charge. But the Indian slave trade proved hard to monitor. As different factions competed over the nature of a trade that had long functioned with only minor oversight, most regulatory laws faced resistance in Charles Town. In Indian country, they were almost impossible to enforce.

As the first commissioner of the Indian trade, Thomas Nairne faced bitter opposition from English traders as well as South Carolina officials. One of Nairne's main challengers was Governor Nathaniel Johnson, who was not only deeply involved in the Indian slave trade but also greatly benefitted from the trade's unfettered nature.[110] The governor routinely challenged Nairne's efforts to regulate the access, extent, and profits of the Indian trade. Under Johnson's orders, traders John Dickson and Edward Griffin accused Nairne of treason. Nairne was briefly imprisoned but quickly found support from Johnson's many enemies. He fought the allegations levied against him and even secured a seat in the House of Commons from jail. Rather than imposing order, the act to regulate the Indian trade revealed the chaos behind South Carolina's engine for growth.[111]

The English experience during the Tuscarora War further exposed this disarray. On September 22, 1711, a group of Indians led by Chief Hancock attacked the town of Bath, North Carolina. This initial assault was followed by a series of violent raids against English planters along the Neuse and Trent Rivers. North Carolina, overwhelmed by this sudden violence, asked Virginia and South Carolina for aid. Virginia traders vowed that they would keep the peace among their Indians. Short of not adding fuel to a burning fire, however, Jamestown officials offered little help. South Carolinians, in sharp contrast, proved ready to aid their debilitated neighbor.[112] Colonel John Barnwell led the first of two military expectations, arriving in January 1712. The second expedition, commanded by James Moore (son of the former governor), reached Tuscarora country six months later.[113] Indians, mostly Yamasee, Yuchi, Cusabo, and Essaw, comprised the vast majority of Barnwell's 500 men and of Moore's 800 soldiers.[114] This rare moment of intercolonial cooperation showcased South Carolina's military might and displayed the reach and strength of their networks.

Barnwell particularly praised the efforts of his loyal "Yamasee Company." Unlike other Indian groups, "my brave Yamasees told me they would go wherever I led them. They will live and die with me," declared Barnwell.[115] In June 1711, one group of Yamasees delivered into English hands two Spanish spies they had apprehended. The English officials commended and rewarded the Yamasees for their actions. "Great is the consequences of the Spaniards at St. Augustine knowing of this Indian War and the preparations we are making," explained the South Carolinians. The English had feared that San Agustín, on learning of the Tuscarora "War and the preparations ... [the English were] making," would attack a distracted Charles Town. By capturing the Spanish spies, these Yamasees had helped protect South Carolina during a time of war. Yamasee mobilization and loyalty during the Tuscarora War convinced Barnwell, as well as many other Charles Town officials, that the Indian alliances made through their trade network were strong and working to benefit the English.[116]

In the late spring of 1711, the speaker of the House proclaimed that "the Country (praised be God for it) is in a flourishing condition, abounding with a great trade."[117] But South Carolina's success in the Tuscarora War, as well as its "great trade," was fraught with strain. At the end of the war, the South Carolina government prosecuted six traders who worked with the Cherokees and five traders who exchanged goods with the Creeks for "stopping the Indians from marching against the Tusqueroras." These men had tried to use the chaos of war for their own financial gain. Governor Charles Craven decried these actions as "the highest contempt that can be shown to the Government, and what is more a growing Evil & of so pernicious consequences that if not timely prevented will endanger the safety of this province."[118] But this "growing Evil" proved hard to prevent. Working far away from Charles Town, most traders remained unscathed by the government's fines or threats; some, like John Dickson and Thomas Welch, were so well connected that their contemptuous actions often went unpunished or simply ignored.[119] After all, these were the very traders who not only developed and maintained the profitable Indian slave trade but had also helped South Carolina win the Tuscarora War.

～

Who carried and moved news in the late seventeenth and early eighteenth centuries? There were English traders, Spanish sentinels, runaway slaves, and Indian agents (and double agents). There were also soldiers, friars, messengers, diplomats, sailors, and planters. The variety and diversity of informers emphasizes the chaotic and interrelated arrangements of information networks in the early South. From the 1670s to the mid-1710s, the Indian slave trade was the primary product and producer of these power struggles. For every informer detailing the destruction and loss of this violent trade, there were other, more sanguine reporters describing the connections and possibilities afforded by Indian slavery. For all the extensive and lucrative alliances the English built through Indian nodes and links, there were also African runaways using these far-reaching connections to escape slavery. And for each fugitive slave incorporated into San Agustín, there were tens of Indian nodes moving away from Spanish networks. Focusing on *who* carried information does not compartmentalize the violence, opportunity, and change brought on by the Indian slave trade; it brings these factors together, revealing an increasingly interconnected world that had more links and nodes than any one particular group could control or even properly discern.

Examining *who* moved and spread information helps center the role of human actors in the transmission of news. This seemingly minor point destabilizes a rather pervasive assumption about the autonomous agency of information. It serves as an important reminder that information did not move freely or independently; information was (and is) contingent on people—on the decisions and actions of individuals like cacica Pamini, Don Patricio, Thomás de la Torre, and chief Altamaha. The ingenious arrangements created by the different inhabitants of the early South to solve their information problems, especially those caused by the Indian slave trade, reveals the careful connections among Indians, Europeans, and Africans. These inclusive networks show fluid ties and diverse nodes but also render almost tactile the rhythms of power that punctuated that world. The focus on *who*—on both individuals and their connections—explains how peoples' lives in the early South could shatter apart even as their networks bound them together.[120]

CHAPTER FIVE

THE INFORMATION RACE

❧

I am very sorry that I came with so small a following that I cannot
wait your arrival. Be informed that I came to get acquainted with the
country, its mountains, the seacoast, and Apalachee. I trust in God
that I shall meet you gentlemen later when I have a larger following.

Henry Woodward to Antonio Matheos, September 2, 1685

THIS IS THE STORY of three men: Henry Woodward, Antonio Matheos,
and Marcos Delgado. But it is not exclusively about them. It is also about
Niquisaya, Pentocolo, four unnamed Yamasee spies, and a handful of
Mobile diplomats—all of whom shaped what Woodward, Matheos, and
Delgado accomplished or even knew. Only fragments are known about the
experiences of Woodward, Matheos, and Delgado—and only fragments of
those fragments detail anything about the Indians who abetted them.

Woodward never officially met Matheos or Delgado. But they all traveled
the same paths, visited the same towns, and spoke to the same Indian caciques as they reconnoitered Apalachee and Apalachicola for their various
governments in the mid-1680s. Woodward lived intermittently in Carolina
for two decades. Born in England or perhaps Barbados, contemporary
accounts often refer to him as "doctor," indicating that he had some degree
of education. Woodward spent much of his life in Carolina working as an
Indian agent and trader. In 1685, as Woodward traveled and traded goods
all over Apalachicola and Apalachee, a rather persistent Spanish lieutenant
began nipping at his heels.[1] Little is known about Antonio Matheos, who
had arrived in San Agustín at the end of 1680.[2] In September 1685, Matheos
followed Woodward's shadow all the way to the town of Coweta. As the
Spanish lieutenant approached the town, three Indian men bearing "a white
cross" came to greet him. Matheos probably thought this a strange sight.

There were no nor had there ever been missions or Franciscans residing in Coweta. Without prompting from Florida officials, these Indians imitated a common Spanish ritual to showcase their want for diplomacy and nonviolence—Spanish delegations often traveled holding a cross to signal their peaceful intentions.[3] But if seeing the cross at first calmed Matheos, what the Coweta greeting delegation did next left him seething: They handed Matheos a letter.

This "written paper" was in English. Matheos could not read it, but he was eager to know what it said. He had another Spaniard translate it quickly and discovered that this note came from Woodward himself. The letter, quoted in the chapter-opening epigraph, mocked Spanish efforts to secure Apalachee, in particular taunting Matheos's failure to apprehend any of the English traders in the region. Woodward cheekily apologized for not waiting for the lieutenant's arrival, but he promised that, at their next meeting, the English would boast "a larger following." Matheos was furious—furious with what the letter said and furious that such a document existed in the first place. Evidence of Woodward's savvy and insolent character, the "written paper" also demonstrated the alliances and lines of communication that the English traders had managed to establish with Coweta. Woodward's ability to send and obtain information helped explain Matheos's inability to capture his English rival.[4]

It is possible that the Coweta delegates who handed Matheos the "written paper" were unaware of its insulting content. Or maybe Woodward had convinced them that the letter offered an olive branch to the Spanish. But even if that had been the case, the Cowetas knew that the Spanish were opposed to the English presence, peaceful or not, in Apalachee and Apalachicola. Matheos, in particular, had made his feelings on the subject widely known. In delivering this letter, the Cowetas both defied the lieutenant's explicit orders and revealed Coweta's open paths to South Carolina. Hence the white cross. The Indians wanted peace with Florida but on their terms. An alliance with the Spanish would not come at the expense of trade with South Carolina. The Cowetas' actions were intended to remind Matheos as well as Woodward that communication in Apalachicola moved through them—through the paths and alliances they chose to keep open.[5]

Less than a year later, Marcos Delgado tried his luck at using these Apalachicola controlled paths, as he led an expedition first to find and then to remove the rumored French colony in the area. Delgado, a Spanish soldier and rancher in Apalachee, worked with Pensacola, Tawasa, and Mobile

Indians to expand Spanish information about and access to the west of Apalachee.[6] While he did manage to establish new alliances and paths, he exerted little control over where those connections led or who they included. Closely examining the actions of Delgado, Matheos, and Woodward, as well as those of the Indians who facilitated, impeded, and circumvented their efforts, helps recount the everyday experiences of informers.

The race to network Apalachicola affords a more in-depth answer to the question of *who* carried and spread information in the early South. For Matheos, information was about control; it granted him the ability to know the intentions of his allies and block the advances of his enemies. For Woodward, information was about expansion; it enabled him to extend English trade routes and find new allies. For Delgado, information was about options; it enabled both the Spanish and the Indians to navigate an increasingly volatile landscape. Zooming in on the late 1680s offers a way, first, to illuminate the different yet concurrent and politically charged approaches to gathering information, and, second, to underscore the connectedness of Indian and European experiences. The decisions, actions, and networks of one informed the other. Through the struggles of these men, both native and European, emerges a larger story about both the imagined and implemented strategies for networking *la tierra adentro* and the power—the asymmetrical and variable power—that information held.

The Spanish hold in western Florida, a region they considered *el más alla* ("what is beyond"), had never been particularly strong.[7] The Franciscans were the only ones who had made any inroads in Apalachicola. But the missionizing efforts that began in 1633 fell apart as Indian resistance rose, culminating in an uprising in 1647.[8] It would be over thirty years before the Spanish attempted to enter Apalachicola again. Much in the same way that French Huguenot efforts in the 1560s had prompted the Spanish to establish San Agustín, English activities in Apalachicola in the late 1670s helped reignite Spanish interest in a place they had long neglected. In 1679, Franciscan friars ventured to Apalachicola and, once again, quickly clashed with the local populations. Governor Juan Márquez Cabrera was discouraged, but not deterred, by the Franciscan failures in Sabacola, a vibrant Apalachicola town on the Chattahoochee River.[9] Convinced by reports that Apalachicola Indians "had shown great inclining" to conversion before the Franciscans departed, the governor prepared to send another group of friars into Apalachicola.

In the 1680s, the Apalachicola Indians, who would later become part of the Indian nation known as the Creeks, were composed of two distinct groups.[10] The first consisted of nine or ten villages along the Chattahoochee River. The Spanish grouped these towns together under the label Apalachicola.[11] The second included several northern towns, which the Spanish called the Province of Coweta or Cussita, after the main towns in the area. Taken together, these two groups of Apalachicola Indians were numerous and growing, and they had access to vast hunting lands and deerskins. In the Creek migration legend recorded in Savannah, Georgia, in 1735, Chigelly, mico (town chief) of Coweta, detailed the long connection between Cussita and Apalachicolas. Apalachicolas were once a hostile rival but had slowly become an important, peaceful "white" town integrated into the Creek nation. By continually strengthening kinship ties, Apalachicolas had managed to bind relatively independent towns into a coherent system of reciprocal obligations and exchange.[12]

San Agustín officials wanted in. With violent slaving raids from South Carolina destabilizing missions in Timucua and Guale, the Spanish believed it was "imperative to keep them [Apalachicola Indians] happy."[13] But how exactly the Spanish intended to find, let alone keep, "happy Indians" was not clear. In March 1681, the Franciscans were ready to try missionizing in Apalachicola one more time. Accompanied by a group of soldiers, friars Francisco Gutiérrez de la Vega and Miguel Abengojar headed to Sabacola. Their efforts were better received than the previous two Franciscan endeavors. By the summer months, the friars had managed to convert over thirty people. Encouraged by their success, Fray Gutiérrez urged Governor Cabrera "to come visit the province . . . and persuade" the Indians of Spanish commitment to the region. But before Florida's governor could even consider embarking on this journey, the tide had once again turned in Apalachicola.[14]

The tense relations between friars and Indians, exacerbated by the brash leadership of Antonio Matheos, the highest-ranking Spanish official in the region, prompted Apalachicola Indians to demand the removal of all friars and Spanish officials from their towns. But this time a handful of Indian converts wanted to relocate with the Franciscans. To house these neophytes, the Spanish established the mission of Santa Cruz de Sabacola in the last months of 1681. Located below the confluences of the Flint and

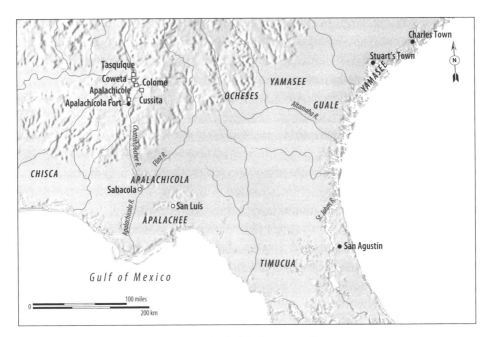

MAP 5.1. Apalachicola towns, 1680s

Chattahoochee Rivers, this mission was eighty miles south of where the friars had originally hoped to conduct their conversion efforts, and it was even further removed from the main Indian towns in Apalachicola. (See Map 5.1.) From here and from the existing mission posts, such as San Luís de Apalachee (near present-day Tallahassee), the Spanish began rebuilding their ecclesiastical and military influence over the region.[15]

Yet reinvigorating the mission program in Apalachee put the Spanish in a bind. Sending gifts, supplies, and men to Apalachicola left little for Guale and Timucua Indians at a time when devastating slaving raids were crippling their towns and livelihoods. In a pleading letter to the Spanish king, the Guale cacique of Santa María described how "the whole province" was "destroyed, annihilated, and reduced." Since Guale "had always done what was commanded," he only asked that "the regiment currently assisting in the maintenance of the province of Apalachee be sent" back to eastern Florida.[16] Guale and Timucua Indians were longtime Spanish allies and were in dire need of aid and protection. Apalachee and Apalachicola Indians, on the other hand, welcomed English and French traders into their towns and launched attacks against Spanish missions.[17] To Guale and Timucua caciques, it seemed that the Spanish were abetting, rather than remedying, their worsening situation. San Agustín officials insisted that they had few options and even fewer resources at their disposal. The best way to lessen the effects of the Indian slave trade, they claimed, was to gain some footing in Apalachicola.[18]

But instead of recruiting new Indian allies and building missions, the Spanish in Apalachicola faced native opposition and European competition at every turn. In 1684, Robert Cavalier de La Salle led a French expedition from France that was intended to establish a French outpost near the mouth of the Mississippi River.[19] Though La Salle's colony was short-lived, French efforts in the area persisted, with the French hoping "to profit from the disarray of the Spanish monarchy."[20] And profit they did. In 1699, the French established Fort Maurepas (near present-day Biloxi, Mississippi) and began trading with Indian populations who lived beyond San Agustín's sphere of influence. The impact of these early French ventures cannot be overstated. However small and tentative these efforts were, it was obvious to nearby Indians that the "French assisted their allies better than did the Spaniards." By "furnishing arms" and goods, and by not interfering in social-cultural practices, the French established lasting alliances with Indian groups, like the Natchez, Chickasaws, and Choctaws, who had stayed away from Spanish initiatives.[21]

French officials, like Jean-Baptiste Le Moyne, known by his inherited title Sieur de Bienville, carefully cultivated these alliances. A French soldier and explorer, Bienville eventually became governor of colonial Louisiana in 1701.[22] In his long tenure in the region, Bienville led many expeditions to reconnoiter the Gulf Coast and the Mississippi River. In his journeys, Bienville detailed both Spanish and English undertakings, particularly noting the devastating effects of the Indian slave trade on local populations. Bienville's descriptions of the English attacks against Louisiana and its Indian allies mirror the reports from San Agustín detailing South Carolina's sponsored incursions into Guale, Timucua, and Apalachee. Though Bienville considered the Spanish as competitors, he also regarded them as a necessary buffer between Louisiana and the better-armed English and English-allied Indians. As much as the Spanish and the French distrusted each other, they both agreed that the English posed the biggest threat.[23]

As we saw in the previous chapter, South Carolinians made great strides into Apalachicola in the 1680s.[24] But the grand expectations of South

Carolina traders like Henry Woodward would have amounted to little without Indian support.[25] Apalachicola Indians led the charge in establishing these lucrative trading partnerships. William Dunlop, one of the founders and leaders of Port Royal, reported how Apalachicola Indians instigated these exchanges.

> [T]he Indians of that countrie [Apalachicola and Coweta] . . . are desyrous of trade and comerice [sic] with his Majestie's subjects here, which if effectuated wold be a matter of vast importance . . . We are in order to this plan laying down a method for correspondence and trade with *Cuita* [Coweta] and *Cussita* nations of Indians, who leive upon the passages betwixt us and New Mexico, and who have for severall yeirs left off any Comercie with the Spaniards.[26]

These Indians on the Chattahoochee were "desyrous of trade and comerice," and Dunlop wanted nothing more than to nurture this desire. He insisted that South Carolina could not afford to miss the opportunity to open trade with Cowetas and Cussitas. Securing access to Apalachicola offered a double victory for South Carolina. "[L]aying down a method for correspondence and trade" with these Indians not only enriched Port Royal and Charles Town but also limited Spanish and French influence over the region.[27]

Coweta and Cussita Indians had never considered their homeland *el más alla*. But as the Spanish, French, and English players raced through their lands in the 1680s and 1690s, Apalachicolas increasingly saw their towns and connections at the center of interimperial contests.[28] Apalachicola Indians had witnessed the evolution of the Indian slave trade and had no intention of ending on the wrong side of this violent exchange. In the 1670s, they opened some paths to San Agustín, but the Spanish left them unimpressed. Florida officials had few goods, offered no guns, and proved incapable of providing protection from English slaving raids. Eager to protect their sovereignty as well as expand their "trade and comerice," Apalachicola Indians began welcoming English traders into select towns. The Apalachicolas fostered these new connections carefully, but dismayed Spanish officials simply remarked that Indians throughout Apalachicola "left and took all their subjects, and all those of their nation who were in other towns, and many Christian [Indians], and with all that went to the enemy." Once they joined the English, Apalachicolas received "arms . . . and knowledgeable of these lands they entered them, devastating the Christian towns of these provinces killing and taking captives, which they sell for guns, to the enemies."²⁹ But this Spanish rendition of events, which credited guns and slaving with reshaping the Chattahoochee valley, over-looked Apalachicola agency.

Apalachicola was not a united land or group of peoples. As Coweta, Cussita, and other Indians who lived in the northern towns of the Chattahoochee River opened paths to Charles Town and Port Royal, many southern towns, including the towns of Apalachicola, Sabacola, and Tallapoosa, continued looking to Florida and even to the new French forts for goods and trade. Apalachicola networks supported this internal division of interests and alliances, allowing both southern and northern towns to foster their own Indian–European and inter-Indian connections. Consider, for instance, the welcome a southern Apalachicola town gave a group of Franciscans in October 1679. Both the Apalachicola Indians and the Spanish hoped to improve communication between southern Apalachicola Indians and San Agustín. The Franciscans had even sent Jacinto Barreda, the definidor of Florida (a leading figure of the religious order). But within weeks of the Franciscans' arrival, a group of Indians from Coweta (and possibly from other northern towns) arrived. These northern delegates were unhappy to learn of these southern Apalachicola–Spanish connections and threatened to "set the Chichimecos [the Westos] against" the friars. The Cowetas' purported ability to mobilize the Westos intimidated both the Franciscans, who hurried back to San Agustín, and the southern Apalachicolas, who were forced to acquiesce to the Cowetas' demand and temporarily severed ties with Florida.³⁰

The expulsion of the Franciscans from Apalachicola sheds light on how these networks—Indian–European, inter-Indian, and north–south Apalachicola—actually played out. As the Spanish struggled to regain some control in the Chattahoochee valley, as the English attempted to secure unmediated access into Apalachicola, and as the French endeavored to make headway into this contested region, they all relied on Apalachicola connections. Apalachicolas and Apalachicola networks determined not only *who* could and did move in *la tierra adentro* but also who did so successfully.

~

The trouble in Apalachicola did not begin with Henry Woodward, but he offers a good place to start. Only scattered and somewhat fantastical details are known about Woodward. He traveled to North America in the 1666 expedition led by Robert Sandford. Before making landfall, Woodward had informed Sandford that he intended to stay and explore the region. Sandford wrote, "Mr. Henry Woodward, a Chirurgeon, had before I settout assured mee his resolucon to stay with the Indians if I should thinke convenient."[31] Sandford thought it convenient enough, and Woodward stayed in Carolina for roughly two years. Woodward found a kind welcome among the Cusabo Indians, but his efforts to learn Indian languages and customs were quickly interrupted. Spanish Indians captured the English "Chirurgeon" and took him to San Agustín as a prisoner. Woodward's time in the Spanish presidio also proved brief. He soon escaped on Robert Searles's pirate vessel, which had attacked Florida in 1668. Shortly thereafter, Woodward, along with Searles's crew, were shipwrecked on the island of Nevis. During his brief time in Nevis, Woodward met and married his wife. Unfazed by his trials, Woodward returned to Carolina in 1670—affirming that his "resolucon to stay" in the region was indeed strong.[32]

During the early days of the English colony, Woodward worked as an interpreter, quickly assuming a role in the governor's council. In 1670 and 1671, he reconnoitered Carolina searching for gold and silver, privately communicating his findings to proprietor Anthony Ashley Cooper. Carolina's governor, Sir John Yeamans, then sent Woodward to explore the lands to the north of the colony, near Virginia. The South Carolina government immediately recognized the value of Woodward's connections and information, paying him £100 for his endeavors in 1671. Until his death in 1686, Woodward was one of the most influential traders in the region.[33]

If in many ways exceptional, Henry Woodward was not unique. His story serves as a model for understanding how traders moved and worked through *la tierra adentro,* how they forged alliances and connections with Indian populations, and ultimately how they came to establish an expansive network. But Woodward's story—the few, incomplete, and episodic facts that make up his story—serve as a model in another way. It reveals the complications of reconstructing, let alone documenting, the experiences of early traders. This difficulty is as much the product of the historical record as it is an artifact of the type of movement, alliances, and networks that the traders participated in. As difficult as it is to retrace Woodward's steps now, his actions also proved elusive at the time.

In December 1674, Woodward led a small trading party to Westo towns. He hoped to gain the favor, alliance, and trade of this powerful Indian nation.

Woodward wanted to bring the Indian trade to the center of English activity, and English activity to the heart of the Indian world. He eagerly exchanged "arms, amunition, tradeing cloath and other trade [goods] from" Charles Town for "deare skins furrs and young Indian Slaves."[34] For Woodward, trade, friendship, and open communication were one and the same. Though it is unclear how well he spoke the Westo language, once he understood that the Westos wanted "freinship, and comerse wth us," he began paying attention to their "long-speeches" and to the inter-Indian relations that fueled the Westos' growing power.[35] Woodward's connections revealed that, for the English, information could not be separated from trade or power. On the contrary, news was both a prerequisite and product of both.

This understanding served Woodward well during his visit to Westo towns.[36] While he was trying to court the powerful Westos, a Savannah delegation arrived. The timing of the Savannahs' delegation had not been coincidental. Living between Carolina and the large Apalachicola Indian groups settled along the Chattahoochee River, both Westos and Savannahs exerted significant influence over a key geographic region. They were the gatekeepers of a larger Indian trade.[37] The Savannahs had purposely traveled to Westo towns during Woodward's visit in hopes of establishing a stronger alliance with both their Indian and English neighbors. The Savannahs came before Westo leaders and Woodward, eager to share some pressing information. They revealed that a joint force of Cherokee, Chickasaw, and Cussetaw was plotting against the Westos.[38] By communicating this important piece of news at this particular moment, the Savannahs were signaling their intentions for friendship and peace. As with the exchange of captives and goods, the exchange of information afforded Indian groups a way to express their intentions and expectations. But the Savannahs' message conveyed something else: their access to the latest developments in the region. They were showing themselves not just as allies to the Westos but also as well-connected players whom English traders, like Henry Woodward, would do well to heed, support, and supply.

The Westos, for their part, responded carefully to the Savannahs' warning.[39] Receiving a message was just as much performance as conveying one. A wholehearted acceptance of the Savannahs' news would expose Westo vulnerability by revealing that they had failed to learn about the attack themselves. The Westos thus made a point to prepare for the attack by showcasing their strength, refortifying their homes, and displaying their access to both English and Spanish goods. Woodward readily recognized the Westos' strategy. By flaunting their connections and "commerce wth white people like unto mee [Woodward]," the Westos would prove to the Cherokee, Chickasaw, and Cussetaw attackers as well as to Woodward that they were well prepared, and even better supplied.[40] If the Westos' message was not lost on Woodward, neither were the Savannahs' intentions. The English trader, much like the Indian leaders, valued information. By sharing news of a coming attack, the Savannahs were revealing their far-reaching connections to Coweta and other Apalachicola towns—connections Woodward longed to exploit.[41]

Woodward drew one other lesson from the exchange. By acknowledging the war among the Westos and the Cherokee, Chickasaw, and Cussetaw, the Savannahs revealed that Westo influence, though wide, operated within clear boundaries. Woodward was ready to push the limits of these boundaries. He worked to find and then carefully reorient these extensive and far-reaching inter-Indian alliances to serve English interest. Woodward heeded the Savannahs' message of friendship and, when relations deteriorated between the Westos and Carolinians, the English were ready to start a new arrangement with the all-too-willing Savannahs.[42]

Woodward needed information to understand and manipulate the connections that bound the region. But for all his knowledge of Indian practices, Woodward noted that he was not the only one making these evaluations. Indians as far as Coweta were working to understand who the English were, what they intended to accomplish, and how South Carolina's networks functioned. And what's more, Woodward remarked in a letter to John Locke, they were doing so successfully: "They say they have knowledge of our comeing into these parts severall yeares before wee arrived."[43] Just as Woodward was trying to figure with whom and how to connect, the Apalachicola Indians were doing the same.

Woodward continued to cultivate Indian connections in southern areas of Carolina. His luck improved when he befriended Niquisaya, a Yamasee chief who, like the powerful cacique of Altamaha, had recently settled near Port Royal.[44] Niquisaya had moved closer to Scottish and English towns and, like many Yamasee leaders, was also working to open paths to key Apalachicola towns. But he was careful. He did not want these new connections to come at the expense of the paths he had previously opened to San Agustín. Niquisaya managed to keep his old and new alliances in play.[45] With Niquisaya's help,

Woodward was able to push English trade further west and even gain access to the prominent town of Coweta.[46] For Woodward, this is what good communication and friendship was supposed to do. It was supposed to open paths and foster trade. Information was neither the goal nor the reward; it was the means through which trade functioned.

The Spanish watched in horror. The native groups they had barely managed to get acquainted with were now becoming fast partners with South Carolina. By the mid-1680s, Woodward traveled regularly into Apalachicola and even Apalachee. There were rumors that he had even made headway with the Chickasaws. These new inter-Indian and English–Indian alliances threatened to block Spanish access to Apalachicola, as they had at Santa Catalina. Governor Cabrera realized that the Spanish needed to fight back. It was now or never.[47]

Lieutenant Antonio Matheos thought he was the man for the job. Though little is known about his life before he arrived in Florida, his writings reveal the outlines of an inflexible, condescending, and self-assured officer. Tasked with the defense of the western provinces of La Florida, Matheos had a poor understanding of the land and people under his jurisdiction, and even less sympathy for them. The lieutenant did not bother to hide his disdain toward the Indian populations he served and supposedly governed. He often called them "dogs" and thought them childlike. The surge of English and French traders in western Florida had done little to change Matheos's mind. Apalachee and Apalachicola Indians had never been particularly steadfast allies, but now they openly defied San Agustín's authority by trading with other Europeans. Convinced that the Indians were *gente sin razón* ("peoples without reason") who could not be trusted, Matheos believed that his only course of action was to remove all English and French traders from the region. Rather than trying to gain Indian friendship, Matheos needed to eliminate all competition.

Governor Cabrera encouraged Matheos to cast his net a bit wider. The governor of Florida knew that capturing a handful of foreign traders without finding and punishing their Indian allies would not provide a permanent solution. The Spanish needed to learn where the English and French were making headway; what Indian towns facilitated and enabled their successes; and which groups, if any, opposed them. Governor Cabrera was trying to keep Apalachicola within Spanish influence. Matheos simply wanted to catch Henry Woodward.[48]

In the fall of 1685, Matheos led his first expedition up the Chattahoochee River to find and apprehend English traders. But the task proved more difficult than Matheos had envisioned. As he traveled north, he encountered only abandoned towns, false reports, and Indians reluctant to cooperate.[49] No one offered to guide him. No one seemed willing to tell him where the English were hiding. Matheos captured and interrogated some Indians holding English goods, but in "their declarations none spoke with clarity." The lieutenant complained, "[L]istening to them would have left me without better judgment."[50] The gifts Matheos had brought and the promises he made were not enough to acquire the information he needed. *Noticias ciertas* ("truthful news") about the English traders eluded him. He could spread goods and gain access to some leading Apalachicola towns, but "the Indians would still not reveal the path that led to the English." The lieutenant had "to keep moving inland until the place in Apalachicola [where the English were] or until he found certain news."[51]

Matheos, an impatient man, quickly became frustrated by the Apalachicolas' convoluted answers to what he believed were rather simple questions about Carolina traders. From the Apalachicolas' vantage point, however, there was nothing simple about reporting on English whereabouts. Matheos's demands that the Apalachicolas first reveal and then relinquish their connections to the English were, in essence, asking the Apalachicolas to redraw their communication networks and alliances. The Apalachicolas, the Spanish slowly came to understand, were more willing to close their paths to San Agustín than to allow Matheos to determine how their networks should function.[52] By watching Matheos struggle to keep his wits about him while trying to find *nuevas* about the English, Apalachicola Indians realized how little the Spanish actually knew and how desperate they were for information. Matheos spent most of his time in Apalachicola taking declarations, reconnoitering trails, and recruiting spies. Almost every page of his correspondence remarks on his efforts to acquire and secure information. Knowing when, if, and how much news to share allowed the Apalachicola not only to obtain goods from Matheos and keep "the path that led to the English" hidden but also to network information from a position of power.[53]

After a slow journey, Matheos entered Coweta in the early fall of 1685. The lieutenant had hoped that, by distributing goods, he could loosen both

Indian tongues and whatever agreement Coweta had reached with Charles Town. If the powerful cacique in Coweta embraced the Spaniards, then other Apalachicola towns would surely follow suit; a failure at Coweta could spell disaster for Matheos's expedition. The subtlety required for this operation eluded Matheos. As soon as he entered Coweta, he resorted to violence. He "grabbed a woman, and thinking that I was going to kill her, the Indians who had been with me, came to me, and, without me asking anything, they told me the English and [their] Indians were in a Palenque, but did not know where it was." The only way Matheos extracted information from the Cowetas involved threatening a woman's life.[54]

Following this tip, Matheos headed to Tasquique, a Muskogean-speaking town in northern Apalachicola. But by the time the Spanish party arrived, the English were nowhere to be found. Angry, Matheos called to the woman he had "grabbed" earlier—apparently, he had taken her as his prisoner. Matheos ordered her to "speak with clarity and reveal where the Palenque was." Matheos believed that this woman knew the location of the English traders not because she had previous or even personal relations with them but because she "had been daily talking with all her relatives and neighbors." It was through this inter-Indian communication network along the Chattahoochee River that Matheos believed he would find Woodward and the other seven (some reports list four) English traders.[55] Much like the English trader, the Spanish lieutenant wanted access to these far-reaching Indian connections and paths. In contrast to Woodward, however, Matheos seems to have valued this network more for its ability to control Indian expansion than to expand trade networks.

After his failures at Coweta and Tasquique, Matheos tried a different approach. He called for a *junta general* (large council meeting) with the caciques from all the major Apalachicola towns. With the caciques of Coweta, Cussita, and several other Apalachicola towns gathered in one place, Matheos hoped to achieve the two goals that had eluded him as he journeyed from town to town. He first showcased renewed Spanish interest in and support of Apalachicola. Then he instructed the Indian leaders to sever ties with Charles Town. Met by a welcoming reception and promises of loyalty, Matheos attempted to convince the caciques that the best way to prove Apalachicola–Spanish friendship would be to give him "certain news" of the whereabouts of the English. To this, they all agreed—but no one told Matheos anything. The lieutenant thus ended the council meeting with a threat. He warned that if the caciques of Apalachicola were not honest and their promises of friendship proved false, "everything would turn to blood and fire." The caciques conceded to these terms, or so Matheos believed.[56]

As if waiting in the shadows, Woodward returned to Apalachicola as soon as Matheos left. The only one surprised by the sudden reappearance of the English trader seems to have been Matheos. Sergeant Major Domingo Leturiondo, who had recently been appointed Defender of the Indians, pointed out the serious disjuncture between what Matheos wanted to accomplish and what the Indians were willing to do. The sergeant major and several Apalachicola caciques, including Pentocolo of Apalachicole, Chief Achito of Acolanque, and a minor chief of Sabacola, explained to San Agustín's governor that the Apalachicolas had no intention of allying exclusively with one particular European power.[57] Leturiondo feared that Matheos's determination to limit the Apalachicola's networks would backfire. In the first of his many critiques of Matheos's vision of Apalachicola, Leturiondo argued that the Spanish should cease any efforts to apprehend English traders and instead focus on promoting better relations with the Indians in the region. Leturiondo wanted to network Spanish needs with Indian interests, and vice versa.[58]

News that "the English enemy was still in Apalchicoli" infuriated the already hot-blooded Matheos. He had been in San Luís de Apalachee for only a couple of days when Juan Mercado, friar of the Santa Cruz de Sabacola mission, reported that Woodward had once again begun trading in the region. Mercado wrote: "an Indian native to Sabacola . . . says he saw four Englishmen who were helping the Indians in the place of Osuchi . . . [Father Argüelles and I] persuaded and ordered said Indian, who, because he had seen them, he himself should go and tell it to your honor."[59] Matheos's *junta* and violent threats had failed to keep the English away. Subsequent reports hinted at even further English involvement in Apalachicola and detailed South Carolina's efforts to build a trading house and possibly even a fortification near Coweta.[60]

Matheos responded to this news with uncharacteristic care. Knowing that he would get neither the authorization nor the supplies and soldiers for another expedition, the lieutenant decided to learn as much as he could about the traders' whereabouts before acting. Matheos wanted better control over the location, movement, and intentions of the enemy; in short, he wanted better information. He turned to the Franciscans first. The friars stationed in Santa Cruz de Sabacola had reported on English activities in the past. They were the first to mention the new trading house erected to the north of Coweta.[61] This *nuevas* troubled Matheos because it showed that the English were not merely defying Spanish authority; English traders intended to stake a permanent claim in the province.

Given the distance between Sabacola and Coweta, Matheos decided to employ spies to get a closer look at the English. At first he hired the same Indians who had guided him during his previous expedition through Apalachicola. Soon enough, Matheos realized his mistake. Though loyal to the Spanish, these Indians proved incapable or unwilling to locate the English. Eventually the lieutenant recruited additional spies from Sabacola and Apalachee. Unsatisfied with their reports as well, Matheos decided to reconnoiter the region himself. High-ranking officials rarely ventured into regions destabilized by Indian slaving and raiding, but with so many conflicting and incomplete reports, Matheos wanted to gather his own *nuevas*.[62]

During his time away from San Luís, Matheos met and befriended Pentocolo, chief of the town of Apalachicole. Pentocolo quickly allied himself with Matheos, in much the same way that Niquisaya had with Henry Woodward, and accompanied him during subsequent reconnaissance and diplomatic missions. Pentocolo fashioned himself a mediator between Florida and the increasingly factious Apalachicola province. But while Matheos allowed Pentocolo to travel with him, the lieutenant remained wary of his newfound ally. Matheos feared that Pentocolo was working for the cacique of Coweta or for other Indian leaders aligned with South Carolina and intended to trick the Spanish. Pentocolo did not fully trust Matheos either. The Indian cacique was careful about what he revealed to Matheos, almost never speaking of English activities and thus not jeopardizing his relations with either the powerful Coweta or the well-supplied Charles Town. This position as both a Spanish ally and an English sympathizer gave Pentocolo some authority within Indian country (especially vis-à-vis the mightier cacique of Coweta). He kept the English interested in supplying his town, and his ties to Matheos proved lifesaving during the lieutenant's second and more violent expedition into Apalachicola.[63]

By January 1686, Matheos felt prepared for a second journey. He had gathered intelligence from Franciscans, ordered Indians to spy on nearby towns, reconnoitered the area personally, and even established new friendships. From all these different reports, Matheos had reached a singular and very familiar conclusion: The Spanish needed to remove English traders from Apalachicola. Matheos had vowed that "blood and fire" would befall those who welcomed South Carolina traders.[64] He was now ready to carry out his threat.

The Spanish lieutenant began his second expedition by calling another *junta*. Though Pentocolo and other leading chiefs attended this council, the four most northern towns did not send delegates. The absence of Coweta, Cussita, Colome, and Tasquique interfered with Spanish plans, discredited Matheos's authority, and offered a blatant confirmation of the northern towns' alliance with South Carolina. In response, Matheos ordered the destruction of Coweta, Cussita, Colome, and Tasquique, but he spared most of the southern Apalachicola towns, including Pentocolo's town of Apalchicole. By the time Matheos's forces reached northern Apalachicola, the four offending towns were empty. Matheos reduced them to ashes all the same, sending a clear message: Either align with Florida exclusively or suffer the consequences.

Destruction was the only alternative to friendship with San Agustín. During the attack against the four northern Apalachicola towns, Matheos found an English store and gladly ransacked it. But in the hands of this rash lieutenant, even this windfall turned into a debacle. Instead of giving these appropriated goods to the leading Indian caciques, Matheos distributed the bounty as he saw fit. Abandoning protocol and precedent, he gave the goods to those Indians who were openly loyal and friendly to Florida. In the process, Matheos alienated key native leaders and many important Indian towns.[65] Meanwhile, Woodward, who remained in the area, was also using gift giving to secure Indian alliances. But by favoring the leading caciques, this English trader gained more and more powerful allies than the Spanish ever could. The burning of towns that had refused to attend the *junta* and the arbitrary distribution of valuable gifts limited what the Spanish could accomplish in Apalachicola. Matheos's very narrow definition of who constituted a Spanish ally tightened an already shrinking network.

Though Governor Cabrera had sanctioned Matheos's expeditions, his successor, Governor Diego de Quiroga Losada, was appalled by the violence of the whole affair. In a scathing review of Matheos's second expedition, Quiroga Losada dubbed the lieutenant's actions "excessive" and blamed him for "breaking communication" with the Apalachee.[66] Sergeant Major Leturiondo, who had long opposed Matheos, produced an official report that sided with the governor. Leturiondo argued that Matheos's strategy was ill conceived, at best. The sergeant major advocated for peace and believed that trade, rather than violent raids, would persuade the powerful towns of Cussita and Coweta to welcome the Spanish once again. A delegation of caciques from the town of Abalahchi, who traveled to San Agustín around the time Leturiondo finished his account, echoed the sergeant major's concerns. These caciques vowed that they would stay loyal to San Agustín if the Spanish stopped burning Indian towns and commenced trading goods, two propositions that seemed basic enough.[67] But these new promises came a little too late. Many Apalachicola towns, like Coweta, had already severed their ties with the Spanish—most of their paths would remain closed until the start of the Yamasee War (1715–1717). Only minor towns, like Apalachicole, kept their paths open. Matheos had secured more foes than friends.

Eager to remedy the situation in Apalachicola, San Agustín officials ordered Matheos to survey Apalachicola through other means. A disgraced Matheos turned to four Yamasee spies, asking them to scout Apalachicola and locate any Apalachicola towns still interested in allying with the Spanish. Little is known about these four men beyond the fact that all were identified as Yamasee. At least one is given the title of chief, but the social ranking of the other three is unclear. Connected to the Spanish and the English, these Yamasee spies traveled with relative ease along the Chattahoochee River and among Apalachicola towns, revealing some familiarity with the region. These men perhaps belonged to the Upper Yamasee towns that had relocated away from San Agustín and the coast.[68] These four spies also understood several Indian languages, Spanish, and probably some English. The four Yamasee spies received orders to survey as many towns along the Chattahoochee as they could manage, including the towns attacked by Matheos.

Unsurprisingly, the spies received a chilly welcome in the northern Apalachicola towns. Coweta and Cussita caciques readily identified the Yamasees as spies as "from Apalache and, consequently, their enemies."[69] When the spies arrived, Coweta and Cussita Indians were "playing *el juego de la pelota*," long an issue of contention between Indians and Franciscans. Towns often played the physically demanding ballgame to solidify relations or mitigate tensions.[70] The fact that Coweta and Cussita were engaged in this relationship-strengthening activity when the spies arrived is particularly revealing.[71] Unmoved by the presence of the spies, Coweta and Cussita

Indians continued to play. The spies sat waiting for the game to finish, "without anyone having come to speak to them during this meantime, although one of these spies had some relatives there."[72] Coweta and Cussita Indians displayed their unity, ignoring the Yamasee spies. Not even the kinship ties of these spies helped them gain access into these northern towns. Coweta and Cussita Indians were not ready to forgive the Spanish or the Indians who allied with San Agustín. The spies reported that "no one would speak to them because they knew that they were coming on some investigation." Coweta and Cussita rebuffed Matheos's efforts with an impenetrable silence.[73]

The other two towns attacked by the Spanish, Tasquique and Colome, proved far more welcoming to the Yamasee spies. The caciques of Tasquique and Colome told the spies that, "although the Christians had burned their villages, they had patience [with them], because they [themselves] had their guilt, although the ones entirely responsible were the caciques of Cussita and Coweta, who had deceived and entangled all the rest in bringing the Englishmen and forcing them to receiving them."[74] In this complex speech, the caciques of Tasquique and Colome accepted some of "the guilt" for the tense relations with the Spanish, but they placed most of the blame on Cussita and Coweta. The caciques of Tasquique and Colome believed that Cussita's and Coweta's desire for English goods had "entangled" all of Apalachicola in a network that enriched some towns at the expense of others. Cussita and Coweta gained influence and firepower, while Colome and Tasquique had paid the cost.

Tasquique and Colome Indians offered Matheos's spies vital information. The caciques told the Yamasee spies about an English trader who had been hunting near "the Chicassa of Calosa" and about the gunshots they had heard across the Flint River—only several miles east of the Chattahoochee.[75] The Tasquique and Colome Indians acknowledged that they did not know whether the English or hostile Indians, perhaps Chichimecos or Chiscas, had fired those shots. However, they were certain that English traders and soldiers were hiding near their towns.

The Yamasee spies thanked the caciques for their news and rushed to share their findings with Matheos. The reports of the Yamasee spies described a deeply fractured Apalachicola. The welcoming declarations from the caciques of Colome and Tasquique and the acute silence from Coweta and Cussita demonstrated as much. This disunity undermined efforts to incorporate Apalachicola into a single sphere of influence. Charles Town and San Agustín officials could only establish individual connections to specific towns.[76]

The Yamasee spies carried the reports from Colome and Tasquique back to Matheos. But the lieutenant rejected this intelligence. Experience had taught Matheos that Indian informers communicated what the Spanish wanted to hear and not the truth. After careful consideration, the lieutenant dismissed the reports of the caciques of Tasquique and Colome as having "little foundation." Matheos told his Yamasee spies that, because "their brothers and relatives there [in the town rumored to be housing the English] . . . [have] said nothing at all to them," the reports from Tasquique and Colome were mostly likely false. As he had done with the Coweta woman he had captured during his first expedition, Matheos placed his trust not on individual Indian informers but on Indian kinship networks.[77] It was his spies' "brothers and relatives" who could ascertain the truth in the reports from northern Apalachicola. Matheos instructed that, "as to the gifts that your lordship says are to be given to them [loyal Indians], it appears to me that it will be better not to give them anything unless one shows signs that he deserves it."[78] The uncorroborated warning Colome and Tasquique caciques had provided did not, according to Matheos, "deserve" to be rewarded.

Of the four Yamasee spies, only one brought information that Matheos deemed worthy. The first two spies to return carried the tantalizing but speculative news from Tasquique and Colome that Matheos had eventually dismissed. The third Yamasee spy, who was identified as a cacique, traveled to Ocute and supposedly surveyed the region from that town—his reports, if ever delivered, have not been found. The final news to reach Matheos came from a spy who traveled past Coweta and into Yamasee towns. Unlike those who had journeyed to Coweta, Cussita, Colome, and Tasquique, this spy did not reveal his intentions or identity. Rather than acting as a Spanish agent and sending introductory *correos* (letters) to the caciques of the towns (as the three other spies had done), the fourth spy approached the Yamasee *casillas* (little houses) with care. He also "placed a Gamusa [skins] over his shoulders to disguise himself . . . for everyone in that place ordinarily dressed in this fashion." The disguise fooled a young warrior, who "took the spy to be a native of that country since neither his tongue nor dress was strange."[79] Once in the town, the spy was asked where he was traveling from and why he journeyed alone. The Yamasee spy responded that he had departed from Apalachee for he had wanted to leave Spanish influence behind "and that he had fled from his companions for this reason."[80] This reply suited his Yamasee hosts well. This group of Yamasees had recently severed ties with San Agustín and relocated closer to the lucrative English trade.[81]

Matheos's spy clearly knew what he was doing. From his physical disguise to his cover story, he understood and manipulated the geopolitics of the region. He was also the only one of Matheos's spies to find concrete evidence of South Carolina's commercial links in the region. The spy saw that "the Yameses were carrying twenty-seven muskets (escopetas) and thirty pistols (pesttolas) and one machete, each one had a hat and waist-jackets (justadores)."[82] English goods as well as English traders were everywhere. The spy even conversed with one such trader, who commended the Indian for leaving the Spanish and told him to be in "good cheer" because more goods and trade were on the way. After learning that the Yamasee were planning to raid Spanish missions, the spy rushed back to San Luís in Apalachee.

Matheos readily welcomed this spy and all his information. As the lieutenant listened to the Yamasee's report, Matheos realized that he had gained something far greater than news about English activities. It so happened that before the final spy arrived in San Luís, Matheos had received word from several Apalachicola caciques, including the cacique of Coweta, that they wanted friendship with Spanish Florida and would prove their loyalty by sending word as soon as they heard or knew of English activity in the region. The reports from the fourth Yamasee spy gave Matheos a way to test the strength of the recent promises from Coweta. Because Matheos now had evidence of English activity and knowledge of their whereabouts, he expected to receive similar reports from his Indian allies, "and if he [the cacique of Coweta] does not do so, there is no need to provide proofs of his tricks (trapanzas)."[83] The reports from his Yamasee spy allowed Matheos to know if these supposed Apalachicola allies were truly loyal to the Spanish.

The lieutenant waited a long time, but Coweta's warnings never came. It would take Coweta and the other northern towns over thirty years to reopen communication with San Agustín. In the meantime, northern Apalachicola towns fostered connections with Charles Town and with Indians allied with the English, like the Westos and the Yamasees. But

Apalachicola was not completely lost to the Spanish. Matheos had secured the loyalty of key southern Apalachicola towns and the friendship of some important caciques, like Pentocolo. The welcome Matheos's Yamasee spies received in the towns of Ocute, Tasquique, and Colome revealed that not all of Apalachicola was loyal to South Carolina. The growing fault lines of Apalachicola, which some Florida officials like Leturiondo feared would push the Spanish away, proved a mixed blessing. San Agustín officials definitely had less access to Apalachicola than they had hoped, but their alliances also became tighter and easier to regulate—these were the direct and exclusive connections Matheos had long wanted.

After 1684, the Spanish faced another European threat—albeit largely a phantom threat—in Apalachicola. In that year, La Salle attempted to establish a French colony on the Mississippi River. Overshooting his intended destination by several hundred miles, the party landed instead near present-day Galveston, Texas.[84] Within three years, the colony had crumbled. The French leaders had been murdered, and the few colonists who had managed to survive the disease-ridden area had joined the neighboring Indians. It would not be for another fifteen years before the French were able to establish a permanent colony in the area. The Spanish were unaware of the tragic fate of this colony, however. Florida officials remained convinced that there was a French stronghold in the region and that it would not only block Spanish access to the Mississippi but would also allow France to form a unified colony that extended from the Great Lakes to the Gulf of México. The Spanish crown therefore ordered over ten expeditions to find and destroy La Salle's efforts. Marcos Delgado led the only expedition against the French colony that departed from Florida; the rest and equally unsuccessful ventures were organized from México.[85]

This is the context in which Delgado's story is usually told. But his expedition also took place within months of Matheos's devastating second march into Apalachicola in the summer of 1686. Letters from Matheos appeared in Delgado's official reports. And the two men even had an important meeting in San Luís de Apalachee before Delgado proceeded further west. Fueled by rumors of a coming French invasion, Delgado's expedition took place at a time when San Agustín officials were trying to figure out how best to tread the ground already shifting beneath their feet.

Delgado's expedition, much like Matheos's march, was part of an evolving Spanish effort to stabilize the region's ever-changing and increasingly connected networks.[86] Delgado's mission had, at its core, a strategic goal of opening communication and access to *el más alla*.

Delgado's journey into western Florida (and present-day Alabama) was the first Spanish *entrada* into this region since the journey of Hernando de Soto and Tristán de Luna in the mid-sixteenth century.[87] The region had welcomed these early conquistadors with hardship, violence, and disappointment. Delgado seemed poised for a similar fate. He failed to find the French or any trace of European settlement. He did not reach México, his secondary objective. He spent a large part of the journey ill and the remaining time bartering for basic necessities such as food and water. Delgado did manage some minor triumphs, however. First, he and his men survived the journey, a remarkable feat compared to the experiences of the early conquistadores. Delgado made new alliances with Tawasa and Mobile Indians.[88] And he created, or at least attempted to create, a Spanish-allied network that linked Apalachee with the Mississippi River.[89]

Offering goods and promises, Delgado tried a less violent approach than Matheos's to open communications and secure Indian friendship. This strategy was as much rooted in Delgado's belief that peaceful dealings would bring better relations as it was necessitated by the fact that this small Spanish delegation was in Indian country, far away from San Agustín and San Luís de Apalachee. As Delgado made his way westward from Apalachee, his official objective to find and expel the French morphed into an equally ambitious, but perhaps more practical, need to establish good and clear communications with Indians to the west of Apalachee. When Delgado's men were not searching for food, means of transportation, and guides who could lead them to the French settlement, they were trying to obtain reliable news about the hardships that awaited them as they marched ahead.[90] Delgado knew that having good communication would not magically transport him to the French, ensure the loyalty of all Indians, or even produce the corn he needed to survive. But he also knew that open paths and *nuevas* were necessary if he wanted to survive his journey west of Apalachee.[91]

Before departing San Luís de Apalachee, Delgado met with a delegation of ten Pensacola Indians who attempted to dissuade the Spanish agent from heading overland to Pensacola. The Indians insisted that there was no food along the trail and that, without Indian provisions, Delgado would never be able to reach Pensacola. The Pensacola Indians declared the roads closed. As Delgado weighed his options, he consulted with Matheos, who was in San Luís and openly upset that he had not been chosen to lead this new expedition.[92] Matheos distrusted the Pensacolas' report and wondered if the roads were indeed closed or merely closed to the Spanish. True to his uncompromising character, Matheos issued an ultimatum to the Pensacolas: Either let Delgado travel through their paths and towns or they would "have to lose his friendship." To retain Spanish amity and goods, the Pensacola Indians would need to help Delgado march west. After making his position clear, the lieutenant gleefully remarked that the Indians "knew not where to turn nor how to mollify him," and they eventually agreed to Delgado's request.[93] Matheos's threats kept the road opened for the Spanish.

But not all paths could be maintained by menace and violence. Delgado endured a difficult journey because, as the Pensacolas had stated, the paths were unkempt due to the bad harvest and drought. When he finally reached the western edge of the Apalachicola province, the Spanish agent expressed interest in continuing west to Mobile. His Indian guides discouraged him from doing so. Four chiefs met Delgado in Culassa, a town on the Coosa River, and warned him that "Movilia Indians" had recently killed some Spanish Indians, "and one of them was a Christian called Clemente."[94] Mobile Indians were warlike and had no regard for Christians. The four caciques, Miculasa, Yaimuna, Pagna, and Cusachet, explained that their province of Tiquipache was at war with Mobile. These Indians refused to take Delgado any further, insisting that it would surely lead to his and possibly their deaths. Delgado, having learned from Matheos not to take Indian threats at face value, decided to conduct his own reconnaissance of the region. He sent couriers and spies toward Mobile. Instead of hostile Indians, he found "provinces very deficient in provisions" and in need of support.[95] Mobile Indians might have once been destructive, but now they were destitute.

Delgado saw a simple solution to the Indians' misery that would also relieve tensions between Mobile and Coosa Indians and possibly allow the Spanish to continue their journey west. Delgado believed that, by sharing whatever provisions he had with the Mobile, he could forge a successful alliance. Though the Spanish had struggled to secure enough food and water throughout their entire trip, by serving (or at least attempting to serve) as benefactors, they hoped to both reconnect a severed path and extend San Agustín's connections west of Apalachicola.

Against the advice of the Indians of Tavasa, Delgado summoned the Mobile chiefs. Chiefs from Thome, Ysachi, Ygsusta, Canuca, and Guassa arrived, and

> as soon as they saw the Spaniards they rejoiced much and to me they said that it appeared that they had come forth from a very dark night, for they came very gloomy and melancholy fearing treachery that might be plotted to kill them as at other times had attempted those of this province because they are their mortal enemies and that at all times they kill them.[96]

The "dark night" was over. The Mobiles were very much relieved to see the Spanish, especially to find that they were not part of a ploy to continue the war.[97] Delgado made the case that peace and good communication would resolve the mistrust between the two native groups and would also improve Spanish access to the land. As Mobile and Coosa chiefs embraced and "clasped hands in friendship," Delgado declared the path to the west open and cried victory.

But it was an empty cry. When Delgado asked the chiefs of the now-friendly Mobile towns for help crossing their lands, they kindly and honorably declined. Peace or no peace with the Indians of the province of Tiquipache, the Mobile caciques insisted that there simply was not enough food in the province to sustain the Spanish party. Furthermore, there was the issue of the Chata (Choctaw) Indians. Enemies of the Mobile, the powerful Chata had no intentions of allowing the Spanish through their lands, or so the Mobile caciques claimed. Delgado was now faced with the exact same predicament he had just resolved. This time it was the Mobiles, rather than Pensacolas or Coosas, who vowed friendship to the Spanish but still refused to assist Delgado across their lands. The roads were open, but not to the Spanish.

The Mobile Indians explained to Delgado that their hesitation was rooted in their firsthand experiences with the Spanish. They had "heard of the friendliness of the Christians," but when they decided to visit Apalachicola, they had witnessed Matheos's attack on Coweta, Cussita, Colome, and Tasquique. The fact that the Mobiles learned about the Spanish from Indian towns on the Chattahoochee River, rather than from San Luís, the main Spanish hub in the area, is itself noteworthy. The Apalachicolas' extensive networks, which encompassed contacts with Spanish, English, and a wide variety of native groups, gave the Mobiles a way to see exactly where, with whom, and how Spanish "friendliness" played out. From what they saw, the Mobiles concluded that the Spanish were worse than the English, for at least "the presents of the English were better, that in trading gave more powder, balls, and muskets."[98] If they had to choose between two aggressive European partners, the Mobiles preferred the one who supplied them with weapons.

Delgado could not deny the violence of Matheos's campaigns or even that the English traded guns, but he reminded the Mobile Indians that English aggression was far more devastating than anything San Agustín had ever done.[99] It had been the English and the English-supplied "Chalaque" and "Chichimecos" who had pushed the Mobile from their lands. Delgado insisted that, while Matheos's attacks represented a targeted act of violence, the English were indiscriminate. South Carolina had a lust for land and trade that could never be satisfied. Delgado did not portray the Spanish as good; he merely portrayed them as better than the English. The Spanish agent promised that relations with Florida "would be quiet and peaceful, and that the friendship of the Christians was not like that of the English." In a world fraught with uncertainty, "quiet and peace" were desirable qualities.[100]

Delgado decided not to press his luck any further. He did not threaten the Mobiles, as Matheos had done with the Pensacolas. Instead, Delgado acquiesced to his new allies and merely requested information about other European overtures in the region. The Spanish agent recorded with relief that the Mobile chiefs "have never [even] heard rumors of a settlement of Spaniards, neither of English nor of any other nation."[101] Long ago a vessel had been seen off the gulf, but it had been years since any European had entered the land. Delgado was satisfied. He had not reached La Salle's colony simply because, as the Mobiles reported, there was no French outpost to reach. In the conclusion of his official report, the Spanish agent proudly declared: "we have passed to overcome the greater difficulties so that today communication will be easy."[102] By clearing difficult paths and establishing new alliances, he had secured peace and friendship. By securing peace and friendship, he had made communication "easy." Or so Delgado hoped.[103]

Three years after Delgado's journey, Florida officials built Fort Apalachicola to preserve that hope. This garrison was intended to showcase Spanish dedication to the region as well as to deter any future English and French incursions.[104] Constructed under the guidance of Captain Enrique Primo de Ribera, the garrison enjoyed some early successes. From Fort

Apalachicola, the Spanish established more regular trading and military alliances with the region's Indians. Officials and soldiers from the garrison reported a growing native support for this new Spanish outpost, and for a brief moment it seemed that Fort Aplachicola would help undo the damage caused by Matheos's violent excursions in 1686.[105] Though Guale, Timucua, and increasingly Apalachee continued to bear the brunt of Indian slaving, the Spanish had managed to regain some access into Apalachicola. In 1690, San Agustín officials were cautiously optimistic about their prospects.

Appearances, however, proved deceiving. In the same year the Spanish built the garrison, Don Francisco de Romo, Captain of Apalachee, produced a worrisome report arguing that, in spite of Spanish initiative, "commerce" between the English and the Apalachicolas was only expanding. Fort Apalachicola's second commander, Don Faviano de Ángelo, dismissed Captain Romo's preoccupations and praised the many successes of the garrison. Ángelo either believed that the fort had tangible influence over the region or simply hid any unfavorable reports from his supervisors. All was quiet in Apalachicola, Ángelo insisted, and Fort Apalachicola was instrumental in keeping this peace.[106]

That story held until 1691, when the Spanish officers in Fort Apalachicola awoke one day to find the Apalachicolas gone. The Apalachicolas, the very same Indians who had vowed loyalty to Florida and had benefitted from trade with Fort Apalachicola, were no longer in their towns. The Cowetas and Apalachicolas had relocated near the Ocmulgee, Oconee, Ogechee, and Savannah Rivers—closer to South Carolina's profitable Indian slave trade.[107] John Stewart, a Carolina trader, reported that the Coweta, "being 2500 fighting men, [had] deserted the Spanish protection and com'd setl'd 10 days Jurnay nearer us to Injoy the English frier protection."[108] As Stewart rejoiced in the relocation of the Apalachicolas and Cowetas, San Agustín officials reeled from the shock. They had missed a mass exodus occurring under the supposedly watchful eyes of Fort Apalachicola. There was no value in a fort that could not even keep track of the very Indians it was supplying.

The Apalachicolas had concealed their intentions with great care and had given only subtle hints of their plans. Both Fort Apalachicola commanders and San Agustín officials had received reports that the Indians of Coweta and Cussita, two major Apalachicola towns, were not preparing for the harvest. Only in retrospect did it become clear that these two towns had intended to leave the area. The cleverness of the Apalachicolas' deception afforded the Spanish little comfort.[109] Governor Quiroga Losada quickly ordered the dismantling of the fort so that "enemy Indians could not be capable of making the fort theirs." Flustered by the garrison's inadequacies, the governor wanted to make sure that this useless fort could in no way be turned against Florida.[110] By mid-1692, Fort Apalachicola, one of the last Spanish endeavors in the region, was gone.

~

The Spanish had not won the race to network Apalachicola, but neither had they lost. Henry Woodward and Antonio Matheos had pursued each other through the Chattahoochee valley, while Marcos Delgado had chased French ghosts further west. Their efforts underscored the competing and at times contrasting value that information held. For Woodward, information represented the possibility of expanding English trade connections; for Matheos and Delgado, it promised more influence over their Indian allies. The race to network Apalachicola, however, was not merely taking place among Woodward, Matheos, and Delgado. The journeys of these European informers rendered visible Apalachicola trails, relations, and rivalries—networks that operated beyond and outside Spanish, English, or French control.

The Apalachicolas left only hints of what were far more intricate and extensive inter-Indian networks—like the growing northern Apalachicola–Yamasee connections, discernible when Niquisaya led Woodward from Port Royal to Coweta; the timely northern Apalachicola–Westo alliance, which was revealed when Coweta chiefs used threats of slaving raids both to expel Franciscan friars and to reorient the friendships of southern Apalachicola towns; or even the Apalachicolas' position as a central node between Mississippian groups and the European powers along the coast, which was visible when Mobile Indians decided to journey to Apalachicola towns on the Chattahoochee River rather than to San Luís or San Agustín to learn about the Spanish. During the late seventeenth century, Apalachicola communication networks proved elastic and dynamic. The increased Spanish, French, and English competition in the region reaffirmed, rather than compromised, the political and military power manifested by Apalachicolas through their paths and connections. Examining *who* spread and acquired news offers more than mere details on an interesting and often understudied set of actors; it reveals the inner workings of a palimpsest of networks that connected the early South.

PART III

HOW

New Ways of Articulating Power,

1710–1740

❧

That there were now large grounds for suspicion, he could no longer doubt; but how to proceed in arousing the people . . . and how to inform them in time for the crisis which he now felt was at hand . . . all depended upon the correctness of his acquired information.

Gabriel Harrison, protagonist of the novel
***The Yemassee* (1835) by William Gilmore Simms**

CHAPTER SIX

NETWORKS IN WARTIME

∼

The Indians seemed very ready to come to a good agreement and reconciliation, and having prepared a good supper for our Messengers, all went quietly to rest; but early next morning their lodging was beset with a great number of Indians, who barbarously murdered Captain Nairn [*sic*] and Messieurs John Wight, and Thomas Ruffy, Mr. Cockran and his wife they kept prisoners, whom they afterwards slew.

"An Account of the Breaking out of the
Yamasee War in South Carolina," 1715

WHEN THOMAS NAIRNE and John Wright, two respected Indian agents, were killed in the Yamasee town of Pocotaligo on Good Friday, 1715, it called into question everything the English had known (or thought they knew) about South Carolina. Indians regarded as allies quickly overwhelmed South Carolina. The relations that had allowed the English to gain access to Apalachee and Apalachicola and even to reach the Mississippi River were now spinning out of control. South Carolinians suddenly saw the limits of their expansive trade networks. Now the English feared the whole world had turned against them, and a "barbarous and inhumane Indian Warr formed and carried on by a universal Confederacy of the Indian Nations" was here to destroy them.[1] Though it would be both an exaggeration and an oversimplification to label the Yamasee War "universal," many English colonists experienced the war in this way.[2] The war showed the English that, for all their strength and connections, they could be, and almost were, overpowered.

For South Carolinians, the Yamasee War began with an abrupt end in communication. The networks of trade and information that had enabled South Carolina's exponential growth suddenly stopped working. English links failed, and South Carolina's nodes were eliminated, one by one, as the English traders scattered throughout Indian country were targeted and killed. The use of the passive voice here is intentional. The English knew that traders *were* killed, but they were less certain of when, where, or who bore responsibility. From 1715 to 1717, the main years of fighting of the Yamasee War, officials in Charles Town struggled to grasp the extent and meaning of these orchestrated killings—especially because all the people who normally provided information about Indian affairs were dead.

It would take South Carolina almost a decade to rebuild its alliances and reopen the paths disrupted by warfare, in part because the Yamasee War destabilized English–African relations as well as English–Indian alliances. African slaves played important roles in the fighting and legacy of this war. As many as 400 were recruited to fight alongside the English. Although slaves had served in South Carolina's militia during previous conflicts, the numbers who participated in the Yamasee War were striking.[3] Some blacks fought with the English, some with the Yamasees, and some used the chaos of war to seek freedom elsewhere. As the paths and relations that supported any form of movement through Indian country collapsed under the weight of war, African slaves began to realize the extent of both their dependence on and the limitations of networks defined by the Indian slave trade.[4]

Folded inside this narrative of disruption and opportunity lies a different story, one of functioning, interconnected, and clearly demarcated communication networks. Yamasees, Creeks, Catawbas, and Cherokees did not begin the war in the dark. For them, the Yamasee War demonstrated the expansive and clearly demarcated reach of their information networks. These connections helped Indians coordinate battles; recruit allies; and negotiate with Spanish, French, and English officials. Native information networks allowed the Yamasee War to unfold in the way it did.

Particularly for the English, the war descended with terrifying suddenness. After the murders of Nairne and Wright at Pocotaligo in April 1715, Yamasee and Creek soldiers killed other English traders and colonists, attacked the town of Port Royal, and raided the plantations in St. Bartholomew's Parish. By May, the English feared the Catawbas and the Cherokees had joined the Yamasees and the Creeks. Not wanting this "Confederacy of the Indian Nations" to grow, the South Carolina militia rallied against these northern groups.[5] The Catawbas agreed to peace in July; the English spent the following six months trying to convince the powerful Cherokee to do the same. As South Carolina attempted to control the conflict's northern front, Creek and Yamasee attacks continued. The

English suspected that the Creek–Yamasee alliance had grown to include San Agustín officials as well as Chickasaws, Choctaws, and French traders.

The murder of a Creek delegation in the Cherokee town of Tugaloo in January 1716 prolonged the fighting. The increasingly militarized animosity between Creeks and Cherokees made peace between the Creeks and the English, who allied with the Cherokees in the last months of 1715, difficult to negotiate. It would take another year for most Creek attacks to cease. At the end of 1717, the remaining Yamasees severed ties with the English and found refuge in certain Apalachicola and Spanish towns. Though South Carolina conducted several punitive expeditions against the Yamasees during the 1720s, the main fighting of the war ended in 1717.

The shifting alliances of the Yamasee War underscore the many and different players that comprised the early South and their equally numerous and diverse networks. Focusing on the responses to two particular moments during the war—the assassination of Nairne and Wright at the start of the conflict and the murders of the Creek delegates in the Cherokee town of Tugaloo at a defining moment of the war—helps trace *how* information spread across Indian, European, and African networks. The Yamasee War offers a way to take apart the components of this convoluted process, revealing not only the inner workings of different networks but also the ways these connections overlapped and intersected.

The war began with two ends: the end of English lives, and the end of an alliance and exchange network that had enabled those killed to access Indian country in the first place. The deaths of Thomas Nairne, John Wright, and two other traders (Samuel Warner and William Bray) at Pocotaligo was both a product and a reflection of the complex communication system in place at the onset of the Yamasee War. Nairne had lived in South Carolina since before 1695; though he had worked as a surveyor, a magistrate, and even a judge, his most prominent role was as an Indian agent. He had actively participated in the Indian slave trade, taking a leading role in the 1704–1706 raids on the Apalachee missions. As South Carolina's first commissioner of Indian trade, Nairne had sought to regulate the expansive trade, to establish standard rates of exchange, and to require traders to carry proper licenses.[6]

In 1715, Nairne headed to Pocotaligo eager to ease trade relations with the Yamasees. John Wright, the other trader assigned to this delegation, had different plans. Wright had succeeded Nairne as Indian commissioner. Wright was abrasive, self-interested, and more careful with his money-lending practices than with his own borrowing.[7] In 1715, Wright traveled to Pocotaligo to reprimand and threaten the Yamasees for failing to pay their debts. The Yamasees recalled, "Mr. Wright said that the white men would come and [fetch] [illegible] the Yamasees in one night, and that they would hang four of their head men and take all the rest of them for Slaves, and that he would send them all off the Country."[8] As Nairne promised peace and tried to work with the Yamasees, Wright threatened the lives of Yamasee caciques and sought to assert English authority. One agent vowed that Charles Town meant no harm, while the other declared that the English would enslave the Yamasees unless they paid their debts.

Contradictory communication was emblematic of Yamasee–South Carolina relations. The growing number of unregulated traders in Indian country, each with his own set of concerns and ambitions, created a disjointed Indian policy. As different voices competed for prominence in Indian country, English diplomacy had become muddled and unclear. These mixed messages created frustration among Carolina's Indian part-ners. By April 1715, the Yamasees had had enough. Nairne, Wright, Warner, and Bray became some of the first victims of this cluttered communication. Their murders in Pocotaligo set off a wave of violence across the early South, in which Yamasees and their allies targeted South Carolina traders. By eliminating Indian agents—the very people the English relied on for access to trade and talk with Indian leaders—the Yamasees disrupted English net-works of information.[9]

Not all traders perished. Some South Carolinians with fortuitous connec-tions avoided the initial violence. John Fraser was one. Not much is known about Fraser except that he sold goods to the Yamasee in the 1710s and, more important, that he had managed to escape the fate afforded most traders at the war's outbreak. Fraser learned of the impending attack on English traders via his wife, who in turn heard it from Sanute, a Yamasee Indian. Sanute told Fraser's wife "that there would be a terrible war with the English . . . that the Yamassees, the Creeks, the Cherokees, and many other nations, together with the Spaniards, were all to engage in it." She had quickly reported Sanute's news to her husband, but Fraser doubted the report and decided to question Sanute further. When Fraser asked how long the Yamasees "had formed this horrid design," Sanute calmly explained that it had been months in the making. "Do not you remember about twelve months ago that Ishiagaska, one of our chief warriors, with four more Indians, went to the Creeks . . . Then it was, said Sanute, he carried with him a Spanish talk for destroying all the English inhabitants of the province."[10]

Fraser did not know what to believe. Trade had been good, and there had been no other signs that pointed to "this horrid design." He doubted that he had somehow missed the Creeks conspiring with the Yamasees, the Yamasees extending their alliance to the Cherokees, and the growing influence of Spanish officials. He trusted his information over Sanute's warning. His wife, however, believed Sanute and urged her husband to relocate the family to Charles Town for their safety. There are some indications that Sanute and Mrs. Fraser had an established relationship, perhaps one of kinship or blood, but not much else is known about her or why she chose to trust a piece of news that her husband was not too keen to believe at first (Figure 6.1).[11] Her instincts proved right—the Frasers lived, as one after another of the English Indian traders died.

The wife of William Bray, another Indian trader, also informed her husband about the developing conflict. At the outbreak of the war, Bray was in northern Florida trying to catch runaway slaves. He reported how his wife had heard from a "friendly Yamasee" that the Creeks, frustrated by the current trade conditions, intended to turn against the English.[12] That Mrs. Bray learned this news before her husband raises questions not only about Bray's ability to read ongoing development in Indian country but also about exactly whom the friendliness of this "friendly Yamasee" was intended to aid. It is possible that Mrs. Bray was Creek or Yamasee (or both) and had known her informer personally. The lack of information about Mrs. Bray and Mrs. Fraser makes answering these questions nearly impossible, but it nonetheless hints at *how* South Carolina's communication networks worked. While some of the nodes were English—stores, outposts, and, more often than not, traders themselves—the ties that bound them together were Indian and were operated on Indian terms.[13]

Bray, unlike Fraser, reported what he heard to Charles Town officials. Samuel Warner, a trader in Apalachicola who had also received warnings of a coming war, corroborated Bray's news, and together both traders cautioned that "the Creek Indians had a designe to Cut of the Traders first and then to fall on the settlement, and that it was very neare."[14] Charles Town officials quickly grasped the severity of these reports. More troubling than

FIGURE 6.1. Sanute warns of coming war.
("Sanute and Mrs. Fraser," Picture Collection, The New York Public Library,
Astor Lenox, and Tilden Foundations.)

the murmurs of Indian unrest and unhappiness was the difficulty of hearing these whispers in the first place. South Carolinians needed to get a better handle on the situation, and they needed to do so fast. The South Carolina government ordered Bray and Warner to join Nairne and Wright, who had already departed for the main Yamasee town of Pocotaligo. There were also two other English traders, including Seymour Burroughs, doing business in the Yamasee town. If the Creeks were indeed planning an attack, South Carolinians needed to rally and secure the friendship of the Yamasees. The logic was sound; it just came too late.

Four of the six Englishmen were killed in Pocotaligo in April 1715. Unbeknown to the South Carolinians, an alliance between Lower Creeks and Yamasees had already been forged, a dual Creek–Yamasee delegation had already obtained assurances of Spanish support, and the caciques of both nations were working to secure the support of their neighbors both near, like the Cherokee and Catawba, and far, like the Choctaws and Seneca.[15] Some of these connections were new and tentative. Others had much deeper roots and had developed, as Sanute had indicated, over the course of many months and even more council fires. Like the thin threads of a spider web made suddenly visible by the morning dew, these connections became exposed with the outbreak of war. South Carolinians had thought themselves in charge, spinning the webs. The murder of the agents disoriented and unsettled the English. They were not weaving the webs; they were tangled in them.[16]

Charles Craven, the governor of South Carolina, had arrived to the colony only three years earlier. He had received praise for aiding North Carolina during the Tuscarora War and for strengthening English control of the Port Royal River. Craven, who one eighteenth-century historian described as "deeply interested in the prosperity of Carolina," had known about the mounting unrest in Yamasee towns but was convinced that Nairne and Wright, two of the colony's most experienced agents, could calm the situation.[17] Craven learned of the murders in Pocotaligo just as Cuffy, a Yamasee (possibly from the Lower Town of Euhaw), came with "the first intelligence of the Yamasee Indians' design to massacre the English."[18] This "first intelligence" proved dated; soon after Cuffy's warning, other reports began trickling into Charles Town about other attacks and murders. These grim messages generally concurred that the abuses of Indian traders and the destabilizing practice of Indian slaving had pushed the Yamasees and Creeks to war.[19]

After the murders at Pocotaligo, Yamasee and Creek forces carried out devastating attacks against English settlements in St. Bartholomew's Parish and Port Royal. In Port Royal, "several hundred of English lives were saved" by Seymour Burroughs's frantic warning.[20] Burroughs was a trader stationed in Pocotaligo. He had gladly welcomed Nairne and Wright to town, only to bear witness to their deaths. His Yamasee allies also turned on him, and though "One [shot] took him though [*sic*] the cheek," Burrough escaped. Not for naught described as "a strong robust man," Burroughs managed to race to the coast and share the latest news with John Barnwell, the largest planter and landholder in the Port Royal area.[21] Together Burroughs and Barnwell traveled quickly, warning colonists and ushering about 400 people onto a vessel away from harm's way. From their anchorage not far from the shore—just out of range of the Yamasees' guns—the colonists saw their homes and possessions destroyed. The inhabitants of St. Bartholomew's Parish suffered a far bloodier fate. They received no warnings, and Yamasee forces laid waste to their plantations, killed their cattle and horses, and "burned the men . . . [and] made them die in torture."[22]

In May 1715, just a couple of weeks after these attacks, George Rodd, a colonist in Charles Town, wrote to his employer in London about the alarming situation in South Carolina. He detailed how individual traders were "overwhelmed in this disaster" and how the English were struggling to make sense of this sudden violence.[23] Another early historian of South Carolina reported that "the planters scattered here and there." Charles Town seemed the only safe place to go, and "every one who came in brought the governor different accounts" of the war.[24] South Carolina officials waded through these conflicting, fear-filled reports in order to discern the actual "number and strength" of the Indians involved in the attacks. The word *consternation* makes its way into many English accounts of the Yamasee War. It encapsulates perfectly the dismay, alarm, and anxiety with which South Carolinians experienced the war. In a rather awkward description of the attacks, an unnamed Indian trader revealed the difficulties of even describing this violence. The trader claimed that he had seen what could not be seen and heard "unheard of things."[25]

Governor Craven soon relinquished any hope of a diplomatic solution. Before the start of summer, he had ordered an armed response against hostile Indians. But the English were playing catch-up, responding and retaliating to attacks rather than developing a cohesive military strategy. The missteps of militia Captain Thomas Barker offer a telling example. He led one of the first English attacks in the north of South Carolina after a group of Catawba soldiers killed John Hearn, an English trader in the area. Until Hearn's murder, South Carolina officials were unaware of the Catawbas' involvement in the rising conflict. Captain Barker received orders to attack or, at the very least, intimidate the Catawbas. But he was quickly betrayed "by the treachery of an Indian, whom he unluckily trusted." The ninety men under his command fell "into a dangerous ambuscade in a thicket," and a third of the English forces perished.[26] "We lost the Capt. and 26 very pretty young men," Francis Le Jau, a missionary in St. James's Parish, lamented. "This Accident did put the whole Country, & ym chiefly who layd most expos'd into a great Consternation."[27] Le Jau's description of the incident as an "Accident" is telling because no part of the expedition, from the reason behind the captain's march to the loyal Indian guide turned traitor, had been under English control.

Other English "Accidents" soon followed. Commander Redwood was also "foolishly betray'd by credulity." "Listening too much to the insinuations of making peace [he] disarmed his own men, and suffered the Indians to come amongst them." The Indian forces then proceeded to massacre the English regiment.[28] South Carolinians were unsure of whom to trust; the mechanisms the English had previously employed to evaluate native promises were gone as well. Charles Town officials discussed the need to manage war and reassert control over the region, or "we may expect a long and bloody war."[29] The English not only needed to institute a short-term plan for organizing the army and defending the colony, South Carolina officials also needed a new way of conceptualizing their place and alliances in the region now that their trading network had collapsed.

Luckily for South Carolina, the "consternation" of the first few months of the Yamasee War did not prove permanent. In late spring and early summer of 1715, the English delivered a devastating blow to the Yamasees in an open battle near the head of the Combahee River. Subsequent assaults led by the unfortunately named Colonel George Chicken and Maurice Mathews destabilized Indian communities in the Carolina Piedmont. Other South Carolina militia attacked the Upper Town of Pocotaligo as well as other northern Yamasee towns.[30] By midsummer, South Carolina forces had targeted some Lower Yamasee towns and forced the remaining ones to relocate away from the English.

As they moved south and west, Yamasees carried with them more than their scattered possessions. They also took Africans slaves. Yamasees and Creeks used the chaos of war to capture many Africans and encouraged many others to desert. Or so the English bemoaned. It is clear, however, that many slaves fled during the Yamasee War of their own accord. Several of these slaves made their way to San Agustín, leaving behind some of the best (and only firsthand) accounts of African experiences during the Yamasee War. The war generated opportunities for slaves—to fight alongside the Yamasees, to escape their masters, and to obtain freedom—but it also disrupted existing avenues for escape. The slaves who managed to reach Florida during the war and its immediate aftermath would be the last large wave to do so for almost ten years.

In 1720, during what became known as the Primus Plot, a large group of slaves in South Carolina planned to rebel against their masters. Instead of "rising with a designe to destroy all the white people," as their English masters feared, these slaves decided to flee to San Agustín. They did not make it very far. First they failed to secure Indian guides, and then they struggled to find open paths that led to Spanish Florida. By the time they finally reached Savannah Town, these slaves were "half starved."[31] The Yamasee War had removed some key nodes and links connecting Charles Town with San Agustín.[32] The Yamasee War exposed the important connections between Indian networks and black freedom.

The war also shaped the experiences of those runaways who made it to Florida. Once in San Agustín, these fugitives enlisted (or were enlisted) in the Spanish militia and soon played an integral part in the defense of Florida. In an ironic twist, when Colonel John Palmer led a punitive expedition from South Carolina against Yamasees still living near San Agustín, it was these runaways turned soldiers who helped defeat the English. Palmer, who had been a scout during the Yamasee War, had spent the subsequent decade eradicating Yamasee strongholds in South Carolina. In 1727, he traveled to Florida to battle Indians but instead came face to face with runaway slaves now living in and protected by Spanish Florida. Spanish officials had long acknowledged the tactical and military importance of the black militia in Florida, but it was the fierce efforts of runaway slaves during both the Yamasee War and the retaliatory Palmer raids that convinced Governor Manuel de Montiano finally (in 1738) to free all fugitives who reached San Agustín.[33] Later that year, Captain Francisco Menéndez, a former slave who had fought alongside the Yamasees during both the war and Colonel Palmer's raids, became governor of Fort Mose, a free black community established just outside San Agustín. Military experience and close connections to Yamasee Indians were the cornerstones of Menéndez's rising political position in Florida.[34]

Taken together, the African and English experiences during the Yamasee War emphasize two important (albeit not new) features of the communication networks in the early South. First, Africans and Europeans depended on Indian paths and connections to move, travel, and spread information. Second, these Indian networks operated outside and often beyond European control. What changed during the Yamasee War was the visibility of both those features, enabling the historian a glimpse not only of where those information networks reached but also of *how* they worked. Besides reminding the English that they were neither in control of nor at the center of these connections, the Yamasee War exposed the scope, complexity, and limitations of Indian networks that otherwise remained hidden in plain sight.

The collapse of English networks is easier to see than the many crisscrossing Indian connections that remained operational at the exact same time. On the eve of the Yamasee War, Yamasee networks connected Ochese Creeks, Abecas, Tallapoosas, Alabamas, Charles Town officials and traders, Lower Cherokees, Middle and Overhill Cherokees, Virginia traders, Catawbas, French officials, San Agustín agents, and some Iroquoian groups. But within a year, the Yamasee network had completely transformed. It shrank and, as the experiences of the fugitive slaves headed to San Agustín revealed, failed to keep many of its important paths open.[35] Reconstructing these Indian information networks is difficult, but this difficulty is not necessarily because of the challenge of finding sources. A single sentence in the report of an English Indian delegation can offer clues into the inter-Indian connections forged beyond the European gaze.[36] A brief mention of an imminent raid can show both how far Indian networks extended and how fast news moved through them.[37] Conflicting reports by Indians from the same nation can help reveal the internal divisions within an Indian polity and the competing channels through which information traveled.[38] Indian-authored maps offer visual representations of these complex connections.[39] The challenge for the historian then lies in deciphering *how* and if these network fragments functioned as a whole.

The murders of Nairne, Wright, Warner, and Bray at the start of the Yamasee War offer a way in. For the Yamasees, killing these traders in Pocotaligo was like throwing a stone into a pond. The rock sank quickly, but the impact caused small waves. These ripples of war soon inundated Indian paths and towns. They pushed Yamasees and Ochese Creeks closer together and tore Yamasees and the English apart.[40] The bellicose undulations from Pocotaligo soon crashed and eddied into other waves originating from Cherokee, Catawba, and Creek towns. Following these waves as they moved through the early South shows a complex network in action.

The Yamasees had been close English allies since the 1680s. This native group had risen to power as one of South Carolina's most active Indian trading partners. Lucrative in the short term, the enslaving and the selling of people to obtain English guns and goods proved destabilizing, trapping the Yamasees in a cycle of crushing debt. As the first decade of the eighteenth century came to a close, the Yamasees saw their influence within English trade networks wane. In 1711, South Carolinians built a road between Charles Town and Port Royal, cutting through Yamasee lands and encouraging an influx of "white Men setling among them." Tensions flared between Yamasees and these new arrivals. The "Complaints being of soe high and grievous a Nature," warned English agents to the Yamasee, that unless relations with the Yamasees improved, it could lead "to the utter Ruin and Desolation of the Government."[41] The pressure amplified when a Yamasee delegation arrived in Charles Town in 1712. The Yamasees had come to demand payment for their service during the Tuscarora War, and they had arrived in much larger numbers than the English had anticipated. The size of their delegation was not coincidental; the Yamasees were trying to display their nation's might and discredit reports of their imminent decline and loss.[42]

But the English were already rehearsing the narrative of Yamasee declension. In 1713, Le Jau explained that the Yamasee "Nation was formerly very numerous but by degrees they are come to very little . . . they decrease apace, the Reason of it is the continual Warr they all make."[43] A census conducted right before the outbreak of the war confirmed Le Jau's assessment. The ten Yamasee towns listed, which housed a population of slightly over 1,200, were clustered mostly in the Port Royal area. These numbers were not insignificant, but there was a noticeable drop in the number of Yamasee warriors, from 500 recorded in 1708 to 350 in 1715.[44] The Yamasees understood both the practical and political problems of population loss. South Carolina would not ally with or aid weak Indian groups. On the contrary, the English would enslave them.

The Yamasees attempted to reverse this pattern, in particular by strengthening their connections to the Lower Creeks. In 1713, the Yamasees petitioned to incorporate the Cheehawes back into their towns. They explained that the "Cheehawes . . . ware formerly belonging to the Yamasees and now settled att [*sic*] the Creek might return." Once Yamasee, now Creek, the Cheehawes revealed the intimate connections between these two nations.[45]

The alliance between Yamasee and Apalachicola was not new. In 1691, when the Apalachicolas decided to abandon Fort Apalachicola, which was erected by the Spanish, their connections to both the Yamasees and South Carolina facilitated their relocation. In the 1700s, Yamasees and Ochese Creeks worked alongside each other capturing and selling Indian slaves, in particular during the 1704–1706 raids on Apalachee.[46] The importance of these links became even more pronounced in 1715 and 1716, as the ravaging violence of the war destroyed most Yamasee towns and forced Yamasees to flee their homelands. Many of them went south, toward San Agustín— a phenomenon that attracted English and Spanish notice.[47] For South Carolinians, the Yamasees' removal closer to Florida confirmed English suspicions about Spanish involvement in the Yamasee War.[48] The Spanish, in contrast, greeted news of Yamasee and Creek movement into the Chattahoochee area with great excitement. Florida officials hoped for the rebirth of southern Apalachicola, a province devastated by the slaving raids of a decade earlier. But a 1717 census conducted by Joseph Primo de Rivera revealed that most Yamasees had not set up towns "close to the presidio." Instead, more than half of the Yamasees had relocated near or in Creek settlements (Figure 6.2). By the end of the Yamasee War, Spanish–Yamasee connections were weak and English–Yamasee commercial networks were shattered, but the paths between Yamasees and Creeks, established over thirty years earlier, remained open and active.[49]

This alliance fell far short of unity. In the summer of 1715, a Creek and Yamasee delegation traveled to San Agustín to ask for Spanish support to wage war against South Carolina. The Indian delegates began by giving Florida's governor, Francisco Córcoles Martínez, eight strips of deerskin with knots tied in them. The Spanish governor was elated. Holding the knotted deerskin strands in his hand, Córcoles Martínez counted 161 knots, for the 161 towns that supported this joint delegation. But even as the governor excitedly ran his fingers through the knots, imagining the many Indian towns now under Spanish protection, the Indian delegates pointedly

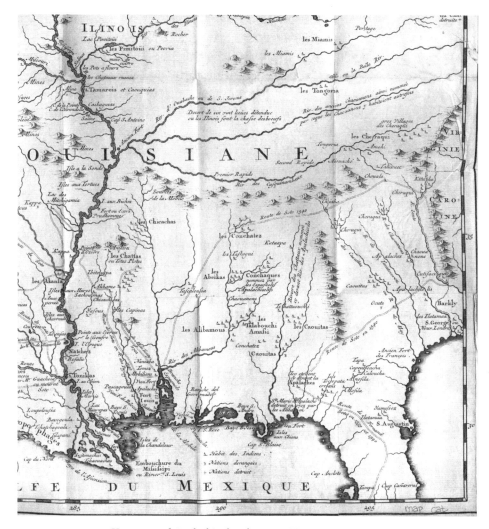

FIGURE 6.2. Yamasee and Apalachicola relocation. New Yamasee towns appear near
San Agustín. Section from *Le Carte de la Louisiane*.
(Photo courtesy of the Newberry Library, Chicago. Call no. Case G81.091.)

emphasized the autonomy of each knot and the individuality of each
town. They used the plural, speaking of "micos," "caciques," "towns," and
"Provinces." Brave Dog, one of the main delegates, even explained that he
represented the interests of *two* main chiefs: Brims and Chislacaliche.
Governor Córcoles Martínez wholeheartedly welcomed the Creeks and
Yamasees into Spanish care, ignoring or failing to see the divisions and

power struggles within the Creek nation that Brave Dog had so clearly articulated.[50]

The different responses to the same news from Pocotaligo revealed just how carefully defined and demarcated these divisions were. Each town had to decide whether or not they would support their longtime Yamasee allies and then what that support, or lack of support, would actually entail. The Upper Creek towns, keen on preserving their trading partnerships with South Carolina, held back when they received word of the murders of Nairne, Wright, Warner, and Bray. The Upper Creeks' reluctance to join the war was as deliberate and calculated as the Yamasee attack on Pocotaligo. An Abeika headman explained how the Upper Creeks had been "brought into" the Yamasee War against their "Desire . . . by the Tallapoosas, Cowetas, and other Lower people."[51] The headman's statement before an English audience suggested a not-so-subtle comparison between the loyalty of the Upper Creeks to South Carolina and the far more fickle actions of the Lower Creeks. The Lower Creek, as the Abeika headman remarked, lived close to both Yamasee and English towns. An alliance with one side could push them into open warfare with the other. The Lower Creeks needed to tread with utmost care, which made the complex networks of alliances they proceeded to establish even more remarkable.

Brims, mico of the Lower town of Coweta, was a central node in this Lower Creek network. Practically no details are known about Brims's upbringing and early life, but by the 1700s, he was an important Lower Creek figure. In 1711, he participated in an English-led expedition against the Choctaws and afterward swore "his Loyalty and Obedience to the British Nation."[52] But the Yamasee War forced the mico to reconsider his allegiances. If Brims chose to fight alongside South Carolina, as he had previously promised, he would be sent to kill people he regarded as close allies. If he chose to side with the Yamasees, the Lower Creeks would become prime targets of English aggression. As Brims contemplated his position, his priorities became clear: His first and true "Loyalty and Obedience" was to neither the English nor the Yamasees, but to Coweta. To protect and strengthen Coweta, Brims transformed the town's transversal pattern of alliances into a network that was as wide as it was flexible. Even as the Lower towns under his guidance lent their support to the Yamasees—reaffirming an alliance that had been in place before the war and would remain strong long after official hostilities ended—Brims sent delegates to the Upper Creeks, who refused to join the war as Yamasee allies. Coweta's embassies to the Alabamas and Abeikas kept communication open among Upper and Lower Creek towns. Brims managed to connect peoples and places pursuing clashing policies, in the process extending the Lower Creeks' networks further west and south.[53]

In 1716, Lieutenant Diego Peña got an intimate look at Brims's networking prowess. Peña was the leader of the first Spanish delegation to the Chattahoochee River since Antonio Matheos's violent campaigns against the Creeks in 1686. The Spanish had high hopes for Peña's mission. The Spanish lieutenant was to journey through Creek towns, convince them of Spanish friendliness, and reestablish good communication between San Agustín and Apalachicola. Peña was eager to meet Brims, who held "the key" to all Lower Creek towns. Brims kindly welcomed the lieutenant, but his welcome was meant more to showcase his own influence than to comply with any Spanish demand.[54] By the time Peña arrived, Brims had already opened paths to Pensacola via an alliance with Tickhonabe, a Tallassee cacique.[55] As the Yamasee War pushed English networks to their breaking points and destroyed Yamasee nodes and links, Brims expanded Coweta's connections to the two main Spanish towns in the region. Peña was quick to note the growing number and diversity of nodes in Brims's networks. The mico of Coweta was both architect and manager of this motile web of interrelations.[56]

As a result of Brims's connections, pro-Spanish caciques, like Chipacasi, Chislacaliche, and Tickhonabe, began to gain prominence in Lower Creek towns. But Brims also had Upper Creek interests in mind. The Upper Creeks, who did not want an alliance with the Spanish, also stood to gain from these new paths between Coweta and key Spanish hubs. Abeika and Okfuskee, who were keen on resuming trade with South Carolina, now had a way to excuse and even exonerate Creek involvement in the Yamasee War: They could simply blame the Spanish. Rather than depicting the paths to Pensacola and San Agustín as careful connections made by Brims, Creek leaders sympathetic to the English could point to Spanish interference in Creek affairs.

And that is exactly what the pro–South Carolina Creeks did. In early 1717, some Lower Creeks welcomed John Jones, the first English trader into their towns since the outbreak of hostilities. They expressed their eagerness to resume trade with South Carolina and proceeded to explain how the Spanish had pushed the Creeks into fighting against the English.[57] Probably neither Jones nor the Creeks truly believed this rendition of events, but what mattered was that Florida officials proved a convenient and plausible scapegoat for both sides. The networks that Brims linked together did not eliminate the differences among Creek towns; rather, the connections acknowledged and drew strength from the autonomy of each node.

For the English, the Creeks' insistence on autonomy complicated their negotiations. In early 1717, Bocatio, an Upper Creek Indian, arrived at Savannah Fort and spoke of peace with South Carolina. The English, ready to end the ongoing war, were initially delighted. Their enthusiasm quickly dampened, however, as Bocatio began speaking of conditions, not offers. The Creek delegate made clear that peace would not come "before their corn is ripe." Peace would happen when, and only when, the Indians were ready. Furthermore, Bocatio outlined the boundaries of Creek friendship. The Creeks would ally with South Carolina, but that friendship would not shape how Creeks interacted with other Indians—in particular the Cherokee and the Catawba, who the Creeks now regarded as enemies. If the English wanted friendship with the Creeks, they would have to comply with Creek requests. "We are in such a straight," complained Indian agent Joseph Boone, "that we know not what to do, nor how to turn our selves."[58] Refusing Bocatio's friendship would mean condemning South Carolina to prolonged fighting with a powerful enemy, but accepting his conditions implied agreeing to peace and diplomacy on Creek terms.

The ripples from Pocotaligo reached all the way to Chickasaw and Choctaw towns. In July 1715, three months after the traders' deaths, the English confessed that they remained unsure "whether any of the Nations living beyond those [Creeks] be combined with them, but . . . they very much fear the Chacktaws [sic], a numerous and warlike People, is in the Confederacy."[59] Uncertainty quickly turned to fear when reports reached Charles Town that both Choctaws and Chickasaws had murdered English traders in their towns. According to Alexander Spotswood, lieutenant governor of Virginia, these attacks were evidence of "the late Peace concluded between their Neighbouring Indians [the Creeks] and those Chacktaws, (who were always very good friends with the French)."[60] Though the French-backed Creek–Choctaw force that Spotswood feared did not descend on Charles Town, Choctaw involvement in the Yamasee War nevertheless was a double blow to South Carolina. It implied, first, that the Choctaws had closed their paths to English traders— paths that South Carolina had only managed to open the year before the war started.[61] And second, it meant that Choctaws had strengthened their paths to

French and Creek towns.[62] As English networks contracted, Creek, Choctaw, and French connections expanded.

News of Pocotaligo reached French Louisiana in July 1715. The first accounts were vague, detailing how "several of the Indian tribes in Carolina had fallen upon the English in their towns and had massacred them, including those of Port Royal."[63] But then a subsequent report came that some young Chickasaw soldiers had mistaken a French trader for an English agent and murdered him. The French interpreted this incident as evidence that the budding alliance between the Chickasaw and the English had run aground.[64] South Carolina officials, for their part, feared that the murder of this trader was an outright declaration of war. But the Chickasaws' involvement in the Yamasee War proved as tepid as it was strategic. Killing a trader in their lands allowed the Chickasaws to display an anti-English sentiment before Louisiana agents, granting them access to French trade and goods that had previously only benefitted their Choctaw rivals. But the Chickasaws had no intention of severing ties with South Carolina completely. To the English, the Chickasaws pointed to their restraint and loyalty. They had killed only one trader and had launched no other offensive raids. In their dealings with anxious South Carolinians, the Chickasaws parlayed this one murder and display of strength into tangible gains. They negotiated for better exchange rates and more favorable trading terms than had been in place before the Yamasee War.[65]

Bienville, the governor of Louisiana, also hoped to take advantage of the hostilities to expand his networks. He sent French agents beyond the familiar Chickasaw and Choctaw towns to establish direct trade with Alabama and Upper Creek towns. The French moved quickly to improve their access and connections to the Creeks, exploring both the feasibility and potential profitability of constructing a French node in the area.[66] The Creeks welcomed these French inroads. Though French goods paled in comparison to what the English could provide, the possibility of a bourgeoning French alliance increased the parameters and stakes of Indian connections with European colonists.[67]

South Carolinians soon realized that to win, or even to weather, the Yamasee War, they would need to forge new networks. By the fall of 1715, Charles Town officials focused their efforts on securing an alliance with Cherokees or, at the very least, on preventing this large Indian nation from joining Creek–Yamasee forces.[68] "The Northern Indians have not since appeared against Us," wrote George Rodd, "we are in hopes, the Cheroquese will be Our Friends."[69] But South Carolina–Cherokee connections were not particularly strong. Two years before the Yamasee War some English traders had helped the Cherokee wage war against the Yuchis. South Carolina had also supported, and maybe even supplied, a Cherokee attack against French Indians.[70] But neither raid was carried out at English behest, and the Cherokees had proven more ambivalent than friendly in the aftermath of Pocotaligo. English traders had been killed in Lower Cherokee towns, but Middle and Overhill Cherokees had shown no interest in joining the war.[71] Everyone, from the Yamasees to the English, wanted to exploit the deep divisions within Cherokee towns.[72]

The decisions and actions of the Cherokees after Pocotaligo reflect the unique geographical and political position of the Cherokees. Unlike South Carolinians, the Cherokees were not consumed by the war; they felt little urgency to find new or to reaffirm existing connections. And unlike the Creeks and Yamasees, the Cherokees were not scrambling to increase the size and scope of their alliances.[73] The Cherokees, who had previously figured only marginally in these competing networks, suddenly found themselves acting as central nodes. This is not to say that Cherokees had somehow failed to appreciate their own importance until the Creeks, Yamasees, and English attempted to bring them under more direct control. But as both their European and Indian neighbors tried to integrate the Cherokees into their own networks, the Cherokees began weighing the value of each connection differently. They did not need to fold their interests into those of the powerful and nearby Lower Creek towns or to maintain the peace with the Catawba, as South Carolina requested.[74] Instead, they would follow their own paths.

In the winter of 1715, Colonel George Chicken traveled to the Lower Cherokee town of Tugaloo to establish friendship with the Cherokees and, more important, to determine whether this nation "would assist us against our Enemies or no."[75] Chicken needed to offer the Cherokees a clear message of strength, unity, and friendship. But as luck would have it, Alexander Longe, a trader to the Cherokee, had already begun spreading some rather disturbing news to Lower Cherokee towns. At "the war's first breaking out," Longe had "told these people that ye English was going to make wars with them and that they did design to kill all their head warriors."[76] Longe had carried out an unsanctioned attack against a Euchee town; his reckless lies were intended to secure his refuge with the Cherokees—a strategy that would work only if the Cherokee refused to welcome any other English agent. Longe's actions placed Colonel Chicken in the position of not only having to persuade the Cherokees that they would benefit from an alliance with South Carolina but also that he, and not Longe, was the true voice of Charles Town. Supporting Chicken's authority was a force of 300 colonists led by Colonel Maurice Moore, younger brother of former governor James Moore. The English had hoped that marching with a sizable force would compel the Cherokees not to join the Yamasees. The theatrics worked. The Cherokees dismissed Longe's reports and, after a brief debate, agreed to an alliance with the English.

The Cherokee were perfectly happy to extend "white flags" to the English delegation and offer proof of their friendship (for instance, by not killing South Carolinian traders). But Cherokee chiefs showed no inkling of reworking or relinquishing their existing connections. Opening communication, Chicken discovered, was not the same as controlling how information flowed. The English could be included as allies, but on Cherokee terms. The colonel urged the Cherokees to consult or at least inform the English before making any major decisions, and "not to make war or peace wthout ye Consent of ye English."[77] The Cherokees understood the importance of this request. They had firsthand experience with the problems caused by rumors and their own efforts to open relations with South Carolina had been "hindered" by self-serving informers carrying "a parcel of Lies."[78] To eliminate the dangers of misleading reports, Chicken insisted that the Cherokee establish a straight path to Charles Town. Too many voices, as the Cherokees themselves had learned in their dealings with trader Alexander Longe, could tangle talks and complicate friendships.

The Cherokees agreed with Chicken's message but refused his terms. They vowed to "make war or peace" as they saw fit and, in an act that seemed nothing short of open defiance, the Cherokees prepared for an unsanctioned war against the Creeks. Though the Cherokee headmen had not received English "Consent" for this attack, they argued that their actions were necessary for they had "no [other] way of getting Slaves to buy ammunition & Clothing."[79] Ironically, Cherokee leaders cited the trade with South Carolina as their reason to refuse Chicken's request. The Cherokees then proceeded to attack a Creek delegation visiting the town of Tugaloo on January 27, 1716.[80] As had the murders of the English traders not a year earlier, the slaying of the Creek delegation in a supposedly friendly Cherokee town caused waves of unrest that rippled through the region. The massacre at Tugaloo forced a massive reorganization of the networks that had taken shape since the start of the war.

For the English, the attack at Tugaloo was a mixed blessing. The murder of the Creek delegation demonstrated Cherokee support for South Carolina. Colonel Moore recalled how the "Charikees were upon the point of falling upon Our men but as providence Order'd it they chang'd their minds and fell upon the Creeks and Yamasee who were in their Town and killed every man . . . since which the Cherokees have been carry[ing] on the war against their and our enemies."[81] Though Moore celebrated the fact that South Carolinians and Cherokees now shared common enemies, the events at Tugaloo also displayed Cherokee willingness to act without and even against English approval. Cherokees had "chang'd their minds" and made their own decisions. Cherokee actions were a reminder that this powerful nation would not seek English "Consent" before making "war or peace." As Nicholas Trott, Francis Yonge, Samuel Eveleigh, and some of the other leading traders to the Cherokee soon complained, "the demands they make are so unreasonable that we may properly say, We are become their tributaries." The Cherokee exerted significant sway over how South Carolina could reconstitute its alliances and influence.[82]

For the Creek, the murders at Tugaloo proved unpardonable, a horrible betrayal, and an act of war. Chigelly, an Indian from the Lower town of Coweta, recalled how delegates had barely started talks in Tugaloo when they were killed without provocation or just cause. Speaking a decade after the war, Chigelly downplayed the antagonism between the Creeks and their neighbors, both Indian and European. He insisted that the Creek delegates had come to Tugaloo neither to spy on the English nor to push the Cherokees into waging war against South Carolina.[83] The Creek party wanted to establish peace with the Cherokees and, more important, with the English. To make his case, Chigelly pointed to the many personal connections and friendships the Creek delegates had with English traders.[84] But even in his version of the Tugaloo massacre, in which the Creeks were innocent and the Cherokees deceitful, the peace-seeking Creek delegates appeared determined, strong, and capable of exerting significant influence as they traveled through Cherokee paths.

The Cherokee showed more unity in their antagonism toward Ochese Creeks than in their partnership with South Carolina.[85] The murders at

Tugaloo were soon followed by a series of attacks against the Creeks, who returned in kind and nearly decimated the Cherokee town of Naguchee.[86] This violence, in which no Carolina traders died or even participated, was very much part of the Yamasee War— an expansive conflict that involved people, places, and fighting well beyond South Carolina's control.

The Cherokee attacks on the Catawbas were a case in point. The Catawbas had initially decided to fight in the Yamasee War, but their stance against South Carolina proved brief.[87] The Catawbas quickly realized, first, that the Virginians, though very much enraged by the abrasive incursions and abuses of South Carolina traders, were not going to supply any native group that intended to wage war against their English neighbors.[88] And second, while the Creeks had used "talk" to convince the Catawbas to join the war, the Cherokees, who lived much closer, used violence and intimidation to persuade the Catawbas to cease fighting.[89] The Cherokees used their involvement in the Yamasee War to exploit Catawba paths and gain more direct access to Virginia—objectives that had little to do with South Carolina's ambitions during the war and everything to do with Cherokee efforts to expand their networks.[90]

The effects of the Yamasee War extended as far as the Iroquois. The murders at Tugaloo forced the Creeks to reexamine their networks. Since the Cherokee would not be their allies, staining red the paths between them, the Creeks sought to strengthen their ties with other Cherokee enemies. In the fall of 1717, Indian agent Joseph Boone lamented,

> I am now to inform you of melancholy newes in relation to our Indian warr, we have two white men lately come from the Creeke Indians that brings acct. that the Senecas or Mohocks are joined with them, and resolve to fall on the Charchees and Cuttabaws that are now our friends.[91]

Creek delegates had traveled north, past Cherokee, Catawba, and Virginia lands, in their search for more powerful allies.[92] Though large-scale Iroquois participation in the Yamasee War never materialized, mention of Creek delegates in Iroquoia and of Seneca and Mohawk emissaries in the southern towns appear in the minutes of several assembly proceedings, including those of South Carolina, Virginia, New York, and Connecticut.[93] The English feared not only an Iroquois attack on South Carolina but also that the Creeks, Senecas, and Mohawks would use their networks to collapse distance and unite under a common anti-Cherokee banner. In a time of heightened uncertainty, when it was unclear who was allied with whom or how strong or lasting those connections would prove, "talk" of friendship and rumors of violence were often enough to transform potential alliances into concrete ones.

The same was true in Creek networks. During the first months of 1718, Don Juan Fernández de la Orta arrived in Coweta. The Spanish official wanted to reaffirm the connections between Pensacola and the Lower Creeks, which Brims and Tickhonabe had worked to establish at the start of the war. But no sooner had Don Orta begun communicating his message than word reached Brims that Colonel John Musgrove and Theophilus Hastings had arrived in Creek country and wanted access to Coweta. Both traders had spent the previous years trying to rebuild the paths and connections between Charles Town and the Lower Creeks. While the English were still not welcomed at every Creek town, Musgrove and Hastings had used their kinship ties to gain access to both Brims and Coweta.[94] As the mico of Coweta attempted to balance both Spanish and English delegations, a third agent arrived at Coweta from Fort Toulouse, a French holding below the confluences of the Coosa and Tallapoosa Rivers. The French were eager to continue expanding their networks and start a partnership with the Creeks.[95] Three rival empires appeared before the mico—each promising great opportunities and each issuing equally as restrictive demands. If the mico felt overwhelmed or worried, he did not let it show. On March 23, 1718, Brims convened a general meeting among the Creek in which it was decided that all of the competing nodes would be integrated into Creek networks.[96]

Maintaining these complicated networks required constant adaption and reevaluation. Creek–Yamasee relations offer a case in point. Though the two nations were allies, Creek violence against the Yamasee increased after 1717, especially when South Carolinians vowed to embargo Indian towns that refused to attack the Yamasees. Creeks towns like Cussita, Tallapoosas, and Abeika never had strong connections to the Yamasees and had no desire of losing their access to English goods, so they balked at Brims's attempts to maintain earlier connections between Creeks and Yamasees.[97] But Brims understood that, while Creek–Yamasee ties weakened, Creek–Cherokee aggression grew only stronger. Brims could not keep Creeks from raiding the Yamasees, but he could persuade them to target a more imminent foe. When South Carolina officials forcibly demanded that the Creeks organize war parties against the Yamasees, Brims issued "a false report that the Cherokees were discovered in the Woods," forcing the Tallapoosas and Abeika to switch their focus from the Yamasees to the Cherokees.[98] Brims used a rumor of a Cherokee attack to preserve Lower Creek–Yamasee ties.

In an account recorded two centuries after these events, Fulotkee, a Lower Creek Indian, recalled Coweta's importance in making and controlling alliances.

> In olden times two Coweta men came from the northwest, each carrying a war club (atåså). They ran and whooped, so that the earth quaked and echoes rolled in all directions. In some mysterious manner this produced more people who came flocking around . . . They talked to these people, and presently they came down and accompanied them back. They were the Tukabahchee. Then the men of the two towns said[,] "We have seen each other's power; let us unite. The Coweta shall be the leaders."

By the 1720s, the power of Coweta was not merely spreading across Indian country; it was making the "earth quake."[99]

The Yamasee War ended gradually. By 1717, most of the fighting had subsided, but, as Brims's efforts to prevent Tallapoosas and Abeikas from raiding Yamasee towns showed, violent reverberations from the war continued for another two decades.[100] The connections and rivalries made during the war proved long-lasting. Creeks and Yamasees remained linked, even as the balance of power between the two shifted to privilege the former. The Creeks would eventually reconnect with South Carolina, but with a new sense of place and power. The massacre at Tugaloo had helped create more paths between the Cherokees and Charles Town, but it unlinked the Cherokees from the Creeks and encouraged a rivalry that persisted for many years. After the war, the Chickasaws reopened their paths to the English and forged new connections with the Cherokees as a way to counter a growing Choctaw–French threat. The Catawbas, after briefly cutting ties with Charles Town, saw their networks shrink, attacked by both English and Cherokee forces.[101] Runaway slaves also noted their dependence on these Indian paths and connections. The Yamasee War did more than open opportunities for enslaved persons to escape; it affected the direction of their flight and redefined both the trials and the possibilities afforded to the fugitive slaves who reached San Agustín.

The experience of the Yamasee War offers a way to see *how* these networks were made, unmade, and remade—processes that proved continual and dynamic. These connections were local and often personal, but their impact rippled across large areas touching hundreds, if not thousands, of people. Exploring how these networks operated helps explain not only what information spread and who carried it but also why the understanding, interpretation, and implementation of one piece of news, say, the murder of English traders in Pocotaligo, could vary so widely. Considered alongside each other, European, African, and Indian networks reveal the importance and autonomy of individual nodes and, in turn, the connectedness and influence of one particular town or person in a larger network.[102] Constraints, rivalries, and violence underlay the struggles to make sense of this rapidly changing world. Considering *how* information networks functioned and faltered offers an argument less about the importance of having the latest news and more about the different (political, military, economic, and kinship) connections that helped articulate and maintain power in the early South.

CHAPTER SEVEN

DISSONANT CONNECTIONS

~

In the first Place, we return you hearty Thanks for your Readiness in
sending your Negroes to assist our Trade, but we expected you would
send some *Wineau* Indians instead of them . . . it would be very
inconvenient to you and chargeable to us, to keep your Negroes for so
long a Voyage . . . Agreed with Col. John Barnwell for the Hire of his
two Indian Slaves, for Oarsmen for the Periago designed for the
Northward Indian Trade.

Board of Trade to Captain Bartholomew Gallard, 1716

IN JULY 1716, as the Yamasee War raged on, South Carolina officials wanted
to hire some slaves to "assist our Trade" in Indian country. They needed
oarsmen to help deliver goods from Charles Town to the trading outpost on
the Santee River. Captain Bartholomew Gallard had sent some of his
"Negroes" to complete the task, but the Commissioner of the Indian Trade
quickly returned them. South Carolina officials worried about the cost of
employing "Negroes for so long a Voyage" and decided to "send some *Wineau*
Indians instead of them." Colonel John Barnwell agreed to supply "two Indian
Slaves," and the matter was resolved.

Consistent with English efforts and laws to limit the participation of
African slaves in the Indian trade, the officials' decision to favor Barnwell's
Indians over Gallard's "Negroes" seemed perfectly reasonable. But that con-
sistency and logic changed in the course of five short years. In the summer
of 1721, South Carolina officials once again addressed a request for slaves to
travel to Indian country and help construct a fort. Colonel Barnwell, this
time doing the requesting rather than the supplying, refused to employ
Indian slaves. He even turned away some Creek Indians who volunteered
their services. Instead, Barnwell hired two African slaves, "two sawyers."[1]
His decision marked an important transition in the early South from Indian

to African slave labor that took place without much fanfare. What had been considered "chargeable" and dangerous in 1716 had become acceptable and commonplace five years later. Barnwell's decision, which was in many ways personal and circumstantial, echoed the larger changes in South Carolina after the Yamasee War.

Almost all parties in the early South reevaluated and realigned their priorities after the war. Like the English, key Indian nations, in particular the Yamasees, Creeks, Cherokees, Choctaws, and Chickasaws, were also wrestling with the war's aftermath. All five groups were involved in bitter intertribal wars and equally contentious internal struggles. In the two decades following the end of the Yamasee War, the once-clear alliance between the Creeks and the Yamasees became tangled and bloody. An increasing number of Creek towns chose to support South Carolina and turned away from their close, and sometimes even familial, ties with the Yamasees. At the same time, the conflict between the Cherokees and the Creeks, which had begun with the murder of the Creek delegation at the Cherokee town of Tugaloo, had escalated. The violence of these raids and counter-raids reverberated across the early South. The Chickasaws, who needed support against the growing Choctaw–French attacks, folded their interests into the Cherokee side of the mounting Cherokee–Creek war. The Creeks in turn considered this Chickasaw–Cherokee alliance to be a threat. To counter the initiatives of their Cherokee rivals, the Creeks began opening paths to both the Choctaws and the French. And to complicate matters further, none of these alliances were clear-cut. Not all Cherokees agreed to war against the Creeks, not all Creeks agreed to welcome the French, not all Chickasaws sided with the English, and not all Choctaws allied with the Creeks. As native towns belonging to the same nation made different political and military decisions, the wider network dependent on these nodes became increasingly factionalized.

South Carolina agents and traders compelled to work through all these divisions made slow and uneven progress in Indian country in the 1720s and 1730s. The English had less success in reconstructing their previous alliances than they did in simply taking native lands that were abandoned and depopulated as a result of the Yamasee War. With powerful Yamasee groups no longer surrounding English holdings in St. Bartholomew's Parish and Port Royal, for example, South Carolina colonists seized the opportunity to expand. Plantation slavery was at the vanguard of that expansion. Though

African slavery had long been a fixture of South Carolina, the production of rice, a staple since the 1690s, grew drastically in the first decades of the eighteenth century—the 200,000 pounds of rice exported in the 1700s increased to over 16 million pounds by the 1730s. But for Governor James Glen to conclude confidently in 1761 that "the only commodity of consequence produced in South Carolina is rice," the enslaved African population that produced this staple also needed to expand.[2] And expand it did. Between 1710 and 1720, South Carolinians almost quadrupled the numbers of slaves imported into the colony. They also started buying slaves directly from Africa.[3] By 1730, there were 21,000 black slaves in the colony, more than twice the number of white persons living in South Carolina. In a letter back to his family in Switzerland, new arrival Samuel Dyssli commented, "Carolina looks more like a negro country than a country settled by white people."[4]

Florida officials also had to reshuffle their alliances and priorities. The Spanish experienced growth in the number of runaway slaves fleeing into San Agustín and Indian groups seeking Spanish friendship. After the Yamasee War, the boom of African slavery and the reshuffling of Indian alliances allowed the Spanish to establish new nodes and to reconnect old paths to both Creek and Yamasee towns—paths that had been closed since the 1704–1706 slaving raids had devastated the missions in Apalachee. For the first time in over a decade, Spanish influence was expanding in *la tierra adentro*. As Florida's connections grew, the Spanish struggled to find ways to preserve these new alliances without either overextending Florida's limited resources or leaving San Agustín exposed to English attacks. Navigating this contested landscape required the Spanish to reconsider *how* to make, sustain, and evaluate these expanding connections.

The English, Spanish, and Indian struggles to navigate the tenuous, static-ridden networks of the postwar South reveal some important differences. Florida officials, much like their South Carolina neighbors, wanted connections that would ensure safety and avoid conflict and confusion. But unlike their English counterparts, the Spanish continued favoring Indian alliances, rather than African slavery, as the way to maintain their hold over the region. The different approaches to reconstituting the networks disrupted by the Yamasee War generated competing visions of safety, control, and empire. These notions, however, were not forged in isolation. The dynamic ties between African slavery and Indian alliances were like two sides of the same coin; only when considered together can the contrasting conclusions that South Carolina officials reached about which type of slave was best, Indian or African, make any sense. Examining the information networks created in the aftermath of the Yamasee War not only centers the concomitant experiences of Indians and African slaves but also connects them to a larger struggle to produce and protect power in the early South.

The English adopted a more somber and cautious tone after the Yamasee War. Safety, not just from the immediate violence but also for the long-term development of the colony, became a growing concern.[5] South Carolinians began carefully monitoring Indian affairs, establishing a military cordon along the frontier, and creating English towns in key regions, all in an attempt to ensure better defense and control of the area between the Edisto and the Savannah River.[6] The colonists in postwar South Carolina were trying to rebuild more than old paths and towns; they were piecing together their shattered territorial ambitions and expectations. Painfully aware of the vulnerability of their colony, especially their land claims to the south of Charles Town, the English adopted a new networking strategy that recognized the need for more defendable nodes and more responsive ties.[7]

Between 1715 and 1730, South Carolina constructed over 30 forts. Fort Moore, for example, was built in 1715 to protect Savannah Town, a major trading outpost. Although built during the Yamasee War, Fort Moore proved to be an important node in English relations with Creeks, Cherokees, and Chickasaws—almost all traders and Indians moving from those Indian nations to Charles Town in the 1720s and 1730s passed through Fort Moore.[8] While the majority of these forts were garrisoned as temporary war measures, at least ten were built or refortified in the postwar period to establish clear hubs of English power in Indian country.[9] The development of several townships, and concurrent efforts to claim what the English considered the Carolina backcountry, soon followed.[10] More loudly than ever before, Charles Town officials began clamoring for the establishment of a permanent colony to serve as a buffer between themselves (their plantations, slaves, and sources of profit) and San Agustín.

In 1732, James Oglethorpe founded the colony of Georgia for that purpose. Though some South Carolina traders complained about Oglethorpe's efforts to regulate the Indian trade, many Charles Town officials and planters were quick to praise the "good Effects" of this colony, especially in monitoring the movement of African slaves. No longer was there "Shelter in vast Woods to the Southward" for runaways.[11] Captain Edward Massey, who had spent years of his military service patrolling the southern border of Carolina apprehending fugitive slaves, "told the Trustees that, since the Establishment of Georgia, the Price of Lands has greatly rais'd in Carolina, and the Plantations there increas'd."[12] After the Yamasee War, many South Carolinians measured their safety by how comfortable they felt investing in African slavery. Though Georgia eventually came to symbolize that promised security, in the fifteen years between the end of the Yamasee War and the colony's founding, both that investment and safety depended on the protection afforded by forts and soldiers. Strategically scattered throughout the region, these garrisons embodied the English strategy of expansion and protection.[13]

Fort King George was one such post. South Carolina built this garrison on the mouth of the Altamaha River, a region formerly controlled by Yamasees. Fort King George was actually located on the southernmost edge of this region recently acquired by the bloody war—clearly the English had no intention to tiptoe where they believed they had earned the right to tread.[14] Completed in 1721, this garrison had the dual purpose of monitoring "the Southward" of Carolina and curbing the influence of French and Spanish Indian traders, who, since the Yamasee War, had been making inroads into Creek towns.[15] Colonel John Barnwell, known as Tuscarora Jack for his involvement in the Tuscarora War, oversaw the construction of the garrison. This three-story wooden structure watched over the waters of the Altamaha, St. Simons Island (to the east), and the vast marshes that seemed to engulf the garrison.[16] Barnwell, though no stranger to this particular area, was "perplexed" by the large cypress swamps that extended for miles.[17] Five years after Barnwell had reconnoitered the area in search of an elusive and hostile Yamasee faction, he found the area nearly unrecognizable. He detected some lingering traces of Indian presence, but the "Indian field [had] gown [sic] up with Small Bushes," and he could not find any Indian towns or their residents. Whether he knew it or not, Barnwell was staring directly at the devastating effects of the Yamasee War.

Warfare had pushed Indian groups farther south and west. Fort King George was remote from both Charles Town *and* most Indian towns. Although this isolation posed a problem for supplying the fort, it did not otherwise concern Barnwell, whose distrust and disgust for his own company was only rivaled by his contempt for Indians. By 1721, the fifty-one-year-old

Barnwell had served South Carolina in a variety of gubernatorial and military roles. From deputy surveyor to commissioner of Indian affairs, Barnwell's jobs had kept him well connected to Indian matters. In 1711, he helped establish the town of Beaufort, near Port Royal, and had developed close connections to the Yamasees. That same year, as Barnwell led a regiment during the Tuscarora War, he commended the bravery and loyalty of his Yamasee allies. Four years later, Barnwell would take back all his praise. During the Yamasee War, Barnwell led a series of attacks against Indians he had once considered loyal. His experiences during the Tuscarora and Yamasee Wars left him mistrustful of Indians, a feeling that was only exacerbated when the six Creeks hired to guide the English down to the location of the future Fort King George quickly abandoned the expedition.[18] Flustered by their departure, Barnwell deemed it indicative of the inconsistent and unpredictable nature of Indians.

The Creek guides, however, interpreted the events differently. Their decision to leave Barnwell and his men behind had more to do with the South Carolinians' nature than with their own. The colonel and his men, a disorderly and drunken group, had done little to recommend themselves and had provided no assurance that this fort would, in fact, materialize. The Creeks probably decided that it was not worth their time and effort to aid this ill-advised project.[19] Barnwell eventually found two Indians, one Tuscarora and one Creek, who agreed to help the English. As the construction of the fort got underway, another group of Creek Indians approached Barnwell and offered their help. These Creeks, now convinced that South Carolina truly intended to build an outpost in the region, wanted to gain better access to the commodities that would soon be traded from Fort King George. But Barnwell was skeptical. He did not trust the Creeks' intentions and, after some deliberation, the colonel declined any further Indian involvement in the project.

Barnwell's decision angered the soldiers at the dangerously understaffed garrison and shocked members of the House of Commons, who had been trying, with limited success, to court and secure trading partnerships with the Creeks.[20] When asked to explain his dismissal of Indian aid, Barnwell responded that he "did not much Care, that they [Tuscarora] and the Creeks Should be much more acquainted then they are."[21] While he wanted to open paths to the Creeks, Barnwell believed that it was not in South Carolina's interest to have those connections depend on inter-Indian relations. The colonel insisted that if Indians were going to forge alliances that involved

South Carolina, those accords needed be made through the English. South Carolina had to monitor or, preferably still, dictate the terms of those "acquaintances." The whole point of Fort King George was to establish English influence over the region, not foster intertribal communication.

Barnwell's decision reflected a larger change in *how* the English approached Indian affairs in the aftermath of the Yamasee War. In the 1720s, as English traders struggled to rebuild the extensive commercial connections that had crumbled as a result of the fighting, South Carolina officials envisioned a different type of network based on talk, not trade. To establish this new type of connection, the House of Commons hired two veterans of the Yamasee War, Captain Tobias Fitch and Colonel George Chicken. Fitch traveled to both Lower and Upper Creek towns and, though he had some understanding of Indian affairs, he was younger, more impatient, and less experienced than Chicken, who had participated for decades in South Carolina's Indian trade and had already served as a delegate to the Cherokee during the Yamasee War. Before departing Charles Town in 1725, both Fitch and Chicken received instructions to establish "straight paths" and "good communication" with the Creeks and Cherokees. The directions were simple enough, but neither delegate was sure *how* to accomplish this new task.[22]

At first, both men floundered. Even Chicken, who was dealing with familiar peoples and places, struggled with this new type of network. After traveling through several Cherokee towns without much success, Chicken convened a council of "the whole [Cherokee] Nation" and appointed a "King." The colonel "informed them [Cherokee] that Crow was their King and made by them and Approved off by the English, that [he] Expected they would look upon him as such, otherwise they would be no people."[23] Chicken hoped that by designating one Cherokee leader as king, he could streamline and regulate the talk between South Carolina and the Cherokees. But King Crow did not possess any tangible authority; he could not properly represent the multiple and at times conflicting interests of the Cherokees. Chicken was the first to concede that King Crow was "more under the Comands of his Subjects than they are under him."[24]

Fitch faced an equally divided Creek country. The English had previously relied on Brims, the mico or chief of Coweta, to establish "straight paths" between Charles Town and the leading Creek towns, but Brims was getting older, and his influence was fading. Fitch's efforts to improve communication with the Creeks exposed the growing conflicts between Upper and Lower Creek towns. Fitch realized that the Creeks were split on many important issues. There was no unified Creek policy for aiding the refugee Yamasee groups; for responding to Cherokee threats; or even for balancing the new Creek alliances with the Spanish, French, and Choctaws.[25] Despite Creeks' and Cherokees' lack of receptivity to South Carolina's call for "good communication," Fitch and Chicken maintained their message and tone. After the Yamasee War, the English entered Indian country to dictate, not negotiate, the terms of exchange.[26]

As the most southern node in the new English network, Fort King George was to give South Carolina a way to control the strength and nature of some of its most strategic connections.[27] Colonel Barnwell had already chosen to limit Creek involvement in the building of the garrison. Barnwell saw no point in rewarding Indians who were not inclined to take their talk or trade directly, exclusively, or even readily to the English.[28] Instead Barnwell hired two African slaves to finish construction of Fort King George, showing his preference for a labor force he felt was easier to control.[29]

Slavery was a not uncommon feature of South Carolina's backcountry. Despite the regulations against and penalties for using African slaves in Indian country, many traders took their slaves with them, using them as packhorse-men, guides, guards, and even as interpreters.[30] Colonel Chicken remarked on both the frequency with which he saw traders bring African slaves into Cherokee towns and the problems that subsequently arose. Chicken detailed how "the Slav's that are now come up talk good English as well as the Cherokee language[,] and I am Afraid too often tell falsities to the Indians which they are very apt to believe, they being so much among the English."[31] The colonel fretted about the repercussions of Indian–African communication, which was difficult for the English to understand or police.

Captain Fitch faced a similar predicament in Creek towns, where he also witnessed the ability of African slaves to interfere with Creek–South Carolina relations. He became intent on regulating the mobility and opportunities of black men and women in Creek towns.[32] The amount of time, energy, and pages in Fitch's short journal devoted to the apprehension and control of what appear to be a small number of African slaves in Indian country at first seems surprising, even distracting from the "straight paths" Fitch supposedly needed to establish with the Creeks.[33] But for Fitch, as for Colonel Barnwell, these two goals were related. The efforts to regulate the mobility of African slaves and the attempts to establish more direct communication and access to Indian towns were complementary. English networks, supported and operated through Indian paths, were now also intended to protect African slavery.

Arthur Middleton, South Carolina's governor, also viewed these two goals as connected. Arguing that, without "Guarding our Southern Frontiers," slaves could readily flee from their plantations and, even worse, could turn "against us, to Rob and Plunder us," Middleton considered the outposts erected in Indian country and the protection of African slavery as intertwined. Without Fort King George or other garrisons, South Carolina's most important source of wealth could also become its most obvious vulnerability.[34]

For close to three decades, San Agustín officials had offered freedom to all runaway slaves who reached San Agustín and converted to Catholicism—though the religious clause was eventually dropped from the law.[35] San Agustín officials did not, however, automatically free every slave who reached the presidio's gates. Some slaves were enslaved again and others hovered in limbo. Antonio de Benavides, governor of Florida from 1718 to 1734, supported this ambivalent approach. During his first years in office, he suggested forgoing any official policy. He proposed that San Agustín officials "make resolutions that his Majesty considered most beneficial to the nature of each case, and to the circumstances in which it [the arrival of the slaves] occurred."[36] Benavides insisted that, by treating runaway slaves on a case-by-case basis, the Spanish could better accommodate the changing circumstances.

Benavides's reasoning began to change in the mid-1720s. Florida officials had a hard time ignoring the emphasis that South Carolinians placed on their African slaves and an even harder time pushing aside the new waves of fugitives who arrived in San Agustín seeking freedom. In this environment, Benavides began advocating for a more coherent and welcoming policy regarding fugitives. San Agustín officials, like their English counterparts, developed new strategies for protecting the colony, its allies, and its connections. Tired of South Carolina's advances into Spanish lands and particularly enraged by English-sponsored attacks on Indians allied with Florida, Benavides decided in 1724 to take action against South Carolina.[37] Fort King George offered him the perfect target.

In the first week of February 1724, and much to the surprise of the English soldiers manning Fort King George, a Spanish diplomatic party marched undetected to the very entrance of the garrison.[38] Don Juan Mexía, Don

Juan de Ayala, Juan de Sandoval, Don Josef Rodríguez Menéndez, Don Alonzo de Avila Saavedra, and Don Francisco Menéndez Marqués reached the shadow of the fort's gates before the English apprehended them.[39] As Captain Edward Massey, the second commander of the fort, had sarcastically noted, Fort King George was so "incapable of defence" and so incapable of monitoring "any part of its trade [that] it might as usefully have been place[d] in Japan."[40] Once within the fort, the Spanish delegation made three demands: The English must dismantle the garrison; remove any and all English presence from Florida territory; and, more important, establish a clear boundary between South Carolina and Florida. With no sense of what they should do or say in response, the soldiers of Fort King George hurriedly sent the Spanish delegation to Charles Town.

Governor Francis Nicholson graciously received the Spanish delegation and, just as graciously, refused to address any of their demands. Nicholson had a long career in the North American colonies before becoming South Carolina's first royal governor. He had served as lieutenant-governor of New York, captain general of Virginia, and governor of Nova Scotia. A decorated military officer, Nicholson focused on developing South Carolina's military defenses.[41] He understood the strategic position of Fort King George and feared that any agreement he reached with the Spanish, however beneficial this treaty might prove to South Carolina in the short term, could potentially curtail future English expansion in the area. Nicholson dismissed all three Spanish demands, explaining that he lacked permission to negotiate on such issues. But in the spirit of peace and "good communication," the English governor vowed to continue diplomatic talks with Florida.

It was unclear, however, what those talks would be about. Florida wanted a border; South Carolina refused to discuss the issue. Governor Benavides wanted Fort King George dismantled; Nicholson argued that the removal of the fort was not an option. South Carolina and Florida could only agree to disagree. The diplomatic talks could have ended there, but Nicholson used Fort King George as an excuse to demand an explanation, if not reparations, for what he considered Florida's most grievous offense: refusing to return the colony's fugitive slaves. In his letter to Benavides, Nicholson expressed the following:

> [I was] much surprised at the treatment given to Capt. Watson when I sent him in a Publik [sic] capacity, to make a Demand of some

slaves that run from this Government and that not long since that Cherekeeleechee with a party came into this settlement, killed some of our People and carried a Negro Slave, which he presented to Your Excellency and likewise that some of our runaways from Fort King George and other places are now Entertained at San Agustín therefore I hope and Expect your Excellency will cause all those people to be Sent hither by Sea, or Secured till wee can send for them.[42]

Nicholson accused the Spanish governor of both "entertaining" slaves and supporting notorious Yamasee chiefs, like Cherekeeleechee, who had threatened South Carolina. After demanding the return of these runaway slaves, the governor presented the Spanish diplomats with "a paper with the names of seven slaves who have fled said government and also [the names] of their masters who demand their return."[43]

Menéndez Marqués, who had led the Spanish party, found himself suddenly on the defensive. Instructed to negotiate the fate of a garrison on the Altamaha River, he was now pressed to account for Florida's slave policy. Menéndez Marqués quickly turned the tables on the governor. Instead of addressing the issue of the runaway slaves, the Spanish delegates rallied against what they considered to be the most grievous offense committed by South Carolina: inciting Indians against Florida colonists and native allies, especially the Yamasees, who had relocated near San Agustín after the Yamasee War. Menéndez Marqués recalled how "in that same council," in which the fate of the fugitive slaves was addressed, "we discussed the hostilities by Uchises [Creeks] Indians and others who take actions against this [Spanish] jurisdictions carrying out English goals."[44] The more Nicholson clamored for the return of fugitive slaves, the more Menéndez Marqués accused South Carolina of raiding Indians allied with or living close to Florida.

The lively discussion about fugitive slaves and Yamasee Indians relegated the issue of Fort King George to the background.[45] Yamasees and runaways became the centerpiece of the negotiations, providing insight into the most fundamental needs of each colony. Fort or no fort, Florida wanted the English to stop harassing its Indian allies, in particular, the Yamasees. The Spanish knew that they needed to curb English incursions if they were to maintain their new inroads into Creek and Apalachicola towns.[46] South Carolina insisted on the return of runaway slaves above all else. For them, the struggle over Fort King George exposed a new type of network that protected African slavery by expanding the English hold over the region and, in turn, protected English interests by expanding African slavery.[47] Nicholson and Menéndez Marqués were not merely speaking past each other, seeing who could shout louder about what mattered to them most. They understood that their priorities were bound together.

In a surprising turn, Nicholson conceded first. The governor had probably run out of money, patience, or both after hosting the Spanish delegation for several weeks at his own expense. In 1724, Nicholson vowed to issue "clear orders . . . so that no damage whatsoever would befall this [San Agustín] presidio" or Spanish Indians.[48] He never explained his reasoning, but the governor had apparently come to realize that only by stopping or, at the very least, pledging to stop the attacks against Spanish holdings and Indians would Florida officials return the runaway slaves. Menéndez Marqués and the other delegates were pleased. The South Carolina governor had vowed to respect Spanish–Indian alliances and, in the process, had inadvertently shown the Spanish delegates a way to enforce South Carolina's promises. In their runaway slave policy, the Spanish had found a way to assert some influence over the expanding English colony.

In September 1725, with South Carolina showing no signs of abandoning Fort King George, Governor Benavides sent a second delegation to Charles Town. Menéndez Marqués once again led the diplomatic party and this time Joseph Primo de Rivera was with him. Rivera had conducted a detailed survey of the Yamasees who had relocated closer to San Agustín after the Yamasee War. Rivera had seen firsthand the devastation that the Yamasees had endured and the threats they continued to face. Rivera also knew that there was an even larger number of Yamasees who had relocated away from San Agustín, in Apalachee and Apalachicola towns. The Yamasee–Creek connection was key for the Spanish, who were endeavoring to keep the paths to Apalachicola open. For Rivera, as for most Spanish officials, keeping the Yamasees safe seemed like a vital first step.

The instructions that Menéndez Marqués and Rivera received before heading to Charles Town were familiar. Governor Benavides wanted the delegates to demand the destruction of Fort King George and establishment of a clear boundary between the colonies; however, there was one important addition. Benavides instructed the second delegation to use Florida's runaway slave policy as leverage during the negotiations. He gave orders to Menéndez Marqués and Rivera to spread word of San Agustín's welcoming slave policies while in Charles Town. In so doing, the Spanish governor sought to challenge *how* South Carolina was building, expanding, and networking its power.[49] The insignificance of the fort itself became painfully clear when Fort King George was destroyed in a fire, but the debates continued and ended without a clear resolution.

Even after Fort King George burned to the ground and the English soldiers left the region, Florida officials continued welcoming and freeing runaway slaves. With Yamasee Indians still suffering from English attacks, the Spanish had no plans to return the runaway slaves to South Carolina.[50] In 1726, "fourteen Slaves [had] Runaway to St. Augustine"; in 1727, "six runaway Slaves and the rest Indians" seized two small boats and then proceeded to make their way to the Spanish. Governor Benavides even began paying Yamasee Indians to capture and bring South Carolina slaves to San Agustín. The Yamasees, who, in the 1680s had attacked Spanish missions and enslaved Spanish Indians, were now raiding South Carolina and were rewarded "for every live Negro they should bring."[51] Benavides further petitioned the Council of the Indies for permission to send Yamasees and former slaves to raid and intimidate South Carolina planters. The council thought that Benavides's plan, which included payment for every English scalp that this joint African–Yamasee force brought back, was too extreme.

Benavides continued to use runaway slaves to harass the English throughout his tenure as governor. In November 1733, he "published by beat of Drum round the town of St. Augustine (where many Negroes belonging to English Vessels . . . had the Opportunity of hearing it)" the edict "promising Liberty and Protection to all slaves that should desert."[52] Benavides's initiatives to broadcast Florida's fugitive slave policies seemed to have worked because the black population in Florida grew in the 1720s and 1730s. In 1735, Benavides was named governor of Venezuela and replaced by Francisco del Moral y Sánchez, but Florida continued to use runaway slaves to undermine English authority. In 1738, San Agustín allowed the construction of Fort Mose, an independent black township, on the outskirts of San Agustín. Mose had its own officials and militia, boasting "the largest concentration of blacks, both slave and free, in the Spanish borderlands."[53]

At least a few English traders were surprised to find that the Spanish policy toward freeing slaves applied even to them. The experience of Captain Caleb Davis offers a case in point. Davis was English, but he "had been a Trader several Years at St. Augustine, and lived there great Part of the Time."[54] He had a close relationship with the Spanish governor and, in addition to supplying the governor with food and goods, furnished Florida officials with information. Davis played both sides, keeping the English informed of Spanish movements, too, and was "said to be grown wealthy" from this double dealing.[55] Almost overnight, his wealth diminished when "no less than nineteen Negro Slaves, which he had in Carolina, run away from him lately all at once."[56] The slaves fled to San Agustín. Some had probably accompanied Davis to Florida in the past, but now, "under that strong Temptation of the Spaniards" committed to "making all free," the slaves had taken matters into their own hands. Davis quickly made his way to San Agustín, where "he found verified" his fears, "for he saw all his said Negroes." These men were now living as freemen; they "laughed at him" when he attempted to reclaim them.[57]

Davis was familiar with Spanish laws regarding fugitives but, having acquired the trust and, more important, the debts of Florida's governors and prominent officials, he assumed that his slaves would be returned upon his request.[58] They were not. As greatly appreciated as Davis's goods and news were, they were not more valuable than his African slaves. These nineteen "laughing" runaways not only confirmed Spanish determination to use runaways' own initiatives for Florida's gain but also made the English doubt their ability to control or even maintain their slave property with San Agustín so close. Commenting on the mounting danger that the Spanish slave policy posed for South Carolina, Lieutenant-Governor William Bull concluded, "their Negroes which were their chief support may in little time become their Enemies, if not their Masters."[59]

Indian groups, in particular Creeks and Cherokees, also began using the return of (or the refusal to return) fugitive slaves as bargaining chips in their relationships with South Carolina. When Augustus, the chief of Tama, abandoned his alliance with South Carolina, he decided that the best way to prove his newfound loyalty to the Spanish was to present them with the slaves he had captured from South Carolina.[60] Lieutenant Diego Peña received the chief's gift with open arms. Peña had led several Spanish expeditions to Apalachicola in the aftermath of the Yamasee War and had convinced the Creeks to extend their paths to San Agustín. Peña had seen Creeks pledge their support for Florida only to turn around and encourage French or English initiatives, but even so he believed Augustus was sincere. According to Peña, the cacique's decision to give these African slaves to the Spanish was a clear indication that Augustus and other Tama Indians would no longer ally with South Carolina because nothing could offend the English more than refusing to return runaway slaves. Peña's assessment proved right on point: The Tama cacique proved a loyal Spanish ally.[61]

It was not always so simple. The question of whether or not to return English slaves to their owners divided Creek leaders, although, or maybe because, all recognized the issue as central to their relation with South Carolina. In 1725, Brims, the mico of Coweta, had proven his friendship to South Carolina by helping Captain Fitch capture a "Spanish negro." But around the same time, Squire Mickeo, a contemporary of Brims and also a Lower Creek chief, not only refused to return a slave to Captain Fitch but also "Imediately assisted him [the runaway slave] with Cunnue and provisions." Squire Mickeo had aided a "French slave" who had eluded English capture for some time. This "French slave" had traveled to Creek country from Fort Toulouse, and Fitch believed him to be dangerous. He had supposedly persuaded a Creek war party sent by the English to attack Yamasee strongholds in Florida to abandon their plans.[62] Captain Fitch, who was still on his expedition to establish "straight paths" between Charles Town and Creek towns, demanded that Squire Mickeo hand over the French slave. The Creek mico refused. Instead, he "Cutt the Rope [that bound the slave] and threw it into the fire . . . [and] Told the White men that they [Creeks] had as good Guns as they, and Could make as good use of them."[63] For the Creeks, and for Squire Mickeo in particular, runaways offered a new way both to challenge South Carolina and to assert Creek sovereignty.

Brims and Squire Mickeo adopted opposite strategies when it came to returning slaves to the English. Both micos understood, however, that their actions would resonate well beyond their council fires. In the last speech of his expedition, Captain Fitch voiced his displeasure with the Creeks. The Creeks had conceded to two of the most important requests by the English: They had finally agreed to attack Yamasee settlements, and they agreed to end their ongoing war with the Cherokees. But the issue of runaway slaves remained unresolved. Captain Fitch considered the Creeks undependable allies because they refused to return fugitive slaves to South Carolina consistently. The English expected their native allies to help enforce the parameters of plantation slavery. Fitch evaluated the Creeks' connection to Charles Town not only in terms of the inter-Indian paths the Creeks maintained or severed but also through their relation to African slaves.[64]

In a meeting with Captain Fitch, the Dog King, a principal of the Lower Creek town of Pallachocola, attempted to parlay English demand for African slaves into Indian terms. The Dog King told the English captain, "I have heard that the Chocktawes makes as good slaves as Negroes."[65] Comparing Choctaws to "negro slaves," the Dog King showcased an acute understanding of what the English valued and, more important, of *how* they articulated that value.[66] This meant that both Indians and English could have a conversation about slavery, but they could speak about radically different things. The comments of a 1730 Cherokee delegation in response to English complaints about Cherokee lack of assistance in apprehending runaway slaves is similarly telling. The Cherokee delegates explained, "this Small Rope which We shew you is all We have to bind our slaves with, and may be broken; but you have Iron Chains for yours. However if we catch your slaves, We shall bind them as We can."[67] Cherokee bonds of slavery were different than English ones. They would endeavor to "catch slaves" who fled, but only on Cherokee terms. In the 1670s, Sewees had used Spanish Florida as a point of reference from which to help the newly arrived English colonists distinguish friendly native groups from hostile ones; over fifty years later, Creeks and Cherokees used slavery in much the same way: to communicate to South Carolina their intentions and alliances.

The English had shown their hand. In their dealings with neighboring Indians as well as in their negotiations over Fort King George, they had slowly, but decidedly, placed their growing plantation economy at center stage. In the aftermath of the devastating Yamasee War, South Carolinians had managed their loss and disorientation by creating new networks that both recognized and promoted slavery's importance in fostering English dominion over the early South. But the protection, expansion, and even maintenance of slavery did not and could not occur in a vacuum. Spanish policies to welcome fugitive slaves; lackluster Creek and Cherokee commitment to return runaways; and, more important, the actions and struggles of Africans themselves deeply affected how the English could enforce their commitment to slavery. As South Carolina officials attempted to work through these limitations, they felt the constraints of relying on networks that supported other and at times conflicting interests.

In the 1720s, the view from San Agustín seemed better than it had in decades. The Yamasee War had reversed what seemed like an irreversible trend of Spanish decline. For the first time in forty years, the Spanish were welcoming Indian groups into their decrepit networks, receiving invitations into Indian country, and enjoying an increased presence in *la tierra adentro*. Indian leaders like Chislacaliche, mico of Sabacola Old Town, had come to San Agustín officials promising the friendship of their towns as well as the support of many other Indian towns along the Chattahoochee River.[68] San Agustín officials knew that they needed to protect their expanding connections or they would just as quickly retract.

Suddenly South Carolina and Florida's networking strategies seemed to mirror each other: Both European powers built nodes and established ties that prioritized safety, clarity, and control.[69] But a closer look at how the Spanish sought to extend their influence over the newly relocated Yamasee towns and to reestablish a presence in Apalachee and Apalachicola reveals that Florida and South Carolina took different approaches to their similar ambitions. The differences between Spanish and English networking strategies in the post–Yamasee War South speak to the complex legacies of this far-reaching conflict. Examining *how* San Agustín officials articulated and, more important, implemented their new priorities uncovers the continuing and dialogic relations between the English and the Spanish imperial projects in the region.

As South Carolinians built forts and opened "straight paths," San Agustín officials invested in individual Indian informers. Florida officials attempted to learn about developments in Apalachee and Apalachicola through the *nuevas* of Indians like Francisco Jospoque. Jospoque was an Apalachee Indian in his mid-thirties who had been placed in a position of power by the Spanish. His authority over the mission town of Nombre de Díos came from his connections to both San Agustín officials and the Franciscans, not his role in intra- or inter-Indian alliances. The Spanish had appointed Jospoque to his leadership role and, in return, he had a stake in protecting Spanish interests in the region.[70] In San Marcos de Apalachee, "Don Captain Jul., a Christian Indian of the Uchise Nation" served as an official messenger and informer, rewarded for both his "punctuality" and loyalty.[71] In other cases, the Spanish cultivated Indian leaders. Quilate, the cacique of Apalachee; Ysques, the cacique of Achito; Chislacaliche, of Coweta; and Chocate and Yahoulakee, the pro-Spanish leader of Coweta, had all promised that "if there was any news among the nations they would immediately reveal it" only to the Spanish.[72]

Several related patterns can be discerned from the experiences of the Spanish in dealing with these caciques. First, the Spanish began recruiting and increasingly relied on a specific type of informer. While Florida officials had a long tradition of accepting and heeding reports from a wide array of individuals, the Yamasee War had pushed them to reconsider *how* they acquired and maintained these many connections. The Spanish began preferring the regular and exclusive correspondence of select Indian leaders. Second, the Spanish expected more from their allies than they had in the past. Loyalty and information were the non-negotiable price these Indians paid to establish ties with Spanish nodes. Third, Spanish Indians received clear incentives, from coveted goods to appointments, to positions of power, in exchange for their information.[73] More than in previous decades, the Spanish understood and treated information as a commodity that could be purchased and then, they hoped, secured. But by investing in particular Indians, the Spanish became complicit in the information these Indian leaders provided. The more San Agustín officials rewarded particular informers, the more willing the Spanish were to believe their reports.[74]

One of the most prominent of these informants was Juan Ygnacio (sometimes spelled Ignacio). Born in 1703 in the town of Pocotalaca, Juan had made a name for himself as a reliable and efficient information gatherer.[75] Governor Manuel de Montiano bluntly declared that if Juan Ygnacio could not find the needed information, no one could. In the late 1730s, the Spanish governor sent Juan to spy on English activities.[76] Juan traveled through the open roads without a disguise, hoping for an encounter with the rumored enemy. It did not take long before he stumbled onto an English party. Juan approached the South Carolina traders and introduced himself as a Spanish fugitive. He explained that he had murdered another Indian and now needed protection from San Agustín officials. Juan then placed himself at the mercy of these traders, making the English feel in charge. As the Yamasee spy hired by Captain Antonio Matheos in 1686 had done, Juan had selected this false identity carefully and, according to his testimony, the traders proved easy to fool.

The English agreed to protect Juan, but in return, they wanted information about San Agustín. Juan, hired by Montiano to spy on South Carolina, now had to furnish the English with news about the Spanish. Colonel John Cochran, who was heading the English operations near San Simón Island, eagerly interrogated this supposed Indian fugitive. The English colonel began by inquiring after the military strength of the Spanish. At first, Juan responded coyly, claiming he knew little of military matters. But his ability to answer questions about the state of the San Agustín garrison seemed to betray him. Cochran was pleased and, believing he had stumbled upon a knowledgeable and unbiased informer, listened attentively to Juan's misleading report. Juan exaggerated the military capacity of Florida, overstating numbers for the armaments, equipment, and men in the Spanish garrison and hoping to intimidate the English colonel and his men. The Spanish spy was careful, however, not to overplay the strength of the Spanish lest his English audience grow suspicious.

As Juan described the presidio's might, he also revealed that the impressive forces at San Agustín were still waiting for the *situado* (the royal subsidies).[77] Juan depicted Florida as militarily strong but nonetheless dependent on outside support. This reference to the *situado* was brief, and it is unclear if the English took note of this particular detail. Indeed, Juan's comment seemed targeted more at Montiano than at Cochran. Juan was letting the Spanish governor know that he understood how Florida worked: The informer was privy to Spanish strengths as well as weaknesses.

After his brief meeting with Colonel Cochran, Juan moved through English lands without difficulty. Just like the cacica of Yspo in the 1670s or the Apalachicola Indians in the 1690s, Juan entered and exited English spaces without any complication. In the fifty years between Pamini, cacica of Yspo, and Juan's travels, South Carolinians had developed a more careful understanding of the South, exerted more control over the region, and forged alliances with powerful Indian nations like the Creek and Cherokee. But Juan's experience demonstrated the difficulty the English still had deciphering Indian loyalties and intentions. As easily as he had entered into English confidence, the Spanish spy left his trusting hosts behind. Before departing, Juan told Colonel Cochran he intended to go hunting and then fishing but would return in a couple of days. Announcing his arrival and explaining his departure, Juan Ygnacio was not a very subtle spy—nor did he need to be. His openness granted him access to the very information the San Agustín officials wanted him to acquire. Juan returned with reports that the English "not by day or by night do they cease their talks of [invading] Florida."[78]

No English sources found to date mention Juan Ygnacio. Colonel Cochran might not have wanted to record his interactions with a Spanish Indian, especially an Indian who disappeared from English control just as quickly as he had entered into it. South Carolina officials often bemoaned the threat posed by Indians like Juan and commented that "the greatest

Danger we imagine ourselves exposed to in this Colony, may be from such Indians as are in the Spanish interest; whom it is pretty hard to distinguish from our Friends."[79] There is also the possibility that Colonel Cochran never realized Juan's deception and simply chose not to record his brief interaction with a random Uchise Indian. But perhaps it was Juan who was lying. Maybe his success with the English was so impeccable because, in fact, it had never taken place; perhaps Juan was simply telling Governor Montiano what he wanted to hear. The evidence does not fully support either possibility, but it does reveal the limitations of the new type of communication networks developed by the Spanish. With only a handful of trusted informers in their employ, San Agustín officials had few ways of corroborating Juan's account and thus tended to give credence to news that supported Florida's existing concerns and fears.[80]

In 1738, Juan served as the main Indian guide for Alonso Márquez del Toro's expedition. Toro led a well-supplied diplomatic mission that was part of a joint Florida–Cuba endeavor to establish a trading outpost in San Marcos, in Apalachee. The Spanish, eager to secure their alliances with the Creeks, decided to use Juan's expertise to help Toro negotiate the region's complex relations. Though instructed to guide the Spanish to the main Creek towns, Juan carefully selected the places Toro visited.[81] Since Juan was Uchise and had close kin and linguistic connections to the Lower Creeks, he led Toro through paths that reinforced the importance of Coweta, a leading Lower Creek town. As a guide and informer, Juan constantly made choices, prioritizing certain types of information over others. But by simply trusting Juan, the information he brought, and the networks he traveled, Spanish officials made Juan Ygnacio's preferences seem natural.[82]

Apalachicola and Apalachee Indians viewed Juan's selections differently. The Tallapoosa Indians were furious that Juan had not come among their towns to deliver the Spanish talk or Toro's goods. The Tallapoosas had wanted to establish clear connections with the Spanish, but Juan had gone to "Cowetas and to the Uchieses" instead. The Tallapoosas' complaints further emphasized the power of this informer. Because Juan had supposedly traveled to the towns that the Spanish considered the most important, his visit (or lack thereof) served as a litmus test of how San Agustín valued each Indian group or town. The Tallapoosas interpreted Juan's route, which did not go through their towns, to imply that San Agustín officials had little regard for the Tallapoosas.

Tickhonabe, a Tallapoosa chief, also expressed frustration with *how* the had Spanish had recently reconstituted their information networks. Tickhonabe had close contact with the Spanish since the Yamasee War. He had helped open paths between Pensacola and Lower Creek towns. In 1717, he had even traveled to México City, where he met with the viceroy, the Marquis de Valero. But by the 1720s, Tickhonabe had grown disenchanted with the poor quality and limited number of Spanish goods that filtered into his town. He began siding with Upper Creeks and favored an alliance with South Carolina. In 1738, he appeared once again before Spanish officials seeking friendship and, more important, goods.[83] Tickhonabe praised the virtues of the decentralized connections of the past. The Tallapoosa chief recalled a time when he could have forged alliances with multiple European powers without jeopardizing his relations with any particular group. Tickhonabe admitted that "he was allies with the French . . . but that [alliance] did not deprive him of having communication with the Spanish."[84] The Spanish governor disagreed with that assessment. Friendship with the French implied no connection with San Agustín. But it had been Juan Ygnacio, not Montiano, who had excluded the Tallapoosa from Toro's journey.

Juan's choices, though rooted in intra-Indian relations, reflected larger changes to Florida's communication network. Like Juan, Spanish officials were making choices about the paths that would allow "straight talk," the Indian groups that would sustain an exclusive partnership with Florida, and the individual informers that would help forge these strong ties.[85] The networks created after the Yamasee War had given the Spanish access to more Indian allies and nodes, but now Florida officials needed to decide *how* to maintain and profit from these connections. In 1738, Governor Juan Francisco Güemes Horcasitas of Cuba described the "seven conditions" required for a Spanish communication network to thrive in Florida. Of the seven criteria, two required the Indians who corresponded with the Spanish to ban "English or other foreigners in their pueblos." Three were concerned with establishing a "perfect friendship and obedience" between Spanish and Indian nodes. And the remaining two outlined the consequences for any Indian who refused the aforementioned terms.[86]

The Spanish clearly wanted a network in which loyalty and exclusivity were prerequisites for formalizing connections. Güemes Horcasitas argued that these clear and strong ties with Indian allies would not only afford the Spanish better control over the region but would also supply Florida with more reliable and regular information. He was partly right. A network built on trustworthy nodes would provide Florida officials with more dependable alliances and news. But by favoring exclusive connections to loyal Indians, the Spanish were confined to the biases of their allies. San Agustín officials could better monitor the sources of their information, but the type and variety of news they received became increasingly constricted. As Florida officials privileged a specific type of Indian spy, they began to bias a specific type of news. In other words, these reliable reports were not always accurate and were usually far from complete.

∽

South Carolina's and Florida's new networking strategies came to a head when England and Spain went to war in 1739. This conflict over territorial claims and shipping rights, which much later became known as the War of Jenkins' Ear, also tested South Carolina–Georgia relations. The Walpole government in England pushed for an empire of commerce and, at least initially, wanted trade rather than war with the Spanish colonies. In contrast, the Patriot opposition, which had funded a substantial part of Oglethorpe's colonial venture in Georgia, rallied for war. These clashing political views created important tensions within and between the colonists of South Carolina and Georgia.[87]

Oglethorpe, an experienced military officer, rallied a sizable force against San Agustín. Oglethorpe was determined to succeed where the previous English expedition of 1702 had failed.[88] In January 1740, he traveled to Charles Town to request men and weaponry for his attack. South Carolina officials debated Oglethorpe's plan at length, and Governor William Bull seemed to drag his feet on the matter. South Carolina eventually agreed to supply the expedition, and Oglethorpe was, at first, "well satisfied with his reception in Carolina, and the Aid he was assured."[89] But when the siege failed, Oglethorpe no longer seemed "satisfied" with South Carolina, and blamed the expedition's failure on the delayed and parsimonious aid from Charles Town. South Carolinians retaliated with their own accusations.[90] The mounting dispute between South Carolina and Georgia hinted at the different English political interests and competing imperial strategies at play in the early South.

Florida's governor, Manuel de Montiano, felt helpless as English forces attacked and blockaded Florida once again. Montiano was convinced that this bout of English aggression would prove San Agustín's last. The Spanish were weak, and their pleas for additional weaponry, soldiers, or any type of supplies had fallen on deaf ears. Making matters worse, in the early days of the siege English soldiers had intercepted one of Montiano's most candid letters detailing the frail state of the Spanish defenses. With the communication channels to *la tierra adentro* and Cuba closed, Montiano believed that San Agustín had little hope for survival.[91]

Before Oglethorpe attacked, Montiano had gathered information about the coming English forces. The Spanish governor had attempted "to procure by every possible means a knowledge of the condition of the new settlements of Port Royal and Purisburg." Montiano wanted to know "if they [the English] have had any reinforcement of troops, or if any maritime forces have arrived, and of what character they are." As he tried to collect "the most minute accounts . . . from the most faithful and careful channels" to send back to Spain, the governor commented on the difficulty of assessing the situation. "I assure you," concluded Montiano, "that of all the difficulties which surround one here, the greatest is the want of an intelligent person for these intrigues."[92] Montiano needed men; weapons; and, above all else, information to understand "the difficulties which surround" San Agustín. But not any piece of news would suffice. The governor's comments about both the value of news and "the want of an intelligent person for these intrigues" echoed the more selective Spanish approach to information and informers in the 1730s.[93]

Montiano endeavored to protect the "faithful and careful channels" of information and even tried to "establish the communication with Apalache" by constructing two forts: Fort Pupo and Fort Picolata. "The said forts Picalata and Pupo," explained Florida's governor, "were erected for the sole purpose of defending and sheltering the couriers who went to & came from Apalache from the continual attacks of the Indians friendly to the English."[94] Couriers needed protection not only because they suffered from "continual attacks" but also because open (as well as regular and reliable) communication with Apalachee served as Montiano's only means of communication with other Spanish colonies. These "careful channels" were San Agustín's last line of defense against the English.[95] Information would give the comparatively weaker Spanish colony an advantage over the sizable English enemy—or so Montiano hoped.

Oglethorpe understood that to defeat San Agustín, he needed to isolate the garrison and sever its communication networks. His military efforts focused on sieging the Spanish garrison, blockading the port, and capturing Forts Pupo and Picolata (see Figure 7.1). In the first days of the war, the English strategy worked flawlessly. A delighted Oglethorpe detailed how, in the chaos of war, "the Spanish at San Francisco de Pupo . . . seeing some of our [English] Indians took them for Spanish Indians" and opened the fort's gates.[96] Fort Pupo, designed to protect Spanish informers, had welcomed the enemy. "The English have occupied the whole river of St John with their vessels," lamented Montiano, "and . . . their navigation on the southern part tends to embarrass the communication with Apalache, to render the Uchees friendly to them, and to make captive any courier who may go or come."[97] The English controlled the region, constricting the information that moved in and out of San Agustín and limiting the alliances that the Spanish could establish. "I cannot express to you the confusion of this place," Montiano complained, "here the only defence is its fortress, and all the rest is open country."

Montiano even sent his most reliable Indian informer, Juan Ygnacio, to "learn the state and condition of the citizens of those colonies, as well as their ideas and intentions." But "the said Juan Ignacio assured me he could not accomplish that object."[98] Without forts or allies, without safe channels of communication, and without the reliable Juan, the Spanish were faced with the daunting task of controlling the "open country." Seeing his "safe channels" destroyed, Montiano decided that receiving and sending no news was safer than having Spanish information intercepted by the enemy. He severed all lines of communication and simply hoped that word about Florida's predicament had reached Cuba. Montiano found some relief when he confiscated a copy of the *South Carolina Gazette*. After reading the brief paper, the governor happily concluded that the English, though better supplied, "had not the least knowledge of what was going on, as may be seen by their Gazette." Montiano realized that he was not the only one struggling to make sense of "what was going on."[99]

Information played an important, albeit different, role for Oglethorpe's invading forces. The English governor, much like his Spanish counterpart, struggled to establish "safe channels" to communicate. He attempted to forge connections with Apalachee and also suffered setbacks when his correspondence was intercepted.[100] But if the Spanish viewed information as an

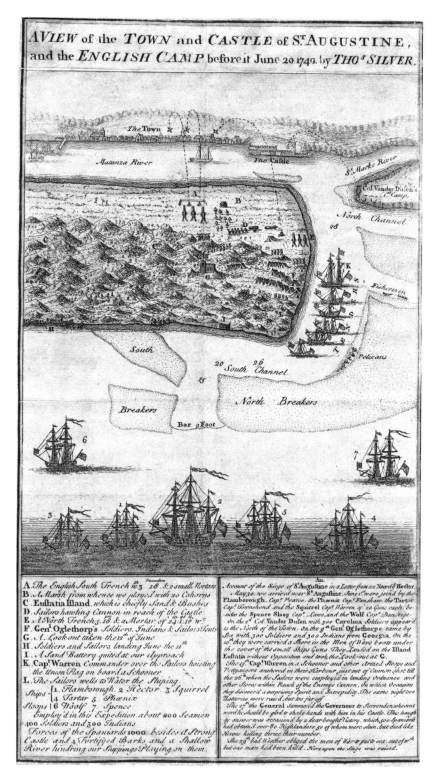

FIGURE 7.1. Oglethorpe's attack on San Agustín.
("A View of the Town and Castle of St. Augustine, and the English Camp before It,
June 20, 1740" by Thos. Silver. Originally published in *Gentleman's Magazine*, London,
1740. Photo courtesy Hargrett Rare Book and Manuscript Library, Georgia.)

end unto itself, the English considered it only a means. Information was necessary to conquer the Spanish and to destroy hostile Indian groups, but information alone was not sufficient for the task.[101] Unlike the correspondence of Montiano, which was replete with references to acquiring, spreading, and retaining news, Oglethorpe discussed the value and importance of information only tangentially during the 1739 siege.[102]

Instead, Oglethorpe concerned himself with slavery and the reclaiming of fugitive slaves.[103] Montiano anticipated as much and had evacuated Fort Mose before the English forces reached San Agustín. The Spanish did not want members of this booming free black community to be captured and enslaved again. During the 1739 siege, the Fort Mose militia fiercely defended San Agustín, knowing that, if Oglethorpe breached the Spanish presidio, their newly secured freedom would be taken away. Employing black soldiers, scouts, and officers throughout the conflict, Montiano praised their valor and initiative.[104] In 1742, when Florida officials launched retaliatory raids against the English, a former South Carolina slave used his knowledge of the land and language to trick a small English regiment into disembarking from their piraguas. When the soldiers were close to the shore, this unnamed black man led a violent attack against them. The struggles and stories of these black men and women challenged, in a very fundamental way, *how* the English chose to expand, control, and network the South.[105]

In the end, Governor Oglethorpe, much like Colonel Moore thirty-seven years earlier, could not take the Spanish presidio.[106] After a two-week blockade, the English forces had drained their supplies and, fearing the coming hurricane season, withdrew. Spanish Florida had managed to survive yet another English invasion. Montiano wasted no time in trying to reconnect the severed communication networks and, with the help of Juan Ygnacio, "t[ook] care to send immediately an express to the Uchees to give them information of all that they may separate themselves from the friendship and service of the English, and to offer to regale them if they chose to come and visit me." The Spanish hoped to remedy the damage caused by the English attack by, once again, reestablishing these Indian alliances.[107] As Oglethorpe's forces departed, Juan Ygnacio went back to work.

CONCLUSION

~

THIS BOOK is about European, Indian, and African men and women, and how they communicated among themselves and with one another. At its core, *Informed Power: Communication in the Early South* tells a human story. Its protagonists are many and varied: Etowah Indians struggling to maintain their political autonomy in the late fourteenth century; Timucua chiefs negotiating with Franciscan friars over the extent of Catholic missions in the early seventeenth century; English traders and agents traveling to Creek towns in the 1690s; and runaway African slaves fleeing to San Agustín in the 1730s, among many others. The daily interactions among the very different groups and individuals in the early South show the nexus of information and power in action.

The spread and acquisition of news was not simply a matter of messages reaching the intended recipients but rather a contested process inextricably tied to the region's social and geopolitical contexts. Like a prism, communication helps refract a common experience and need into a broad spectrum, allowing the individuals and methods necessary for information exchange to be both differentiated and compared. Studying how people communicated thus offers a new framework for the history of the early South.

In his second official letter to King Charles V, dated October 30, 1520, Hernán Cortés asked for forgiveness. The conquistador explained that his account of México did not include "every detail of these lands and new realms" because that would require him "to continue almost forever." Cortés begged "Your Highness' pardon if I do not render as long an account as I should. Neither my natural aptitudes nor the conditions in which I find myself favor me in the task." These "conditions," not the least of which was the bloody invasion of the Aztec capital Tenochtitlan, interfered with his ability to give a more correct account. As he later explained in his fourth letter, "the many new things which we have learnt from these discoveries make it necessary that for new circumstances there be new considerations and decisions."[1]

Always careful of how he presented himself, Cortés was trying to justify the inaccuracies and incompleteness of his accounts. His excuses also spoke, however, to the arduous process of acquiring and interpreting new information. He needed "new considerations and decisions," new logics and processes, to understand the complicated and ever-changing milieu of New Spain. Because to truly grapple with the "new discoveries" and realities in the emerging colonial world, Indians as well as Spaniards, Africans, and later French and English colonists needed to reevaluate how they engaged with and conceived of even the most basic of processes, including acquiring and spreading information.

Communication exchange in the early South was rarely a linear, finite process. Though an emphasis on networks often has positive undertones, implying connectivity, reach, and flexibility, information spread in the early South also shows the limits and challenges to colonial authority. Consider, for example, the experiences of a group of Franciscans who sailed in 1697 from Cuba to Florida to reestablish missions among the Calusa Indians. This native group, who lived on the southwest tip of Florida and had resisted the intermittent waves of Spanish colonialism since the 1510s, would also foil the efforts of this late seventeenth-century expedition. The Calusas offered no help to the Franciscans who were trying to build new missions and plant crops; instead they "asked why they had not brought blacks who dig with the hoes."[2] This simple rebuttal, which perhaps alluded to the Calusas' knowledge of Cuba's slave plantation economy or maybe hinted at the Calusas' awareness of a black labor regime in South Carolina, showed not only the far-reaching networks this native group had developed but also the subversive power that those connections could have on European colonial projects. Tracing such stories and histories reveals an early South defined not by borders but by fluidity and by the often-failed struggles to regulate that fluidity

Indian networks offer the best way to reconstruct the interconnections of the colonial world without flattening its many complexities. As corridors of interregional trade and communication, Indian paths connected the region in ways that were deeply local and just as deeply contested. Indian chiefs performed a variety of rituals that allowed them to obtain news, keep their communities apprised of the latest political and military developments, and establish balance between This World and the Upper World.[3] But by the time Europeans and Africans arrived in the early sixteenth century, Indian information networks were in flux. The far-reaching and relatively centralized paths that had once sustained powerful chiefdoms like Cahokia had gradually and unevenly given way to more numerous but less extensive connections. These fragmented communication networks reflected the growing regional variation of native polities in the fifteenth- and sixteenth-century South as well as the increasingly violent conflicts that emerged within those polities.

European colonization and encroachment into *la tierra adentro* did not mark the end of these contested and asymmetrical connections. On the contrary, the importance of these dynamic native networks became all the more noticeable when Spanish, French, English, and African newcomers competed, with varying degrees of success, for using and influencing these connections. Only by accessing Indian networks and information could these European *adelantados* and colonists begin to understand who and what comprised La Florida—a process that proved neither easy nor fast. "We are still ignorant," admitted Garcilaso de la Vega, over seventy-five years after the first Spanish explorations of Florida, "as to whether or not it [Florida] is limited on the north by more lands or by the sea itself." Remedying that ignorance required initiative and, more important, Indian allies.[4]

After establishing a permanent base in San Agustín in 1565, the Spanish erected Franciscan missions in seventeenth-century Timucua, Guale, and Apalachee for improving their access to *la tierra adentro*. These missionary inroads into Indian country were intended to provide the Spanish with native land and labor by transforming potentially hostile groups into loyal allies and Catholic converts. But built on Indian towns, connected through Indian paths, and contingent on the goodwill of Indian caciques, Franciscan missions afforded Spanish officials access only to small nodes in otherwise Indian-controlled networks. As the Timucua Rebellion of 1656 made clear, native networks reached people and places beyond the grasp of San Agustín officials and Franciscan friars.

The English were one such people included in these extensive Indian networks. The Spanish first learned of English incursions in the area through native informers and networks. Exchanging guns, ammunition, and other European commodities for deerskins and, more important, Indian slaves, South Carolinians and their native allies, at first Westos and Savannahs and quickly thereafter Yamasees and Creeks, forged a different type of network throughout the early South. Built through the deerskin and Indian slave trade, these commercial connections proved expansive and lucrative but also highly volatile. By the 1710s, paths from Charles Town extended all the way to the Mississippi River; the English had both a reach and an influence that many in the early South—particularly the Spanish—found threatening.

The Yamasee War tested the limits and strengths of the different information networks that connected the early South. This conflict, which pitted the Yamasees and Lower Creeks against South Carolina, produced violent reverberations that echoed throughout the region. Spanish, French, and Africans as well as Catawbas, Cherokees, Iroquois, Choctaws, and Chickasaws all found themselves affected by and partaking in this war. Few found comfort, however, in the realization that their actions and decisions were actually interconnected.

In the wake of the Yamasee War, the different inhabitants of the early South had to do more than repair the paths damaged by the fighting and rebuild the nodes that had been abandoned or destroyed. They had to reconstitute and reconfigure their entire information networks. As Indians, Europeans, and Africans evaluated what connections to restore first and who to include, they revealed the bitter, competing, yet coexisting articulations of power that gave shape to the early South.

This narrative, woven through the lives of a diverse set of actors, a deep chronology, and from a multilingual source base, can be read as a stand-in for the historians' increasingly complex understanding of the tapestry of early America. But this communication story is not just complex and diverse for sake of being complex and diverse. Because simply including Timucuas, Creeks, Spaniards, Apalachees, enslaved Africans, French, and Yspos is not the same as arguing that these non-Anglo actors matter. What is new here (which is, after all, why we historians return to dusty archives and old documents) is the use of communication networks to both reconstruct and deconstruct what happened in the past, who had an impact on the development of the colonial world, and how those struggles unfolded.

To communicate and exchange information, different groups and individuals formed ties with one another. Through these connections, which were sometimes coveted and cultivated, and other times merely tolerated, people built networks that formed the basis for acquiring and transmitting local news in the colonial South before the advent of a more regularized mail system or printing press. Widespread information networks sustained by multiethnic, multilingual, and increasingly multiracial nodes emerge not as the creation of a historian eager to see a more inclusive and diverse past but as historical forces that bound and divided the early South.

The focus on human (as opposed to technological) approaches to communication reveals the importance of information networks neither controlled by European actors nor dependent on the circulation of printed and epistolary formats. These mostly oral information networks render visible the dynamic topology of the colonial world. Understanding how the early South worked requires understanding how people, all different types of people, communicated.

We supposedly live in the age of information, though that label has had traction for at least forty years.[5] With news channels increasingly congested, we are forced to wade through more reports than we can properly process, reconcile vastly conflicting accounts and details, and develop ways of interpreting and implementing policies from our imperfect communication sources. But the uneven and often awkward integration of competing stories that are in no way equal or balanced is a very old problem. To learn the latest, colonists in South Carolina needed to obtain a certain level of comfort with Indian informers and slave networks. Indian groups, like the Yamasees, had to construct networks that linked competing nodes, such as Scottish traders in Stuart's Town, San Agustín officials, and the newly coalescing Muskogean towns. Enslaved Africans had to work through inter-Indian connections and shifting European alliances to obtain news from beyond the rice plantations of South Carolina. Putting these multivalent nodes and ties in some semblance of order was as much a challenge then as it is one now.

∽

James Oglethorpe, governor of Georgia, was trying to improve Indian relations in western Georgia when some Indian traders on board a "Boat going to Fort Augusta" shared some disturbing news. They "told [him that] the Negroes in Carolina has raised up in Arms and killed about forty White People." Choosing caution over panic, Oglethorpe decided to travel away from Indian country to verify the Indian traders' information. As soon as he arrived at an English garrison, the governor found all the proof he needed: "thirty men [had] come from Purysburg t[o] Strengthen the Fort" and protect the province from further damage. The traders' reports were true. The slaves "in Carolina has raised up in Arms" and many renegades were possibly still roaming the countryside. Oglethorpe joined these "Purysburg" men and helped defend the fort, but the story of the Stono Rebellion that the governor chose to write down in his journal did not come from these terrified South Carolinians; rather, it came from an unnamed black man, probably a slave. This man told Oglethorpe,

> what was said of the Negroes Rising in Carolina was True and that they
> had marched to Stono Bridge . . . Burning of House[s] and Committing
> other Outrages, and that One hundred Planters who had assembled
> themselves together pursued . . . [the] Villains [who had] attempted to
> go home but were taken by the Planters who Cutt off their heads and set
> them up at every Mile Post they came to.[6]

The placing of rebels' heads "at every Mile Post" was undoubtedly meant to be a sign of white power and authority. Still, the fact that Oglethorpe had been trying to forge better relations with Indians when he received this information, first from Indian traders heading to Augusta and then from an enslaved African, reveals that the English, even with their grim and bloody mile markers, could not properly control the interconnected dependency required for spreading and acquiring information in the early South.

NOTES

~

AGI   Archivo General de Indias.

AHR   *American Historical Review.*

Banc.   Bancroft Library, University of California Berkeley.

Beinecke   Beinecke Rare Book and Manuscript Archive, Yale University, New Haven, Connecticut.

CO   Colonial Office, Public Record Office, London, England.

CRSG   *The Colonial Records of the State of Georgia,* Vols. 1–5, ed. Allen D. Candler (Atlanta, GA: Franklin Print. and Pub. Co., 1904–1916).

CSCHS   *Collections of the South Carolina Historical Society,* Vols. 1–5 (Charleston, SC: S.G. Courtenay & Co., 1857–1897).

CSP   *The Calendar of State Papers, Colonial: North America and the West Indies 1574–1739,* ProQuest: Online database, http://colonial.chadwyck.com/.

The De Soto Chronicles   *The De Soto Chronicles: The Expedition of Hernando De Soto to North America in 1539–1543,* ed. Lawrence A. Clayton, Edward C. Moore, and Vernon James Knight (Tuscaloosa: University of Alabama Press, 1993).

Documentos Históricos   *Documentos Históricos de La Florida y La Luisiana, Siglos XVI al XVIII,* ed. Manuel Serrano y Sanz (Madrid, Spain: Librería General de Victoriano Suárez, 1912).

FHQ   *Florida Historical Quarterly.*

Fort Caroline Documents   *Laudonniere and Fort Caroline History and Documents,* ed. Charles E. Bennett (Tuscaloosa: University of Alabama Press, 2001).

GDAH   Georgia Department of Archives and History.

GHS   Georgia Historical Society, Savannah, Georgia.

HL   Huntington Library, San Marino, California.

JCB   John Carter Brown Library, Providence, Rhode Island.

JCHA   *Journal of the Commons House of Assembly,* in South Carolina
Department of Archives and History.

JCIT   *Journal of the Commissioner of the Indian Trade, September 20, 1710–*
August 29, 1718, ed. William L. McDowell Jr. (Columbia: South Carolina
Department of Archives and History, 1955).

The Lanning Papers   The John Tate Lanning Papers, Thomas Jefferson Library,
University of Missouri, St. Louis.

LC   Library of Congress, Washington, DC.

The Luna Papers   *The Luna Papers, 1559–1561,* ed. Herbert Ingram Priestley
(Tuscaloosa: University of Alabama Press, 2010).

MPA   *Mississippi Provincial Archives: French Dominion.* Vols. 1–3, ed. Dunbar
Rowland and A. G. Sanders (Jackson: Press of the Mississippi Department of
Archives and History, 1927–1932); Vol. 4, ed. Dunbar Rowland, A. G. Sanders,
and Patricia Galloway (Baton Rouge: Louisiana State University Press, 1984).

NL   Newberry Library.

PKY   P. K. Yonge Library, University of Florida, Gainesville.

PRO   *Records in the British Public Record Office Relating to South Carolina:*
1663–[1710], Vols. 1–5, ed. A. S. Salley Jr. (Columbia: Historical Commission of
South Carolina, 1928–1947).

SCDAH   South Carolina Department of Archives and History, Columbia, South
Carolina.

SCHGM   *South Carolina Historical and Genealogical Magazine.*

SCHM   *South Carolina Historical Magazine.*

SCHS   South Carolina Historical Society, Addlestone Library, College of
Charleston.

SD   Santo Domingo.

SPG   *Letters from the Clergy of the Anglican Church in South Carolina,*
c. 1696–1775, ed. George W. Williams and Gene Waddell (Charleston: College
of Charleston Library, 2008).

The Statutes   *The Statutes at Large of South Carolina,* Vols. 1–10, ed. Thomas
Cooper and David James McCord (Columbia, SC: Printed by A. S. Johnston,
1836–1841).

WMQ   *William and Mary Quarterly.*

YCBA   Yale Center for British Art, Yale University, New Haven, Connecticut.

INTRODUCTION

1. "William Bull to Duke of Newcastle," October 5, 1739. C.O. 5/367, 195–196.
2. "An Act for the Better Strengthening of the Province," in *The Statutes,* Vol. 3, 556–568. "Act for the better ordering and governing of Negroes and other Slaves in the Province," in Vol. 7, 397–417.
3. "Lewis Jones to [David Humphreys]," May 1, 1739, Frank J. Klingberg, *An Appraisal of the Negro in Colonial South Carolina, a Study in Americanization,* 66.
4. "El Gobernador de la Florida D. Manuel Montiano," in Irene A. Wright, "Dispatches of Spanish Officials Bearing in the Free Negro Settlement of Gracia Real De Santa Teresa De Mose, Florida," *The Journal of Negro History* 9, no. 2 (1924): 176.
5. "Joseph Primo de Rivera y Menéndez Marqués . . . ," April 12, 1731, AGI 86–5–21/33 bnd 5310, Reel 40, Stetson Collection, PKY.
6. "El Gobernador de la Florida D. Manuel Montiano," in Wright, "Dispatches of Spanish Officials," 176.
7. Helen Hornbeck Tanner, "The Land and Water Communication Systems of the Southeastern Indians," in *Powhatan's Mantle: Indians in the Colonial Southeast,* ed. Gregory A. Waselkov, Peter H. Wood, and Tom Hatley (Lincoln: University of Nebraska, 1989), 27–42.
8. Most of the relatively few works relating to the subject are situated in New England. Jane Kamensky, *Governing the Tongue : The Politics of Speech in Early New England* (New York: Oxford University Press, 1997); Matt Cohen, *The Networked Wilderness: Communicating in Early New England* (Minneapolis: University of Minnesota Press, 2010); Katherine Grandjean, *American Passage: The Communications Frontier in Early New England* (Cambridge, MA: Harvard University Press, 2014).
9. Michael Warner, *The Letters of the Republic: Publication and the Public Sphere in Eighteenth-Century America* (Cambridge, MA: Harvard University Press, 1990); Alison Games, *The Web of Empire: English Cosmopolitans in an Age of Expansion, 1560–1660* (New York: Oxford University Press, 2008); David Hancock, *Oceans of Wine: Madeira and the Emergence of American Trade and Taste,* Lewis Walpole Series in Eighteenth-Century Culture and History (New Haven, CT: Yale University Press, 2009); Daniela Bleichmar, *Visible Empire: Botanical Expeditions & Visual Culture in the Hispanic Enlightenment* (Chicago, IL: University of Chicago Press, 2012); Susan Scott Parrish, *American Curiosity, Cultures of Natural History in the Colonial British Atlantic World* (Chapel Hill: University of North Carolina, Published for The Institute of Early American History and Culture, Williamsburg, VA, 2006); Christopher Hodson, *The Acadian Diaspora: An Eighteenth-Century History,* Oxford Studies in International History (New York: Oxford University Press, 2012); Susanah Shaw Romney, *New Netherland Connections: Intimate Networks and Atlantic Ties in Seventeenth-Century*

America (Chapel Hill: Omohundro Institute/UNC Press, 2014); Lindsay O'Neill, *The Opened Letter: Networking in the Early Modern British World*, Early Modern Americas (Philadelphia: University of Pennsylvania Press, 2015); Konstantin Dierks, *In My Power: Letter Writing and Communications in Early America* (Philadelphia: University of Pennsylvania Press, 2009); Sarah M. S. Pearsall, *Atlantic Families: Lives and Letters in the Later Eighteenth Century* (Oxford: Oxford University Press, 2008).

10. David G. Anderson, "The Role of Cahokia in the Evolution of the Southeastern Mississippian Society" in *Cahokia: Domination and Ideology in the Mississippian World*, ed. Timothy R. Pauketat and Thomas E. Emerson (Lincoln: University of Nebraska Press, 1997), 248–268.

11. Daniel K. Richter, *Before the Revolution: America's Ancient Pasts* (Cambridge, MA: Belknap Press of Harvard University Press, 2011), 5.

12. Peter H. Wood, "The Changing Population of the Colonial South, an Overview by Race and Region, 1685–1790," in Waselkov, Wood, and Hatley, eds., *Powhatan's Mantle*, Table 1, 60–61.

13. S. Max Edelson, *Plantation Enterprise in Colonial South Carolina* (Cambridge, MA: Harvard University Press, 2006), 13–52.

14. "Lords Proprietors of Carolina to the Governor and Council of Ashley River," March 7, 1681, CO 5/286, 165–168.

15. Bonnie G. McEwan, ed. *The Spanish Missions of La Florida* (Gainesville: The University of Florida Press, 1993), xv.

16. Alan Gallay, *The Indian Slave Trade, the Rise of the English Empire in the American South 1670–1717* (New Haven, CT: Yale University Press, 2002), 288–314; Christina Snyder, *Slavery in Indian Country* (Cambridge, MA: Harvard University Press, 2010), 46–79.

17. Pekka Hämäläinen, "The Shapes of Power: Indians, Europeans, and North American Worlds from the Seventeenth Century to the Nineteenth Century," in *Contested Spaces of Early America*, ed. Juliana Barr and Edward Countryman (Philadelphia: University of Pennsylvania Press, 2014), 33.

PART I. WHAT:

MAKING SENSE OF LA FLORIDA, 1560S–1670S

The Part I epigraph is from *Deuxiem Voyage du Dieppois Jean Ribaut it la Floride en 1565*, edited by Gabriel Gravier (Rouen, 1872), and is reprinted by permission of the publisher from *Laudonniere and Fort Caroline: History and Documents* by Charles E. Bennett, 164. Copyright © 2001 by the University of Alabama Press.

CHAPTER ONE: PATHS AND POWER

Epigraph: John Lawson, *A New Voyage to Carolina* (London: 1709), 205.

1. F. Terry Norris and Timothy R. Pauketat, "A Pre-Columbian Map of the Mississippi?," *Southeastern Archaeology* 27, no. 1 (2008): 87; Alejandra Dubcovsky, "Pre-Contact Sources in Historical Narratives," *Native South* 7 (2014): 108–121.

2. A 2011 *AHR* Conversation called for investigating the "actual modes, techniques, and social interactions that have characterized communication in all times and places." In an attempt to answer this call, I borrow the participants' terminology. Paul N. Edwards et al., "Historical Perspectives on the Circulation of Information," *AHR* 116, no. 5 (2011): 1.

3. Chester B. Depratter, "The Chiefdom of Cofitachequi," in *The Forgotten Centuries: Indians and Europeans in the American South, 1521–1704*, ed. Charles M. Hudson and Carmen Chaves Tesser (Athens: University of Georgia Press, 1994), 197–226; David J. Hally, "The Chiefdom of Coosa," in *The Forgotten Centuries: Indians and Europeans in the American South, 1521–1704*, ed. Charles M. Hudson and Carmen Chaves Tesser (Athens: University of Georgia Press, 1994), 227–236.

4. Birgit Brander Rasmussen, *Queequeg's Coffin: Indigenous Literacies & Early American Literature* (Durham, NC: Duke University Press, 2012); Matt Cohen, Jeffrey Glover, and Paul Chaat Smith, *Colonial Mediascapes: Sensory Worlds of the Early Americas* (Lincoln: University of Nebraska Press, 2014); Joanne Rappaport and Tom Cummins, *Beyond the Lettered City: Indigenous Literacies in the Andes*, Narrating Native Histories (Durham, NC: Duke University Press, 2012); Jeffrey Glover, *Paper Sovereigns: Anglo-Native Treaties and the Law of Nations, 1604–1664* (Philadelphia: University of Pennsylvania Press, 2014), 6, 19–22; Céline Carayon, "'The gesture-speech of Mankind': Old and New Entanglements in the Histories of Indian and European Sign Languages," *AHR* 121, no. 2 (2016), forthcoming.

5. John R. Swanton, "Social Organization and Social Usages of the Indians of the Creek Confederacy," in *Forty-Second Annual Report of the Bureau of American Ethnology, 1924–1925* (Washington, DC: Government Printing Office, 1928), 446–450; James Adair, *The History of the American Indians, Particularly Those Nations Adjoining to the Mississippi, East and West Florida, Georgia, South and North Carolina, and Virginia* (London: Printed for Edward and Charles Dilly, 1775), 299–300. www.americanwest.amdigital.co.uk/Contents/Document-Details.aspx?documentid=1178.

6. James A. Brown, "Exchange and Interaction until 1500," in *Handbook of North American Indians: Southeast,* ed. Raymond D. Fogelson and William C. Sturtevant (Washington, DC: Smithsonian Institution, 2004), 677–685; Greg A.

Waselkov, "Exchange and Interaction since 1500," in *Handbook of North American Indians: Southeast,* ed. Raymond D. Fogelson and William C. Sturtevant (Washington, DC: Smithsonian Institution, 2004), 686–695; Juliana Barr and Edward Countryman, "Maps and Spaces, Paths to Connect, and Lines to Divide," in *Contested Spaces of Early America,* ed. Juliana Barr and Edward Countryman (Philadelphia: University of Pennsylvania Press, 2014), 1–28.

7. William E. Myer, "Indian Trails of the Southeast," in *Forty-Second Annual Report of the Bureau of American Ethnology, 1924–1925* (Washington, DC: Government Printing Office, 1928), 735–825. For efforts to remedy war-ravaged paths, see Wendy St. Jean, "Trading Paths: Mapping Chickasaw History in the Eighteenth Century," *American Indian Quarterly* 27, no. 3 (2003): 762–763.

8. John H. Goff, "Some Major Indian Trading Paths across the Georgia Piedmont," *Georgia Mineral News Letter* 6, no. 4 (1953): 122–131; Louis DeVorsey, "Indian Trails," *The New Georgia Encyclopedia* (2003), www.georgiaencyclopedia.org /nge/Article.jsp?id=h-790. For parallels in Latin America, see Sylvia Sellers-García, "The Mail in Time: Postal Routes and Conceptions of Distance in Colonial Guatemala," *Colonial Latin American Review* 21, no. 1 (2012): 80.

9. Angela Pulley Hudson, *Creek Paths and Federal Roads: Indians, Settlers, and Slaves and the Making of the American South* (Chapel Hill: University of North Carolina Press, 2010), 12–13.

10. Personal correspondence with Jack Martin, May 24, 2013. Creek dictionary, circa 1758, Moravian Archives, Bethlehem, PA, Box 3382. Courtesy of Steven C. Hahn.

11. Gladys Rebecca Dobbs, "The Indian Trading Path and Colonial Settlement Development in the North Carolina Piedmont" (Ph.D. diss., University of North Carolina at Chapel Hill, 2007), 6; Tom Fowler, *Carolina Journeys: Exploring the Trails of the Carolinas—Both Real and Imagined* (Boone, NC: Parkway Publishers, 2004), 12–18.

12. William E. Myer, "Indian Trials of the Southeast," in *Forty-Second Annual Report of the Bureau of American Ethnology, 1924–1925* (Washington, DC: Government Printing Office, 1928), 823; Jane Merritt, *At the Crossroads: Indians and Empires on a Mid-Atlantic Frontier, 1700–1763* (Chapel Hill: University of North Carolina Press, 2003), 2–3, 33.

13. "Visitation of Timucua," February 13, 1657. In Testimonio de Visita of Governor Diego de Rebolledo. Escribanía de Cámara Legajo 15. No 188 bnd 1467. Reel 12, Stetson Collection, PKY.

14. The most comprehensive study on these paths identified 125 individual trails but focused mostly on Tennessee and Kentucky. For work on Georgia, see Goff, "Some Major Indian Trading Paths across the Georgia Piedmont." For an overview, see Hornbeck Tanner, "The Land and Water Communication Systems of the Southeastern Indians," in *Powhatan's Mantle: Indians in the Colonial Southeast,* ed. Gregory A. Waselkov, Peter H. Wood, and Tom Hatley (Lincoln: University of Nebraska, 1989), 27–42; Joshua A. Piker, "White &

Clean" & Contested: Creek Towns and Trading Paths in the Aftermath of the Seven Years' War," *Ethnohistory* 50, no. 2 (2003): 315–347.

15. Piker, "White & Clean" & Contested, 315–347; Hudson, *Creek Paths and Federal Roads,* 11–35.

16. Timothy R. Pauketat, *Cahokia: Ancient America's Great City on the Mississippi,* The Penguin Library of American Indian History (New York, NY: Viking, 2009), 143. For comparisons to other sites in North America, see: Fred E. Coy Jr., "Native American Dendroglyphs of the Eastern Woodlands," in *The Rock-Art of Eastern North America: Capturing Images and Insight,* ed. Carol Diaz-Granados and James Richard Duncan (Tuscaloosa: University of Alabama Press, 2004), 4–16; Pratz du Le Page, *The History of Louisiana,* Louisiana Bicentennial Reprint Series (1774, repr. Baton Rouge: Published for the Louisiana American Revolution Bicentennial Commission by the Louisiana State University Press, 1975), 373–374.

17. Timothy R. Pauketat, *Ancient Cahokia and the Mississippians,* Case Studies in Early Societies (Cambridge: Cambridge University Press, 2004), 10.

18. Thomas Emerson and Timothy R. Pauketat, "Embodying Power and Resistance at Cahokia," in *The Dynamics of Power,* ed. Maria O'Donovan (Carbondale, IL: Center for Archaeological Investigations, Southern Illinois University Carbondale, 2002) , 105–125. For a different perspective, see James A. Brown, "Where's the Power in Mound Building? An Eastern Woodlands Perspective," in *Leadership and Polity in Mississippian Society,* ed. Brian M. Butler, Paul D. Welch, and Southern Illinois University Carbondale. Center for Archaeological Investigations (Carbondale: Center for Archaeological Investigations, Southern Illinois University, Carbondale, 2006), 197–213.

19. F. Kent Reilly III, "People of Earth, People of Skys . . ." in *Hero, Hawk, and Open Hand: American Indian Art of the Ancient Midwest and South,* ed. Richard F. Townsend, Robert V. Sharp, Garrick Alan Bailey, and Art Institute of Chicago (Chicago, IL: Art Institute of Chicago, in Association with Yale University Press, 2004), 126–128; Christina Snyder, *Slavery in Indian Country* (Cambridge, MA: Harvard University Press, 2010), 13–46; Robbie Ethridge, *From Chicaza to Chickasaw: The European Invasion and the Transformation of the Mississippian World, 1540–1715* (Chapel Hill: University of North Carolina Press, 2010), 11–41.

20. Claudine Payne, "Mississippian Capitals: An Archaeological Investigation of Precolumbian Political Structure" (Ph.D. diss., University of Florida, 1994), 91–114; Adam King, "Leadership Strategies and the Nature of Mississippian Chiefdoms in Northern Georgia," in *Leadership and Polity in Mississippian Society,* 81.

21. Charles R. Cobb and Adam King, "Re-Inventing Mississippian Tradition at Etowah, Georgia," *Journal of Archaeological Method and Theory* 12, no. 3 (2005): 180.

22. Adam King, "Long Term Histories of Mississippian Centerss . . ." *Southeastern Archaeology* 20, no. 1 (2001): 1–17. For a parallel example in Coosa, see Thomas J.

Pluckhahn and David A. McKivergan, "A Critical Appraisal of Middle Mississippian Settlement and Social Organization on the Georgia Coast," *Southeastern Archaeology* 21, no. 2 (2002): 149–161.

23. Joseph M. Hall, *Zamumo's Gifts: Indian-European Exchange in the Colonial Southeast* (Philadelphia: University of Pennsylvania Press, 2009), 20.

24. Kathryn E. Holland Braund, *Deerskins and Duffels, the Creek Indian Trade with Anglo-America, 1685–1815* (Lincoln: University of Nebraska Press, 1993), 61; Robbie Franklyn Ethridge, *Creek Country: The Creek Indians and Their World* (Chapel Hill: University of North Carolina Press, 2003), 135–137.

25. Amy Bushnell, "Patricio De Hinachuba: Defender of the Word of God, the Crown of the King, and the Little Children of Ivitachuco," *American Indian Culture and Research Journal* 3, no. 3 (1979): 2–3; Verner W. Crane, *The Southern Frontier, 1670–1732* (Durham, NC: Duke University Press, 1928), 36–37.

26. David H. Dye, "Art, Ritual, and Chiefly Warfare in the Mississippian World," *Hero, Hawk, and Open Hand*, 191–206; Wayne William Van Horne, "The Warclub: Weapon and Symbol in Southeastern Indian Societies" (Ph.D. diss., University of Georgia, 1993), 149; David G. Anderson, *The Savannah River Chiefdoms: Political Change in the Late Prehistoric Southeast* (Tuscaloosa: University of Alabama Press, 1994), 149.

27. Louis de Vorsey Jr., "Maps in Colonial Promotion: James Edward Oglethorpe's Use of Maps in 'Selling' the Georgia Scheme," *Imago Mundi* 38 (1986): 35–45, quote on 37.

28. Myer, "Indian Trails of the Southeast," 765.

29. St. Jean, "Trading Paths," 763–764.

30. Jose Rabasa, *Writing Violence on the Northern Frontier: The Historiography of Sixteenth Century New Mexico and Florida and the Legacy of Conquest* (Durham, NC: Duke University Press, 2000), 179–182. For a parallel and later example, see "Testimonio de los actos hechos a constesta del Corornel Don Miguel Román de Castilla y Lugo," July 6, 1759, AGN, Reel 144G, PKY.

31. Depratter, "The Chiefdom of Cofitachequi," in *The Forgotten Centuries: Indians and Europeans in the American South, 1521–1704*, ed. Charles M. Hudson and Carmen Chaves Tesser (Athens: University of Georgia Press, 1994), 197–226; David J. Hally, "The Chiefdom of Coosa," in *The Forgotten Centuries: Indians and Europeans in the American South, 1521–1704*, ed. Charles M. Hudson and Carmen Chaves Tesser (Athens: University of Georgia Press, 1994) 227–236; Paul W. Mapp, *The Elusive West and the Contest for Empire, 1713–1763* (The Omohundro Institute of Early American History and Culture and Chapel Hill: University of North Carolina, 2011), 72–98.

32. "Letter from Coosa," August 1, 1560. in *The Luna Papers*, 2010. V.1, 231.

33. Lawson, *A New Voyage to Carolina* (London: 1709), 59–60.

34. Gregory A. Waselkov, "Indian Maps of the Colonial Southeast," in Waselkov, Wood, and Hatley, eds., *Powhatan's Mantle,* 444.

35. John O. E. Clark, ed. *100 Maps: The Science, Art and Politics of Cartography throughout History* (New York: Sterling Publishing, 2005), 132; G. Malcolm Lewis, *Cartographic Encounters: Perspectives on Native American Mapmaking and Map Use* (Chicago, IL: University of Chicago Press, 1998); Cynthia Jean Van Zandt, *Brothers among Nations: The Pursuit of Intercultural Alliances in Early America, 1580–1660* (Oxford: Oxford University Press, 2008), 19–43.

36. Waselkov, "Indian Maps of the Colonial Southeast," 444.

37. Daniel Lord Smail and Andrew Shryock, "History and the 'Pre,'" *AHA* 118, no. 3 (2013): 709–737.

38. James Adair explained the "war whoop" as helping to "denot[e] good or bad news." Adair, *The History of the American Indians,* 298–300. For a general overview, see Brown, "Exchange and Interaction until 1500," in *Handbook of North American Indians: Southeast,* 677–685; and Greg A. Waselkov, "Exchange and Interaction since 1500," in *Handbook of North American Indians: Southeast,* 686–696.

39. Lawson, *A New Voyage to Carolina,* 181.

40. Ibid. (emphasis added).

41. Ibid, 43.

42. Jean Bernard Bossu, *Nouveaux Voyages aux Indes Occidentales; Contenant une Relation des différent Peuples qui habitent les environs du grand Fleuve Saint-Louis, appellé vulgairement le Mississippi; leur religion; leur gouvernement; leurs moeurs; leurs guerres et leur commerce.* Paris: 1768, quoted from Swanton, "Religious Beliefs and Medical Practices of the Creek Indians," in *Forty-Second Annual Report of the Bureau of American Ethnology, 1924–1925* (Washington, DC: Government Printing Office, 1928), 543.

43. Benjamin Hawkins in Swanton's "Social Organization and Social Usages of the Indians of the Creek Confederacy," 306.

44. *Discovering the New World, Based on the Works of Theodore de Bry,* ed. Michael Alexander (New York: Harper & Row, 1976), 46.

45. John Worth, "Ethnicity and Ceramics on the Southeastern Atlantic Coast: An Ethnohistorical Analysis," in *From Santa Elena to St. Augustine . . .* ed. Kathleen Deagan and David Hurst Thomas, vol. 90, American Museum of Natural History Anthropological Papers (2009), 179–203.

46. Lawson, *A New Voyage to Carolina,* 37.

47. For Iroquois greeting rituals, see Jon Parmenter, *The Edge of the Woods: Iroquioa, 1534–1701* (East Lansing: Michigan State University Press, 2010), 41–76, 90; John Lederer and William Talbot, *The Discoveries of John Lederer . . .* (London: Printed by J. C. for S. Heyrick, 1672), 46.

48. Lawson, *A New Voyage to Carolina,* 231.

49. Jane Kamensky, *Governing the Tongue: The Politics of Speech in Early New England* (New York: Oxford University Press, 1997), 5–10.

50. Emanuel Drechsel, "An Integrated Vocabulary of Mobilian Jargon, a Native American Pidgin of the Mississippi Valley," *Anthropological Linguistics* 38, no. 2 (1996): 248–354.

51. James Merrell, *Into the American Woods, Negotiators on the Pennsylvania Frontier* (New York: W. W. Norton & Company, 1999), 58–72. See also Claudio Saunt, *A New Order of Things, Property, Power, and the Transformation of the Creek Indians, 1733–1816* (Cambridge: Cambridge University Press, 1999), 33–34.

52. "A 17th century letter of Gabriel Díaz Vara Calderón," ed. Lucy L. Wenhold and John Reed Swanton. (Washington D.C.: Smithsonian Institution, 1936).

53. Lawson, *A New Voyage to Carolina,* 225.

54. John H. Hann, "Translation of the Ecija Voyages of 1605 and 1609 and the González Derrotero of 1609," *Florida Archaeology* 2(1986): 24–45; Carroll L. Riley, "Early Spanish-Indian Communication in the Greater Southwest," *New Mexico Historical Review* 46, no. 4 (October 1, 1971): 285–314.

55. Julian Granberry, *A Grammar and Dictionary of the Timucua Language,* 3rd ed. (Tuscaloosa: University of Alabama Press, 1993), 2. For the importance of native place names, see Lisa Brooks, *The Common Pot: The Recovery of Native Space in the Northeast* (Minneapolis: University of Minnesota Press, 2008), xxii–xxvi; Keith Basso, *Wisdom Sits in Places, Landscapes and Language among the Western Apache* (Albuquerque: University of New Mexico Press, 1996), 6–26.

56. Lawson, *A New Voyage to Carolina,* 225.

57. Henry Woodward, "A Faithfull Relations of My Westoe Voaige, by Henry Woodward, 1674," in *Narratives of Early Carolina, 1650–1708,* ed. Alexander S. Salley (New York: Charles Scribner's Sons, 1911), 130, 131–133.

58. Garcilaso de la Vega, *The Florida of the Inca . . .* (Austin: University of Texas Press, 1951), 75. For a closer look at this incident, see Lisa Voigt, "Captivity, Exile, and Interpretation in La Florida Del Inca," *Colonial Latin American Review* 11, no. 2 (2002): 115–116.

59. Garcilaso de la Vega, *The Florida of the Inca,* 250, 253–255; Charles Hudson, *Warriors of the Sun: Hernando de Soto and the South's Ancient Chiefdoms* (Athens: University of Georgia Press, 1997), 367.

60. Rabasa, *Writing Violence on the Northern Frontier,* 196.

61. Hudson, *Warriors of the Sun,* 455.

62. Garcilaso de la Vega, *The Florida of the Inca,* 143; Stephen Greenblatt, *Marvelous Possessions, the Wonder of the New World* (Chicago, IL: University of Chicago Press, 1991), 104–108.

63. Thomas Hariot, *Narrative of the First English Plantation of Virginia* (London: Bernard Quaritch, 1893), 41–42.

64. Paul Kelton, *Epidemics and Enslavement: Biological Catastrophe in the Native Southeast, 1492–1715* (Lincoln: University of Nebraska Press, 2007), 47–100.

65. *Alvar Núñez Cabeza De Vaca: His Account, His Life, and the Expedition of Pánfilo De Narváez,* ed. Rolena Adorno and Patrick Charles Pautz (Lincoln: University of Nebraska Press, 1999), 70–72, 113–114.

66. Raquel Chang-Rodríguez, *Beyond Books and Borders: Garcilaso De La Vega and La Florida Del Inca* (Lewisburg, PA: Bucknell University Press, 2006), 15–32.

67. Rolena Adorno, *The Polemics of Possession in Spanish American Narrative* (New Haven, CT: Yale University Press, 2007), 295–302.

68. Garcilaso de la Vega, *The Florida of the Inca,* 482–483.

69. Charles Hudson, *Knights of Spain, Warriors of the Sun: Hernando de Soto and the South's Ancient Chiefdoms* (Athens: The University of Georgia Press, 1997), 370, footnote 53. Rolena Adorno, "El Inca Garcilaso: Writer of Hernando De Soto, Readers of Cabeza De Vaca," in *Beyond Books and Borders: Garcilaso De La Vega and La Florida Del Inca,* ed. Raquel Chang-Rodríguez (Lewisburg, PA: Bucknell University Press, 2006): 119-133.

70. Matt Cohen, *The Networked Wilderness: Communicating in Early New England* (Minneapolis: University of Minnesota Press, 2010), 68–71.

71. *Ecija Voyage,* 33.

72. *Ecija Voyage,* 43–47 (emphasis added).

73. *Alvar Núñez Cabeza De Vaca,* ed. Rolena Adorno and Patrick Charles Pautz (Lincoln: University of Nebraska Press, 1999), 56 (emphasis added).

74. Garcilaso de la Vega, *The Florida of the Inca,* 134.

75. "Relación de la Tama y Su Tierra," November 9, 1588, in *Documentos Históricos,* 141–160.

76. Agustín Dávila y Padilla, *Historia De La Fundacion y Discurso . . . ,* 1625, 217. For Spanish communication strategies during Coronado's expedition, see Richard Flint and Shirley Cushing Flint, *Documents of the Coronado Expedition, 1539–1542: "They Were Not Familiar with His Majesty, nor Did They Wish to Be His Subjects,"* 1st ed. (Dallas, TX: Southern Medthodist University Press, 2005), 68–76. For similar strategies employed throughout the Southwest, see Juliana Barr, *Peace Came in the Form of a Woman: Indians and Spaniards in the Texas Borderlands* (Chapel Hill: University of North Carolina Press, 2007), 113–114.

77. "An account by a Gentleman from Elvas," in *The De Soto Chronicles,* 82. For French examples, see Pierre Le Moyne d'Iberville and Richebourg Gaillard McWilliams, *Iberville's Gulf Journals* (Tuscaloosa: University of Alabama Press, 1950), 87–89.

78. Luys Hernández de Biedma, "Relation of the Island of Florida," in *The De Soto Chronicles,* 225; Snyder, *Slavery in Indian Country,* 40.

79. *"An account by a Gentleman from Elvas,"* in *The De Soto Chronicles,* 60. Andrés Reséndez, *A Land So Strange: The Epic Journey of Cabeza De Vaca* (New York: Basic Books, 2007), 91–92, 106–108; Snyder, *Slavery in Indian Country,* 35–36.

80. "Memoir of S d'Escalante Fontaneda, Respecting to Florida, Written in Spain, about the year 1575," in Jerald T. Milanich, ed. *Earliest Hispanic/ Native American Interactions in the American Southeast,* vol. 12, Spanish Borderlands Sourcebooks (New York: Garland Publishing Inc., 1991), 300; Anna Brickhouse, "Toward a Theory of Narrative Unsettlement: The Ladino Account of Hernando De Escalante Fontaneda," *Clio: A Journal of Literature, History, and the Philosophy of History* 40, no. 1 (2010): 35-61; John E. Worth, "Fontaneda Revisited: Five Descriptions of Sixteenth-Century Florida," *FHQ* 73, no. 3 (1995): 339-352.

81. "Memoir of S d'Escalante Fontaneda," 300; Brickhouse, "Toward a Theory of Narrative Unsettlement," 35-61.

82. *"An account by a Gentleman from Elvas,"* in *The De Soto Chronicles,* 76–77.

83. Ibid.

84. John R. Bratten and John E. Worth, "Shipwrecked History," *American Heritage* 2009.

85. "Luna to his Majesty," May 1, 1559, in *The Luna Papers,* 2010, V. 2, 213.

86. Ibid.

87. "Luna to his Majesty," September 24, 1559, in *The Luna Papers,* 2010, V. 2, 245.

88. Ibid.

89. Patricia Galloway, *Choctaw Genesis 1500–1700* (Lincoln: University of Nebraska Press, 1995), 143–160.

90. *"An account by a Gentleman from Elvas,"* in *The De Soto Chronicles,* 93; Charles Hudson et al., "Coosa: A Chiefdom in the Sixteenth-Century Southeastern United States," *American Antiquity* 50, no. 4 (1985): 723–737; Marvin T. Smith, *Coosa: The Rise and Fall of a Southeastern Mississippian Chiefdom* (Gainesville: University Press of Florida, 2000), 95; Adam King, "The Historic Period Transformation of Mississippian Societies," in *Light on the Path: The Anthropology of the Southeastern Indians,* ed. Robbie Ethridge and Thomas J. Puckhahn (Tuscaloosa: University of Alabama Press, 2006), 179–195; "De Soto's Itaba and the Nature of Sixteenth Century Paramount Chiefdoms," *Southeastern Archaeology* 18, no. 2 (1999): 110–123.

91. "Declaration made by Luna," in *The Luna Papers,* 2010, v. 1, 149.

92. Smith, *Coosa,* 118–121; Charles Hudson, "A Spanish-Coosa Alliance in Sixteenth-Century North Georgia," *The Georgia Historical Quarterly* 72, no. 4 (1988): 618; David J. Hally, Marvin T. Smith, and James B. Langford Jr., "The Archaeological Reality of de Soto's Coosa," in *Archaeological and Historical Perspectives on the Spanish Borderlands East. Columbian Consequences,* vol. 2, ed. David Hurst Thomas (Washington, DC: Smithsonian Institution Press, 1990): 121–138.

93. "Mateo del Sauz to Luna," July 6, 1590, in *The Luna Papers*, 2010. V. 1, 218–221. For Coosa participation in Mabila, see Charles Hudson, Marvin Smith, and Chester DePratter, "The King Site Massacre Victims: A Historical Detectives' Report," in *The King Site: Biocultural Adaptation in Sixteenth-Century Georgia*, ed. Robert L. Blakely (Athens: University of Georgia Press, 1984): 117–134.

94. Agustín Dávila y Padilla, *Historia De La Fundación y Discurso*, 1625, 201–207, quote on 204; Translation from Swanton, *Early History of Creek Indians . . .* Bulletin 73, 256.

95. Stephen A. Kowalewski, "Coalescent Societies," in *Light on the Path: The Anthropology of the Southeastern Indians*, ed. Robbie Ethridge and Thomas J. Puckhahn (Tuscaloosa: University of Alabama Press, 2006), 94–122.

CHAPTER TWO: INFORMATION CONTESTS

Epigraph: Melchor Portocarrero to Francisco Salazar, September 15, 1683.
　　　AGI 58–1–37/1 bnd 2342, Reel 16, Stetson Collection, PKY.

1. "Memorial de Pedro Menéndez de Avilés . . ." in Eugenio Ruidíaz y Caravia, *La Florida: Su Conquista Y Colonizacion Por Pedro Menéndez De Avilés* (Madrid: Imp. de los hijos de J. A. Garcia, 1893), 320–326.

2. "Capitulación y Asiento . . ." March 20, 1565, in Caravia, *La Florida*, 415–427.

3. "Relación del Suceso de la Armada Francesa que fue a poblar la tierra de la Florida," in *Fort Caroline Documents*, 87–93.

4. Paul E. Hoffman, *A New Andalucia and a Way to the Orient: The American Southeast During the Sixteenth Century* (Baton Rouge: Louisiana State University, 1990), 169.

5. Andrew Pettegree, *The Invention of News: How the World Came to Know about Itself* (New Haven, CT: Yale University Press, 2014), 208–229.

6. Steven C. Hahn, *The Life and Times of Mary Musgrove* (Gainesville: University Press of Florida, 2012), 41; Jack B. Martin, "How to Tell a Creek Story in Five Past Tenses," *International Journal of American Linguistics* 76, no. 1 (2010): 43–70; Geoffrey D. Kimball and Bel Abbey, *Koasati Grammar, Studies in the Anthropology of North American Indians* (Lincoln: University of Nebraska Press, 1991), 572; Ives Goddard, "The Indigenous Languages of the Southeast," *Anthropological Linguistics* 47, no. 1 (Spring 2005): 1–60.

7. For a general overview, see James A. Brown, "Exchange and Interaction until 1500," in *Handbook of North American Indians*, 677–685; Greg A. Waselkov, "Exchange and Interaction since 1500," in *Handbook of North American Indians: Southeast*, ed. Raymond D. Fogelson and William C. Sturtevant (Washington, DC: Smithsonian Institution 2004), 686–695.

8. David J. Hally, *King: The Social Archaeology of a Late Mississippian Town in Northwestern Georgia* (Tuscaloosa: University of Alabama Press, 2008), chapter 6, 170; Lewis H. Larson Jr., "Functional Considerations of Warfare in

the Southeast during the Mississippi Period," *American Antiquity* 37, no. 3 (1972): 390; Wayne William Van Horne, "The Warclub: Weapon and Symbol in Southeastern Indian Societies" (Ph.D. diss., University of Georgia, 1993).

9. Cameron B. Wesson, "Chiefly Power and Foodstorage in Southeastern North America," *World Archeology* 31, no. 1 (1999): 145–164; David G. Anderson, *The Savannah River Chiefdoms: Political Change in the Late Prehistoric Southeast* (Tuscaloosa: University of Alabama Press, 1994), 44; Cohen, Glover, and Chaat Smith, *Colonial Mediascapes: Sensory Worlds of the Early Americas* (Lincoln: University of Nebraska Press, 2014), 233–321.

10. Patricia Galloway, "A Storied Land: Choctaw Place-Names and the Emplotment of Land Use," in *Practicing Ethnohistory: Mining Archives, Hearing Testimony, Constructing Narrative* (Lincoln: University of Nebraska, 2006), 175–201; Keith H. Basso, *Wisdom Sits in Places: Landscape and Language among the Western Apache* (Albuquerque: University of New Mexico Press, 1996), 3–27; Lisa Brooks, *The Common Pot: The Recovery of Native Space in the Northeast* (Minneapolis: University of Minnesota Press, 2008), 28–50.

11. Willet A. Boyer, III, "The Acuera of the Ocklawaha River Valley: Keepers of Time in the Land of the Waters" (Ph.D. diss., University of Florida, 2010), 71–72.

12. Christina Snyder, *Slavery in Indian Country* (Cambridge, MA: Harvard University Press, 2010), 57.

13. "Hernán Pérez to King," November 28, 1567, bnd, 53–6–5, Reel 3, Stetson Collection, PKY.

14. "Pedro Menéndez to the King," September 11, 1565, in *Pedro Menéndez De Avilés, Cartas Sobre La Florida (1555–1574),* ed. Juan Carlos Mercado (Madrid: Iberoamericana, 2002), 129.

15. "Deposition of Stefano Rojomonte, 1564," in *Fort Caroline Documents,* 94–98.

16. "Pedro Menéndez to the King," October 15, 1565, in *Cartas Sobre La Florida,* 129.

17. "Gonzalo Solís de Merás," in *Pedro Menéndez De Avilés, Adelantado, Governor and Captain-General of Florida: Memorial,* trans. Jeannette M. Thurber Connor, Publications of the Florida State Historical Society No. 3 (Deland: The Florida State Historical Society, 1923), 104.

18. René Goulaine de Laudonnière. *A notable historie containing foure voyages made by certayne French captaynes vnto Florida . . .* London: Imprinted by Thomas Dawson, 1587, 33.

19. "Fort Matanzas Massacre, 1565" in *Pedro Menéndez De Avilés;* A. M. Brooks, *The Unwritten History of Old St. Augustine.* (St. Augustine, FL: The Record Co., 1909), 15.

20. For letters of René Goulaine de Laudonnière's in French, see Paul Gaffarel, *Histoire De La Floride Française* (Firmin-Didot et cie, 1875), 141.

21. "Pedro Menéndez to the King," September 11, 1565 in *Cartas Sobre La Florida,* 130.

22. James M. Crawford, "Timucua and Yuchi: Two Language Isolates of the

Southeast," in *The Languages of Native America: Historical and Comparative Assessment,* ed. Lyle Campbell and Marianne Mithun (Austin: University of Texas Press, 1979), 327–354; Ives Goddard, "The Classification of Native Languages of North America" (Washington, DC: Smithsonian Institution, 1996), 290–323.

23. John E. Worth, *The Timucuan Chiefdoms of Spanish Florida, Volume 2: Resistance and Destruction,* vol. 2 (Gainesville: University of Florida, 1998), 9–10; Jerald Milanich, "Timucua," in *Handbook of North American Indians,* 219–228; John H. Hann, "1630 Memorial of Fray Francisco Alonso De Jesus on Spanish Florida's Missions and Natives," *The Americas* 50, no. 1 (1993): 85–105.

24. The terms *paracoussi, olata,* and *utina* were all used to identify different types of Timucua leaders. DeCoster, "Entangled Borderlands: Europeans and Timucuans in Sixteenth-Century Florida," *FHQ* 91, no. 3 (2013): 378.

25. For the meaning of Saturiwa's name and a discussion of his political power, see Boyer, "The Acuera of the Ocklawaha River Valley," 72. For the complicated relation of Saturiwa with the French, see Eugene Lyon, *The Enterprise of Florida: Pedro Menéndez De Avilés and the Spanish Conquest of 1565–1568* (Gainesville: University of Florida Press, 1976), 199; René Goulaine de Laudonnière, *A Notable Historie Containing Foure Voyages Made by Certayne French Captaynes Vnto Florida* . . . (London: Imprinted by Thomas Dawson, 1587), 45.

26. René de Laudonnière and Bennett, *Three Voyages* . . . trans. Charles E. Bennett (Tuscaloosa: University of Alabama Press, 2001), 125.

27. "Deposition of Stefano Rojomonte, 1564," in *Fort Caroline Documents,* 94–98; André Thevet, *Les vrais pourtraits et vies des hommes* (Paris, 1584), 663–664.

28. Bartolomé de Flores, *Obra Nueuamente Compuesta* . . . (Sevilla: En casa de Hernando Diaz . . . a la Calle de la Sierpe, 1571), in John Carter Brown Library, Providence, RI (hereafter known as JCB).

29. "Gonzalo Solís de Merás," in *Pedro Menéndez De Avilés, Adelantado* . . . trans. Jeannette M. Thurber Connor, 80–106.

30. "Carta del Adelantado Pedro Menéndez de Avilés," October 15, 1565, in *Cartas Sobre La Florida,* 141–146; "Francisco Lopez de Mendoza Grajales," in *Fort Caroline Documents,* 141–163.

31. Laudonnière, *A Notable Historie Containing Foure Voyages Made by Certayne French Captaynes Vnto Floridas* . . . (London: Imprinted by Thomas Dawson, 1587), 56.

32. "Pedro de Valdés to King," September 12, 1566, AGI-SD, Reel 5, Stetson Collection, PKY. For more on nonverbal communication, see James Axtell, *Natives and Newcomers: The Cultural Origins of North America* (New York: Oxford University Press, 2001), Chapter 2; Nancy Shoemaker, *A Strange Likeness: Becoming Red and White in Eighteenth-Century North America* (Oxford: Oxford University Press, 2004), 64–68.

33. Andrés Gonzalez de Barcía Carballido y Zúñiga, *Chronological History of the*

Continent of Florida . . . trans. Anthony Kerrigan and Introduced with a Foreword by Herbert E. Bolton (Gainesville: University of Florida Press, 1951), 145; Herbert E. Bolton, *The Spanish Borderlands, a Chronicle of Old Florida and the Southwest,* ed. Allen Johnson, vol. 23, The Chronicles of America Series (New Haven, CT: Yale University Press, 1921), 156.

34. *Histoire memorable de la reprise de l'isle de la Floride, faicte par les Francois, sous la conduite du Capitaine Gorgues,* April 27 and 28, 1568, Massachusetts Historical Society, Boston, 1928; Bartolomé de Barrientos, *Vida y Hechos de Pedro Menéndez de Avilés,* printed in Genaro García, Bartolomé Barrientos, and Miguel Andrés de San, *Dos Antiguas Relaciones De La Florida* (México: Tip. y lit. de J. Auilar vera y Comp. [S. en C.], 1902), 141.

35. Clifford Merle and Albert J. Loomie Lewis, *The Spanish Jesuit Mission in Virginia, 1570–1572* (Chapel Hill, NC: Published for the Virginia Historical Society by the University of North Carolina Press, 1953), 90–92.

36. "Letter from Jesuit Father Quirós," in Mary Letitia Ross papers AC 73–163, GDAH; Anna Brickhouse, *The Unsettlement of America: Translation, Interpretation, and the Story of Don Luis De Velasco, 1560–1945* (Oxford: Oxford University Press, 2015), 46–92.

37. Lisa Voigt, *Writing Captivity in the Early Modern Atlantic: Circulations of Knowledge and Authority in the Iberian and English Imperial Worlds* (The Omohundro Institute of Early American History and Culture and Chapel Hill: University of North Carolina Press, 2009), 99–102, 50–52; Seth Mallios, *The Deadly Politics of Giving: Exchange and Violence at Ajacan, Roanoke, and Jamestown* (Tuscaloosa: University of Alabama Press, 2006), 37–57.

38. Merle and Lewis, *The Spanish Jesuit Mission in Virginia,* 90–92.

39. Mathias Tanner, Melchior Küsel, and Karel Škréta, *Societas Jesu Usque Ad Sanguinis Et Vitae* . . . (Pragae: Typis Universitatis Carolo-Ferdinandeae, in Collegio Societatis Jesu ad S. Clementem, per Joannem Nicolaum Hampel Factorem, 1675), 448.

40. Luís Gerónimo de Oré, "The Martyrs of Florida (1513–1616)," *Franciscan Studies,* no. 18 (1936): 29 (emphasis added); Noble David Cook, "Beyond the Martyrs of Florida: The Versatile Career of Luis Gerónimo De Oré," *FHQ* 71, no. 2 (1992): 187

41. de Oré, "The Martyrs of Florida (1513–1616)," 29.

42. "Relacion muy verdadera de lo sucedido en la Florida en el mes de Jullio" July 1580, AGI-SD Reel 5, Stetson Collection, PKY.

43. Ibid.

44. Ibid.

45. "Deposition taken in San Agustin of French captives," July 24, 1580, in Mary Letitia Ross papers AC 73–163, GDAH.

46. Fray Andrés de San Miguel, *An Early Florida Adventure Story,* trans. John H. Hann (Gainesville: University of Florida, 2000), 81; Paul E. Hoffman, *Florida's*

Frontiers (Bloomington: Indiana University Press, 2002), 151–159; Fred Lamar Pearson Jr., "Spanish-Indian Relations in Florida, 1602–1675: Some Aspects of Selected Visitas," *FHQ* 52, no. 3 (1974):261–73; J. Leitch Wright Jr., "Andrew Ranson: Seventeenth Century Pirate?," *FHQ* 39, no. 2 (1960): 264–265; "Papeles precedentes a varios corsarios franceses, 1533–1596," August 30, 1564, Simancas, Real Armada, 2–5–1/22; Pirates in Santa Elena, September 1586, AGI SD 54–2–4; Agramont's attack, September 30, 1686, AGI-SD 54–5–19; Pirates attacking Apalache, see July 8, 1682, AGI SD 54–1–23, all in Mary Letitia Ross papers AC 73–163, GDAH.

47. Capt. Vicente Gonzalez, June 11, 1586, AGI, Stetson, Reel 6, PKY. For the connection between Indian and *nuevas,* see also Luís Gerónimo de Oré, "The Martyrs of Florida (1513–1616)," "Letter from Jesuit Father Quirós," in Mary Letitia Ross papers AC 73–163, GDAH.

48. *A Summarie and True Discourse of Sir Frances Drakes* (Imprinted at London: By Richard Field, dwelling in the Blacke-Friars by Ludgate, 1589), 42–48, http:// gateway.proquest.com/openurl?ctx_ver=Z39.88–2003&res_id=xri:eebo&rft _val_fmt=&rft_id=xri:eebo:image:23483.

49. *Further English Voyages to Spanish America, 1583–1594. Documents from the Archives of the Indies at Seville Illustrating English Voyages to the Caribbean, the Spanish Main, Florida, and Virginia,* Works Issued by the Hakluyt Society, 2d Ser., (London: Printed for the Hakluyt Society, 1951), 163–164, 80–84, 90–92.

50. "Carta XXIV," January 30, 1566, in *Cartas Sobre La Florida,* 186.

51. For native peoples' connections to the larger Atlantic world, see Jace Weaver, *The Red Atlantic: American Indigenes and the Making of the Modern World, 1000–1927* (Chapel Hill: University of North Carolina Press, 2014), 35–85; Nancy E. van Deusen, *Global Indios: The Indigenous Struggle for Justice in Sixteenth-Century Spain* (Durham, NC: Duke University Press, 2015), 34–98.

52. "San Augustine dilegencias for friendships with Indians of Ays. Horruque and Oribia," 1605, Stetson Collection, Reel 8, bdn 896, 54–5–9; Jerald Milanich, "Early Groups of South and Central Florida," in *Handbook of North American Indians,* vol. 14, 214–216.

53. "San Augustine dilegencias for friendships with Indians of Ays. Horruque and Oribia," 1605, Stetson Collection, Reel 8, bdn 896, 54–5–9.

54. "Horruque, Ays, Oribia, Abia, and Caparaca," July 10, 1605, bnd 896 54–5–9, Reel 8, Stetson Collection, PKY.

55. *Jonathan Dickinson's Journal; or, God's Protecting Providence* ed. Evangeline Walker Andrews and Charles McLean Andrews (New Haven, CT: Yale University Press, 1945). For the Indians' connections to different peoples in the region, see "Gov Aranguiz y Cotes reporting on English settlement," September 8, 1662, bnd 1565, 54–5–10, Reel 12, Stetson Collection PKY; Amy Turner Bushnell, "Escape of Nickaleers, European-Indian Relations on the Wild Coast of Florida in 1696, from Jonathan Dickinson's Journal," in *Coastal*

Encounters: The Transformation of the Gulf South in the Eighteenth Century, ed. Richmond F. Brown (Lincoln: University of Nebraska Press, 2007), 58.

56. "Governor Ybarra inquiries into the Chesapeake," September 13, 1608, AGI-SD 87-5-2, in Mary Letitia Ross papers AC 73–163, GDAH.

57. *Ecija Voyage,* 45.

58. Ibid., 72 ff25; Joseph Hall, "Glimpses of Roanoke, Visions of New Mexico, and Dreams of Empire in the Mixed-Up Memories of Gerónimo de la Cruz," *WMQ* 72, no. 2 (2015): 323–350.

59. August 28, 1609. *Ecija Voyage,* 45. For an earlier reconnaissance of the Guale, see "Al Capt Luis de la Cruz Piloto Mayor," 1600c. Derrotero. "Capítulo 13, Detalles de cómo navegar por San Agustín y Santa Elena" [pp. 30–34.]. HM 30957. HL.

60. August 28, 1609, *Ecija Voyage,* 44–45; "Sgt. Fransisco de Salazar y Cuñiga to spy on the English," May 22, 1610. 1610 May 22, bdn 943, 87-5-2, Reel 9, Stetson Collection, PKY; Index of Letter, undated 1600 ca., bnd 54–5-9/30, Reel 7, Stetson Collection, PKY; Irene A. Wright, "Spanish Policy toward Virginia, 1606-1612; Jamestown, Ecija, and John Clark of the Mayflower," *AHR* 25, no. 3 (1920). For lessons learned from early Florida, see Peter C. Mancall, *Hakluyt's Promise: An Elizabethan's Obsession for an English America* (New Haven, CT: Yale University Press, 2007), 172.

61. "Diego de Rebolledo," September 18, 1657, AGI, Stetson, Reel 12, PKY.

62. John Archdale, *A New Description of That Fertile and Pleasant Province of Carolina: With a Brief Account of Its Discovery and Settling, and the Government Thereof to This Time.* (Charleston, SC: Re-Printed in 1822 and Sold by A. E. Miller, 1707); Samuel Wilson, "An Account of the Province of Carolina, in America . . . (1682)," in *Historical Collections of South Carolina . . . ,* vol. 2, ed. B. R. Carroll (New York: Harper & Bros., 1836): 19–35; Thomas Ash, *Carolina; or a Description of the Present State of the That Country . . .* (1682, repr. Tarrytown, New York: Reprinted W., 1917), 6-14 [178-186]; S. Max Edelson, *Plantation Enterprise in Colonial South Carolina* (Cambridge, MA: Harvard University Press, 2006), 15–24.

63. "Extracts from the Journal of William Edmundson's Second Visit to Carolina," in *The Colonial State Records of the State of North Carolina, Vol. 1* (1886), 226–227; Documenting the American South, University of North Carolina.

64. Joseph Dalton, "Joseph Dalton to Lord Ashley," in *CSCHS Vol. 5,* 183.

65. "William Owen to Lord Ashley," September 15, 1670, PRO 30/24/48, No. 37, 93–94; Timothy Paul Grady, *Anglo-Spanish Rivalry in Colonial South-East America, 1650-1725, Empires in Perspective* (London: Pickering & Chatto, 2010), 24–30.

66. "Mr. Mathews Relation of St. Katherina" in *CSCHS Vol. 5,* 169–171.

67. Samuel Wilson, *An account of the province of Carolina in America . . .* (London: Printed by G. Larkin for Francis Smith . . . 1682). NL.

68. William Hilton, "A Relation of Discovery by William Hilton, 1664," in *Narratives of Early Carolina, 1650–1708,* ed. Alexander S. Salley (New York: Charles Scribner's Sons, 1911), 54–57; Edelson, *Plantation Enterprise in Colonial South Carolina,* 25–30; Elizabeth A. Fenn, Peter H. Wood, and Sydney Nathans, *Natives & Newcomers: The Way We Lived in North Carolina before 1770* (Chapel Hill: University of North Carolina Press, 1983), 33.

69. Jeanette Thurber Connor, *Colonial Records of Spanish Florida, Letters and Reports of Governors and Secular Persons,* vol. 1, 1570–1577 (Deland: The Florida State Historical Society, 1925), 144–185.

70. "H. Woodward to Sir John Yeamans," enclosure in "Sir John Yeamans to Lord Dudley," PRO 30/24/48, No. 33, 131–132.

71. Hilton, "A Relation of Discovery by William Hilton, 1664," 54.

72. Gene Waddell, *Indians of the South Carolina Lowcountry, 1562–1751* (Columbia: University of South Carolina, Southern Studies Programs, 1980), 286–297.

73. John Lawson, *A New Voyage to Carolina* (London: 1709), 10; Documenting the American South, University of North Carolina.

74. For more on Captain Brayne, see Patrick Melvin, "Captain Florence O'Sullivan and the Origins of Carolina," *SCHM* 76, no. 4 (1975): 235–249.

75. Waddell, *Indians of the South Carolina Lowcountry,* 286–298.

76. Stephen Bull, "Stephen Bull to Lord Ashley," Setptember 12, 1670, in *CSCHS Vol. 5,* 195.

77. Ibid.

78. For a similar experience in Roanoke, see Kathleen Donegan, *Seasons of Misery: Catastrophe and Colonial Settlement in Early America* (Philadelphia: University of Pennsylvania Press, 2014), 28.

79. Eliga H. Gould, "Entangled Histories, Entangled Worlds: The English-Speaking Atlantic as a Spanish Periphery," *AHR* 112, no. 3 (2007), 764–786.

80. "Reports on English . . . by Bernardo Medina of Guale," Nov 10, 1678 bnd 2081, 58-1-26/52a Stetson Collection, Reel 15, PKY.

CHAPTER THREE: REBELLIOUS NEWS

Epigraph: "Jesus Maria Letter," Fray Alonso Cuaderas and Cacique Manuel, December 9, 1651, NAA MS 2446-f. Reel 6-i in the National Anthropological Archives, Smithsonian Museum Support Center, Suitland, Maryland. Many thanks to George Aaron Broadwell for a copy of the document.

1. "Menéndez de Avilés to King Philip II," September 11, 1565, in *Pedro Menéndez De Avilés, Cartas Sobre La Florida (1555–1574),* ed. Juan Carlos Mercado (Madrid: Iberoamericana, 2002), 130–140.

2. Bonnie G. McEwan, ed. *The Spanish Missions of La Florida* (Gainesville: The University of Florida Press, 1993), xv; Charles W. Spellman, "The 'Golden Age'

of the Florida Missions, 1632–1674," *The Catholic Historical Review* 51, no. 3 (1965): 358.

3. Jerald T. Milanich, *Laboring in the Fields of the Lord: Spanish Missions and Southeastern Indians* (Washington, DC: Smithsonian Institution Press, 1999), xiv.

4. "Carta de Fray Gómez de Engraba que envió al Padre Fr. Francisco Martínez," March 13, 1657, in Spellman, "The 'Golden Age' of the Florida Missions, 1632–1674," 362.

5. John E. Worth, *The Timucuan Chiefdoms of Spanish Florida, Volume 2: Resistance and Destruction,* vol. 2 (Gainesville: University of Florida, 1998), 9–10; John H. Hann, "1630 Memorial of Fray Francisco Alonso De Jesus on Spanish Florida's Missions and Natives," *The Americas* 50, no. 1 (1993): 85–105.

6. Fred Lamar Pearson Jr., "Spanish-Indian Relations in Florida, 1602–1675: Some Aspects of Selected Visitas," *FHQ* 52, no. 3 (1974): 267; Robert Allen Matter, "The Spanish Missions of Florida: The Friars Versus the Governors in the 'Golden Age,' 1606–1690" (Ph.D. diss., University of Washington, 1972), 441; Michael Gannon, *The Cross in the Sand; the Early Catholic Church in Florida, 1513–1870* (Gainesville: University of Florida Press, 1965), 51, 59–60.

7. Theodore G. Corbett, "Population Structure in Hispanic St. Augustine, 1629–1763," *FHQ* 54, no. 3 (1976): 267.

8. Juan Diez de la Calle. *Memorial Informatorio al Rey* . . . Madrid: 1645, 1–12, JCB; Conde de Juan Francisco Güemes y Horcasitas Revilla Gigedo, *Reglamento Para Las Peculiares* . . . Mexico, 1753, JCB; John R. Dunkle, "Population Change as an Element in the Historical Geography of St. Augustine," *FHQ* 37, no. 1 (1958): 3–10; Theodore G. Corbett, "Migration to a Spanish Imperial Frontier in the Seventeenth and Eighteenth Centuries: St. Augustine," *AHR* 54, no. 3 (1974): 414–430; Kathleen A. Deagan, "Mestizaje in Colonial St. Augustine," *Ethnohistory* 20, no. 1 (1973): 55–65.

9. Amy Turner Bushnell, "The Menéndez Marquéz Cattle Barony at La Chua and the Determinants of Economic Expansion in Seventeenth-Century Florida," *FHQ* 56, no. 4 (1978): 407–431.

10. "Suárez Toledo to King Philip II," July 3, 1586, quoted from Charles W. Arnade, "Florida on Trial, 1593–1602," *Hispanic American Studies,* no. 16 (1959): 11.

11. Kathleen Deagan, "St. Augustine and the Mission Frontier," in *The Spanish Missions of La Florida,* ed. Bonnie G. McEwan, 91; Paul E. Hoffman, *Florida's Frontiers* (Bloomington: Indiana University Press, 2002), 82.

12. Luís Gerónimo de Oré, "The Martyrs of Florida (1513–1616)," *Franciscan Studies,* no. 18 (1936): 23, 100–114, 119, 126–134; John H. Hann, "Church Furnishings, Sacred Vessels and Vestments Held by the Missions of Florida: Translation of Two Inventories," *Florida Archaeology* 2 (1986): 146–164.

13. "Planta de las Pensiones y cargas anuales . . ." 1697, Sp-33 Codex, inn JCB; Gannon, *The Cross in the Sand,* 37.

14. J. Michael Francis, Kathleen M. Kole, and David Hurst Thomas, *Murder and Martyrdom in Spanish Florida Don Juan and the Guale Uprising of 1597,* vol. 95, American Museum of Natural History Anthropological Papers (2011), 32–34.

15. "Letter from Gonzalo Méndez de Canzo," February 23, 1598, AGI SD 224, cited in Francis, Kole, and Thomas, *Murder and Martyrdom in Spanish Florida,* 97–101; Sarah M. S. Pearsall, "'Having Many Wives' in Two American Rebellions: the Politics of Households and the Radically Conservative," *AHR,* 118, no. 4 (2013): 1001–1028.

16. John E. Worth, *The Timucuan Chiefdoms of Spanish Florida, Volume 1: Assimilation,* (Gainesville: University of Florida, 1998), 35–54.

17. "Juego de la Pelota," November 29, 1677, Escribanía de Cámara, Legajo 156, fols 519–615, bnd 2035-a, Reel 14, Stetson Collection, PKY. See also Amy Bushnell, "That Demonic Game": The Campaign to Stop Indian Pelota Playing in Spanish Florida, 1675–1684," *The Americas* 35, no. 1 (1978): 1–19.

18. John Worth, "Spanish Missions and the Persistence of Chiefly Power," in *The Transformation of the Southeastern Indians, 1540-1760,* ed. Robbie Ethridge and Charles Hudson (Jackson: University Press of Mississippi, 2002), 39–65. For *gasto de Indios,* see Amy Turner Bushnell, *Situado and Sabana, Spain's Support System for the Presidio and Mission Provinces of Florida,* vol. 3, Anthropological Papers of the American Museum of Natural History (1994), 46.

19. "Visitation of Timucua," February 13, 1657, in Testimonio de Visita of Governor Diego de Rebolledo, Escribanía de Cámara. Legajo 15, no 188, bnd 1467, Reel 12, Stetson Collection, PKY (cited as *Visita* from now on). See also John H. Hann, "Translation of Governor de Rebolledo's 1657 Visitation of Three Florida Provinces and Related Documents," *Florida Archaeology* 2 (1986): 104.

20. Jerald Milanich, "Timucua," in *Handbook of North American Indians: Southeast,* ed. Raymond D. Fogelson and William C. Sturtevant (Washington, DC: Smithsonian Institution, 2004), 219–228.

21. Ibid, 219. George Aaron Broadwell, "Invisible Authors: Uncovering Native Identity and Intention in Timucua Religious Texts," paper given in the Linguistic Society of America Conference, Minneapolis, 2014.

22. "Junta in San Pedro de Potohiriba, 1670," in Worth, *The Timucuan Chiefdoms of Spanish Florida, Volume 2: Resistance and Destruction,* 193–206.

23. Paul Kelton, *Epidemics and Enslavement: Biological Catastrophe in the Native Southeast, 1492-1715* (Lincoln: University of Nebraska Press, 2007), 82–87; Clark Spencer Larsen, "Colonialism and Decline in the American Southeast: the Remarkable Record of La Florida," in *Beyond Germs: Native Depopulation in North America,* ed. Catherine M. Cameron, Paul Kelton, and Alan C. Swedlund (Phoenix: University of Arizona Press, 2015).

24. "Governor de Rebolledo's reply to the Franciscans," August 5, 1657, in *Visita*, Reel 12, Stetson Collection, PKY. See also Hann, "Translation of Governor de Rebolledo's 1657 Visitation of Three Florida Provinces and Related Documents," 111.

25. "Captain Martín Alcayde de Cordoba," May 2, 1660, in *Visita*, Reel 12, Stetson Collection, PKY.

26. Nicole Greenspan, "News and the Politics of Information in the Mid Seventeenth Century: The Western Design and the Conquest of Jamaica," *History Workshop Journal*, no. 69 (2010): 1–26; Irene A. Wright, *Spanish Narratives of the English Attack on Santo Domingo, 1655* (London: Offices of the Society, 1926); Irene A. Wright, "The Spanish Resistance to the English Occupation of Jamaica, 1655–1660," *Transactions of the Royal Historical Society* 13 (1930): 117–147.

27. *Visita*, Reel 12, Stetson Collection, PKY; John H. Hann, *Apalachee: The Land between the Rivers* (Gainesville: University of Florida Press, 1988), 14–20.

28. *Murder and Martyrdom in Spanish Florida*, 95, 13–27. For the 1647 Apalachee revolt, see Hann, *Apalachee: The Land between the Rivers*, 15, 17–20.

29. Bushnell, "The Menéndez Marquéz Cattle Barony at La Chua and the Determinants of Economic Expansion in Seventeenth-Century Florida," 407–431.

30. Worth, *The Timucuan Chiefdoms of Spanish Florida, Volume 2: Resistance and Destruction*, 2, 92.

31. "Testimony of Manuel Calderón, May 7, 1660, in Caja de San Agustín de Florida. Residencia a Diego de Rebolledo," AGI Contaduría, 963; Worth, *The Timucuan Chiefdoms of Spanish Florida, Volume 2: Resistance and Destruction*, 2, 66–87.

32. For a more in-depth analysis of this document, see Linda Suzanne Cecelia Borgen, "Prelude to Rebellion: Diego De Rebolledo Vs. Lucas Menéndez in Mid-17th Century Spanish Florida" (master's thesis, University of West Florida, Department of Anthropology, 2011), 50–79.

33. Milanich, *Laboring in the Fields of the Lord*, 191; Jerald T. Milanich, "The Timucua Indians of Northern Florida and Southern Georgia," in *Indians of the Greater Southeast: Historical Archaeology and Ethnohistory*, ed. Bonnie G. McEwan (Gainesville: University Press of Florida, 2000), 12–13, 21.

34. *Visita*, Reel 12, Stetson Collection, PKY.

35. Worth, *The Timucuan Chiefdoms of Spanish Florida, Volume 2: Resistance and Destruction*, 2, 77.

36. Robert Allen Matter, "Missions in the Defense of Spanish Florida, 1566–1710," *FHQ* 54, no. 1 (1975): 22–24.

37. Lucy L. Wenhold, "The First Fort of San Marcos De Apalache," *FHQ* 34, no. 4 (1956): 301–314.

38. "Visitation to San Luís," January 22, 1657, in *Visita*, Reel 12, Stetson Collection, PKY; Hann, "Translation of Governor de Rebolledo's 1657 Visitation of Three Florida Provinces and Related Documents," 95.

39. "Visitation to Bacucua," January 19, 1657, in *Visita*, Reel 12, Stetson Collection, PKY; Hann, "Translation of Governor de Rebolledo's 1657 Visitation . . .", 90–91.

40. "Visitation to San Luís," January 22, 1657, in *Visita*, Reel 12, Stetson Collection, PKY; Hann, "Translation of Governor de Rebolledo's 1657 Visitation . . .", 95.

41. "Visitation to San Luís," January 22, 1657, in *Visita*, Reel 12, Stetson Collection, PKY; Hann, "Translation of Governor de Rebolledo's 1657 Visitation . . .", 95.

42. Arnade, "Florida on Trial," 61–70. For a later report on the cost of maintaining the colony, see Juan Diez de la Calle, *Memorial Informatorio Al Rey Nuestro Señor* . . . ([Madrid?], 1645), in JCB.

43. "Governor Pedro Ibarra a Pedro Vermejo," July 27, 1605, Reel 8, Stetson Collection, PKY.

44. John H. Hann, "Evidence Pertinent to the Florida Cabildo Controversy and the Misdating of the Juan Márquez Cabrera Governorship," *FHQ* 79, no. 1 (2000): 71.

45. For examples, see Pedro Menéndez de Avilés, (1565–1574) Escribanía de Cámara. Legajo 156-A, Reel 27-A and 27-B, PKY; Pablo de Hita y Salazar (1675–1680), Escribanía. Legajo 156-A, Reel 27-I [Roll 8], PKY; Diego de Quiroga y Losada (1687–1693) and Laureano de Torres y Ayala (1693–1699), Escribanía de Cámara. Legajo 157-A, Reel 27-O [Roll 14], PKY.

46. "Letter from Jesuit Father Quirós," in Mary Letitia Ross papers AC 73–163, GDAH; Charlotte M. Gradie, "Spanish Jesuits in Virginia: The Mission That Failed," *The Virginia Magazine of History and Biography* 96, no. 2 (1988): 131–156; Lisa Voigt, *Writing Captivity in the Early Modern Atlantic: Circulations of Knowledge and Authority in the Iberian and English Imperial Worlds* (Chapel Hill: The University of North Carolina Press, 2009), 50–52, 99–102.

47. Luís Gerónimo de Oré, "The Martyrs of Florida (1513–1616)," *Franciscan Studies*, no. 18 (1936): 29. For the quote, see Hann, "The 1630 Memorial of Fray Francisco Alonso De Jesus on Spanish Florida's Missions and Natives," 101.

48. Gabriel Díaz Vara Calderón, *A 17th Century Letter of Gabriel Díaz Vara Calderón, Bishop of Cuba, Describing the Indians and Indian Missions of Florida*, ed. Lucy L. Wenhold, and John Reed Swanton, Smithsonian Miscellaneous Collections (Washington, DC: Smithsonian Institution, 1936). For population figures, see Peter H. Wood, "The Changing Population of the Colonial South, an Overview by Race and Region, 1685–1790," in *Powhatan's Mantle: Indians in the Colonial Southeast*, ed. Gregory A. Waselkov, Peter H. Wood, and Tom Hatley (Lincoln: University of Nebraska, 1989), Table 1, 61.

49. Díaz Vara Calderón, *A 17th Century Letter of Gabriel Díaz Vara Calderón, Bishop of Cuba, Describing the Indians and Indian Missions of Florida*, 10; Milanich, *Laboring in the Fields of the Lord*, 134–135.

50. Díaz Vara Calderón, *A 17th Century Letter of Gabriel Díaz Vara Calderón*, 10. For the Chiscas, see Jennifer Baszile, "Apalachee Testimony in Florida, a View of Slavery from the Spanish Archives," in *Indian Slavery in Colonial America*, ed. Alan Gallay (Lincoln: University of Nebraska Press, 2009), 189.

51. "Letter of Provincial and his Council," "Francisco de San Antonio counter reply to Governor de Rebolledo," July 15, 1657, AGI, SD 235; Hann, "Visitations and Revolts in Florida, 1656–1695," *Florida Archaeology* 7 (1993), 21–24. See also Matter, "The Spanish Missions of Florida," 220–229.

52. "Cartas de los religiosos," September 20 and October 6, 1657, Lowery Collection, Banc.

53. Ibid.

54. A. M. Brooks, *The Unwritten History of Old St. Augustine*, trans. Annie Averette (St. Augustine, FL: The Record Co., 1909), 102–105.

55. "Juego de la Pelota." November 29, 1677, Escribanía de Cámara. Legajo, 156, fols 519–615, bnd 2035-a, Reel 14, Stetson Collection, PKY.

56. "Franciscan Petición to de Rebolledo," August 4, 1657. See also "Visita del lugar [San Antonio] de Bacuqua," January 19, 1657; "Visita del lugar de San Pedro de Patali," January 19, 1657; "Visita del lugar de San Juan de Azpalaga," January 22, 1657. AGI Escribanía de Cámara, Legajo 155, Stetson Collection, PKY.

57. "Francisco de San Antonio counter reply to Governor de Rebolledo," July 15, 1657, AGI, SD 235, in Hann, "Visitations and Revolts in Florida, 1656–1695," 21–24.

58. Fred Lamar Pearson Jr., "Timucuan Rebellion of 1656: The de Rebolledo Investigation and the Civil-Religious Controversy," *FHQ* 61, no. 3 (1983): 274.

59. "Adj. Pedro de la Puerta to Governor de Rebolledo," July 12, 1657, in Hann, "Translation of Governor de Rebolledo's 1657 Visitation of Three Florida Provinces and Related Documents," 118.

60. For more details of this debate, see ibid., 81–147; Matter, "The Spanish Missions of Florida," 171–288; Fred Lamar Pearson Jr., "Spanish–Indian Relations in Florida: A Study of Two Visitas, 1657–1678" (Ph.D. diss., The University of Alabama, 1968).

61. Cameron B. Strang, "Indian Storytelling, Scientific Knowledge, and Power in the Florida Borderlands," *WMQ* 70, no. 4 (2013): 671–700.

62. "Testimony of Don Joseph de Prado, Royal Treasurer," "Testimony of Adjutant Pedro de la Puerta," "Testimony of Captain Augustín Pérez de Villa Real," April, 1660, in Caja de San Agustín de Florida. Residencia a Diego de Rebolledo," AGI Contaduría, 963.

63. "Testimony of Captain Francisco de la Rocha," May 6, 1660, in Caja de San Agustín de Florida. Residencia a Diego de Rebolledo," AGI Contaduría, 963.

64. "Testimony of Captain Alonso de Argüelles," May 2, 1660, in Caja de San Agustín de Florida. Residencia a Diego de Rebolledo," AGI Contaduría, 963. From transcriptions of Borgen, "Prelude to Rebellion," 121–129.

65. For the meeting at San Pedro, see "Carta de los religiosos de la Florida," June 16, 1664, AGI, SD 233 in Lanning Papers no. 701. For Lucas and Diego communicating via letters, see "Testimony of Juan Alejo," May 17, 1660, in Caja de San Agustín de Florida. Residencia a Diego de Rebolledo," AGI Contaduría , 963.

66. "Jesus Maria Letter," Fray Alonso Cuaderas and Cacique Manuel, December 9, 1651, Don Patricio Indian to Captain Don Juan de Ayala Escobar, February 28, 1701, SD 840, in the Jeanette Thurber Connor Papers, PKY; Amy Bushnell, "Patricio De Hinachuba: Defender of the Word of God, the Crown of the King, and the Little Children of Ivitachuco," *American Indian Culture and Research Journal* 3, no. 3 (1979): 1–21.
67. "Testimony of Captain Francisco de la Rocha," May 6, 1660, in Caja de San Agustín de Florida. Residencia a Diego de Rebolledo," AGI Contaduría, 963.
68. Worth, *The Timucuan Chiefdoms of Spanish Florida, Volume 2: Resistance and Destruction,* 2, 42.
69. "Testimony of Cacique Clemente Bernal of San Juan del Puerto," May 16, 1660, in Caja de San Agustín de Florida. Residencia a Diego de Rebolledo," AGI Contaduría, 963. From transcriptions in Borgen, "Prelude to Rebellion," 189–190.
70. "Testimony of Cacique Clemente Bernal of San Juan del Puerto," May 16, 1660.
71. Hann, *Apalachee: The Land between the Rivers,* 15, 17–20.
72. Christina Snyder, *Slavery in Indian Country* (Cambridge, MA: Harvard University Press, 2010), 28–45.
73. For the importance of Don Luís, see "Testimony of Don Cosme Catalán," May 3, 1660, and "Testimony of Adjutant Francisco de Monzon" May 4, 1660, in Caja de San Agustín de Florida. Residencia a Diego de Rebolledo, AGI Contaduría, 963.
74. "Testimony of Captain Alonso de Argüelles," May 2, 1660, in Caja de San Agustín de Florida. Residencia a Diego de Rebolledo, AGI Contaduría, 963.
75. "Testimony of Adjutant Francisco de Monzon," May 4, 1660, in Caja de San Agustín de Florida. Residencia a Diego de Rebolledo, AGI Contaduría, 963.
76. "Visitation to San Pedro," February 13, 1657, in *Visita;* Worth, *The Timucuan Chiefdoms of Spanish Florida, Volume 2: Resistance and Destruction,* 91.
77. Snyder, *Slavery in Indian Country,* 13–46.
78. "Visitation to Xinayca," January 22, 1657, in *Visita,* Reel 12, Stetson Collection, PKY. See also Hann, "Translation of Governor de Rebolledo's 1657 Visitation of Three Florida Provinces and Related Documents," 93–94.
79. "Visitation to Ayubale," February 6, 1657, in *Visita,* Reel 12, Stetson Collection, PKY. See also Hann, "Translation of Governor de Rebolledo's 1657 Visitation . . .", 99–100.

PART II. WHO:

THE MANY FACES OF INFORMATION, 1660S–1710S

The Part II epigraph is from Garcilaso de la Vega, *The Florida of the Inca,* trans. and ed. John Grier Varner and Jeannette Johnson Varner (Austin: University of Texas Press, 1951), 641. Copyright © 1951 by the University of Texas Press.

CHAPTER FOUR: INFORMERS AND SLAVES

Epigraph: John H. Hann, "Translation of Alonso de Leturiondo's Memorial to the King of Spain," *Florida Archaeology,* no. 2 (Tallahassee: Florida Bureau of Archaeological Research, 1986), 175. Courtesy of the Florida Department of State.

1. John H. Hann, "Florida's Terra Incognita: West Florida's Natives in the Sixteenth and Seventeenth Century," *The Florida Anthropologist* 40, no. 1 (1988): 73–79.

2. John H. Hann, "Twilight of the Mocamo and Guale Aborigines as Portrayed in the 1695 Spanish Visitation," *FHQ* 66, no. 1 (1987): 10–12.

3. "Indios Chichimecos and relations with San Jorge," June 8, 1675 bnd 1919, 58-1-26/30, Reel 15, Stetson Collection, PKY.

4. "Testimonio de Andrés de Escobedo," May 23 1675, AGI SD 839, fol 193–194, in "Plans for the Colonization of and Defense of Apalachee, 1675," trans. Katherine Redding, *Georgia Historical Quarterly* 9 (1925): 169–175. For similar reports from Guale, see "Letter from Diego Agusti and Juan Chicasli, Chiefs, to His Majesty," March 1, 1699, Santa Elena, AGI-SD 54-5-19, in Mary Letitia Ross papers, AC 73–163, GDAH.

5. John E. Worth, "Razing Florida: The Indian Slave Trade and the Devastation of Spanish Florida, 1659–1715," in *Mapping the Mississippian Shatter Zone: The Colonial Indian Slave Trade and the Regional Transformation in the American South,* ed. Robbie Ethridge and Sheri M. Shuck-Hall (Lincoln: University of Nebraska Press, 2009), 295–311; Eric Browne, *The Westo Indians, Slave Traders of the Early Colonial South* (Tuscaloosa: University of Alabama Press, 2005), 35.

6. Alan Gallay, *The Indian Slave Trade, the Rise of the English Empire in the American South 1670–1717* (New Haven, CT: Yale University Press, 2002), 288–314.

7. "Visitation to Xinayca," January 22, 1657, in *Visita,* Reel 12, Stetson Collection, PKY. See also John H. Hann, "Translation of Governor de Rebolledo's 1657 Visitation of Three Florida Provinces and Related Documents," *Florida Archaeology,* no. 2 (Tallahassee: Florida Bureau of Archaeological Research, 1986): 93–94.

8. Browne, *The Westo Indians,* 20–27.

9. "Carta a Su Magestad," September 8, 1662, in Folder 3, Bolton Papers, Banc.

10. Extracts from "A Letter from Governor Zúñiga to King," March 30, 1704, in Mark F. Boyd, Hale G. Smith, and John W. Griffin, *Here They Once Stood; the Tragic End of the Apalachee Missions* (Gainesville: University of Florida Press, 1951), 48.

11. Gallay, *The Indian Slave Trade,* 70–100; Robbie Ethridge, *From Chicaza to Chickasaw: The European Invasion and the Transformation of the Mississippian World,* 1540-1715 (Chapel Hill: University of North Carolina Press, 2010), 89–116. For a more specific case study, see John H. Hann, "Demise of the Pojoy and Bomto," *FHQ* 74, no. 2 (1995): 184–200.

12. "Letter from Sergeant Major Domingo de Leturiondo," November 5, 1685, Folder 4, Bolton Papers, Banc. For the destruction of Guale, see John E. Worth, *The Struggle for the Georgia Coast: An 18th-Century Spanish Retrospective on Guale and Mocama* (New York: American Museum of Natural History; distributed by the University of Georgia, 1995), 9–55.

13. "Menéndez de Avilés to King," January 30, 1566, in *Pedro Menéndez De Avilés, Cartas Sobre La Florida (1555–1574),* ed. Juan Carlos Mercado (Madrid: Iberoamericana, 2002), 186–191; Karen Lynn Paar, "To Settle Is to Conquer: Spaniards, Native Americans and the Colonization of Santa Elena in the Sixteenth-Century Florida" (Ph.D. diss., University of North Carolina, Chapel Hill, 1999), 273–274; Hann, "Translation of Alonso de Leturiondo's Memorial to the King of Spain," *Florida Archaeology,* no. 2, 171; "Zúñiga y Cerda, General Visitation at Santa Maria," February 7, 1701, cited in "Summary Guide to Spanish Florida Missions and Visitas . . . ," *The Americas* 66, no. 4 (1990): 500.

14. "Cartas Oficiales Reales," June 20, 1668, Lowery Transcripts, Banc.; "Captian Andres Perez," March 26, 1685, AGI54-5-12/14, bnd 2404, Reel 17, Stetson Collection, PKY; "Governor Márquez Cabrera to King," April 8, 1683, AGI-SD 54-5-10, in Mary Letitia Ross papers, AC 73-163, GDAH.

15. "Los Oficiales Reales a SM," July 10, 1685, bnd 2434, 58-2-6/1, Stetson Collection, Reel 17, PKY.

16. "Testimony . . ." April 16, 1683, bnd 2313, 54-5-14/154, Reel 16, Stetson Collection, PKY.

17. "English invasion," March 20 1685, bnd 2463, Reel 17, Stetson Collection, PKY.

18. "Report of attack," May 24, 1683, bnd 2315, 54-5-11/99, Reel 16, Stetson Collection, PKY.

19. "William Owen to Lord Ashley," September 15, 1670, in *CSCHS* 5: 198.

20. "Memorandum from the Virginia Governor's Council to the Board of Trade of Great Britain Concerning Trade and Emigration to Carolina. October 19, 1708," in *The Colonial State Records of the State of North Carolina,* 690–691. Documenting the American South, University of North Carolina.

21. S. Max Edelson, *Plantation Enterprise in Colonial South Carolina* (Cambridge, MA: Harvard University Press, 2006), 50–52.

22. Francis Oldfield, "Deposition regarding John Dixon," June 16, 1708, HM 1386, HL; "To Sir Nathaniel Johnson," September 7, 1708. Petition from Colleton County. HM 1389, HL; "A Certificate . . . [regarding Capt. Thomas Nairne.]," George Smith, September 22, 1708 [written and sent October 16, 1708] HM 1387, HL. For the quote, see "Report of John Stuart to the Lords Commissioners of Trade and Plantations on the Southern Indian Department," March 9, 1764, in Braund, *Deerskins and Duffels: The Creek Indian Trade with Anglo-America, 1685-1815* (Lincoln: University of Nebraska Press, 1993), 26.

23. Eirlys M. Barker, "Pryce Hughes, Colony Planner, of Charles Town and Wales,"

SCHM 95, no. 4 (1994): 302–313; Denise I. Bossy, "Godin & Co.: Charleston Merchants and the Indian Trade, 1674–1715," *SCHM* 114 (2013): 96–131.

24. Though most traders' letterbooks from before the 1730s have not been found, some of the records that do exist include "An edition of Daniel Axtell's account book, 1699–1707," 43/2103; Ravenel, Henry, 1729–1785, Henry Ravenel papers, 1752–1777 (43/709); Sindrey, Elizabeth, d. 1705. Elizabeth Sindrey estate account book, 1705–1721 (34/355 OvrSz), all in SCHS. Henry Woodward's Account Book, SCDAH.

25. *South Carolina Gazette,* July 3, 1736, as quoted in Verner W. Crane, *The Southern Frontier, 1670–1732* (Durham, NC: Duke University Press, 1928), 115.

26. Ibid.

27. "That the Governor be Advised," April 27, 1704, *JCHA,* 232.

28. Steven J. A. Oatis, *A Colonial Complex, South Carolina's Frontiers in the Era of the Yamasee War, 1680–1730* (Lincoln: University of Nebraska Press, 2004), 35; Eugene M. Sirmans, *Colonial South Carolina, a Political History, 1663–1763* (Chapel Hill: University of North Carolina Press, 1966), 19–35.

29. "Lords Proprietors of Carolina to the Governor and Council of Ashley River," March 7, 1681, CO 5/286, 165–168, in *CSP;* "Journal of the Grand Council," September 27, 1671, in William J. Rivers, *A Sketch of the History of South Carolina . . .* (Charleston, SC: McCarter & Co, 1856), 372; Jessic Stern, "The Economic Philosophies of Indian Trade Regulation Policy in Early South Carolina," in *Creating and Contesting Carolina: Proprietary Era Histories,* ed. Michelle LeMaster and Bradford J. Wood (Columbia: University of South Carolina Press), 97–117.

30. Edelson, *Plantation Enterprise in Colonial South Carolina,* 50–52.

31. "May it Pleased your Lordship," October 1, 1700, *Commissions and Instructions from the Lord Proprietors of Carolina to Public Officials of South Carolina, 1685–1715,* ed. A. S. Salley (Columbia: The Historical Commission of South Carolina, 1916), 144.

32. "From Bienville and Salmon to Maurepas," September 1, 1736, *MPA, French Dominion,* vol. 1, 321.

33. "Governor Francisco de Córcoles y Martínez . . . ," January 22, 1710, 58-1-28/72, bnd 4545 Stetson Collection, Reel 34, PKY.

34. "Report," September 17, 1708, PRO, vol. 9, 207 [82], SCDAH; Robert Paulett, *An Empire of Small Places: Mapping the Southeastern Anglo-Indian Trade, 1732-1795* (Athens: University of Georgia Press, 2012), 12–35.

35. "Ordered . . ." November 15, 1700, 272 [359], *JCHA;* Bossy, "Godin & Co.," 101–113.

36. "Robert Stevens . . . to the Secretary," n.d., 1703, SPG Series A, volume I, 29.

37. "Gideon Johnston to Lord Bishop of Sarum," September 20, 1708, SPG Series A, volume I, 81–85.

38. "Francis Le Jau the Society," August 5, 1709, SPG Series A, volume I, 94–96.

39. Jennifer Baszile, "Communities at the Crossroads: Chiefdoms, Colonies, and Empires in Colonial Florida, 1670-1741" (Ph.D. diss., Princeton University, 1991), 212.

40. *Ecija Voyage*, 44–45; Francis, Kole, and Hurst Thomas, *Murder and Martyrdom in Spanish Florida, Don Juan and the Guale Uprising of 1597.* vol. 95, American Museum of Natural History Anthropological Papers (2011), 20–30.

41. "Testimonio de Antonio Argüelles," in "Governor Manuel de Cendoya to the Queen," October 31, 1671, AGI 58–1–26, bnd 1741, Stetson Collection, Reel 13, PKY.

42. "Testimonio de la cacica," in Governor Manuel de Cendoya to the Queen, October 31, 1671, AGI 58–1–26, bnd 1741, Stetson Collection, Reel 13, PKY.

43. "Testimonio de Antonio Argüelles," in Governor Manuel de Cendoya to the Queen, October 31, 1671, AGI 58–1–26, bnd 1741, Stetson Collection, Reel 13, PKY.

44. "Testimonio of Antonio Camuñas," Governor Manuel de Cendoya to the Queen, October 31, 1671, AGI 58–1–26, bnd 1741, Stetson Collection, Reel 13, PKY.

45. "William Owen to Lord Ashley," September 15, 1670, in *CSCHS* 5: 196–202.

46. "Manuel Cendoya to the Crown," March 24, 1672, AGI-SD 839, folio 273–274, Reel 8, PKY.

47. "Governor Manuel de Cendoya to the Queen," October 31, 1671, AGI 58–1–26, bnd 1741, Stetson Collection, Reel 13, PKY.

48. Ibid.

49. "Testimonio de Antonio Argüelles," in Governor Manuel de Cendoya to the Queen, October 31, 1671, AGI 58–1–26, bnd 1741, Stetson Collection, Reel 13, PKY; "Letters from governor," March 24, 1672, bnd 1759, 58–1–26, Stetson Collection, Reel 13, PKY.

50. William Green, Chester B. DePratter, and Bobby Southerlin, "The Yamasee in South Carolina: Native American Adaptation and Interaction along the Carolina Frontier," in *Another's Country: Archaeological and Historical Perspectives on Cultural Interactions in the Southern Colonies* (Tuscaloosa: University of Alabama Press, 2001), 19–29; John E. Worth, "Yamasee," in *Handbook of North American Indians: Southeast,* ed. Raymond D. Fogelson and William C. Sturtevant (Washington, DC: Smithsonian Institution, 2004), 245–256.

51. Crane, *The Southern Frontier,* 26; George Pratt Insh, "Arrival of the Cardoss Settlers," *The South Carolina Genealogical Magazine* 30, no. 2 (1929): 69–80; Gallay, *The Indian Slave Trade,* 76–79; Lawrence Sanders Rowland, *The History of Beaufort County, South Carolina: 1514–1861* (Columbia: University of South Carolina Press, 1996), 67–75.

52. Ethridge, *From Chicaza to Chickasaw,* 100–102.

53. "Dr. Henry Woodward to Deputy Governor Colonel John Godfrey," March 21, 1685, CO 5/287, 143, in *CSP.*

54. "The Examination of Severall Yamasee Indians," May 6, 1685, PRO, 66.

55. Hann, "Twilight of the Mocamo and Guale Aborigines," 12.

56. Kowalewski, "Coalescent Societies," in *Light on the Path: The Anthropology*

of the Southeastern Indians, ed. Robbie Ethridge and Thomas J. Puckhahn (Tuscaloosa: The University of Alabama Press, 2006), 94–122.

57. Often called the "Province of Apalichicole, Cauetta, and Cassitta." See "Juan Márquez Cabrera," March 18, 1687, AGI-SD 54-5-12, in Lanning Papers no. 702. The Spanish continued using these names into the 1740s; see "Alonso Márquez del Toro," April 18, 1738, Stetson Collection, Reel 43 PKY.

58. Oatis, *A Colonial Complex,* 120; Steve C. Hahn, "'They Look Upon the Yuchis as Their Vassals': An Early History of Yuchi-Creek Political Relations," in *Yuchi Indian Histories before the Removal Era,* ed. Jason Baird Jackson (Lincoln: University of Nebraska Press, 2012), 123–154.

59. "Antonio Matheos to Márquez Cabrera," February 8, 1686, AGI SD 839, in Lanning Papers no. 702. For the English, see "Caleb Westbrook to Gov. West," February 21, 1685, Folder 3, Bolton Papers, Banc.

60. "Craven to the Grand Council," October 10, 1687, in *PRO,* Vol. 4, 221–228.

61. "Melchor Portocarrero to Francisco Salazar," September 15, 1683, St AGI 58-1-37/1, bnd 2342, Reel 16, Stetson Collection, PKY.

62. Crane, *The Southern Frontier,* 31–33; Peter Wood, *Black Majority, Negroes in Colonial South Carolina from 1670 through the Stono Rebellion* (New York: W. W. Norton & Company, 1974), 50; Worth, *The Struggle for the Georgia Coast,* 146–171; "Letter from Mr. Randolph to the Board, March 16, 1698/9," in *PRO,* Vol. 4, 88–95; J. G. Dunlop, "Spanish Depredations, 1686," *The South Carolina Genealogical Magazine* 30, no. 2 (1929): 81-89; Jane Landers, *Black Society in Spanish Florida, Blacks in the New World* (Urbana: University of Illinois Press, 1999), 23.

63. "The Examination of Severall Yamasee Indians," May 6, 1685, PRO, Vol.2, 66.

64. J. G. Dunlop, "Journal, Capt Dunlop's Voyage to the Southward, 1687," *The South Carolina Genealogical Magazine* 30, no. 3 (1929): 132–133.

65. "Testimonio de Blauacacy" in Governor Manuel de Cendoya to the Queen, October 31, 1671, AGI 58-1-26, bnd 1741, Stetson Collection, Reel 13, PKY; Wood, *Black Majority,* 35–55; Ira Berlin, *Many Thousands Gone, the First Two Centuries of Slavery in North America* (Cambridge, MA: Belknap Press of Harvard University, 1998), 64–71.

66. "Governor Quiroga addressed the crown, reporting the arrival of certain Negro slaves who came from San Jorge to become Christians," February 24, 1688, in Wright, "Dispatches of Spanish Officials Bearing in the Free Negro Settlement of Gracia Real De Santa Teresa De Mose, Florida," *The Journal of Negro History* 9, no. 2 (1924), 150; Landers, *Black Society in Spanish Florida,* 24.

67. J. G. Dunlop, "William Dunlop's Mission to St. Augustine in 1688," *SCHGM* 34, no. 1 (1933): 1–30.

68. "Quiroga y Losada a SM," August 16, 1689, in Wright, "Dispatches of Spanish Officials," 153–154; "Quiroga y Losada a SM," June 8, 1690, in Wright,

"Dispatches of Spanish Officials," 156–157; "Recommendations on how to deal with English slaves," April 12, 1731, AGI 86–5–21/33, bnd 5310, Reel 40, Stetson Collection, PKY.

69. Edward B. Rugemer, "The Development of Mastery and Race in the Comprehensive Slave Codes of the Greater Caribbean During the Seventeenth Century," *WMQ* 70, no. 3 (2013): 429–458.

70. "Quiroga y Losada to the King transmitting a statement relative to the Bay of Espiritu Santo," Febuary 24, 1688, Reel 19, Stetson Collection, PKY; Alejandra Dubcovsky, "The Testimony of Thomás De La Torre, a Spanish Slave," *WMQ* 70, no. 3 (2013): 559–580.

71. "A Bill for Governing of Negroes," October 8, 1737, *JCHA*, 362–365.

72. Dunlop, "Spanish Depredations, 1686," 82.

73. Dunlop, "Spanish Depredations, 1686," 84.

74. Ibid.

75. Dunlop, "Spanish Depredations, 1686," 84; Christopher Gale, "Memorial from Inhabitants of South Carolina to Seth Sothell Concerning the State of Government," in *The Colonial State Records of the State of North Carolina*, 839–852. Documenting the American South, University of North Carolina.

76. "An act for the defense of the Country," February 20, 1686, *The Statutes at Large of South Carolina*, Vol. 2. (Columbia: Printed by A. S. Johnston, 1837), 23–24 (emphasis added).

77. Ibid.

78. "James Moore . . . ," February 19, 1709, *JCHA*, 413.

79. John TePaske, "The Fugitive Slave, Intercolonial Rivalry and Spanish Policy, 1687–1764," in *Eighteenth-Century Florida and Its Borderlands*, ed. Samuel Proctor (Gainesville: University of Florida Press, 1975), 7.

80. "Thom. Smith," September 12, 1603, *JCHA*, 27.

81. "John Archdale for Thomas Archdale," June 5, 1682, PRO, Colonial Entry Book, 173–174 [195].

82. Gallay, *The Indian Slave Trade*, 70–98.

83. Ian K. Steele, *The English Atlantic: An Exploration of Communication and Community* (Oxford: Oxford University Press, 1986), 168, 204–206.

84. Charles W. Arnade, *The Siege of St. Augustine in 1702* (Gainesville: University of Florida Press, 1959), 11.

85. Governor Zúñiga y Cerda, "The Siege of St. Augustine in 1702: A Report to the King of Spain by the Governor of East Florida," trans. Mark F. Boyd *FHQ* 26, no. 4 (1948): 348.

86. "Diego de Florencia to Governor Zúñiga," January 25, 1703, in Boyd, Smith, and Griffin, *Here They Once Stood*, 39–40.

87. "Capt Jacinto Roque Perez to Governor Zúñiga," May 25, 1703, in Boyd, Smith, and Griffin, *Here They Once Stood*, 42–44.

88. "Governor Zúñiga y Cerda to King," September 30, 1702, Folder 7, Bolton Papers, Banc.

89. "Several Servants . . ." September 6, 1703, in *Journals of the Commons House of Assembly, for 1703,* ed. A. S. Salley Jr. (Columbia, SC: The State Company, 1934), 103; Steven C. Hahn, *The Invention of the Creek Nation, 1670–1763* (Lincoln: University of Nebraska Press, 2004), 58–65.

90. "Opinion of the House," January 27, 1703, in *Journals of the Commons House of Assembly,* 25; Charles W. Arnade, "The English Invasion of Spanish Florida, 1700–1706," *FHQ* 41, no. 1 (1962): 29–38.

91. "Colonel Moore To Sir Nathaniel Johnston," in Boyd, Smith, and Griffin, *Here They Once Stood,* 91–93; "Letter from Governor Zúñiga to King," in Boyd, Smith, and Griffin, *Here They Once Stood,* 48–50; Antonio Bizarròn, *Primera y Breve Relacion De Las Favorables Noticias . . .* (Madrid, 1703), in JCB.

92. William Hammerton, "Map of the Southeastern Part of North America, 1721," YCBA.

93. Boyd, "Further Consideration of the Apalachee Missions," *The Americas* 9, no. 4 (1953), 469.

94. "Auto of an inquiry into the deaths of the Friars of Apalachee," June 5, 1705, in Boyd, Smith, and Griffin, *Here They Once Stood,* 74–82, quote on page 77.

95. Myra Jehlen, "History before the Fact; or, Captain John Smith's Unfinished Symphony," *Critical Inquiry* 19, no. 4 (1993): 677–692.

96. "Governor Zúñiga to King," San Agustín, September 3, 1704, Jehlen, "History before the Fact," 66.

97. "Manuel Solana to Governor Zúñiga," July 8, 1704, in Boyd, Smith, and Griffin, *Here They Once Stood,* 51–55, quote on page 53.

98. "Manuel Solana to Governor Zúñiga," July 8, 1704, in Boyd, Smith, and Griffin, *Here They Once Stood,* 51–55.

99. Gallay, *The Indian Slave Trade,* 145; Hahn, *The Invention of the Creek Nation,* 63; Ethridge, *From Chicaza to Chickasaw,* 209; Hall, *Zamumo's Gifts: Indian-European Exchange in the Colonial Southeast* (Philadelphia: University of Pennsylvania Press, 2009), 107–108.

100. MAP/IR-237, William Hammerton (d. 1732), "Map of the Southeastern Part of North America, 1721," YCBA.

101. Ibid.

102. "Colonel Moore To Sir Nathaniel Johnston," April 16, 1704, in Boyd, Smith, and Griffin, *Here They Once Stood,* 91–93, quote on page 92.

103. John H. Hann, "Church Furnishings, Sacred Vessels and Vestments Held by the Missions of Florida: Translation of Two Inventories," *Florida Archaeology* no. 2 (Tallahassee: Florida Bureau of Archaeological Research, 1986): 146–164.

104. "Manuel Solana to Governor Zúñiga," July 8, 1704, in Boyd, Smith, and Griffin, *Here They Once Stood,* 51–55.

105. "Council of War, San Agustín," July 13, 1704, in Boyd, Smith, and Griffin, *Here They Once Stood,* 58–59.

106. "Colonel Moore To Sir Nathaniel Johnston," April 16, 1704, in Boyd, Smith, and Griffin, *Here They Once Stood,* 91–93.

107. Hahn, *The Invention of the Creek Nation,* 58–65.

108. Thomas Nairne, *A Letter from South Carolina* (London: Printed for A. Baldwin, 1710), 34.

109. "An Act for Regulating the Indian Trade," June 7, 1712, *The Statutes at Large of South Carolina,* Vol. 2, 381.

110. Crane, *The Southern Frontier,* 89–100.

111. "A Certificate . . . [regarding Capt. Thomas Nairne.]," George Smith, September 22, 1708 [written and sent October 16, 1708] HM 1387, HL; "Petition to Queen Anne," Thomas Nairne. 1708, HM 1384, HL; "To [Earl of Sunderland]," Thomas Nairne, HM 22268, HL.

112. "Letter from Col. A Spotswood Lieut. Governor of Virginia, dated the 15th of October 1711, giving an account of a massacre committed by the Tuscarora Indians and a great many of the palatines in North Carolina of the disobedience of ye Quakers in Virginia and of 2 vacancies in the council there," HM 59962, HL; David La Vere, *The Tuscarora War: Indians, Settlers, and the Fight for the Carolina Colonies* (Chapel Hill: University of North Carolina Press, 2013), 69–95.

113. "An Account of Missionaries Sent to South Carolina," in *CSCHS* Vol. 2, 103; La Vere, *The Tuscarora War,* 153–177.

114. Joseph W. Barnwell, "The Second Tuscarora Expedition," *The South Carolina Genealogical Magazine* 10, no. 1 (1908): 36; "The Tuscarora Expedition, Letters of Colonel John Barnwell," *The South Carolina Genealogical Magazine* 10, no. 1 (1908): 30–31.

115. "The Tuscarora Expedition, Letters of Colonel John Barnwell," *The South Carolina Genealogical Magazine* 10, no. 1 (1908): 32.

116. November 9, 1711, 596, *JCHA,* 596.

117. "Speaker to the House," May 5, 1711, 552, *JCHA.*

118. November 18–20, 1712, *JCHA,* 109–110; Barnwell, "The Second Tuscarora Expedition," 45.

119. Gallay, *The Indian Slave Trade,* 281.

120. Ethridge and Shuck-Hall, *Mapping the Mississippian Shatter Zone,* 2–3.

CHAPTER FIVE: THE INFORMATION RACE

Epigraph: "Papeles de los Yngleses escritos a los Caciques Apalachicola traducidos en Castellano," September 2, 1685, AGI SD 839, folio 515, Reel 18, PKY. Quote from English translation in Herbert E. Bolton and Mary Ross,

The Debatable Land: A Sketch of the Anglo-Spanish Contest for the Georgia Country (Berkeley: University of California Press, 1925), 50.

1. Joseph Dalton, "Joseph Dalton to Lord Ashley," in *CSCHS*, Vol. 5, 183–187; "Henry Woodward to Sir John Yeamas," September 10, 1670, in *CSCHS*, Vol. 5, 186–188; Joseph W. Barnwell, "Dr. Henry Woodward, the First English Settler in South Carolina, and Some of His Descendants," *SCHGM* 8, no. 1 (1907): 29–32.

2. John H. Hann, *The Native American World beyond Apalachee: West Florida and the Chattahoochee Valley* (Gainesville: University of Florida, 2006), 107.

3. For a discussion of the use of the cross and symbols in Spanish delegations see Juliana Barr, *Peace Came in the Form of a Woman: Indians and Spaniards in the Texas Borderlands* (Chapel Hill: The University of North Carolina Press, 2007), 109–119.

4. "Letter of Antonio Matheos," in Folder 4, Bolton Papers, Banc.

5. John H. Hann, "Cloak and Dagger in Apalachicole Province in Early 1686," *FHQ* 78, no. 1 (1999): 74–93.

6. "Delgado's Report . . . ," January 5, 1687, 29, in Mark F. Boyd, "Expedition of Marcos Delgado, 1686," *FHQ* 16, no. 1 (1937): 4–33.

7. For early Spanish efforts in Apalachicola, see Paul E. Hoffman, *Florida's Frontiers* (Bloomington: Indiana University Press, 2002), 109–110; Jennifer Baszile, "Communities at the Crossroads: Chiefdoms, Colonies, and Empires in Colonial Florida, 1670-1741" (Ph.D. diss., Princeton University, 1991), 138–144; Hann, *The Native American World beyond Apalachee*, 106–122.

8. Patrick Lee Johnson, "Apalachee Identity on the Gulf Coast Frontier," *Native South* 6, no. 10 (2013): 110–141; Robert C. Galgano, *Feast of Souls: Indians and Spaniards in the Seventeenth-Century Missions of Florida and New Mexico* (Albuquerque: University of New Mexico Press, 2005), 93.

9. "Don Pablo Hita y Salazar reporting . . ." March 8, 1680, in "Documents Concerning the Settlement of Florida, English Encroachments, and Indian Troubles," in Folder 3, Bolton Papers, Banc.

10. Bonnie G. McEwan, "The Apalachee Indians of Northwest Florida," in *Indians of the Greater Southeast: Historical Archaeology and Ethnohistory,* ed. Bonnie G. McEwan (Gainesville: University Press of Florida, 2000), 57–84.

11. James M. Crawford, "Southeastern Indian Languages," in *Studies in Southeastern Indian Languages,* ed. James M. Crawford (Athens: University of Georgia Press, 1975), 26; Mary R. Haas, "The Position of Apalachee in the Muskogean Family," in *Language, Culture, and History: Essay by Mary R. Haas* (Stanford, CA: Stanford University Press, 1978), 2882–2893.

12. Steven C. Hahn, "Cussita Migration Legend," in *Light on the Path: The Anthropology of the Southeastern Indians,* ed. Robbie Ethridge and Thomas J. Puckhahn (Tuscaloosa: The University of Alabama Press, 2006), 57–93; Joseph Hall, "Anxious Alliances: Apalachicola Efforts to Survive the Slave Trade,

1638–1705," in *Indian Slavery in Colonial America*, ed. Alan Gallay (Lincoln: University of Nebraska Press, 2009), 147–184.

13. "Diego de Quiroda y Losada al Rey," April 1, 1688, AGI-SD 58-1-26, Microfilm 290/69/, Section 4-3, Mary Letitia Ross papers, AC 73-163, GDAH.

14. "Don Juan Márquez Cabrera a SM," December 1680, "Letter from Fray Juan Francisco Gutiérrez de Vega," July 12, 1681, both in Folder 3, Bolton Papers, Banc. See also Hoffman, *Florida's Frontiers*, 160–161.

15. Antonio de Arredondo. Demostración Historiográphica . . . March 20, 1742, in Arredondo's Historical Proof of Spain's Title to Georgia . . . , ed. Herbert E. Bolton (Berkeley: University of California Press, 1925), 45–54; "Report of Quiroga about building fort in Apalachee," June 8, 1690, AGI-SD 54-5-10, Microfilm 290/69/, Section 4-3, Mary Letitia Ross papers, AC 73-163, GDAH.

16. "The cacique of Santa María to the King," March 1, 1699, bnd 54-5-19, Stetson Collection, Reel 26, PKY.

17. "Juan Márquez Cabrera a Su Magestad," November 8, 1686, AGI-SD 54-5-12, in Mary Letitia Ross papers, AC 73-163, GDAH. For destabilization caused by English slaving, see Ethridge, "Creating the Shatter Zone: Indian Slave Traders and Collapse of Southeastern Chiefdoms," in *Light on the Path,* 208.

18. "Los ofiziales Reales," October 4, 1686, bnd 2512 54-5-15/33, Stetson Collection, Reel 18, PKY.

19. "Lettre du sieur Argoud au Ministre de la Marine, Paris," December 10, 1697, in Margry's *Mémoure sur le project d'establir . . .* (1879), 19–45.

20. "Letter from Governor of Saint-Domingue to Ministre de la Marine," October 29, 1699, in Margry's *Mémoure sur le project d'establir . . .* (1879); Robbie Ethridge, *From Chicaza to Chickasaw: The European Invasion and the Transformation of the Mississippian World, 1540-1715* (Chapel Hill: University of North Carolina Press, 2010), 126–148.

21. "Reports on French settlements near Pensacola," March 19, 1699, bnd 3607, 61-6-22/11, Stetson Collection, Reel 26, PKY; Jennifer M. Spear, *Race, Sex, and Social Order in Early New Orleans* (Baltimore, MD: Johns Hopkins University Press, 2008), 9, 19–20.

22. "Abstracts of letters of Mr. Bienville," July 28, 1706, in *MPA: French Dominion*, Vol. 2, 23–25.

23. "From Diron D'artaguette to Maurepas," *MPA: French Dominion,* Vol. 1, 337–342; "Mr. Bienville to the Count of Pontchartrain," October. 12, 1708, in *MPA: French Dominion,* Vol. 1, 39.

24. Worth, "The Lower Creeks: Origins and Early History," in *Indians of the Greater Southeast: Historical Archaeology and Ethnohistory,* ed. Bonnie G. McEwan (Gainesville: University Press of Florida, 2000), 265–298.

25. Christina Snyder, *Slavery in Indian Country* (Cambridge, MA: Harvard University Press, 2010), 46–79.

26. "Lord Cardross and William Dunlop to Peter Colleton," March 27, 1685, cited in

George Pratt Insh, "The 'Carolina Merchant': Advice of Arrival," *The Scottish Historical Review* 25, no. 98 (1928): 98–108, quote from page 104; "Lord Cardross to the Governor and Grand Council of Charlestown," CO 5/287, 134; Alan Gallay, *The Indian Slave Trade, the Rise of the English Empire in the American South 1670–1717* (New Haven, CT: Yale University Press, 2002), 77–80.

27. "Deposition," May 18, 1685, Folder 3, Bolton Papers, Banc; Steven C. Hahn, *The Invention of the Creek Nation, 1670–1763* (Lincoln: University of Nebraska Press, 2004), 42.

28. John H. Hann, "Florida's Terra Incognita: West Florida's Natives in the Sixteenth and Seventeenth Century," *The Florida Anthropologist* 40, no. 1 (1988): 61–107.

29. "Los ofiziales Reales," October 4, 1686, bnd 2512 54–5–15/33, Stetson Collection, Reel 18, PKY.

30. "Don Pablo Hita y Salazar reporting . . . ," Folder 3, Bolton Papers, Banc; "Reports from Apalachicola," January 25, 1682, bnd 2241 54–5–11/95, Stetson Collection, Reel 16, PKY.

31. Robert Sandford, "A Relation of a Voyage on the Coast of the Province of Carolina by Robert Sandford, 1666," in *Narratives of Early Carolina, 1650-1708*, ed. Alexander S. Salley (New York: Charles Scribner's Sons, 1911), 105.

32. "Cartas Oficiales," June 20, 1668, Lowery Collections, Banc. For Searles, see David Marley, *Pirates of the Americas*, 2 vols. (Santa Barbara, CA: ABC-CLIO, 2010), 351–357.

33. Joyce E. Chaplin, "Woodward, Henry," *American National Biography Online*, February 2000; "Juan Márquez Cabrera to King," March 19, 1686, Full Legajos, SD-839, 555–6, Reel 18, PKY.

34. "A Faithfull Relations of My Westoe Voaige, by Henry Woodward, 1674," in *Narratives of Early Carolina*, 133.

35. Ibid., 130; S. Max Edelson, *Plantation Enterprise in Colonial South Carolina* (Cambridge, MA: Harvard University Press, 2006), 24–33.

36. "Order Concerning the Trade with the Westoes and Cussatoes Indians," April 10, 1677, in William J. Rivers, *A Sketch of the History of South Carolina . . .* (Charleston, SC: McCarter & Co, 1856), 388–389.

37. Eric Browne, *The Westo Indians, Slave Traders of the Early Colonial South* (Tuscaloosa: The University of Alabama Press, 2005), 35; John T. Juricek, "The Westo Indians," *Ethnohistory* 11, no. 2 (1964): 134–173.

38. "A Faithfull Relations of My Westoe Voaige, by Henry Woodward, 1674," in *Narratives of Early Carolina*, 133.

39. Browne, *The Westo Indians*, 82–85.

40. "A Faithfull Relations of My Westoe Voaige, by Henry Woodward, 1674," in *Narratives of Early Carolina*, 134.

41. "Henry Woodward's Account Book," in SCDAH.

42. Gallay, *The Indian Slave Trade,* 56–61.

43. "Letter from a Westoe Town," November 12, 1675, published in Gene Waddell, *Indians of the South Carolina Lowcountry, 1562-1751* (Columbia: University of South Carolina Press, 1980), 387–388.

44. "Declaration of Niquisaya," March 22, 1685, AGI SD 839, and "Juan Márquez Cabrera a Su Magestad," November 8, 1686, AGI-SD 54-5-12, in Mary Letitia Ross papers AC 73–163, GDAH; Hahn, *The Invention of the Creek Nation,* 40–47; Arredondo. *Demostración Historiográphica . . . March 20, 1742,* 159. Juan Márquez Cabrera a Su Magestad," November 8, 1686, AGI-SD 54-5-12, in Mary Letitia Ross papers, AC 73–163, GDAH.

45. "Juan Márquez Cabrera a Su Magestad," November 8, 1686, AGI-SD 54-5-12, in Mary Letitia Ross papers, AC 73–163, GDAH; Worth, *The Struggle for the Georgia Coast: An 18th-Century Spanish Retrospective on Guale and Mocama,* (Athens: American Museum of Natural History; distributed by the University of Georgia, 1995), 54, 204.

46. Worth, *The Struggle for the Georgia Coast,* 54, 204; Hahn, *The Invention of the Creek Nation,* 42. For more on the Creek–Yamasee connections, see A. S. Salley, ed., *Journal of Colonel John Herbert . . .* February 10, 1727, 24–40.

47. There are only rumors that Woodward sent his agents to the Chickasaws. The first documented traders with the Chickasaws were Thomas Welch and Anthony Dodsworth in the 1690s. Woodward traveled to Coweta and Cussita; see "Juan Márquez Cabrera a Su Magestad," November 8, 1686, AGI-SD 54-5-12, in Mary Letitia Ross papers, AC 73–163, GDAH; "Bienville to Pontchartrain, September 6, 1704," in *MPA: French Dominion,* Vol. 3, 18–29, especially page 26; Ethridge, "Creating the Shatter Zone: Indian Slave Traders and Collapse of Southeastern Chiefdoms," in *Light on the Path,* 215; Fred Lamar Pearson Jr., "Anglo-Spanish Rivalry in the Chattahoochee Basin and West Florida, 1685–1704," *SCHM* 79, no. 1 (1978): 50–59; Hahn, "The Mother of Necessity: Carolina, the Creeks, and the Making of a New Order in the Southeast, 1670–1763," in *The Transformation of the Southeastern Indians, 1540-1760,* ed. Robbie Ethridge and Charles Hudson (Jackson: University Press of Mississippi, 2002), 94.

48. "Juan Márquez Cabrera a Su Magestad," April 15, 1685, AGI 856, in the Lanning Papers no. 702.

49. For other attempts to coerce Indian informants, see Kathleen DuVal, *The Native Ground, Indians and Colonists in the Heart of the Continent* (Philadelphia, PA: University of Philadelphia Press, 2006), 33–60; Philip Levy, *Fellow Travelers: Indians and Europeans Contesting the Early American Trials* (Gainesville: University of Florida Press, 2007), Chapters 1 and 2.

50. "Carta del Teniente de Apa[lachee] La entrada que hice en Apalachicoli," October 4, 1685, AGI SD 839, folio 517, Reel 18, PKY.

51. "Carta del Teniente de Apa[lachee] La entrada que hice en Apalachicoli," October 4, 1685, AGI SD 839, folio 517, Reel 18, PKY.

52. Ibid.

53. Ibid.

54. Ibid.

55. Ibid.; Hahn, *The Invention of the Creek Nation,* 45.

56. Herbert E. Bolton, *The Spanish Borderlands, a Chronicle of Old Florida and the Southwest* (New Haven: Yale University Press, 1921), 140; Worth, *The Struggle for the Georgia Coast,* 46.

57. Bushnell, *Situado and Sabana,* 155.

58. "Domingo de Leturiondo to Márquez Cabrera," November 28, 1685, AGI, SD 639 Folder 4, Bolton Papers, Banc.

59. "Fray Juan Mercado," November 27, 1685, Folder 4, Bolton Papers, Banc. Translation from Hann, "Cloak and Dagger in Apalachicole Province," 80–81.

60. Hahn, *The Invention of the Creek Nation,* 43.

61. "Fray Juan Mercado," November 27, 1685, Folder 4, Bolton Papers, Banc. For later recollections, see "Expedientes o instancias de partas, años 1720 a 1760," July 29, 1734, AGI SD 86–5–6, Mary Letitia Ross papers, AC 73–163, GDAH.

62. "Carta del Teniente de Apa[lachee] La entrada que hice en Apalachicoli," October 4, 1685, AGI SD 839, folio 517, Reel 18, PKY. For earlier examples, see "Pedro de Ybarra," AGI, SD Legajo 224, Folio 658–920, Full Legajo, Reel 1 28-B, PKY; "The governor's investigations," June 15, 1666, Reel 12, AGI 54–1–20, bnd 1621, Stetson Collection, PKY.

63. "Declaración del Casique de Apalachicola," 1686, AGI SD 839, folio 542, Reel 18, PKY. See also Hahn, *The Invention of the Creek Nation,* 44–47; Herbert Eugene Bolton and John Francis Bannon, *Bolton and the Spanish Borderlands* (Norman: University of Oklahoma Press, 1964), 140–141.

64. "Los ofiziales Reales," October 4, 1686, bnd 2512 54–5–15/33, Stetson Collection, Reel 18, PKY.

65. "Los ofiziales Reales," October 4, 1686, bnd 2512 54–5–15/33, Stetson Collection, Reel 18, PKY.

66. "Diego de Quiroda y Losada al Rey," April 1, 1688, AGI-SD 58–1–26, Microfilm 290/69/, Section 4–3, Mary Letitia Ross papers, AC 73–163, GDAH.

67. Friar Marcelo de San Joseph, February 19, 1688, in Buckingham Smith, *[Documents in the Spanish and Two of the Early Tongues of Florida (Apalachian and Timuquan)],* (Washington, DC, 1860).

68. Joseph M. Hall, *Zamumo's Gifts: Indian-European Exchange in the Colonial Southeast* (Philadelphia: University of Pennsylvania Press, 2009), 85–88.

69. "Antonio Matheos to Juan Márquez Cabrera," May 19, 1686, in Folder 4, Bolton Papers, Banc, quoted from Hann, "Cloak and Dagger in Apalachicole Province," 82.

70. Some Indian groups referred to this game as "Little brother of war." See Thomas Vennum Jr., *American Indian Lacrosse: Little Brother of War* (Washington, DC: Smithsonian Institution, 1994); Bushnell, "'That Demonic Game:' The Campaign to Stop Indian Pelota Playing in Spanish Florida, 1675-1684," *The Americas* 35, no. 1 (1978): 1–19; John H. Hann, "Father Juan De Paiva, Spanish Friar in Colonial Florida," in *Spanish Pathways in Florida, 1492-1992 . . .* ed. Ann L. Henderson and Gary R. Mormino (Sarasota, FL: Pineapple Press, 1991), 140–146.

71. Hahn, "Cussita Migration Legend," in *Light on the Path,* 57–93.

72. "Antonio Matheos to Juan Márquez Cabrera," May 19, 1686, in Folder 4, Bolton Papers, Banc. quoted from Hann, "Cloak and Dagger in Apalachicole Province," 83.

73. Ibid.

74. Ibid.

75. "Antonio Matheos to Juan Márquez Cabrera," May 19, 1686, in Folder 4, Bolton Papers, Banc.

76. Hoffman, *Florida's Frontiers,* 162.

77. Ibid.; Heidi Bohaker, "Nindoodemag: The Significance of Algonquian Kinship Networks in the Eastern Great Lakes Region, 1600-1701," *WMQ* 63, no. 1 (2006): 1–34.

78. "Antonio Matheos to Juan Márquez Cabrera," May 19, 1686, in Folder 4, Bolton Papers, Banc.

79. "Autos y la entrada de los enemigos Yngleses en la provincial de Timucua, Apalachicoli, y Coweta . . ." March 29, 1686, AGI SD 839, folio 630–634, Reel 18, PKY.

80. "Antonio Matheos to Juan Márquez Cabrera," May 21, 1686, translation from Hann, "Cloak and Dagger in Apalachicole Province," 89.

81. "Antonio Matheos to Juan Márquez Cabrera," May 21, 1686, translation from Hann, "Cloak and Dagger in Apalachicole Province," 89.

82. "Juan Márquez Cabrera to King," AGI-SD 839, Folio 494–95, Reel 18, PKY.

83. "Antonio Matheos to Juan Márquez Cabrera," May 21, 1686, translation from Hann, "Cloak and Dagger in Apalachicole Province," 92.

84. John James Clune, "Historical Context and Overview," in *Presidio Santa María de Galve: A Struggle for Survival in Colonial Spanish Florida,* ed. Judith A. Bense (Gainesville: University of Florida, 2003), 17; Margry, *Mémoires et Documents . . .* (Paris: Maisonneuve et cie., 1879), 19–45.

85. For the most detailed reconstruction of Marco Delgado's journey, see Galloway, *Choctaw Genesis 1500-1700,* (Lincoln: University of Nebraska Press, 1995); 177–181; William Edward Dunn, *Spanish and French Rivalry in the Gulf Region of the United States, 1678-1702: The Beginnings of Texas and Pensacola* (Austin: University of Texas Press, 1917), 71–80; Hoffman, *Florida's Frontiers,* 152.

86. "Delgado to Márquez," October 20, 1686, in "Expediente de fortificación de la Bahía del Espíritu Santo," AGI México 616 (61–6–20), document courtesy of Joseph Hall.
87. DuVal, *The Native Ground,* 31–62.
88. Waselkov and Smith, "Upper Creek Archaeology," in *Indians of the Greater Southeast.* Tawasa (also known as Tavasa), on the confluence of Coosa and Tallapoosa Rivers, was the location of the Upper Creeks. John R. Swanton, "Comments on the Delgado Papers," *FHQ* 16, no. 2 (1937): 127.
89. "Delgado to Márquez," October 20, 1686, in "Expediente de fortificación de la Bahía del Espíritu Santo," AGI México 616 (61–6–20).
90. Ibid.
91. "Expedition of Marcos Delgado, 1686," *FHQ* 16, no. 1 (1937, July): 4–33.
92. Galloway, *Choctaw Genesis 1500–1700,* 177–181.
93. "Matheos to Cabrera," August 21, 1686, 13 in "Expedition of Marcos Delgado, 1686"; Angela Pulley Hudson, *Creek Paths and Federal Roads: Indian, Settlers, and Slaves and the Making of the American South* (Chapel Hill: University of North Carolina Press, 2010), 12–23; Joshua A. Piker, "White & Clean & Contested: Creek Towns and Trading Paths in the Aftermath of the Seven Years' War," *Ethnohistory* 50, no. 2 (2003): 315–347.
94. "Expedition of Marcos Delgado, 1686," 15, in "Expedition of Marcos Delgado, 1686."
95. "Letter from Marcos Delgado to Juan Márquez Cabrera," October 15, 1686, 18, in "Expedition of Marcos Delgado, 1686."
96. "Delgado's Report," January 5, 1687, 19, in "Expedition of Marcos Delgado, 1686."
97. John Reed Swanton, *Early History of the Creek Indians and Their Neighbors* (Washington, DC: Government Printing Office, 1922), 124; Verner W. Crane, *The Southern Frontier, 1670–1732* (Durham, NC: Duke University Press, 1928), 78–106.
98. "Delgado's Report," January 5, 1687," 27, in "Expedition of Marcos Delgado, 1686."
99. Galloway, *Choctaw Genesis 1500–1700,* 177–181.
100. "Delgado's Report," January 5, 1687, 27, in "Expedition of Marcos Delgado, 1686;" Hall, *Zamumo's Gifts,* 196, note 51.
101. "Letter from Marcos Delgado to Juan Márquez Cabrera," October 15, 1686, 12, in "Expedition of Marcos Delgado, 1686."
102. "Delgado's Report," January 5, 1687, 29, in "Expedition of Marcos Delgado, 1686."
103. "Patrick Mackay to James Oglethorpe," March 29, 1735, in Kenneth Coleman and Milton Ready, eds., *The Colonial Records of the State of Georgia: Original Papers, Correspondence to the Trustees, James Oglethorpe, and Others, 1732–5,* vol. 20 (Atlanta: University of Georgia Press, 1902), 294–299.

104. "Testimonio sobre la entrada de los Ingleses," AGI, SD 839, in the Lanning Papers no. 700.
105. "Trip to Apalachicola of Capitan Primo Enrique de Ribera," June 8, 1690, AGI 54-5-12/116, bnd 2907, Reel 21, Stetson Collection, PKY.
106. "Don Francisco de Romo, Captain of Apalachee," September 29, 1689, AGI 54-5-12/97, bnd 2852, Reel 20, Stetson Collection, PKY.
107. Hahn, "The Mother of Necessity," in *The Transformation of the Southeastern Indians*, 95.
108. "Letters from John Stewart to William Dunlop," *SCHGM* 32, no. 1 (1931): 30.
109. "Antonio Matheos to Juan Márquez Cabrera," May 19, 1686, translation from Hann, "Cloak and Dagger in Apalachicole Province," 83; Hahn, *The Invention of the Creek Nation*, 49–52.
110. "El gobernador Diego Quiroga y Losada decide Evacuar el presidio de Apalachicola," April 10, 1692, AGI 54-5-13, bnd 3067, Reel 22, Stetson Collection, PKY.

PART III. HOW:
NEW WAYS OF ARTICULATING POWER, 1710–1740

The Part III epigraph is from William Gilmore Simms, *The Yemassee: A Romance of Carolina* (Richmond, VA: Johnson Publishing, 1911), 236.

CHAPTER SIX: NETWORKS IN WARTIME

Epigraph: "An Account of the Breaking out of the Yamasee War in South Carolina Extracted from the Boston News of the 13th of June, 1715," in *Historical Collections,* ed. by B.R. Carroll (New York: Harper & Brothers, 1836), 570–572.

1. "William Rhett to the King," August 1715, PRO, Vol. 6, 116–117, SCDAH.
2. Steven J. Oatis, *A Colonial Complex, South Carolina's Frontiers in the Era of the Yamasee War, 1680-1730* (Lincoln: University of Nebraska Press, 2004), 10; William L. Ramsey, *The Yamasee War, A Study of Culture, Economy, and Conflict in the Colonial South* (Lincoln: University of Nebraska Press, 2008), 97, 124–125.
3. "Francis Le Jau to the Society," August 23, 1715, 246–248, SPG; Langdon Cheves, "A Letter from Carolina in 1715 and Journal of the March of the Carolinians into the Cherokee Mountains in the Yemassee Indian War," in *The Year Book of the City of Charleston* (Charleston, SC: 1894), 338–351.
4. Patrick Riordan, "Finding Freedom in Florida: Native Peoples, African Americans, and Colonists, 1670–1816," *FHQ* 75, no. 1 (Fall 1996): 27; TePaske, "The Fugitive Slave, Intercolonial Rivalry and Spanish Policy, 1687-1764," in

Eighteenth-Century Florida and Its Borderlands, ed. Samuel Proctor (Gainesville: University Presses of Florida, 1975), 2–12.

5. "William Rhett to King," August 1715, PRO, Vol. 6, 116–117, SCDAH.

6. Verner W. Crane, *The Southern Frontier, 1670–1732* (Durham, NC: Duke University Press, 1928), 89–100.

7. Ramsey, *The Yamasee War,* 95–97; Alan Gallay, *The Indian Slave Trade, the Rise of the English Empire in the American South 1670–1717* (New Haven, CT: Yale University Press, 2002) 242–250.

8. "Huspaw King to Charles Craven," July 12, 1715, in Ramsey, *The Yamasee War,* Appendix, 227–228.

9. April 13, 1728, *JCHA,* SCDAH, "George Rodd to his Employer in London (forwarded by him to the King)," May 8, 1715, CO 5/387, 166–169.

10. Alexander Hewatt, *An Historical Account of the Rise and Progress of the Colonies of South Carolina and Georgia,* Vol. 1 (London: Alexander Donaldson, 1779), 214–215.

11. Ramsey, *The Yamasee War,* 49–50; William Bartram, *Travels through North and South Carolina . . .* (Philadelphia: Printed by James and Johnson, 1791), 390.

12. "Board of Commissioners Meeting," April 12, 1715, *JCIT,* 86.

13. Crane, *The Southern Frontier,* 167–168; Ramsey, *The Yamasee War,* 48–50.

14. "Board of Commissioners Meeting," April 12, 1715, *JCIT,* 86.

15. For a Lower Creek–Yamasee alliance, see "El Gobernador Francisco," July 5, 1715, AGI SD 843, fol. 426–436, Reel 13, PKY. For Spanish support, see Alejandra Dubcovsky, "One Hundred Sixty-One Knots, Two Plates, and One Emperor: Creek Information Networks in the Era of the Yamasee War," *Ethnohistory* 59, no. 3 (2012): 489–513. For the Catawba "Board meeting," see February 20, 1717, *JCIT,* 161–163; Ramsey, *The Yamasee War,* 103–113, 28–48; Oatis, *A Colonial Complex,* 177–213; John H. Hann, "St. Augustine's Fallout from the Yamasee War," *FHQ* 68, no. 2 (1989): 181–201.

16. Robbie Ethridge, *From Chicaza to Chickasaw: The European Invasion and the Transformation of the Mississippian World, 1540–1715* (Chapel Hill: University of North Carolina Press, 2010), 241–243.

17. Hewatt, *An Historical Account,* 214–215.

18. "August 12, 1725," *JCHA,* 434, cited in Ramsey, *The Yamasee War,* 46; April 12, 1715, *JCIT,* 65; Crane, *The Southern Frontier,* 167–168. For Cuffy's identity, see William L. Ramsey, "A Coat for 'Indian Cuffy': Mapping the Boundary between Freedom and Slavery in Colonial South Carolina," *SCHM* 103, no. 1 (2002), 48-66.

19. "Francis Le Jau to the Society," August 23, 1715, 246–248, SPG.

20. "An Account of the Breaking out of the Yamasee War," in *Historical Collections,* 569–572.

21. Ramsey, *The Yamasee War,* 116.

22. "George Rodd to his Employer in London (forwarded by him to the King)," May 8, 1715, CO 5/387, 166–169.

23. "George Rodd to his Employer in London (forwarded by him to the King)," May 8, 1715, CO 5/387, 166–169.

24. Carroll, *Historical Collections of South Carolina,* 196–197.

25. "George Rodd to his Employer in London (forwarded by him to the King)," May 8, 1715, CO 5/387, 166–169.

26. "Samuel Eveleigh to Messrs. Boone and Berresford," July 19, 1715, CO 5/1265, 296–302. Quote from *Historical Collections of South Carolina,* 196–197.

27. "Francis Le Jau to Sir," August 22, 1715, 244–246, SPG.

28. "Samuel Eveleigh to Messrs. Boone and Berresford," July 19, 1715, CO 5/1265, 296–302.

29. "Joseph Boone and Richard Beresford . . . to the Council of Trade and Plantations," December 5, 1716, CO 5/1265, 215–226; Crane, *The Southern Frontier,* 178.

30. "An Account of the Breaking out of the Yamasee War . . ." in *Historical Collections,* 570–572; Crane, *The Southern Frontier,* 163–186.

31. "[?] to Mr. Boone," June 24, 1720, CO 5/358, 57–58.

32. "Antonio de Benavides a SM," November 2, 1725, in Wright, "Dispatches of Spanish Officials," 164–165; Riordan, "Finding Freedom in Florida," 25–44.

33. "Robert Johnson, Francis Yonge, Small Wragg to the Council of Trade and Plantations," May 28, 1728, PRO, Vol. 13, *1727–8,* 51–54, SCDAH; "Deposition of Thomas Jones," April 9, 1741, in *CSCHS* Vol. 4, 166–171; Crane, *The Southern Frontier,* 248.

34. Jane Landers, *Black Society in Spanish Florida: Blacks in the New World* (Urbana: University of Illinois Press, 1999), 26–29; Landers, "Gracia Real De Santa Teresa De Mose: A Free Black Town in Spanish Colonial Florida," *AHR* 95, no. 1 (1990): 9–30; "Breve relación del presidio de la Florida y Apalache, formada en 1758 por D. Pedro Sánchez Griñán," July 7, 1756, Ayer MSS 2198, NL.

35. Mark F. Boyd, "Diego Peña's Expedition to Apalachee and Apalachicola in 1716," *FHQ* 28, no. 1 (1949): 1–27; Denise I. Bossy, "Spiritual Diplomacy, the Yamasees, and the Society for the Propagation of the Gospel Reinterpreting Prince George's Eighteenth-Century Voyage to England," *Early American Studies* 12, no. 2 (2014): 366–401.

36. "Yamasee Testimony," July 5, 1715, bnd 4776 58-1-30/42, Reel 36, Stetson Collection, PKY.

37. "Captain Fitch's Journal to the Creeks," in *Travels in the American Colonies,* ed. Newton D. Mereness (New York, 1916), 196–202; Crane, *The Southern Frontier,* 95, 169.

38. "Governor Nicholson's Speech to Ouletta," May 25, 1722 (doc. 16), and "Ouletta's Response to Governor Nicholson," May 26, 1722 (doc. 17), in *North and South Carolina Treaties, 1654–1756,* Vol. 13, ed. W. Sitt Robinson (Bethesda, MD: University Publications of America, 2001), 106–112.

39. Waselkov, "Indian Maps of the Colonial Southeast," in *Powhatan's Mantle: Indians in the Colonial Southeast,* ed. Gregory A. Waselkov, Peter H. Wood, and Tom Hatley (Lincoln: University of Nebraska, 1989), 435–502.

40. For Chickasaws, see Jean Baptiste Bénard de La Harpe, *Historical Journal of the Establishment of the French in Louisiana* (New York, 1851), 44.

41. "John Wright to Board," May 30 1711, *JCIT,* 8–9; Crane, *The Southern Frontier,* 164–165; Edward J. Cashin, *Guardians of the Valley: Chickasaws in Colonial South Carolina and Georgia* (Columbia: University of South Carolina Press, 2009), 2–18.

42. "May it Please your Honor," April 5, 1712, *JCHA,* 12; "The Tuscarora Expedition," November 18, 1712, *JCHA,* 108, SCDAH; Oatis, *A Colonial Complex,* 84–91.

43. "Francis Le Jau to the Society," August 10, 1713, 215–16, SPG; Hann, "St. Augustine's Fallout from the Yamasee War," 181–201.

44. "Governor Johnson to the Council of Trade," January 12, 1720, CO 5/1265, 300–308; John Worth, "The Yamasee," in *Handbook of North American Indians: Southeast,* ed. Raymond D. Fogelson and William C. Sturtevant (Washington, DC: Smithsonian Institution, 2004), 245–253.

45. "Board of Commissioners," May 25, 1713, *JCIT,* 41–42.

46. Steven J. Peach, "Creek Indian Globetrotter: Tomochichi's Trans-Atlantic Quest for Traditional Power in the Colonial Southeast," *Ethnohistory* 60, no. 4 (2013): 605–635.

47. Boyd, "Diego Peña's Expedition," 27.

48. "Ar. Middleton to the Duke of Newcastle," June 13, 1728, PRO, Vol. 13, 61–70, SCDAH.

49. Joseph Primo de Rivera survey in April 18, 1717, Reel 36, Stetson Collection, PKY; Hann, "St. Augustine's Fallout from the Yamasee War," 118.

50. "Yamasee Testimony," July 5, 1715, bnd 4776 58-1-30/42, Reel 36, Stetson Collection, PKY.

51. "Captain Fitch's Journal to the Creeks," in *Travels in the American Colonies,* 188–189.

52. Crane, *The Southern Frontier,* 96.

53. "Lords Proprietors of Carolina to the Council of Trade and Plantations," June 4, 1717, CO 5/1265, 98–101; "To Robert Johnson," April 1720, PRO, Vol. 8, 1–10, SCDAH.

54. Boyd, "Diego Peña's Expedition," 25. Quote from Boyd, "Documents Describing the Second and Third Expeditions of Lieutenant Diego Peña to

Apalachee and Apalachicolo in 1717 and 1718," *FHQ* 31, no. 2 (October 1952): 120.

55. Boyd, "Documents Describing the Second and Third Expeditions of Lieutenant Diego Peña," 126–127; Andrés Gonzalez de Barcía Carballido y Zúñiga, *Chronological History of the Continent of Florida*, trans. Anthony Kerrigan (Gainesville: University of Florida Press, 1951), 360–365; Steven C. Hahn, *The Invention of the Creek Nation, 1670-1763* (Lincoln: University of Nebraska Press, 2004), 85–86.

56. Boyd, "Documents Describing the Second and Third Expeditions of Lieutenant Diego Peña," 120.

57. "This House . . . ," May 29, 1717, *JCHA*, SCDAH; Crane, *The Southern Frontier*, 257; Hahn, *The Invention of the Creek Nation*, 96; Oatis, *A Colonial Complex*, 209.

58. "To Mr. Joseph Boone," June 8, 1717, PRO, Vol. 7, 49–52, SCDAH.

59. "Lieutenant-Governor Alexander Spotswood," July 15, 1715, in *The Official Letters of Alexander Spotswood*, Collections of the Virginia Historical Society (Richmond, VA: The Society, 1882), 121–125.

60. Ibid.

61. Ramsey, *The Yamasee War*, 128.

62. For English inroads to the Choctaws, see La Harpe, *Historical Journal of the Establishment of the French in Louisiana*, 43; Crane, *The Southern Frontier*, 102–104.

63. *Historical Collections of Louisiana*, Vol. 3, ed. B. F. French (New York: Wiley and Putnam, 1851), 44.

64. Crane, *The Southern Frontier*, 34.

65. "Samuel Eveleigh to Messrs. Boone and Berresford," July 19, 1715, CO 5/1265, 296–302; Christina Snyder, *Slavery in Indian Country* (Cambridge, MA: Harvard University Press, 2010), 68–74.

66. Daniel Thomas, *The French Outpost at the Alabamas on the Coosa* (Tuscaloosa: University of Alabama Press, 1989), 2–5.

67. "Bienville to Pontchartrain," September 1, 1717, *MPA, French Dominion*, Vol. 3, 188. "Bienville to Pontchartrain," June 15, 1715, in *MPA, French Dominion*, Vol. 3, 181. For the limited French goods, see "Bienville to Hubert," September 19, 1717, in *MPA, French Dominion*, Vol. 3, 222–223; La Harpe, *Historical Journal of the Establishment of the French in Louisiana*, 59–60.

68. "Samuel Eveleigh to Messrs. Boone and Berresford," July 19, 1715, CO 5/1265, 296–302.

69. "George Rodd to his Employer in London (forwarded by him to the King)," May 8, 1715, CO 5/387, 166–169.

70. Stephen Warren, *The Worlds the Shawnees Made: Migration and Violence in Early America* (Chapel Hill: University of North Carolina Press, 2014), 100;

Brett Riggs, "Reconsidering Chestowee: The 1713 Raid in Regional Perspective," in *Yuchi Indian Histories before the Removal Era*, 43–72. For the French, see "Bienville to Raudot," January 20, 1715, in *MPA, French Dominion*, Vol. 3, 200.

71. "An Account of the Breaking out of the Yamasee War," in *Historical Collections*, 569–572.

72. "Colonel George Chicken's Journal," November 30, 1715, in Cheves, "A Letter from Carolina in 1715," 330.

73. Theda Perdue, "Cherokee Relations with the Iroquois in the Eighteenth Century," in *Beyond the Covenant Chain: The Iroquois and Their Neighbors in Indian North America, 1600-1800*, ed. Daniel K. Richter and James Hart Merrell, (Syracuse, NY: Syracuse University Press, 1987), 135–149.

74. Rena Vassar, "Some Short Remarkes on the Indian Trade in the Charikees and in Management Thereof since the Year 1717," *Ethnohistory* 8, no. 4 (1961): 401–423.

75. "Colonel George Chicken's Journal," November 30, 1715, in Cheves, "A Letter from Carolina in 1715," 330.

76. Ibid., 334–335.

77. Ibid., 343.

78. Ibid., 343–344.

79. Hahn, *The Invention of the Creek Nation*, 89.

80. "To Messrs. Boone and Berresford, and Thomas Broughton," March 15, 1716, PRO, Vol. 6, 155–161, SCDAH.

81. Ibid.

82. "Governor and Council of Carolina to the Lords Proprietors," January 26, 1717, CO 5/1265, 250.

83. For Creek activity before the murders in Tugaloo, see "Colonel George Chicken's Journal," November 30, 1715, in Cheves, "A Letter from Carolina in 1715," 330–331, 339.

84. Cheves, "A Letter from Carolina in 1715," 345–350; "Minutes of Council and Assembly," January 24–26, 1727, CO 5/387, 209–21; Hahn, "Cussita Migration Legend," in *Light on the Path*, 57–93.

85. "Colonel George Chicken's Journal," November 30, 1715, in Cheves, "A Letter from Carolina in 1715," 333, 342–434.

86. "Letter from Col. Hastings," December 21, 1716, *JCIT*, 141–142.

87. "Spotswood To the Lords Commissioners of Trade," February 16, 1716, in *The Official Letters of Alexander Spotswood*, 140–143.

88. James Hart Merrell, "Our Bond of Peace Patterns of Intercultural Exchange on the Carolina Piedmont, 1650-1750," in *Powhatan's Mantle*, 267–304.

89. "Samuel Eveleigh to Messrs. Boone and Berresford," October 7, 1715, CO 5/1265, 296–302; Creeks "Board Meeting," October 9, 1717, *JCIT*, 216–217.

90. Vassar, "Some Short Remarkes on the Indian Trade," 406–407; "Board Meeting," July 19, 1718, *JCIT*, 306; "Board Meeting," November 23, 1717, *JCIT*,

230–231. Kristofer Ray, "Cherokees and Franco-British Confrontation in the Tennessee Corridor, 1730-1760," *Native South* 7 (2014): 33-67.

91. "Extract of letter from South Carolina to Joseph Boone," September 25, 1717, CO 5/1265, 324-325; Oatis, *A Colonial Complex,* 193.

92. Perdue, "Cherokee Relations with the Iroquois in the Eighteenth Century," 35–49.

93. "Colonel Chicken's Journal to the Cherokees, 1725," in *Travels in the American Colonies,* 112–113; "A council held at Williamsburg," May 26, 1715, in *Executive Journals of the Council of Colonial Virginia,* Vol. 3, (Richmond: Virginia State Library, 1928), 399–400; "At a meeting of the Governour and Council in New London," July 8, 1715, in *The Public Records of the Colony of Connecticut, from October of 1706 to October of 1716,* Vol. 5, ed. Charles J. Hoadly, (Hartford, CT: Press of Case Lockwood and Brainard, 1870), 516.

94. Steven C. Hahn, *The Life and Times of Mary Musgrove* (Gainesville: University Press of Florida, 2012), 55–80; Joshua Piker, *The Four Deaths of Acorn Whistler: Telling Stories in Colonial America* (Cambridge, MA: Harvard University Press, 2013), 189–222.

95. Daniel Thomas, *Fort Toulouse: The French Outpost at the Alabamas on the Coosa* (Tuscaloosa: The University of Alabama Press, 1989), 6–14.

96. Hahn, *The Invention of the Creek Nation,* 114–117.

97. "Theophilus Hastings to Governor Nicholson," September 8, 1723, PRO, Vol. 10, 185–189, SCDAH; "Proceedings of the Committee for Indian affairs," October 25, 1723, CO 5/359, 381-383; Joseph M. Hall, *Zamumo's Gifts: Indian-European Exchange in the Colonial Southeast* (Philadelphia: University of Pennsylvania Press, 2009), 141.

98. "Gerrd Monger to Your Excellency," October 7, 1723, PRO, Vol. 10, 155–158, SCDAH.

99. "Muskogee: Coweta-Tuckabatchee Alliance," recorded by John R. Swanton in "Social Organization and Social Usages of the Indians of the Creek Confederacy," in *Forty-Second Annual Report of the Bureau of American Ethnology, 1924–1925* (Washington, DC: Government Printing Office, 1928), 68.

100. Paul E. Hoffman, *Florida's Frontiers* (Bloomington: Indiana University Press, 2002), 187–188.

101. Joseph Hall, "Anxious Alliances: Apalachicola Efforts to Survive the Slave Trade, 1638–1705," in *Indian Slavery in Colonial America,* ed. Alan Gallay (Lincoln: University of Nebraska Press, 2009), 145–171.

102. Daniel H. Usner Jr., *Indians, Settlers, and Slaves in a Frontier Exchange Economy, the Lower Mississippi Valley before 1783* (Chapel Hill: University of North Carolina, 1990), 30–31.

CHAPTER SEVEN: DISSONANT CONNECTIONS

Epigraph: "Board of Trade to Captain Bartholomew Gallard,"
July 30, 1716, *JCIT,* 92–93.

1. "Fort King George, Journal of Col John Barnwell (Tuscarora) in the Construction of the Fort on the Altamaha in 1721," *SCHGM* 27, no. 4 (1926): 196.

2. James Glen, *A Description of South Carolina,* London, 1761 (reprinted in George Milligen Johnston, ed., *Colonial South Carolina: Two Contemporary Descriptions* (Columbia: University of South Carolina Press, 1951), 95; Peter Wood, *Black Majority, Negroes in Colonial South Carolina from 1670 through the Stono Rebellion* (New York: W. W. Norton & Company, 1974), 35; Voyages Database, 2009, *Voyages: The Trans-Atlantic Slave Trade Database,* http://www.slavevoyages.org (accessed April 15, 2013); special thanks to Ed Rugemer for suggesting this source.

3. Gregory E. O'Malley, *Final Passages: The Intercolonial Slave Trade of British America, 1619–1807* (Chapel Hill: University of North Carolina Press, 2014), 174–187.

4. For population figures, see Peter H. Wood, "The Changing Population of the Colonial South, an Overview by Race and Region, 1685–1790," in *Powhatan's Mantle: Indians in the Colonial Southeast,* ed. Gregory A. Waselkov, Peter H. Wood, and Tom Hatley (Lincoln: University of Nebraska, 1989), 90. Quote from "Letter by Samuel Dyssli," December 3, 1737, in R. W. Kelsey, "Swiss Settlers in South Carolina." *SCHGM* 23, no. 3, (1922): 90.

5. "Address to the lord commissioners for Trade and the Assembly . . . ," January 29, 1719, in William R. Coe Collection, 1699–1741, SCHS.

6. For French mentions of English advances, see "Périer to Maurepas," March 25, 1731, in *MPA: French Dominion,* Vol. 4, 72–74.

7. S. Max Edelson, "Defining Carolina: Cartography and Colonization in the North American Southeast, 1657–1733," in *Creating and Contesting Carolina: Proprietary Era Histories,* ed. Michelle LeMaster and Bradford J. Wood (Columbia: University of South Carolina Press), 27–48.

8. Harold Maness, *Forgotten Outpost: Fort Moore & Savannah Town, 1685–1765* (Beech Island, SC: H. S. Maness, 1986), 107; William Stephens, December 9, 1737, in *Stephen's Journal, 1737–1740,* in *CRSG,* Vol. 4, 47; "To Mr. Speaker and Gent," by James Moore, ca. 1720, Ayer MS 822, NL.

9. Larry E. Ivers, *Colonial Forts of South Carolina, 1670–1775* (Columbia: University of South Carolina Press, 1970), 3, 37–76.

10. M. Eugene Sirmans, *Colonial South Carolina: A Political History, 1663–1763* (Chapel Hill: University of North Carolina Press, 1966), 167; Verner W. Crane, *The Southern Frontier, 1670–1732* (Durham, NC: Duke University Press, 1928), 293–294.

11. Sirmans, *Colonial South Carolina*, 188–191; "Robert Johnson to Oglethorpe," January 28, 1725, *CRSG*, Vol. 20, 203–205, GDAH; Julie Anne Sweet, *Negotiating for Georgia: British-Creek Relations in the Trustee Era, 1733–1752* (Athens: University of Georgia Press, 2005), 61–77. For the quote, see "March 3–10," *South Carolina Gazette* 1733. Published by Thomas Whitmars in Charlestown, South Carolina.

12. "Captain Massey to the Trustees," January 16, 1740, *CRSG*, Vol. 1, 363, GDAH.

13. Daniel Patrick Ingram, *Indians and British Outposts in Eighteenth-Century America* (Gainesville: University Press of Florida, 2012), 10–20.

14. "Law to Appropriate Yamasee Lands," June 13, 1716, Vol. XXIII, in *North and South Carolina Treaties, 1654-1756*. ed. Alden T. Vaughan. *Early American Indian Documents: Treaties and Laws, 1607-1789* (Bethesda, MD: University Publications of America, 2001), 183. See discussion in *The Statutes*, Vol. 3, 30–31.

15. "Council," January 10, 1725, *MPA: French Dominion*, Vol. 3, 477; Daniel H. Usner Jr., *Indians, Settlers, and Slaves in a Frontier Exchange Economy, the Lower Mississippi Valley before 1783* (Chapel Hill: University of North Carolina, 1990), 30–31; "A commutation of the lands belonging between Carolina and the French," John Barnwell, ca. 1720, in William R. Coe Collection, 1699–1741, SCHS.

16. "Journal, July 1720: Journal Book W," in *Journals of the Board of Trade and Plantations*, Vol. 4, November 1718–December 1722, ed. K. H. Ledward (London, 1925), 177–191, http://www.british-history.ac.uk/jrnl-trade-plantations/vol4/pp177-191.

17. "Fort King George: Journal of Colonel John Barnwell in the Construction of the Fort on the Altamaha in 1721," *SCHGM* 27, no. 4 (1926): 189–203; Jeannie Cook, *Fort King George: Step One to Statehood* (Darien, GA: The Darien News, 1990); Bessie Lewis, *Old Fort King George: The First English Settlement in the Land Which Is Now Georgia* (Brunswick, GA: Glover Printing Co, 1973).

18. Joseph W. Barnwell, "The Second Tuscarora Expedition," *SCHGM* 10, no. 1 (1908): 33–48.

19. Verner W. Crane, "Projects for Colonization in the South, 1684–1732," *The Mississippi Valley Historical Review* 12, no. 1 (June 1925): 23–35: Crane, *The Southern Frontier*, 164; Henry A. M. Smith, "Beaufort: The Original Plan and the Earliest Settlers," *SCHGM* 9, no. 3 (1098): 141–160.

20. Joseph M. Hall, *Zamumo's Gifts: Indian-European Exchange in the Colonial Southeast* (Philadelphia: University of Pennsylvania Press, 2009), 141.

21. "Fort King George: Journal of Colonel John Barnwell," 194.

22. "Colonel Chicken's Journal to the Cherokees, 1725," in *Travels in the American Colonies*, ed. Newton D. Mereness (New York: Macmillan Company, 1916), 95–96.

23. Ibid., 109.

24. Ibid., 136.

25. "Captain Fitch's Journal to the Creeks," in *Travels in the American Colonies*, 193.

26. *The Statutes*, Vol. 3, 229–232; Crane, *The Southern Frontier*, 196–205; Hall, *Zamumo's Gifts*, 141.

27. "Journal, August 1720: Journal Book W," in *Journals of the Board of Trade and Plantations*, Vol. 4, November 1718–December 1722, ed. K. H. Ledward (London, 1925), 191–204, http://www.british-history.ac.uk/jrnl-trade-plantations /vol4/pp191–204; Crane, *The Southern Frontier*, 187–235; Sirmans, *Colonial South Carolina*, 131–166.

28. "To Mr. John Bee in Charles Town in South Carolina with Care Deliver from Ocheese River These," July 30, 1723, PRO, Vol. 10, 128–132, SCDAH.

29. "Fort King George, Journal of Col John Barnwell (Tuscarora) in the Construction of the Fort on the Altamaha in 1721," *SCHM* 27, no. 4 (1926), 196.

30. Wood, *Black Majority*, 116; William S. Willis, "Divide and Rule: Red, White, and Black in the Southeast," *The Journal of Negro History* 48, no. 3 (1963): 157–176.

31. "Colonel Chicken's Journal to the Cherokees, 1725," 139.

32. S. Max Edelson, *Plantation Enterprise in Colonial South Carolina* (Cambridge, MA: Harvard University Press, 2006), 151.

33. "Captain Fitch's Journal to the Creeks," 184; "At a Committee of Indian Affairs," November 16, 1723, PRO, Vol. 10, 178–182, SCDAH; Christina Snyder, *Slavery in Indian Country* (Cambridge, MA: Harvard University Press, 2010), 135.

34. "Arthur Middleton to May It Please Your Grace," June 13, 1728, 61–70, PRO, Vol. 13, SCDAH; Wood, *Black Majority*, 277.

35. Irene A. Wright, "Dispatches of Spanish Officials Bearing in the Free Negro Settlement of Gracia Real De Santa Teresa De Mose, Florida," *The Journal of Negro History* 9, no. 2 (1924): 144-195; Landers, "Spanish Sanctuary: Fugitives in Florida, 1687–1790," *FHQ* 62, no. 3 (1984): 297–314; TePaske, "The Fugitive Slave, Intercolonial Rivalry and Spanish Policy, 1687–1764," in *Eighteenth-Century Florida and Its Borderlands*, ed. Samuel Proctor (Gainesville: University Press of Florida, 1975), 5.

36. "Recommendations on how to deal with English slaves," April 12, 1731, AGI 86–5–21/33, bnd 5310, Reel 40, Stetson Collection, PKY.

37. "Pero nunca de notizia a los Ingleses quede los esclavos que se refugianen los dominios de VM." April 12, 1731, AGI 86–5–21/33 bnd 5310, Reel 40, Stetson Collection, PKY; Landers, "Spanish Sanctuary: Fugitives in Florida," 297.

38. "A letter from Fort King George by Charles Huddy," February 9, 1724, 36, PRO, Vol. 11, 1723–25, SCDAH.

39. Antonio de Arredondo, *Demostracion Historiographica . . . March 20, 1742.* Herbert E. Bolton, *Arredondo's Historical Proof of Spain's Title to Georgia* (Berkeley: University of California Press, 1925), 172–173.

40. "Edward Massey to Sir," April 26, 1727, PRO, Vol. 12, 1725–27, 247–250, SCDAH.

41. Stephen Saunders Webb, "The Strange Career of Francis Nicholson," *WMQ* 23, no. 4 (1966): 514–548.
42. "Letter by Francis Nicholson," February 24, 1724, 32. PRO, Vol. 11, SCDAH. For more on Captain Watson, see "John Cockran and Jobth. Drake Committee of the Assembly to Mr. Boone," March 8, 1718, 98–99, PRO, Vol. 7, SCDAH. For more on Cherekleechee, see Boyd, "Diego Peña's Expedition to Apalachee and Apalachicola in 1716," *FHQ* 28, no. 1 (1949): 1-27.
43. "El Gobernador . . . ," November 2, 1725, AGI-SD, AGI 58–1–31/3, bnd 5158, Reel 39, Stetson Collection, PKY.
44. Ibid.
45. "Lord Commissioners of Trade," September 23, 1727, 246, PRO, Vol. 12, SCDAH.
46. "Francis Moore," [37–8]. MS 0573, GHS; Paul E. Hoffman, *Florida's Frontiers* (Bloomington: Indiana University Press, 2002), 182; J. Leitch Wright Jr., *The Only Land They Knew: The Tragic Story of American Indians in the Old South* (New York: The Free Press, 1981), 122–125.
47. Jane Landers, *Black Society in Spanish Florida*. Blacks in the New World (Urbana: University of Illinois Press, 1999), 23–53.
48. "El Gobernador . . . ," November 2, 1725, AGI-SD AGI 58–1–31/3, bnd 5158, Reel 39, Stetson Collection, PKY.
49. "Recommendations to deal with English slaves," April 12, 1731, St AGI 86–5–21/33, bnd 5310, Reel 40, Stetson Collection, PKY; "Testimonio de los autos . . . ," June 10 and August 18, 1724, *Documentos Históricos*, 243–260; For the legacy of this policy, see "Breve relación del presidio de la Florida y Apalache, formada en 1758 por D. Pedro Sánchez Griñán," July, 7, 1756, Ayer MSS 2198, NL.
50. "Antonio de Benavides a SM," November 2, 1725, in Wright, "Dispatches of Spanish Officials," 164.
51. "Arthur Middleton to May It Please Your Grace," June 13, 1728, 61–70, PRO, Vol. 13, SCDAH; Wood, *Black Majority*, 305.
52. "General Oglethorpe's Expedition to St. Augustine," in *CSCHS*, Vol. 2, 356–357. For Black-Indian raids from San Agustín against the English, see "Francis Moore," [87] MS 0573, GHS.
53. Jane Landers, "Gracia Real De Santa Teresa De Mose, A Free Black Town in Spanish Colonial Florida." *AHR* 95, no. 1 (1990): 9-30; Theodore G. Corbett, "Migration to a Spanish Imperial Frontier in the Seventeenth and Eighteenth Centuries: St. Augustine," *The Hispanic American Historical Review* 54, no. 3 (1974): 420.
54. "Stephen's Journal," January 6, 1738, *CRSG*, Vol. 4, 64.
55. "Harman Verlst to James Oglethorpe," September 14, 1739, *CRSG*, Vol. 30, 86–87; "Official letters from Don Manuel de Montiano, Governor of East

Florida, to Don Juan Francisco de Guemes y Horcasitas, Captain-General of the Island of Cuba," Hargrett Rare Book and Manuscript Library, The University of Georgia Libraries (hereafter *Official Letters*), August 31 1738, Letter no. 76.

56. "Stephen's Journal," December 15, 1738, *CRSG*, Vol. 4, 247–248.

57. Ibid.

58. "Discussions," January 19, 1739, *JCHA*, ed. J. H. Easterby (Columbia: The Historical Commission of South Carolina, 1951), 595–597; Landers, *Black Society in Spanish Florida*, 33.

59. "Lieutenant-Governor William Bull to Duke of Newcastle," May 9, 1739, CO 5/388, 90–111.

60. Mark F. Boyd, "Documents Describing the Second and Third Expeditions of Lieutenant Diego Peña to Apalachee and Apalachicolo in 1717 and 1718," *FHQ* 31, no. 2 (1952): 117.

61. Hall, *Zamumo's Gifts*, 41.

62. "Captain Fitch's "Journal to the Creeks," 199.

63. Ibid., 205–206.

64. Snyder, *Slavery in Indian Country*, 135.

65. "Captain Fitch's Journal to the Creeks," 207.

66. Snyder, *Slavery in Indian Country*, 150.

67. "Answer of the Indian Chiefs of the Cherokee Nation," September 9, 1730, CO 37, 291–298, http://www.british-history.ac.uk/cal-state-papers/colonial/america-west-indies/vol37/pp291–298.

68. "Autos y diligencias," July 21, 1716, AGI SD 843, Folio 462–517, PKY.

69. "George Rodd to his Employer in London (forwarded by him to the King)," May 8, 1715, CO 5/387, 166–169. For discussion of Spanish strategy, see "Francis Moore," 1735–1736, MS 0573, GHS.

70. "To Don Antonio Benavides from Francisco Jospoque," January 12, 1734, bnd 86–7–21, Reel 40, Stetson Collection, PKY.

71. "Al Governador Francisco del Moral Sánchez" July 29, 1734, bnd 5376 86–7–21/7, Reel 40, Stetson Collection, PKY.

72. "Letter from San Marcos about Indians," July 29, 1734, bnd 5376 86–7–21/7, Reel 40, Stetson Collection, PKY. See also "The Trials of Captain Don Isidoro De León," *FHQ* 35, no. 3. (1957): 246–265; Hahn, *The Invention of the Creek Nation, 1670-1763* (Lincoln: University of Nebraska Press, 2004), 165.

73. "To Don Antonio Benavides from Francisco Jospoque," January 12, 1734, bnd 86–7–21, Reel 40, Stetson Collection, PKY.

74. "Anonymous diary of an officer, 1738–1742," HM 237, HL.

75. Hahn, *The Invention of the Creek Nation*, 164.

76. "Relacion del Yndio Juan Ygnacio . . . ," August 30, 1738, in *Documentos Históricos*, 260–264.

77. Bushnell, *Situado and Sabana, Spain's Support System for the Presidio and Mission Provinces of Florida*, vol. 3, Anthropological Papers of the American Museum of Natural History (1994), 16–19; TePaske, "Economic Problems of Florida Governors, 1700–1763," *FHQ* 37, no. 1 (1958): 42–52.

78. "Relación del Yndio Juan Ygnacio," August 30, 1738, in *Documentos Históricos*, 260–264.

79. "November 22, 1739," *CRSG*, Vol. 4, 458, GDAH.

80. *Official Letters*, June 17, 1738, Letter no. 57. For the murder of Indian informers, see "Manuel de Montiano [to Son Joseph de la Guntana]," November 21, 1739, bnd 5879 86–7–21/21–22, Reel 45, Stetson Collection, PKY.

81. "Governor Juan Francisco Güemes y Horcasitas to Marqués de Torrenueva," April 14, 1738, St AGI 87–1–2/111, bnd 5716, Reel 43, Stetson Collection, PKY.

82. "Governor Manuel de Montiano," August 14, 1739, St AGI 87–3–12/6, bnd 5855, Reel 45, Stetson Collection, PKY.

83. Hahn, "The Mother of Necessity: Carolina, the Creeks, and the Making of a New Order in the Southeast, 1670–1763," in *The Transformation of the Southeastern Indians, 1540-1760*, ed. Robbie Ethridge and Charles Hudson (Jackson: University Press of Mississippi, 2002), 79–114.

84. "Del Toro's expedition," May 18, 1738, bnd 87–1–3/48, Reel 43, Stetson Collection, PKY.

85. "Breve relación del presidio de la Florida y Apalache, formada en 1758 por D. Pedro Sánchez Griñán," July, 7, 1756, Ayer MSS 2198, NL.

86. "Governor Juan Francisco Güemes y Horcasitas to Marqués de Torrenueva," April 14, 1738, St AGI 87–1–2/111, bnd 5716, Reel 43, Stetson Collection, PKY.

87. Sirmans, *Colonial South Carolina*, 214–217; Geraldine Meroney, "The London Entrepôt Merchants and the Georgia Colony," *WMQ* 25, no. 2 (1968): 230–244.

88. Edward Kimber, *A Relation or a Journal of a Late Expedition to the Gates of St. Augustine on Florida*, reprinted from the original edition, London, 1744 ed. (Boston: Charles E. Goodspeed & Co., 1935), 30; "Francis Moore," [91, 109], MS 0573, GHS.

89. "Stephen's Journal," April 5, 1740, *CRSG*, Vol. 4, 548.

90. "Journal of the Earl of Egmont," April 1741, *CRSG*, Vol. 5, 498–499.

91. *Official Letters*, June 3, 1738, Letter no. 45.

92. Ibid.

93. Francisco De San Buenaventura, *Relación . . . De Lo Sucedido Con D. Diego Obgletorp* [sic], *General Inglés, En La Ciudad De La Florida En El Año De 1740* (Sevilla, 1741), JCB. For the importance of Indian informers during the Spanish retaliation for Oglethorpe's attack, see "Anonymous diary of an officer, 1738–1742." HM 237, HL.

94. *Official Letters*, March 24, 1740, Letter no. 19, and January 31, 1740, Letter no. 180.

95. John M. Goggin, "Fort Pupo: A Spanish Frontier Outpost," *FHQ* 30, no. 2 (1951): 139–192.
96. "A Ranger's Report of Travels with General Oglethorpe, 1739–1742," in *Travels in the American Colonies,* ed. Newton D. Mereness (New York: The Macmillan Company, 1916), 226.
97. *Official Letters,* February, 23, 1740, Letter no. 187.
98. *Official Letters,* August 19, 1739, Letter no. 157; quote from February, 23, 1740, Letter no. 187.
99. *Official Letters,* June 3, 1738, Letter no. 45.
100. "A Ranger's Report of Travels with General Oglethorpe," 227.
101. "To Thomas Broughton Esq. Speaker," April 5, 1728, PRO, Vol. 13, 19–25, SCDAH.
102. "Francis Moore," [87], MS 0573, GHS.
103. "Letters from San Jorge," August 16, 1739, St AGI 86-7-21/18, bnd 5859, Reel 45, Stetson Collection, PKY.
104. *Official Letters,* July 28, 1740, Letter no. 205.
105. "Desertion of Spanish Miguel Soler," May 11, 1746, bnd 6026 87-2-12/3, Reel 46, Stetson Collection, PKY; "Journal of Colonel Charlesworth Glover," December 23, 1727, PRO, Vol. 13, 80–96, SCDAH; John T. Juricek, *Colonial Georgia and the Creeks: Anglo-Indian Diplomacy on the Southern Frontier, 1733–1763* (Gainesville: University Press of Florida, 2010), 114–124.
106. For the difficulty of attacking San Agustín, see "Patrick Mackay to Thomas Causton, March 27, 1735 [from Coweta]," *CRSG,* Vol. 20, 290–291, GDAH.
107. *Official Letters,* February, 23, 1740, Letter no. 187; John Jay TePaske, *The Governorship of Spanish Florida, 1700-1763* (Durham, NC: Duke University Press, 1964), 128.

CONCLUSION

1. Letter II and Letter IV, quotes from Hernán Cortés, *Letters from Mexico,* ed. A. R. Pagden and J. H. Elliott (New Haven/London, CT: Yale Nota Bene, 2001), 47–50, 337.
2. "Statement by the Ensign Francisco Romero," in Testimony of Lay Witnesses Relating to the Calusa Missions, February–March, 1698, AGI, SD 154, in John Hann, *Missions to the Calusa* (Gainesville: University of Florida Press, 1991), 185.
3. Charles M. Hudson, *Elements of Southeastern Indian Religion, Iconography of Religions Section 10, North America* (Leiden, The Netherlands: E. J. Brill, 1984); Clara Sue Kidwell, "Native American Systems of Knowledge," in *A Companion to American Indian History,* ed. Philip Joseph Deloria and Neal Salisbury (Malden, MA, 2002), 88–105; Bill Grantham, *Creation Myths and Legends of the Creek Indians* (Gainesville: University of Florida Press, 2002), 10.
4. Garcilaso de la Vega, *The Florida of the Inca* (Austin: University of Texas Press,

1951), 7. For the difficulty of properly conceiving what was Florida, see Michele Currie Navakas, "Liquid Landscape: Possession and Floridian Geography," *Early American Literature* 47, no. 1 (2012): 89-114; Monique Allewaert, "Swamp Sublime: Ecologies of Resistance in the American Plantation Zone," PMLA 123, no. 2 (2008): 354.

5. John Seely Brown and Paul Duguid, *The Social Life of Information* (Boston, MA: Harvard Business School Press, 2000), 1–10, 17–19.

6. Oglethorpe, "A Ranger's Report of Travels with General Oglethorpe, 1739–1742," in *Travels in the American Colonies,* ed. Newton D. Mereness (New York: The Macmillan Company, 1916), 222–223.

ACKNOWLEDGMENTS

～

This book exists because of the care and support of many people. I want to start by thanking Verena Borton, my first English as a second language (ESL) teacher. It took me far too long to realize that ESL did not actually stand for "extra-special learner," as Mrs. Borton had insisted; her kindness and commitment gave me the courage to tackle a language that I did not grow up speaking. I am eternally grateful and forever inspired.

This book began years ago and many miles away at the University of California, Berkeley. During my time at Cal and in the bay area, I benefitted immensely from the guidance and support of Margaret Chowing, Kathleen Donegan, Paul Duguid, Robin Einhorn, Ellen Harding-O'Connor, David Henkin, Waldo Martin, Tyler Stovall, and Ula Taylor. Jennifer Spear planted the seed that became this project and has graciously helped water it along the way. Mark Peterson was the best kind of adviser anyone could ask for and continues to be a mentor extraordinaire. Mark's generosity, care, and unwavering enthusiasm for this project are just some of the countless reasons I feel fortunate to have him as a friend.

I was very lucky in my next scholarly home: Yale University. Yale has been an invigorating place to complete this book, not least because of the administration's generous support for junior faculty's research. I am grateful to my colleagues Ned Blackhawk, David Blight, Daniel Bostman, Birgit Brander Rasmussen, Marcela Echeverri, Johnny Faragher, Beverly Gage, Naomi Lamoreaux, Mary Lui, Alyssa Mt. Pleasant, Steve Pincus, Stephen Pitti, and Stuart Schwartz. I would especially like to thank Ed Rugemer for all the conversations and thoughts about colonial South Carolina. Joanne Freeman has read multiple drafts of my work and has always been a gracious and kind reader. Jessica Cattelino's advice and kindness lasted far longer than her brief visit to Yale. The Yale History Department also organized a publishing colloquium for this book in which Peter Mancall, Alan Taylor, John Demos, and Joanne Freeman read an initial draft. Their thoughtful and constructive advice gave me the courage to completely rewrite the manuscript (twice!).

My ideas and writing have also greatly improved from the suggestions, questions, and friendly nudges I have received from the audiences of the Rocky Mountain Early

America Seminar, the McNeil Center, the Ethnohistory Conference, the Omohundro Institute for Early America, the Boston Early America Seminar, the Southern Historical Association, the American Indian Series at the Newberry Library in Chicago, and the New York University Atlantic History Workshop. For their feedback in those settings, I would especially like to thank Allison Bigelow, Holly Brewer, Amy Bushnell, Céline Carayon, Nicole Eustace, Antonio Feros, Alan Gallay, Katherine Grandjean, Joseph Hall, Eric Hinderaker, Chris Hodson, Karen Kupperman, Jane Landers, Kerima Lewis, Andrew Lipman, Robert Lockhart, Patricia Marroquin Norby, Marie McDaniel, Jon Parmenter, Chris Parsons, Jenny Pulsipher, Bill Ramsey, Dan Richter, Brett Rushforth, Elena Schneider, David Silverman, Daniel Tortora, Daniel Usner, and Cynthia Van Zandt.

Several kind and obliging friends have read drafts and parts of the project. I would especially like to acknowledge Robbie Ethridge, Hannah Farber, Steven C. Hahn, Sylvia Sellers-García, Christina Snyder, Wendy Warren, and Molly Warsh. Juliana Barr and Josh Piker took the time to read an earlier (and hopefully much improved) full draft. Their insightful comments and suggestions proved invaluable. Their careful advice guided my revisions and pushed this project to the finish line.

I also want to acknowledge Harvard University Press, especially my editor, Kathleen McDermott, and her wonderful assistant, Katrina Vassallo. I am also indebted to the recommendations from Peter Mancall and one anonymous reader. Their generous, insightful, and constructive comments helped make this book much better. Audra Wolfe helped me revise the manuscript, working tirelessly to make my prose and ideas far more legible. I am also thankful to Isabelle Lewis for her wonderful maps.

My family played a large role in the completion of this book. Laura and Jorge, *mi mami y papi,* have cultivated my passion for learning from Tropezón all the way to Yale. They are my strength and inspiration. Martín has always been my avid supporter without losing any of the sarcastic charm that comes with being a younger brother. I am also grateful to my relatives in Argentina. Thank you so much to both the Dubcovsky and Kuperman sides of the family. I was blessed with a wonderful family-in-law. Chuck, Katie, Patrick, Megan, and the rest of the Joseph and Balocca clans have cheered me on at every step of the way. My friends have helped me laugh and endure the whole process; thanks, Becca, Chung-Hay, Monica and Ed, Matt and Kate, Sherry and Alex, and Nga.

My two sons, Joaquín and Santiago, did not really help with the completion of this book, but they did make the process far more enjoyable. They also gave me some daily lessons in humility and some clear perspective on what truly matters. Chaucha and Cuchu, you two are the best parts of every day.

Finally, there is Ryan. He is a true partner and ally. To him, I owe my happiness, sanity, and infinitely more. This book is not simply for you. It is because of you.

INDEX